HASIDISM AND THE STATE OF ISRAEL

THE LITTMAN LIBRARY OF JEWISH CIVILIZATION

EDITORS

David Goldstein
Louis Jacobs
V. D. Lipman

For the love of God
and in memory of

JOSEPH AARON LITTMAN

"Get wisdom, get understanding:
Forsake her not and she shall preserve thee"

Hasidism and the State of Israel

Harry Rabinowicz

Rutherford • Madison • Teaneck
Fairleigh Dickinson University Press
London and Toronto: Associated University Presses

By the same author

The Will and Testament of the Biala Rabbi
A Guide to Hasidism
The Slave Who Saved the City
The Jewish Literary Treasurers of England and America
A Guide to Life
The Legacy of Polish Jewry
The World of Hasidism
Treasures of Judaica

© 1982 by Associated University Presses, Inc.

Associated University Presses, Inc.
4 Cornwall Drive
East Brunswick, N.J. 08816

Associated University Presses Ltd
27 Chancery Lane
London WC2A 1NF, England

Associated University Presses
Toronto M5E 1A7, Canada

Library of Congress Cataloging in Publication Data

Rabinowicz, Harry M., 1919-
Hasidism and the state of Israel.

(The Littman library of Jewish civilization)
Bibliography: p.
Includes index.
1. Hasidism-Israel.   2. Israel-Religion.
3. Religion and state-Israel.   I. Title.
II. Series
BM390.R26   296.8'33   80-70271
ISBN 0-8386-3034-0   AACR2

Printed in the United States of America

Dedicated to Mrs Jane Caplin on
the occasion of her ninetieth birthday

CONTENTS

Preface and Acknowledgments 9

PART ONE

I	The Chosen Land	13
II	The Hasidic Trail-Blazers	22
III	The First Hasidic Aliyah	37
IV	The Flame of Rabbi Nahman	45
V	Exile and Redemption	54
VI	Charity Delivers from Death	67
VII	Hasidism and Zionism	76
VIII	The Return to Zion	89

PART TWO

IX	The Power of Ger	105
X	Kiryat Vizhnitz	119
XI	The Sabra Rabbi	130
XII	He Dreamed a Dream and Built a City	141
XIII	The Kotel and the Rebbe	157
XIV	A Dynasty in the Making	171
XV	Slonim in Jerusalem	176
XVI	Rebbes in the All-Jewish City	180

7

XVII	The Lonely Rabbi	195
XVIII	The Torah Citadel of Bne Brak	199
XIX	The Lion of the Twentieth Century	209
XX	Habad in Israel	212
XXI	A Hasidic Island in a Secular Sea	222
XXII	The Love-Hate Syndrome of Satmar	228
XXIII	From Dan to Beersheba	243
XXIV	The Rebbes of Spinka	257
XXV	The Hasidic Community	263
XXVI	Hasidic Literature	272

Genealogical Tables of Hasidic Dynasties	287
Glossary	299
Notes	311
Bibliography	328
Index	337

PREFACE AND ACKNOWLEDGMENTS

The six years between 1939 and 1945 saw the catastrophic climax of a millennium of East European Jewish culture as Nazi-occupied eastern Europe became the graveyard of six million Jews. As the holocaust raged, the lights of Hasidism were dimmed and the Jewish quarters of Warsaw, Lodz and Lublin, once citadels of piety and learning, became piles of rubble, a physical symbol of the almost total annihilation of their Jewish communities.

But Hasidism refused to die. Out of the ashes it rose again. Today Israel is the home of many great surviving dynasties. Proudly pietists proclaim their identity as Hasidim of Ger, Belz or Vizhnitz. Hasidic courts flourish in Jerusalem, Tel-Aviv and Bne Brak, and new Hasidic yeshivot are being constantly established.

There is today a great demand for Hasidic literature in Israel. Old Hasidic texts are being reprinted and new books are being written. However, there does exist a sizeable communications gap. Little is known about the part that the Hasidim are playing in the rebuilding of the State of Israel. They are no longer, as in the nineteenth century, an unproductive element depending on the *Halukah* (or charity), but are for the most part integrated into the economy of the country. Often the Hasidim are identified

9

with the Neture Karta, a tiny but highly vocal group of militants, followers of Rabbi Joel Teitelbaum of Satmar; yet the vast majority of Hasidim reject the ideology of these active zealots and are repelled by their activities.

Whilst most tourists visit the Meah Shearim quarter of Jerusalem, many miss the picturesque Hasidic district of Geula. They dally in the popular resort of Netanyah, but few are aware of Kiryat Sanz just outside it. Similarly, few visitors to Tel-Aviv visit nearby Kiryat Vizhnitz in Bne Brak.

The Hasidim are not publicity conscious. It is not easy to obtain the biographies of their rebbes, and the compiler of a Who's Who of Hasidism would receive little co-operation. There is, moreover, an occupational hazard in writing about contemporary events.

This study is divided into two parts. The first section describes the deep yearning Hasidim felt for the Holy Land from the time of the founder of Hasidism, Rabbi Israel Baal Shem Tov, to the outbreak of World War II. The second part describes the Hasidic Rabbis now in Israel, their life-styles and their followers. This book attempts to deal with this vast subject within the restricted confines of a single volume.

I am grateful to the Jewish War Memorial Council for awarding me the Sir Robert Waley Cohen scholarship. In the past two years I have visited Israel several times and have met most of the Hasidic rabbis and have visited their institutions and educational establishments. So many people have helped me that it is impossible to list them all, and I am deeply indebted to many Hasidim in Israel and in Britain who have shared their memories with me.

I am deeply grateful to my wife Bella, and my sisters Miriam and Rachel, for reading the manuscript with abundant patience and for their helpful suggestions.

Finally, I wish to thank the editors of the Littman Library of Jewish Civilization, Rabbis L. Jacobs and D. Goldstein, and Mrs C.J. Raab. Their personal and professional help is gratefully acknowledged.

PART ONE

I

THE CHOSEN LAND

The land of Israel, the land that the Almighty calls with possessive tenderness 'my own land', occupies a pivotal role in Jewish theology. It is holier, says the Mishnah,[1] than all other lands, and 'to dwell in its deserts is more desirable than to live in the palaces of the Galut.' 'Unto thy seed will I give this land' was His promise to Abraham (Gen.12:7).

Commenting on the verse 'He rose and measured the earth' (Hab.3:6), the rabbis say, 'The Holy One blessed be He considered all the lands and found no land more suitable for his children than the land of Israel.[2] 'It sometimes happens', say the sages,[3] 'that a man is comely but his clothes are handsomely attired. In the case of Israel, however, the people and the land are admirably suited one to the other, and every Jew has a share in it, a share that it is hard for him to forfeit.'[4]

The love of the people for the land runs like a strand of pearls through the Bible, the Mishnah, the Talmud, the Midrashim, the Prayer-Book, the Selihot, through treatises and Responsa. The imagery is poignant; the Holy Land is 'The bride awaiting the tarrying bridegroom', 'The widow in mourning refusing all consolation', 'The mother waiting for the return of her scattered children.' 'If I forget thee, O Jerusalem, let my right hand forget her cunning' (Ps.137:5-6), wept the exiles by the alien waters of Babylon and also by the shores of the Rhine, the Moselle, the Dnieper and the Vistula.

'Because of our sins', we admit in the liturgy of the Festivals, 'we have been exiled from our land.' Often only after death did the exiles return to be buried in its earth. Jewish tradition generally forbids exhumation, but exception is made when the remains are to be transported to the Holy Land. When a Jew dies in the Diaspora, a handful of hallowed earth, preferably from the Mount of Olives, is placed in his coffin.

Moses b. Nahman (1194-1270), commonly called Nahmanides or *Ramban*, regarded dwelling in the Holy Land as one of the positive commandments of the Pentateuch (Deut.12:13). He himself settled there when seventy-one years old and there he composed the poem which included the lines, 'The land of Israel is the glory of the world, Jerusalem is the glory of the land of Israel, and the Temple is the glory of Jerusalem.' In his *Commentary on the Pentateuch*, he wrote:

It is this belief in the supremacy of the land of Israel and its key position in Judaism that tore me away from my own country and led me to abandon hearth and home. I made myself like a raven which has no feeling for its young. I hardened my heart against my sons and my daughters . . . But the loss of all else which delighted my eyes is compensated by my present joy in a day passed within thy courts, O Jerusalem, visiting the ruins of the Temple and crying over the ruined Sanctuary, where it is granted to me to caress thy stones, to fondle thy dust, and to weep over thy ruins, I wept bitterly, but I found joy in my heart. I rent my garments, but I found solace in doing so.

Even earlier the same concept inspired Judah Halevi (1075-1141), the Spanish-Hebrew poet and religious philosopher, to compose his 'Odes to Zion'. 'Would that I had wings that I could wend my way to thee, O Jerusalem, from afar. My broken heart will find its way amidst your broken ruins.' In the second part of his philosophical work, *Kuzari*, he terms the Holy Land not only 'the centre of the earth', but also 'a gateway to heaven'. For the heart and soul of the land are sanctified as it is by the presence of God.[5]

Yearning to return to the promised land, the Jews clung desperately to their conviction that the Messiah would redeem them and lead them back home. It was a conviction that rendered them pathetically vulnerable. Like shooting stars, false Messiahs flashed across the skies of Jewish history, almost inevitably leaving despair and disillusionment in their wake.

Bar Kochba in Roman times (132-5 CE), Moses of Crete in the fifth century, and Serenus of Syria and Abu Isa of Persia in the eighth century were the first of many. At least eight messianic movements were recorded during the first three Crusades.[6] The appearance of a 'Redeemer' in Yemen in 1172 led the contemporary Maimonides (1135-1204) to warn the Yemenites of the dangers of over-credulity.[7] A pseudo-Messiah who appeared in Kurdistan in the twelfth century, David Alroy, is reputed to have actually raised a Jewish army, and to have planned the recapture of Palestine from its Moslem suzerain by military means.

In Sicily in 1284, Abraham Abulafia (1240-91) of Messina proclaimed himself Messiah, and prophesied that the redemption would come during his lifetime.[8] In 1502, Asher Lamlein of Istria, near Venice announced that the Messiah would come that year. Twenty years later, David Reubeni (1490-after 1535) appeared in Nubia in Egypt, introducing himself as a brother of King Joseph who had reigned in Khaibar in Arabia over 300,000 members of the tribes of Reuben, Gad and half of Manasseh. He presented himself as ambassador to Pope Clement VII in 1524 and offered to help expel the Turks from the Holy Land, proposing to the princes of Europe an alliance with his imaginary brother's forces to this end. He was received by the pope and his offer was favourably considered by King John III of Portugal.

In 1529 Solomon Molcho (1500-32), a Portuguese marrano by birth, predicted that the Messiah would come in the year 1540. 'I have no permission to reveal that which is hidden,' he writes, 'but our deliverance is near at hand and will soon be revealed to all in our days.'[9] In spite of the pope's protection, Molcho as a marrano was found guilty and condemned by the Inquisition to be burnt at the stake. Escaping its clutches, he then conceived the plan of visiting Emperor Charles V in Regensburg, in company with David Reubeni, to plead the Jewish cause. Charles had them both put in chains and carried to Mantua, where Molcho was burnt in accordance with the earlier decree. Reubeni was sent to Portugal, where he disappeared in the prisons of the Inquisition.

In 1648, at the age of twenty-two, Sabbatai Zevi proclaimed himself the long-awaited redeemer who would inaugurate the kingdom of God in Jerusalem. The year 1666 was to see the fulfilment of messianic prophecy. He was supported by men like Moses Pinheiro of Smyrna, Abraham Yakhini of Constantinople, Moses Galanté and Solomon b. Abraham Laniado of Aleppo and above all Nathan Gazzati (or Nathan of Gaza). Sabbatai Zevi made great efforts to enlist the sympathies of Polish and German Jewry, whose sufferings he vowed to avenge. With oriental pomp and ceremony he married the Polish Jewess Sarah in Cairo in 1664. She seems to have lost her parents at the age of six. After living in a convent in Italy she escaped to Amsterdam, where she returned to the faith of her parents. She had earlier travelled to Italy, declaring everywhere that a Messiah was coming to the world and that she was destined to become his bride.

In many communities Jews sold their possessions and waited for the Trumpet of the Messiah. 'It is impossible to describe the rejoicings that occurred when letters were received from Turkey', says Glückel of Hamelin (1646-1724) in her Memoirs.[10]

The Sephardim received most of the letters and immediately rushed with them to their synagogue [in Hamburg] where the news was read aloud; young and old, the Germans too, hastened to the Sephardic synagogue. The young Portuguese put on their best clothes and wore green silk ribbons–Sabbatai Zevi's colours. And thus they all went 'with timbrels and with dances' to the synagogue and with a joy like the 'joy of the Feast of Water-Drawing' they read the letters aloud.

Glückel records that her parents-in-law sent two large cases to Hamburg; one filled with food and the other with linen and clothing. These cases were to be kept in readiness until the summons arrived for the Second Exodus. On 22 Tevet (30 December) 1665 Sabbatai Zevi set sail from Smyrna to the Bosphorus to appear before the sultan. He was, however, arrested by the Turkish authorities as a rebel against the Ottoman Empire and was detained for a time at Abydos, which became known as Migdal Oz (the Tower of Strength). He saved his life by converting to Islam, and the many hopes raised by this charismatic figure were all dashed when he became Mehemed Effendi.

But the messianic dream would not perish, and again and again men rose who fed the fragile hope. Last and most harmful of the pseudo-Messiahs was Jacob Labowitz Frank of Galicia (1726-91) the antinomian, who preached the abrogation of the Talmud, the trinitarianism of the Deity, and that Poland rather than Palestine was the promised land. 'I come', he said, 'to deliver the world from every law and statute which has been in force until now.' Sins of every kind were sanctified, provided that they were committed with religious fervour. Orgies took the place of mystic speculation, and pagan rites became the order of the day. Jewry sighed with relief when Frank and his followers embraced Christianity in 1759.

Innumerable texts cite the exact dates on which the various redemptions were to take place. Needless to say, all these dates were at variance. Nahmanides, basing his prediction on Daniel

12:11, predicted that the Messiah would appear in 1356.[11] In his commentary on the Pentateuch, Isaac b. Judah Halevi of Sens, in France (second half of the thirteenth century), gives the date as 1403.[12] The Zohar ambiguously characterises the years 1300, 1306, 1676 as 'fateful years'.[13] Isaac Abarbanel (1447-1508) was certain that the Messiah had been born before the expulsion of the Jews from Spain,[14] and R. Abraham b. Eliezer Halevi, the Spanish exile and Cabbalist of the early sixteenth century, pointed out that the pangs of the Messiah commenced in 1492.[15] As late as 1861, R. Meir Loeb b. Jehiel Michael Malbim (1809-79) calculated that the Redemption would begin in 1913, and that the process would take fourteen years.[16]

The mystics maintain that, at the time of the Creation, perfect harmony existed between God and His manifestations, between the upper sephirot and the lower sephirah. The concept of the sephirot is first found in the *Sepher Yetzirah (Book of Creation)* composed between the third and sixth centuries. The ten sephirot are *Kether* (crown), *Hochmah* (wisdom), *Binah* (understanding), *Hesed* (lovingkindness), *Gevurah* (power), *Tipheret* (beauty), *Netzah* (victory), *Hod* (majesty), *Yesod* (foundation) and *Malchut* (sovereignty).

The Lights (*Orot*) of the *En Soph* were shattered by a process known as 'the breaking of the vessels' or 'the death of the kings'. Holy sparks were scattered and the Divine Light was trapped by the *kelipot* ('shells'). The vessels and the shells are of paramount importance, for they contain minute particles of the *En Soph*. The exile of the sparks meant the exile of the *Shechinah*. It is the duty of every individual to awaken the dormant sparks and to redeem the lost ones by prayer and by *tikkun* (improvement or rectification). Only when all the holy sparks have been gathered, can the Messiah come. To redeem the scattered sparks, to restore the universe to its original harmony and to reunite the *Shechinah* with the *En Soph*, is the purpose of life.

The Zohar perceives a mystical bond between Israel and the Holy Land, and speaks in rhapsodic terms of 'the inheritance of the Lord', saying: 'Happy is the man who is fortunate enough to dwell there. He causes the dew to fall upon the earth.'[17] The world will be redeemed through the redemption of Israel, and Israel's redemption is contingent upon her reunion with the Creator. The Holy Land will be called in Messianic times 'the Land of God's pleasure'. God will enter into a spiritual marriage with this land and it will be transferred into Paradise, the land of beauty and fertility. 'My heart always burns,' lamented R. Isaiah Horowitz, 'when I behold Jews building houses like fortresses and establishing permanent roots in the land of impurity.'[18]

After the expulsion of the Jews from Spain in 1492, the Holy Land became the scene of a remarkable Cabbalist renaissance. High on the slopes of the graceful Galilean hills, looking towards lofty snow-capped Hermon, lies the picturesque town-let of Safed, which became the home of many celebrated scholars in the sixteenth century. Here lived the far-famed masters of mysticism, men whose vision added new light and new dimension to everyday life. By means of self-afflictions (*siguphim*), fasts (*taaniyot*), ablutions (*tevilot*) and ardent worship, they strove for closer communion with God. For them prayer was a means of ascent. Every word, every gesture, every act, every thought was fraught with untold significance. Every blade of grass, every flower, every element of nature was a manifestation of the Creator and his loving concern for man.

Foremost of the Cabbalists was Yitzhak Luria Ashkenazi (1534-72) known as *Ha-Ari Ha-Kadosh* ('the Holy Lion'). Luria was born in Jerusalem and was brought up by his uncle Mordecai Francis of Cairo. His teachers were Bezalel Ashkenazi and R. David Solomon ibn Abi Zimra, both rabbis of Cairo. He left Egypt with his wife in 1568 and settled in Safed. Luria rejected the divine all-inclusiveness postulated by the Zohar. He developed the concept of *tzimtzum*, meaning 'contraction' or 'withdrawal', which suggests that God initially withdrew part of Himself into Himself to provide an empty space for Creation.

Luria's teachings were disseminated by his disciples, who called themselves 'the lion's whelps', especially Hayyim Vital (1543-1620), who not only gave form and immortality to his master's doctrines but believed that his soul was that of the Messiah, the son of Joseph. Their doctrines were saturated with the theme of national redemption and preparations for the coming of the Redeemer.

The seventeenth century saw the influx of mystical-minded sages. Solomon b. Hayyim Meinstril of Landesberg, drawn by the 'magnificent and holy wisdom to be found in the land of the living', settled in Safed in 1602, founding Talmudic academies and a large synagogue. Eighteen years later R. Isaiah Horowitz, the author of *Shne Luhot Ha-Berit (The Two Tablets of the Covenant)* which became so popular that the name formed from the initials of its title, *Shelah*, replaced the original name of the author, left his family and community in Prague and settled in Jerusalem. To his sons and daughters he wrote in November 1621:[19]

Although Jerusalem lies in ruins now, it is still the glory of the whole earth. There is peace and safety, good food and delicious wine, all much cheaper than in Safed . . . My beloved children, tell everybody who intends to go to the Holy Land to settle in Jerusalem. Let nobody assume that I give this advice because I shall settle there. Far be it from me! But I give this advice in all sincerity because all good is there, and nothing is lacking. The city is enclosed and surrounded by a wall. It is as big as Lvov but the most important point is that it is particularly holy and the gate of heaven. I have firm confidence that the Lord will let much knowledge of Torah spread through me, so that the words: 'Out of Zion shall go forth the Law' may be fulfilled.

In 1699 Judah Hasid Segal (1660-1700), the fiery Maggid of Szydlowiec whom many suspected of being a secret follower of Sabbatai Zevi, left Grodno with 120 people. He, like his disciples, wore a white shroud and as they travelled through Altona, Frankfurt and Vienna, their numbers grew to 1,300.

Then some headed for Constantinople, and Judah Hasid and his party went to Venice. The wealthy Samuel Oppenheimer of Vienna hired two boats for the would-be immigrants, but many did not survive the journey. No more than about 1,000 of them reached the Holy Land, but since there were only 300 Jewish families–some 1,200 people–there already, with the arrival of Judah Hasid and his group on 14 October 1700, the Jewish population was virtually doubled. Unhappily, Judah died five days later. His followers purchased a site on which they erected the Synagogue of Judah He-Hasid and forty homes for the poor. The new settlers borrowed heavily from the Arabs, who in November 1701 attacked them, destroying the synagogue and driving most of them to Safed and Hebron. Only a few remained in the Old City. In 1756-7 Feivish Ashkenazi was sent to Amsterdam, Mainz and London to collect funds for the rebuilding of the synagogue.[20] The rebuilt sanctuary was known as 'Hurvah Rabbi Judah He-Hasid' ('the Ruin of Rabbi Judah the Pious').

II

THE HASIDIC TRAIL-BLAZERS

The eighteenth century has been called 'the century of the true renaissance', or 'the age of science and history, the age of the triumph of the empirical fact.' It was the age of contrasts; of enlightened absolutism and despotism, the age of Louis XVI of France, Peter the Great and Catherine II of Russia, and Maria Theresa of Austria. But it was also the age of humanism, of Rousseau, Newton, Kant and Goethe. Rousseau and his successors examined the problems of human existence in a new and different light. The Methodists, the Quakers and the Evangelists in England, the Swedenborgians in Sweden, the Bohemian Brethren in central Europe and the Quietists in France and in Germany strove in their various ways to foster the inner life through meditation and prayer.

It was in this mid-eighteenth century that eastern Europe gave birth to the greatest revivalist movement in Jewish history. Hasidism was not a new form of Judaism but a revival of quintessential Judaism. Its objective was to establish the kingdom of God. Boldly it proclaimed that every human being has a rightful place in the world.

Poland was the third largest country in Europe, comprising territory which, since the formal merging in 1569 of the crowns of Poland and Lithuania, stretched for nearly a thousand miles from the Dnieper to the Oder, from the Baltic to the Black Sea. Three-quarters of the inhabitants were peasants, most of whom were serfs. The nobility numbered between half to three-quarters of a million people, of whom perhaps only twenty to thirty families were major magnates. They controlled church appointments, the legislature, the Diets and such local councils as existed. They were exempted from taxation and military service. The ruling nobility had neither aptitude nor inclination for commerce. The peasants needed middlemen, the townsfolk needed merchants, and the nobility needed financiers. The Jews were well equipped to play these diverse roles and were consequently welcomed to medieval Poland.

As early as 1264, Boleslaw V (the Pious) of Great Poland (1243-79) granted the Jews inviolability of person and property. For wounding or killing a Jew, the Charter threatened severe penalties. Violation of a Jewish cemetery was punishable by forfeiture of all estates. He safeguarded the interests of Jewish creditors, exempted them from the jurisdiction of the common courts and placed them under the personal protection of the throne.

Allied to these economic opportunities was an unusual degree of religious freedom. On 13 August 1551 Augustus II (1548-72) laid the foundation for autonomous Jewish life. Jews were empowered to elect their own *kahal* which controlled the community from the cradle to the grave. The Vaad Arba Aratzot (the Council of the Four Lands) issued edicts and directives on every phase of life. 'The representatives of the Council of the Four Lands', remarked the chronicler R. Nathan Nata Hanover (d. 1683) in *Yeven Metzula*, 'reminded one of the Sanhedrin ... They dispensed justice to all the Jews of the Polish realm, issued preventive measures and obligatory enactments, and imposed penalties as they saw fit.'

The Jewish community paid dearly for its privileges, and the Diet raised the Jewish poll tax to 105,000 guldens. Every adult Jew was subject to a tax of 1 gulden per head and a general tax based upon his income. In addition, he paid a 'purchase tax' on most of the commodities of daily life. In essence he was paying protection money, but it provided little insurance when the power of the monarch collapsed with catastrophic suddenness in the sixteenth century; instantly the Jews were victimised.

With 'fire and sword' the Cossack leader Chmielnicki (1593-1657) ravaged the defenceless Jewish community. In the Ukraine, over 100,000 Jews were slain and 774 communities were all but annihilated. Only one-tenth of that community survived this holocaust, and one-third of Polish Jewry perished. It was a genocidal devastation that ranked with the destruction of the Second Temple among the major disasters of Jewish history. *Gezerot Tah* ('the fateful events of 1648'), as the Chmielnicki massacres were known, were to be exceeded only by the Hitlerite slaughters of World War II. Jews were forced to leave their rural villages to take refuge in large cities, and their economic conditions degenerated.

The rehabilitation of stricken Jewry was retarded by the Russian and Swedish invasions. The Muscovites swept into Poland from the east, and the Swedes from the west. Warsaw was occupied by the Swedes under Charles Gustav in 1655, and king Jan Kazimierz fled to Silesia. For the next twenty years Poland was the setting for a struggle between Charles XII of Sweden and Augustus the Strong of Saxony. Jews were also the prey of Haidamacks, a gang of murderous bandits who roamed through Podolia and Volhynia between 1734 and 1768. According to some authorities the number of victims reached 20,000. Harassment also came from the 'Confederation of the Bar', an association founded by Polish nobles for 'the Defence of the Fatherland', who exorted war levies from the Jewish communities.

At this time infamous blood-libels were revived at Biala (1710), Dubno (1716), Lvov (1728), Poznan (1736-40), Zaslava (1747) and Zhitomir (1753). Augustus III (1696-1763) in 1739 barred from Poland those Jews whom the Austrian authorities had banished from Breslau and other cities in Silesia.[1]

'Poland's strength lies in anarchy', declared Andrew Maximillian Fredro, Marshal of the Seym. The twin mainsprings of Poland's decline were the elected monarchy and the liberum veto. Poland had a weak executive. The Diet comprised a House of Senators and a House of Deputies. The Senate members were bishops and high government officers. The deputies were culled exclusively from the gentry on a constituency basis. According to the liberum veto (first adopted in 1652), all votes of the Diet had to be unanimous. Should any one member express dissent, the debate would be resumed and continue until such a time as unanimity was achieved. If no such agreement could be reached during the six weeks' session, the Seym was adjourned normally for two years without any decision having been recorded. Between 1652 and 1763 forty-eight of the fifty-five biennial Sessions were unsatisfactorily terminated by the misuse of this pernicious veto. 'With a single word,' wrote Vespazan Kochowski (1633-99), 'God created the world, and with a single word Poland is being destroyed.'[2]

A 1764 census listed 548,777 Jews living in Polish crown domains and 201,191 in Lithuania, a total of 749,968.[3] Nearly one-third of Polish Jewry lived in villages, nine-tenths of them relying for their livelihood on the sale of alcohol and beer. There was fierce competition among the arendars (lessees in general, usually publicans) who were at the scarcely tender mercies of the nobility who granted them their licences. According to the Polish statesman Tadeusz Czachi, 72,000 Jews were unemployed.[4]

The poor were helpless. 'The tax collectors come to their homes and take all they find,' records a contemporary scholar. 'They are left naked and without any utensils and clothing for wife and children. Everything is removed and sold to cover the taxes. The straw is taken out of the beds of the poor and they are left in the cold rain, shivering and crying, each in his corner, husband, wife and children.'[5] In 1764 the government of Poland levied a poll tax of 2 gulden, relieving the Vaad of their task of collecting communal taxes.

Class distinctions among the Jews themselves were clear cut. Their scholars had as little in common with the unlettered Jewish masses as the Polish nobles had with the peasantry. The rabbis were 'little foxes damaging the vineyards of the Lord ... No one enquires after the welfare of his neighbour, but they hate each other.'[6] Many scholars were concerned with fame and honours. The reins were in the hands of a few wealthy oligarchs who were indifferent to the wretched plight of the poor. 'They live in luxury and splendour,' writes R. Joseph Yoske (d. 1702), great-grandfather of the historian Simon Dubnow, 'and do not bear the burden of taxes and other communal levies. They impose heavy burdens. They take the lion's share of all honours and distinctions ... and the congregation of God, the children of Abraham and Jacob, are crushed and humiliated.'

For the great majority, the sole source of instruction was the *heder*. Few had the privilege of attending a yeshiva, and the Talmud was a closed book to most of the country folk. Only for a select handful did the study of the Talmud constitute 'the primary object of education', wrote the philosopher Solomon Maimon (1754-1800). 'A man of wealth, although esteemed by our people cannot compare to the dignity of an erudite Talmudist. He can claim all sorts of offices, and play the leading role in the community. Wherever he attends an assembly, all rise respectfully and escort him to the honoured seat. He is the adviser, the legislator, the judge of the common folk.'[7]

Superstition was rife in Podolia and Volhynia and people were bewildered by the smouldering trails of the pseudo-Messiahs. A popular book at that time was *Kav Ha-Yashar* (*The Just Measure*) by Zevi Hirsch Koidanover (d. 1712). 'Son of man, if you knew how many evil spirits lurk in each drop of blood in your heart, you would immediately dedicate your body and soul to the service of God.' Koidanover theorised that the redemption would start in the north, in Poland and Lithuania.[8] Simone b. Isaac Luzzatto (1580-1663) called Poland the Cabbalist centre,[9] because it produced three great Cabbalists, Isaiah Horowitz, Nathan Spiro and Samson b. Pesah Ostropoler.

Among the people wandered baale shem, itinerant teachers who seemed to perform miracles, healing the sick and driving out dybbukim by means of the Divine Name. Such men were Elijah b. Judah of Chelm (1514-83), Elijah b. Moses Ashkenazi Loanz of Worms (1555-1636), Joel b. Isaac Heilperin of Ostrog (mid-seventeenth century) and Seckel Wormser (1768-1847), the Baal Shem of Michelstadt.

Out of this dark age of religous stagnation, Hasidim was born. The theory that Hasidism was inspired by non-Jewish sources is untenable.[10] In the Golden Age of Spain, the Jews were part of the Arab culture, influenced by the thought and culture of the country in which they lived. Conditions were different in eastern Europe. Although there were no specific ghettos in Poland, the Jews invariably clustered together, building their fragile defences, the morals and the mores, which were an integral part of their religion, and which set them apart from their non-Jewish neighbours.

Fundamentally Judaism was revitalised when Hasidim stressed the cardinal virtues that the prophets had preached; faith and joy in the performance of *mitzvot;* prayer with intention and intensity because the focus was on soul rather than on intellect, on the service of the heart. It raised the unlettered Jew to the spiritual level of the scholar. Everyone was a co-worker with the Almighty in the work of redemption, for every act could be redemptive. God was to be served not solely through the study of the Torah, but also through prayer, through song, through dance, through deeds of lovingkindness. By such deeds man restored the sparks of holiness to the Divine source bringing about unification (*yihud*) in the higher sephirot by *hitbodedut* (solitary communion), *hitlahavut* (fervour or ecstasy) and *kavanah* (concentration).

Hasidism swept away the barrier between the supernatural and natural, the possible and the impossible, the reality and the dream. The Hasidic vision embraced the highest heavens, yet it was rooted in the dreary commonplaces of everyday life. It brought comfort, courage and a form of other-worldly ecstasy to the suffering step-children of humanity.

The Baal Shem Tov (1700-60), or 'the Besht' as he was popularly known, was born in Tluste on the old Polish-Turkish border. Living on the fringe of the Carpathian mountains, he was inspired by the splendour of unravaged nature, and spent many days in total solitude roaming the hills and forests. The historian Simon Dubnow believes that he participated in the Kamenets-Podolski debate with the Frankists in 1757 which resulted in the burning of the Talmud. [11]

Despite our lack of authentic data regarding his parentage, early upbringing and family life, Rabbi Israel Baal Shem Tov is no shadowy figure. Legends have fleshed out the skeletal outlines. 'I have come unto this world', he said, 'to show man how to make the observance of three principles his aim in life, namely love of God, love of Israel, and love of the Torah.' He transformed abstractions into living realities, speaking directly to the masses in a language they understood. The anecdote, the parable and the metaphor took the place of exegesis. His emphasis was on *olam ha-zeh* (this world), whereas the mystics had focused on the transcendental aspects of the Upper Worlds and 'cosmic lights beyond the mortal ken'.

The Besht aimed not to bring man closer to God but to bring God closer to man. He rejected asceticism and self-affliction. As a child of the Cabbalah, he was heir to the doctrines of the Lurian mystics and to their yearning for redemption. Yet Gershom Scholem maintains that after the collapse of the Sabbatian messianic movement in its Frankist form, the Hasidim adopted a neutral stand towards the messianic ideal. Although the Besht yearned for the Messiah, he did not speculate on the exact moment of his arrival. In this respect he followed Isaac Arama (1420-94), who criticised such messianic speculation. A similar attitude had been adopted by such authorities as Azariah dei Rossi (1511-78), Judah Löw b. Bezalel (1525-1609) and Manasseh Ben Israel (1604-57). Maimonides specifically stated: 'It is a fundamental dogma to believe in the coming of the Messiah, even if he is delayed. But no one should attempt to guess or fix the time.'[12]

According to the Besht, exile from the Holy Land was the cause of the Jewish spiritual degeneration. One New Year's Day, he pondered the text (Jer.9:18): 'How we are undone! We are greatly confounded, because we have forsaken the land'. 'O prophet Elijah,' the rabbi exclaimed: 'when will you come and announce the advent of the Messiah? When will the Temple and the altar be rebuilt? When shall we return to our father's table? Woe unto the children who are exiled from their father's table!'[13] On another occasion he remarked: 'Here we do not have the security we enjoyed in the Holy Land. When shall we hear the clarion call of the Messiah?'

Every individual could help to hasten the advent of the Messiah, and national redemption would only be achieved as the result of individual efforts. Every human being had in himself a spark of the soul of the Messiah. By perfecting himself, he hastened the redemption. By engaging in dissension and disputes and causeless hatred he delayed it.[14] 'I asked the Messiah when he would come,' wrote the Besht in 1752 to R. Abraham Gershon b. Ephraim Kutower, his brother-in-law, 'And he answered: "Not until your teachings have spread throughout the world." '

The Besht yearned to fulfil the commandment to live in the land of Israel and to plant the seeds of Hasidism in the hallowed soil, a fusion that could speed the messianic era. 'What shall I do?', he lamented. 'I desire to be buried in the Holy Land.

From there the soul ascends higher.'[15] On another occasion he
said, 'If only one more person would recite "Merciful and
Gracious God answer me" with the same passion that I do, we
could together bring the Messiah.'[16]

According to tradition, the Besht set out three times for the
Holy Land. The *Praise of the Baal Shem Tov*[17] records that once
robbers came to him and said, 'Sir, we know a short cut to the
Land of Israel through caves and underground passages. If you
wish to come with us, we will show you the way.' He agreed to
accompany them. At one point they came to a wide muddy
ditch crossed by a narrow plank. The robbers went first. When
the Besht was about to step onto the plank, a flaming sword
barred his way and he was forced to turn back.

Another legend relates that the Master set out from Miedzyborz on the perilous pilgrimage. This time he was accompanied by his daughter Adel and one of his disciples. The three
pilgrims travelled for many days and after many adventures
they arrived in Istanbul where they celebrated the Passover.
Then they were fortunate enough to find a ship and they
eagerly embarked on the last stage of their journey. Joyfully,
the Besht dreamed of the moment when he would enter
Jerusalem. He would weep as his ancestors had wept at the
Western Wall. He would visit the holy cities of Hebron, Safed
and Tiberias. Every stone, tree and valley would hold mystical
meaning for him.

But on the fourth day a band of pirates fell upon the ship and
took the passengers captive. The Besht's mind became blank.
His learning vanished. He could recall nothing, not a single
passage of the Torah nor a single prayer. He could remember
only the first four letters of the Hebrew alphabet, *aleph*, *bet*,
gimel, *dalet*. The three captives recited these letters with such
great fervour that by the time they had reached the fourth letter
the pirates had vanished and the Rabbi and his companions
were back in Miedzyborz. Although the hour of redemption
was not at hand, the Hasidim maintain that had the Besht set

foot in the land of Israel, nothing could have delayed the coming
of the Messiah. And so the Master's plans were frustrated by
higher forces, and the world still waits for the destined hour.[18]

'God knows', writes the Besht in a letter to his brother-in-
law, 'that I have not given up hope of travelling to the Land of
Israel.'[19] He tried to obtain from the Holy Land such religious
requisites as spices for Havdalah and covers for phylacteries,[20]
and an *etrog*,[21] and he grieved because he was not able to help
the settlers financially.[22] However, a number of his disciples
and associates did make the journey successfully. One such
emigrant was R. Abraham Gershon b. Ephraim Kutower
(named after the town of Kuty, south of Kolomyja), brother-in-
law of the Besht.

Jonathan Eibeschütz (*c.* 1690-1764) of Prague called Abraham
Gershon 'the pious Rabbi',[23] and Ezekiel b. Judah Landau
(1713-93), the *Noda Bi-Yehudah*, described him as 'the perfect
sage, a holy saint'.[24] A judge in one of the four courts in Brody,
R. Abraham Gershon also served for a time as the synagogue
cantor.[25] At first, he had not recognised the hidden greatness of
his sister's husband, but later he became a devoted follower of
the Besht and the teacher of his only son Zevi.[26] R. Abraham
Gershon associated with the Hasidic group in Kuty[27] and
prayed according to Lurian liturgy.[28]

Accompanied by his second wife and his two young sons,
Hayyim Aaron and Yakir,[29] R. Abraham Gershon travelled
through Istanbul where he became acquainted with Moses
Soncino, and arrived in Jerusalem on the eve of the New Year
1747. He was warmly greeted by the Sephardim, especially
those who had been associated with Judah Hasid. He lived in
Hebron for six years (1747-53), visiting Jerusalem from time to
time. His reputation must have preceded him for the Jews of
Jerusalem invited him to become their spiritual leader, a post
which he was reluctant to accept. 'All my life', he wrote to the
Besht, 'I have avoided honour. This must be the work of the
evil power. He caught me in a moment of pride.' He kept in

touch with Yitzhak Zechariah Azulai. In 1757 he moved to Jerusalem. At that time there were twelve small yeshivot in that city, nine for scholars and three for laymen. R. Abraham Gershon was associated with Yeshiva Bet El (situated near the synagogue of Johanan b. Zakkai) which had been founded in 1737 by the Cabbalist R. Gedaliah Hayon (d.1751) and his son-in-law R. Shalom Mizrachi Sharabi (1720-1777), known as *Ha-Reshash*.

Many regarded Sharabi as the spiritual heir of Isaac Luria.[30] Among the scholars at Bet El were Rabbis Hayyim Joseph David Azulai (1724-1806), Yom Tov b. Israel Jacob Algazi[31] and David Samuel b. Jacob Pardo.[32] Bet El had a fraternal association called Ahavat Shalom, whose members pledged to come to one another's aid 'in both spiritual and material matters, in this world and the next'.[33]

Rabbi Abraham Gershon was pleasantly surprised by the cordial relations that existed between the Arabs and the Jews. 'The most distinguished of the Gentiles here,' he wrote, 'like the Jews very much, and when circumcision rites or other festivities take place, they come . . . in the evening and entertain the Jews, beating out rhythms and dancing amongst them—spare the mark–like Jews.'[34] The Besht often wrote to him and occasionally sent him funds. It is, however, difficult to judge the authenticity of many letters that have since appeared.[35]

R. Abraham Gershon venerated his brother-in-law, 'the Divine Cabbalist', and asked him for amulets. 'Pray for me,' responded the Master, 'that I may be worthy to share the inheritance of the Lord.'[36] R. Abraham in turn replied: 'Your fame is known at the Gates. The Sages here have asked me to write to you and urge you to make your home with us.'[37] Long-distance vision served the Besht well. 'One Friday I searched for R. Abraham Gershon throughout the Holy Land,' he said, 'and I could not find him anywhere. But the next morning I found him.' R. Abraham Gershon explained that he had spent that particular Sabbath at Acre, worshipping on the

Friday night in a synagogue which in the Talmudic period was technically outside the northern boundary of the Land of Israel. [38]

News of R. Hayyim b. Moses Ibn Attar (1696-1743) reached the Besht. A native of Morocco, he became a renowned Cabbalist, and lived for a while in Leghorn. His commentary on the Pentateuch *Or Ha-Hayyim* was printed in Venice in 1742 'The zaddikim will redeem the Jews from exile', maintained R. Hayyim, 'for the zaddik is near to God, as it is said (Lev.10:3): "Through them that are nigh unto Me I will be sanctified".'[39] In a public proclamation, R. Hayyim urged his fellow Jews to settle in the Holy Land: 'Come, let us go to the mountain of the Lord.'

In 1741, he left Leghorn with his two wives (as an Oriental, he was not bound by the monogamous enactment of Rabbenu Gershom) and thirty followers. An epidemic in Jerusalem forced him to spend several months at Acre. He visited near-by Kfar Pekiin where he found a number of Jews engaged in agriculture. 'They live in freedom and peace,' he wrote. 'There is no jealousy or hatred among them.' In Jerusalem he established a Bet Hamidrash known as Yeshivat Knesset Yisrael, where a great deal of time was devoted to the study of the Zohar. Among his disciples was Hayyim Joseph David Azulai. R. Hayyim ibn Attar died on 15 Tammuz 1743 and was buried on the Mount of Olives.

According to the Besht, the soul of R. Hayyim was the soul of King David and he was one of the 'Riders of the Chariot' (masters of mysticism). When R. Hayyim died, the Besht proclaimed, 'The Western Light has been extinguished.' The Besht was anxious for him to meet R. Abraham Gershon, but by the time the former arrived, R. Hayyim was dead. Abraham Gershon reported the disappointing news to the Besht: 'He came from the west, and he was a spark from the Messiah, but he was not aware of it. He was a great scholar, well versed in Rabbinics and mysticism. He arrived in Jerusalem with many disciples. Unfortunately he lived there for only one year.'[40] There is a contrary theory, unsupported by fact, that R. Abraham Gershon went to the Holy Land before 1743[41] and did meet R. Hayyim before he died.

R. Abraham Gershon, in Iyyar 1757, was among the signatories of an appeal to the community of Mainz for support of the Holy Land.[42] He died on 25 Adar and was buried on the Mount of Olives.[43] For more than two hundred years the grave could not be found, but it was rediscovered after the Six-Day War.

Hayyim Aaron and Yakir, the two sons of R. Abraham Gershon, were concerned about the welfare of their fellow-Jews. In a letter dated 1763, they appealed once more to the community of Mainz, for conditions had deteriorated after the Russo-Turkish war, and the revolt of Dher el Amr. In 1768 R. Hayyim Aaron himself visited Bamberg and other cities in Germany on behalf of the settlers in the Holy Land.

Four years after the death of the Besht, two of his associates, R. Nahman of Horodenka (d. 1786) and R. Menahem Mendel of Peremyslany (1728-72) settled in 1764-5 in the Holy Land.

R. Nahman was related by marriage to R. Ephraim of Sudylkow, a grandson of the Besht. Like the second-century *tanna*, Nahum of Gimzo, R. Nahman of Horodenka accepted every misfortune with *gam zu letovah* ('This, too, is for the best'), for his faith was 'as strong as a pillar of fire'. He accompanied R. Israel on many journeys. 'I have afflicted my soul and I have immersed myself in the ritual baths,' said R. Nahman, 'but I could not rid myself of evil thoughts until I became attached to Rabbi Israel.'

Rabbi Nahman's companion, Menahem Mendel, was a man of outstanding humility who for twelve years was silent, not uttering a single word. Before his emigration, he visited Gekinowka and Soroki, townlets on the Dniester, where he occupied himself with 'the redemption of captives'. 'If we divert our thoughts from devotion to God, and study excessively,' he maintained, 'we will forget the fear of Heaven . . . Study should therefore be reduced and one should always meditate on the greatness of the Creator.' He was thirty-six years old when he undertook the journey to the Holy Land.[44] Coincidentally, Simhah, son of R. Joshua of Zalosce,[45] was on the same boat. The pilgrims left Galatz on 27 Iyyar and Istanbul on 18 Elul. On the eve of the New Year 1765 they arrived at Jaffa. Some of the Sephardi passengers disembarked, but the Hasidim continued by sea to Acre. The journey should have taken six hours, but a violent storm prolonged it for eight days. In the midst of the storm, R. Nahman assembled a quorum and with a Scroll of the Law in his hand, he declared: 'Lord of the Universe, if it has been decreed by thy Heavenly Court that we should perish, then this Holy congregation jointly with the Divine Presence declares that we refuse to accept the decree. We demand prompt annulment.' They landed at Acre on 12 Tishri.

Tiberias had been resettled by R. Hayyim Abulafia, who had come from Izmir in Turkey at the invitation of Sheikh Dher el Amr. R. Nahman lived there until his death ten years later. In one of his letters he wrote, 'Tradition maintains that the air of the Holy Land makes one wise. Before I came here I hoped I would learn to recite one prayer properly. Now that I am wiser, I would be happy if I could utter one word properly.'[46] R. Nahman yearned to meet the Cabbalist R. Eleazar b. Samuel Rokeah (1665-1742) but the meeting never took place.

Settling in Jerusalem R. Menahem Mendel urged his brother Zevi of Zloczow to follow his example. 'How long will you stay in the Diaspora?', he wrote, and 'How long will you listen to those who speak in derogatory terms of the Holy Land?'[47]

Eleazar, a native of Cracow, was rabbi of Brody for twenty years (1714-34) after which he became rabbi in Amsterdam. A medal was designed in his honour, one side showing his head in relief surrounded by the words, 'Eleazar ben Samuel, rabbi of Brody'. The other side was inscribed with verses from the Psalms. In 1740, at the age of seventy-five, he left for the Holy

Land. In the preface to his work *Maaseh Rokeah* (a Cabbalist commentary on the Mishnah), he writes,[48] 'I was a father to many communities and I had religious and communal responsibilities ... I have resolved to settle in the Holy Land where I can serve the Lord in purity and holiness.' He settled in Safed in 1741, but his stay in the Holy Land brought him no peace, for he became involved in a controversy with a number of Cabbalists who supported Nehemiah Hayun, an adherent of Sabbatai Zevi. In Amsterdam Eleazar had excommunicated the Cabbalist poet Moses Hayyim Luzzatto (1707-47) for claiming to be the forerunner of the Messiah. He was even less tolerant of Nehemiah Hayun. Eleazar died in 1742.

According to the *Praise of the Besht*, R. Eleazar had gone to the Holy Land for the express purpose of meeting R. Nahman, because 'When both of us are in the Holy Land, we will bring the redeemer.' R. Eleazar, however, died before R. Nahman's arrival.[49]

III

THE FIRST HASIDIC ALIYAH

In Adar 1777, 300 Hasidim left eastern Europe for the Holy Land under the leadership of R. Menahem Mendel of Vitebsk.

At first, Hasidism had been confined mainly to Podolia, Volhynia and Galicia, but under R. Israel Baal Shem Tov's successor R. Dov Baer the Maggid of Mezeritz (d. 1773), the movement expanded and his disciples spread Hasidic ideas to even remote villages in Poland and Lithuania. Like all new religious sects throughout the ages, Hasidim were at first persecuted, their principles distorted and their practices maligned. Talmudists put aside the calm deliberations that had cloaked their every utterance, precipitously condemning the movement and excommunicating its followers. Elijah b. Solomon, Gaon of Vilna, probably the greatest *halachic* authority since Maimonides, became Hasidism's greatest opponent.

Though he himself was a mystic and author of commentaries on the mystical work *Sepher Yetzirah* and on the Zohar, the Gaon failed to recognise the value and potential of Hasidism. He regarded it as having more in common with Sabbatianism, Frankism and mystical heresies than with Luria's Cabbalah. In

1772, with the approval of the Gaon, the *kahal* of Vilna issued a *herem* (ban of excommunication) against the 'godless sect'.

With the death of R. Dov Baer, his devoted disciple, Menahem Mendel of Vitebsk tried to maintain the epoch of unified leadership. He believed that only under centralised direction could Hasidism withstand the onslaught of its detractors. As a youth, Menahem Mendel had visited R. Israel twice, but he had studied Hasidism under Dov Baer.

During his master's lifetime, Menahem Mendel was Rabbi of Minsk, a 'fortress of *mitnagdim*'. He was one of Hasidism's most profound thinkers, combining erudition with humility. His closest friend was R. Shneur Zalman b. Baruch of Lyady, founder of Habad Hasidism. In 1775, Menahem Mendel accompanied by Shneur Zalman came to Vilna to seek a personal inverview with the Gaon. They felt that Elijah's knowledge of Hasidic doctrines came to him from devious sources, unreliable and biased, that he had probably never met a Hasid and was probably unfamiliar with Hasidic writings.[1]

However, the Gaon would not consent to meet 'the un-believers', with whom all contact was forbidden. In the words of R. Shneur Zalman: 'He shut the doors on us twice.' Menahem Mendel felt that he could do nothing to stop the fratricidal war that was being unleashed against the Hasidim. The disciples of Dov Baer were establishing their own courts, and the cords that bound the disciples first to Miedzyborz and then to Mezeritz were broken. He still hoped to restore Hasidism to its original glory as one cohesive entity, and thought that he might be able to accomplish this in the Holy Land, which is 'the heart of the world from which salvation and mercy sprout forth'. 'For the Jew who lives in Eretz Yisrael is holy and pure and is able to purify others,' he said. 'Moreover he has the power to influence those who live in the Diaspora.'[2] He ignored those who protested that his departure would deprive them of their spokesman and defender.[3] 'I will be of greater service to you in the Holy Land,' he reasoned.

'For there I will awaken mercy from above and intercede for the congregation of Israel.'[4]

In Adar 1777, Menahem Mendel left Horodok, near Vitebsk, with two colleagues, Abraham b. Alexander Katz of Kalisk (Klyzski) a disciple of Dov Baer, and the fiery preacher Israel b. Peretz of Polotsk. At first they tried to limit the group to those who had means of sustenance, but this restriction proved unrealistic and could not be enforced. For nearly five months they journeyed in leisurely fashion across Volhynia in the Ukraine, and 300 people joined them, including R. Shneur Zalman who accompanied them to Mogilev.

At Galatz, the group embarked for Istanbul. Among them were a number of non-Hasidim, people for whom the climate of eastern Europe had grown unmistakably inhospitable. Many did not have enough money to cover the cost of the journey. 'The Almighty is my witness,' stated R. Menahem Mendel, 'I have not encouraged them. On the contrary, I argued with them . . . I did not even know most of them.'[5] The departure of the emigrants did not please the Polish authorities, since it represented a loss of tax revenue, and it was determined that, as from 27 September 1777, people leaving the country would require special exit permits to be obtained for a fee.[6]

The Jewish community in Istanbul made generous provisions for the pilgrims and arranged their transport to the Holy Land. Tragically one of the vessels capsized near the Crimean peninsula and only thirty of the eighty passengers were rescued. On 5 Elul, the surviving pilgrims arrived in Acre and settled in Safed.

For once, political conditions were favourable for the new settlers. In 1775, the Dher el Amr revolt had been crushed and Ahmad al-Jazzer Pasha, 'the Butcher' (1775-1804), was appointed governor of Sidon. For more than forty years his financial adviser Hayyim Farhi (d. 1820) used his influence to help his fellow-Jews. When R. Menahem Mendel arrived, Safed was still in ruins, the result of the 1759 earthquake in which over 100 Jews perished and four ancient synagogues were destroyed. Five years later, R. Simha of Zalosce estimated that only forty or fifty Jews were left there. The new ruler was anxious to attract new settlers and welcomed R. Menaham Mendel and his people, granting them tax concessions and permission to rebuild their synagogues and their homes. R. Menahem Mendel was overjoyed. 'At last the day has come for which we have waited with such impatience,' he wrote home. 'How happy we are in this Holy Land, the delight of our hearts, the joy of our thoughts, the land which is hallowed by so many different kinds of sanctity.'[7]

They were also welcomed by an unwonted display of cordiality on the part of the Sephardim. In 1763, the Ashkenazim had written to the Jewish community of Mainz complaining bitterly about the ungenerous attitude of the resident Sephardim. 'When we approach them for help, they retort, "Why do you not approach your wealthy Ashkenazim in Germany? What have we in common with you?" ' The erudite R. Menahem Mendel, however, was warmly received and this pleasant relationship was cemented by the marriage of Moses, his son, to a Sephardi girl.[8]

The newcomers were aware of the potential of their new country where they found 'houses without inhabitants'. But although the long-term prospects were bright, ignorance of the vernacular and of local customs hampered their progress. Prices soared, the funds of the settlers were soon exhausted, and R. Menahem Mendel had to concern himself with their material needs. 'Even a man with the heart of a lion melts when he beholds infants begging for bread.' R. Menahem Mendel enlisted the support of his followers in Russia, but letters did not produce any immediate result. So he sent R. Israel ben Peretz of Polotsk, accompanied by Shlomoh Segal and Israel Ber of Lubavitch, to collect funds in eastern Europe. They were the forerunners of many Hasidic meshulahim or shadarim (emissaries).

R. Israel was particularly suited for this role, since he had made the rounds of the villages preaching Hasidism at the behest of Dov Baer. His eloquence won many converts and his pen was as persuasive as his tongue. 'It is your responsibility', he wrote to the heads of Jewish communities in Russia, 'to rebuild the House of God and it is incumbent upon you to support the settlement in the Holy Land . . . Hasten to perform this great *mitzvah* and to sustain the children of Israel, feeding the hungry, and clothing the naked, in order that those who live on holy soil may pray for the scattered community of Israel in exile.'

R. Menahem Mendel stressed the reluctance of R. Israel to leave the Holy Land. 'Even if they were to give him a thousand changes of garments a month, he would not have left of his own free will.' But R. Israel could hardly disobey R. Menahem Mendel. He was sucessful in his mission and sent back large sums of money. Sadly, he never returned home. As he passed Pastov, the burial place of R. Abraham, 'the Angel', he seemed to hear a summons. 'Abraham is calling me,' he said. 'He wants me to be buried at his side.' Abraham's request was granted. Other emissaries of Menahem Mendel were R. Shlomoh Zalman b. Zevi Hirsch Ha-Kohen of Vilna in 1779 or 1780, and seven years later R. Raphael Abraham b. Hayyim Ha-Kohen who was sent to North Africa.[9]

The funds collected in the Diaspora alleviated but did not solve the problems of the settlers. R. Gedaliah of Siemiatycze, a contemporary of R. Menahem Mendel, had his own explanation for the lack of profit-making industries. 'There is also another reason for their inability to make a living . . . Even though liquors are distilled and much wine is manufactured, nevertheless Jews derive no income from them because the Ishmaelites [i.e. the Turks] and the Arabs drink neither wine nor spirits, and if it becomes known that the Jews are producing liquor they are arrested and heavily fined.'[10]

R. Menahem Mendel was in constant contact with R. Shneur Zalman and he tried to stay in touch with his Hasidim. 'You are

my children and I regard you as if I have given birth to you,'
he wrote affectionately to his followers in eastern Europe. 'I
will never forget you. Nothing will divide us. I will never be
oblivious of your needs. Every one of you is inscribed in my
heart.'[11] He regarded himself as 'an ambassador in the court of
the king'. He was, however, reluctant to preoccupy himself
with material matters. 'It is our purpose to help Israel by
means of the Law of God which revives the soul.'[12]

R. Menahem Mendel was grieved to hear of the 'war' that
was being waged against the Hasidim in Russia. He warned
his followers of the dangers of 'hatred without cause ... The
Holy Land was destroyed for this very reason. We are not
guilty of heresy nor do we transgress any Biblical or Rabbinic
ordinances. Surely we can live in peace together? Have we not
all one father, and has not God created us? Why then should
we deal treacherously one against his neighbour?'[13]

Not only did R. Menahem Mendel fail to create peace
among the Hasidim and *mitnagdim* in eastern Europe, but
disharmony followed him even in the Holy Land. The cordiality which first greeted him soon gave way to friction in growing differences between the old settlers and the newcomers.
The Hasidim complained that they did not receive an equitable share of the money collected. The Sephardim counter-
claimed that the Hasidic emissaries were destroying the
centralised agencies. A number of Sephardim, moreover, were
apprehensive about the Sabbatai Zevi heresy, for the allegations levelled against the Hasidim in eastern Europe were
repeated in the Holy Land. People like Sabbetai Leib of Sokal
(Podolia), whom R. Menahem Mendel called 'wicked', and a
certain R. Sabbatai fanned the embers of disagreements into
flames of hatred.[14]

To escape dissension R. Menahem Mendel and some of his
followers settled in Tiberias in 1781. Abraham of Kalisk
remained in Safed and a small number of Hasidim emigrated
to Pekiin (Bekiin), a village in Upper Galilee. Conditions were

not much better in Tiberias, where the local ruler harassed the newcomers.

The Ashkenazim and Hasidim had had to share the same place of worship, and this was not conducive to harmony. The Hasidic adoption of *Nusah Ari* (Lurian liturgy), their different customs and more varied manner of worship aggravated the situation. But gradually conditions improved and R. Menahem Mendel was permitted to hold services in his home and eventually a synagogue was established. R. Baruch of Miedzyborz sent gifts for the new Hasidic place of worship. The Hasidim, despite the opposition of the Sephardim,[15] were able to acquire extra accommodation.

For R. Menahem Mendel, a passionate patriot, the land of Israel was unlike any other country.[16] He did not underestimate the sacrifices that resettlement in the Holy Land involved, but stressed that these sacrifices would be rewarded. He also pointed out that settlers were forbidden to leave the country. Both Mahlon (son of Naomi and first husband of Ruth) and Chilion (husband of Orpah) died because they left the Holy Land, symbolically abandoning any hope of redemption (Ruth 1: 2 and 5).[17]

Human efforts should precede Divine help. There was a precedent for this in Egypt, where the people were required to purify themselves before they were delivered. 'If a man attempts to help himself, he is helped.'[18] However, he discouraged people from immigrating if they were not able to sustain themselves, and R. Joseph Sopher voiced a similar opinion.[19] 'Whoever comes should bring funds with him and not come empty-handed, or else he should be a good artisan, capable of supporting himself.'

In his Last Will and Testament, R. Menahem Mendel suggested that his widow sell the furniture and household effects and utilise the funds for loans to the Ashkenazi Kolel that they might earn a profit and pay her 3 piastres a week.[20] He advised his son Moses not to become a rabbi. No elaborate epitaph was to be inscribed on his tombstone. On the 2 Iyyar 1788 he died and was buried in Tiberias.

After the death of R. Menahem Mendel, his associate R. Abraham of Kalisk (d.1810) became the undisputed leader of the Hasidim in the Holy Land. 'If you only knew', he wrote, 'what a great *mitzvah* it is to sustain the settlers in the Holy Land!' He was a superlative letter-writer and his letters reveal a hard-core pragmatism.[21]

A man who arrives in the Holy Land must adapt himself until it grows upon him and he takes pleasure in her stones and even in the hardships he must endure. He must often be content with a humble cottage ... But if he tries to live in the style to which he was previously accustomed, he may go out of his mind and be induced to blame the land for his misfortune. Therefore, a prospective settler should consider all these things, and question himself to see whether he has the strength to surmount the difficulties, lest he lose even what he had before.

R. Menahem Mendel and his group put the ideals of Hasidism into practice. After a decade only a few were utterly dependant on the Halukah. Others supplemented their income with this extra aid, but most were self-supporting, an extraordinary accomplishment. The economic problems which faced the early Hasidic pioneers discouraged many would-be settlers and inhibited any mass immigration. In the nineteenth century only individuals and small families made the watershed journey to the Holy Land.

IV

THE FLAME OF RABBI NAHMAN

Not since Judah Halevi, that 'fiery pillar of sweet song' to whom Jerusalem was 'the City of the World', had Zion such a lover as R. Nahman of Braclav (1772-1810), the story-teller of Hasidism. The emotions that Judah Halevi expressed in his 'Odes to Zion', R. Nahman voiced in the pithy aphorisms for which he was renowned.

Apart from R. Israel Baal Shem Tov in the eighteenth century, and R. Menahem Mendel of Kotzk in the nineteenth century, no other Hasidic leader has baffled biographers as much as R. Nahman. Despite his voluminous writings and the wealth of material available, this volcanic and complex individual has eluded the grasp of the historians and has remained one of the most intriguing characters in Hasidism. He believed that catastrophe was imminent and that he alone could avert it. Paroxysms of despair alternated with bursts of ebullience, a pattern that continued throughout his brief but tempestuous life.

Nahman was born in Miedzyborz, 'the Jerusalem of Podolia', on Rosh Hodesh Nisan 1772. His father, Simhah, was the son

of R. Nahman of Horodenka, who had settled in the Holy
Land, and his mother Feige was the daughter of Adel, the
only daughter of R. Israel Baal Shem Tov. His uncles were
the scholarly Moses Hayyim Ephraim of Sudylkow and the
turbulent Baruch of Miedzyborz.

Nahman's home was lacking in material comforts, for his
father worked as a pedlar to eke out a meagre existence. Even
as a young child, Nahman showed an inclination to solitude,
which intensified as he grew older. 'Make me worthy to live in
solitude', he prayed, 'so that I may abnegate myself.'[1] His
uncle Moses Ephraim noted the boy's diligence and said at his
bar mitzvah, 'He will be the greatest of all the zaddikim.'

Soon after, the youthful Nahman married the daughter of a
wealthy man, Ephraim Baer of Husiatyn, and at the age of
eighteen he settled in Medvedevka, where he became a highly
non-conformist Rebbe. He did not wish to be indebted to
anyone for anything. 'The world thinks that I owe my attain-
ments to my great-grandfather. That is not so.'[2] 'Every act,
every word is important,' averred R. Nahman. 'A man goes
out into the field and picks flowers one by one and makes them
into a bunch. In this same way, selecting every word carefully, he combines the words of the prayer he presents to
God.'

Following the example of Jacob Joseph of Polonnoye, who
fasted for five years every day until nightfall, Nahman in one
year fasted eighteen times, a week at a time. He leaned
towards the teachings of the Lurian Cabbalists and he derided
the view that a zaddik is born a zaddik and that a 'superior
soul' was a gift from God. Only by strivings and single-
minded intensity could a man acquire a great soul.[3]

Like his great-grandfather, Nahman lived a life of rural
seclusion *(hitbodedut)*, spending his days in mystical study and
meditation. Away from the turmoil of town and townsfolk, he
was never alone and never lonely, for he saw in nature the
power and glory of the Creator. It was said that King Solomon

understood the language of the flowers, the birds and the animals. In a different way, nature spoke to Nahman and through nature spoke God:

'When a man becomes worthy of hearing the songs of the plants, he realises how each plant chants praises to God. How beautiful and sweet it is to hear their singing. Therefore it is good to serve God in their midst, roaming the field amid the growing things and pouring out one's heart before God in truthfulness.'

Unsparing in his criticism, Nahman castigated his fellow-zaddikim as hypocrites. 'Many call themselves "Rabbi", he said, 'but they have no power either over themselves or over others. Yet they aspire to lead the world.'[4] 'Not all who are famous are honest. Many a liar and a scoundrel rides the crest of popular appeal . . . When Satan saw that it was difficult to lead the whole world astray, he appointed a number of such zaddikim in various places to help him in his work.'[5]

Nahman had a high opinion of his own worth. 'I shall make a path through the desert,' he proclaimed. 'I shall hew down one by one the trees which have stood for thousands of years, so that no obstacle stands in our path.' He was certain of his powers. 'I am like the man who wanders in a wilderness and seeks to find a way.' He believed that the Messiah would be one of his descendants[6] and that the holy spirit flowed through him. 'Since the Jews were dispersed from the Holy Land,' he stated, 'there have been four periods of learning. At the centre of each era stood a chosen leader: R. Simon Bar Yohai, R. Isaac Luria, R. Israel Baal Shem Tov and R. Nahman. Each of these leaders gave the Jewish people a deeper insight into the holy Torah through which they derive their inner strength. All who undertake the study of my teachings will be granted the strength needed to cling steadfastly to their faith until the arrival of the Messiah,' for he regarded himself as the fire which cleanses all impurities.[7]

R. Nahman defined the zaddik as one who could perform miracles in heaven as well as on earth, who was able to create a new heaven and a new earth. He was the soul of the people and endowed with 'Divine eyes'; he could hear confessions and grant atonement and only through the zaddik could the ordinary man reach God.

Nahman valued faith above philosophy and simplicity above sophistication. 'It is better to be a believer, although unlettered, than a scholar and a sceptic.' In an age which produced Moses Mendelssohn (1722-86) and Solomon Maimon, Nahman despised philosophers. 'Happy is he who knows nothing of their books, but who walks uprightly and fears retribution.' Even Maimonides, the greatest Jewish philosopher of all time, did not escape censure. 'He who looks into the *Moreh* [Maimonides' *Guide for the Perplexed*]', pronounced R. Nahman severely, 'forfeits the Divine image.'[8] 'There are some who pass today for great thinkers', he added, 'but in the World to Come, it will be revealed that they were in reality nothing more than heretics and unbelievers.'[9] He taught his followers to pray: 'Make me serve Thee in truth, with simplicity, and with wisdom. Guard me and deliver me in Thy great mercy from secular knowledge.'

He disapproved of the acquisition of wealth, for money led to idolatry, and the truly pious man should take no part in the chase after riches. The wealthy were always in debt, slaves to their own desires and ambitions, and slaves to others. 'Would it not be better if they turned away from their idols of gold and silver and learned to serve God?'[10] He also disapproved of physicians. Jestingly, he remarked, 'It was difficult for the Angel of Death to kill the whole world by himself, so he appointed the doctors to be his deputies.'

Nahman stressed the importance of truth. 'It is better for a man to die than to tell a lie. Make me worthy', he prayed, 'of finding goodness in every individual.' Nahman invented his own challenges, and they were not easy to meet.

Passionately, R. Nahman, Hasidism's staunchest Zionist, yearned for the Holy Land. His thoughts on the subject are gathered in a book called *Zimrat Ha-Aretz* (Song of the Land):

The fountain of wisdom and reason is to be found in the Holy Land. There a man comes close to the divine image. The Holy Land and the Torah are one. The holiness of the land strengthens a man's faith, helps him to subdue anger and to banish melancholy. Only in the Holy Land is a man able to pray with true ardour. The Land is the foundation stone of the world, the centre of spiritual life, the well spring of joy, the perfection of faith. The Land exerts a healing and purifying influence on those who settle there.

To settle there involved sufferings, and even a kind of heroism. The zaddik drew his inspiration from the Holy Land which was the source of wisdom, as it was the source of faith for the Jews in the Diaspora. Faith, prayer, miracles and the Holy Land were intermingled. Only through unity would the Messiah come, and he would come suddenly. 'People imagine', said Nahman, 'that after the Messiah has come, they will no longer die. But even the Messiah will die.' He prayed:

Make me and Thy people Israel sincere in our yearning for the Land of Israel; and grant me the strength to satisfy my heart's desire. Thou alone knowest how great is my need of the land because of the distractions, confusions, and imperfections which beset my life and remove me from Thee. Therefore my heart hungers for the Land which is the foundation of our holy faith.

In the accounts of R. Israel Baal Shem Tov's attempts to reach the Holy Land, it is difficult to distinguish fact from fiction. However, Nahman's journey was documented by R. Nathan ben Naphthali Sternharz (d.1830) of Nemirov, who became his Boswell. It was R. Nathan who minutely recorded his aphorisms, his discourses, his prayers and his stories.

Before the journey, Nahman visited Kamenetz-Podolsk, the centre of the conflict between the Talmudists and Frankists, where Bishop Dembowski had burnt tractates of the Talmud in 1757. As was his custom, Nathan endowed the visit with mysterious and mystical significance. 'If people knew the purpose of my journey,' said R. Nahman, 'they would kiss the soles of my feet.'

At the age of twenty-seven, on the eve of Passover 1798, he made the sudden announcement: 'This year I shall arrive in the Holy Land. I shall set forth immediately, whatever the conditions, and even without money. Perhaps people will have pity on me and help me.'

This decision distressed his family. 'Who will look after us while you are gone?' pleaded his young daughter, but her cry was in vain. Nahman refused to be dissuaded. 'Your older sister will become a maidservant. Some kind person will have compassion on your sister and take care of her. Your mother will work as a cook. I must sell all my household goods for travelling expenses.'[11] It was a painful decision but he was willing to risk everything. 'Every step that I took in my journey to the Land of Israel involved sacrifice.'

The knowledge that R. Israel Baal Shem Tov had not succeeded in reaching the Holy Land strengthened the resolve of his great-grandson. 'He who wants to go should go, even if he has to walk all the way. As long as my soul is within me and the breath of life is in my nostrils, I will not give up,' said Rabbi Nahman. 'I am willing to die in order to reach the Land of Israel.'

In poor health and almost penniless, accompanied only by his disciple Simeon,[12] Nahman left his home on 18 Iyyar. First they went to Nikolayev where they celebrated Shavuot. Then, travelling incognito, they embarked at Odessa. Four days later, after a stormy voyage they reached Istanbul. 'What we have related here is only a drop in the ocean,' chronicled Nathan; 'a mere fragment of the tremendous troubles and the sufferings and the perils and the vast miseries that our Rabbi of blessed memory endured on his journey to Eretz Yisrael.'

Nahman behaved strangely in Istanbul, attracting unfavourable attention. He went barefoot, clad in a loose ungirdled garment. These actions had a purpose, a purpose about which he was a little vague. 'Before one can rise to greatness,' he said, 'one must first descend to smallness.'

Meanwhile the world was changing. Early in 1799, Napoleon set out for Egypt with 10,000 men. By March 1799 he had captured Jaffa, and on the 19th he arrived at Acre. While he was in the East, he is said to have invited the Jews of Asia and Africa to rally to his standard, in order to regain possession of Palestine. 'We call upon you', states the Napoleonic proclamation of 20 April 1799, 'not indeed to conquer your patrimony, nay, only to take back that which has been taken away from you.'[13] As a result, visitors from the East were suspected by the Turks of conspiring with the French.

With difficulty Nahman managed to obtain a passage on a boat. Some four months after leaving home, he arrived at Haifa on the eve of Rosh Hashanah 1799. Now the young mystic was in his element. After he had walked four cubits on the hallowed soil, he felt that he had already attained a high degree of spirituality and was ready to return home. However, his companion persuaded him to spend the winter in the Holy Land. He declined the invitation of the Hasidim of Tiberias to spend the festival of Sukkot with them. After the festival he went to Tiberias and later he lived in Safed.

He felt at ease in the holy cities of Safed, and Tiberias, the home of his spiritual counsellors, the Cabbalists. Wherever he went, he was honoured and made many friends, among them R. Abraham of Kalisk whom he greatly revered. He even assumed the role of peacemaker and brought about a reconciliation between R. Abraham and R. Jacob Samson of Shepetovka. Nahman betrothed his daughter to the grandson of R. Menahem Mendel of Vitebsk.

One city Nahman did not visit was Jerusalem. Minutely Nathan describes his visits to Elijah's Cave on Mount Carmel, the tombs of R. Simon bar Yohai and the grave of his grandfather Nahman of Horodenka. After the French withdrawal from Acre in 1799, the Jewish quarter in Safed was ransacked by the Turks. 'They came with axes and began to break down the doors and windows,' records an eye-witness, 'robbing and pillaging, seizing money and property, even shirts and trousers.'[14]

The return journey took Nahman to Rhodes, where he spent the Passover, then to Istanbul, Galatz and Jassy. He arrived home before Pentecost. In spirit, however, he remained in the Holy Land. 'My place is the land of Israel,' he declared. 'If I travel anywhere, I shall travel there. The air I breathe and my very being and whatever holiness I possess come from the Holy Land.' He constantly relived every detail of the visit.

Wholeheartedly he supported fund-raising for settlers: 'By giving to the Holy Land we become a part of the Holy Land.'[15] He composed a special prayer for the benefactors who substantially supported the worthy poor who lived there. Nahman visited a number of Hasidic rabbis, including R. Shneur Zalman, to encourage their work for this cause.

In 1800, eighteen months after his return from the Holy Land, he settled in Zlatopol near Shpola. In 1802 he moved to Braclav and finally, in 1810, he settled in Uman, a city in which the martyrs of the 1768 massacre were buried. It was there that he came into contact with a number of *maskilim* including Hirsch Ber Hurwitz (1785-1857) of Uman, who changed his name to Hermann Hedwig Bernard and taught Hebrew for twenty-seven years at the University of Cambridge.[16] Nahman died on 18 Tishri (16 October) 1810. In 1807 he had considered returning to the Holy Land to live out the rest of his life. However, he decided that he had to die among his Hasidim as well as to live among them: death could not sever the bonds between them.

Nahman had no surviving son, and no rabbi succeeded him. His followers became known as the Toite Hasidim (the 'Dead Hasidim') because they remained faithful to the living memory of their departed Rebbe. His disciple R. Nathan, together with R. Jehudah Eliezer, visited the Holy Land in 1822.

In Jerusalem today the Hasidim of Braclav have erected a magnificent yeshiva and synagogue where they study the works of their teacher. Each service is concluded with a dance. Worshippers join hands in a circle and sing verses from the Psalms. The chair on which R. Nahman sat in Uman has been smuggled out from Russia piece by piece and reconstructed in Jerusalem.

In Bne Brak there is also a Braclav centre and a publication department where the works of R. Nahman are being reprinted. Thirteen students study his works in the Kolel. They like to name their children Nahman and they wear a cord of blue in their fringes.

Before the Russian Revolution, the Hasidim of Braclav gathered in Uman to commemorate their master. Until the outbreak of World War II, the 'Dead Hasidim' met in Lublin in the yeshiva founded by R. Meir Shapira. 'I am a Rebbe without Hasidim,' said R. Meir. 'You are Hasidim without a Rebbe. Let us join forces.' Today the Holy Land has the largest gathering of Hasidim of Braclav.

On his return from the Land of Israel, R. Nahman had said:

I have brought my followers a present and this present is called 'Controversy'. I can foresee that many of my teachings will be disputed, even amongst religious Jews. Satan himself will wage a tireless battle against my adherents and against me. He will succeed in influencing some zaddikim who will turn the masses against my teaching. A time will come when there will be only five of my followers left. But by strengthening their hearts and clinging to my advice they will ultimately cause others to recognise the truth of my teachings. The fire which I have kindled will burn until the coming of the Messiah.

V

EXILE AND REDEMPTION

Primary themes in Hasidic literature are the land of Israel, the
Exile and the Redemption. Although only a small number of
Hasidim actually settled there over the last two centuries, many
links were forged between Hasidism and the Holy Land.

R. Dov Baer, Maggid of Mezeritz, inherited not only the
mantle of R. Israel but also his master's love of Zion. The court
of the Maggid at Mezeritz and at Annopol was a training ground
for future Hasidic leaders. From the Ukraine came Levi
Yitzhak of Berdichev, Menahem Mendel of Vitebsk, Nahum of
Czernobil, Zeev Wolf of Zhitomir; from Lithuania came Aaron
of Karlin, Shneur Zalman of Lyady and Hayyim Heikel of
Amdur. Like the Besht, R. Dov Baer did not himself write
books. His discourses were published in three volumes[1] by one
of his disciples, Solomon of Lutsk (d.1813). Another disciple,
Zeev Wolf of Zhitomir (d.1808), quotes his teacher extensively
in his own work.[2]

For Dov Baer, Zion was the spiritual centre of the world.[3]
The *Shechinah* which accompanied the Jew into Exile after the
destruction of the Temple had shared the tribulations of the

children of Israel. 'We are concerned mainly with our own sufferings but we should also remember that the *Shechinah*, too, yearns for Redemption.'[4] The role of the zaddik is to help to restore the *Shechinah* to its original glory. The bondage of Egypt was the prototypal exile. 'The departure from Egypt did not signify the end of bondage. As long as we are in exile, we are in Egypt. Spiritual Redemption and physical Redemption are interwoven.[5] We are all of us responsible for the Exile and the fact that it lasted so long. By purifying ourselves and overcoming our faults, we can hasten the Redemption.'[6]

Solomon, Rabbi of Lutsk, Koretz and Sokal, anticipated Eliezer Ben Yehuda (1858-1922), one of the pioneers of the modern Hebrew renascence. In his *Divrat Shlomoh*, published in 1859, he writes: 'It is essential that the people living in the Holy Land should use the holy tongue, the language in which the Universe was created. If they do not speak the holy tongue, then the land does not really belong to them and they can easily be banished.' The milk and honey with which the Bible endowed the Land of Israel was interpreted in spiritual terms. He believed that the Redemption would take place by natural means rather than through 'miracles'.[7]

This idea is favoured by many of the sages. 'The sole difference between the present and the Messianic era', said the Babylonian scholar Samuel (165-257), 'is deliverance from foreign powers.'[8] Maimonides warned:

Let no one think that in the days of the Messiah any of the laws of nature will be set aside or that any innovation will be introduced into the Creation. The world will follow its normal course. The words of Isaiah [11:6]: 'And the wolf shall dwell with the lamb, and the leopard shall lie down with the kid', mean that Israel will live in peace among the heathen.

Maimonides[9] avers that the Messiah is the leader under whose guidance Israel will achieve political independence.

In a commentary attributed to Moses b. Nahman (Nahmanides),[10] this idea is amplified: 'By permission of the rulers of the nations and with their aid, the Jews shall proceed to the Land of Israel.' Similarly, R. David Kimhi, the *Redak* (1160-1235), writes in his commentary on Psalm 146:[11] 'He brought about the redemption from the Babylonian exile through Cyrus. In future he will redeem Israel through the rulers of the nations.' R. Hayyim ibn Attar, who was greatly revered by the Hasidim, expressed a similar view: 'Concerning the redemption which will come at the end and in its proper time, it is written "And a sceptre shall arise out of Israel, and shall smite through the corners of Moab", which implies that Israel will be delivered in a natural manner.'[12]

While the Besht gave birth to Hasidism and Dov Baer developed and organised the movement, R. Jacob Joseph Katz of Polonnoye formulated its literature. After the death of the Besht, he produced four monumental works, the greatest of which is *Toledot Yaakov Yosef (The History of Jacob Joseph)*.[13] Commenting on the words in the Passover Haggadah: 'Why is this night different from all other nights?', R. Jacob Joseph cried: 'Why is the present exile longer than all the previous exiles?'[14] 'When will the Messiah come? When will we hear the *shofar* (ram's horn) of the Messiah and when will the outcasts be brought home from the land of Ashur?'[15]

R. Jacob Joseph made careful preparations for his pilgrimage to the Holy Land, and the Besht gave him a letter to deliver personally to his brother-in-law. However, for reasons unknown to us, the journey was never made and the letter was never delivered. Later R. Jacob Joseph included it in his book *Ben Porat Yosef*.

'Eretz Yisrael is an exalted land,' he wrote, 'and the Holy One blessed be He gave it to Israel as a perpetual gift. It is reserved for them and belongs exclusively to them.[16] There are three evils; the exile of the *Shechinah*, the exile of the spirit and physical exile.'[17] Bitterly he deplored the dissension that prolonged the exile.[18] Redemption can be achieved by natural means or by supernatural means,[19] but not without repentance. 'The son of David will not come until pride is eliminated.'[20]

An outstanding personality was R. Phinehas Shapira of Koretz (1726-91). He met the Besht several times and these meetings changed his life. Commenting on Moses' prayer, 'Let me go over, I pray Thee, and see the good land' (Deut. 3:25), R. Phinehas remarked: 'Moses said to God: "I do not want to be like the ten spies who brought back an unfavourable report. I want to see only the good aspects." ' As a tangible reminder of the destruction of the Temple, he lived in a room that was virtually windowless. R. Phinehas collected money for the support of the poor in the Holy Land and in 1791 himself set out on the pilgrimage. However, he died in mid-journey, at the frontier at Shepetovka on 10 Elul 1791.

R. Phinehas felt that anyone who was in a position to settle in the Holy Land should do so. The reason so many zaddikim did not move there was because the Diaspora needed them. He illustrated this idea with a parable. The areas near the king's residence do not need special protection, they are supervised by the king himself. Distant places, however, are garrisoned with troops.[21]

R. Jacob Samson, a descendant of R. Samson Ostropoler, corresponded with many Talmudists and is mentioned in many Responsa. His considerable erudition gave him access to rabbinic circles where he staunchly defended Hasidism.

R. Ezekiel Landau,[22] one of the foremost rabbinic authorities of the eighteenth century, had substituted 'Hasidim' for the word 'poshim' (transgressors) in the verse (Hos. 14:10): 'For the ways of the Lord are right, and the just do walk in them; but transgressors do stumble therein.' R. Jacob Samson managed to convince Landau that he had been overly hasty in his judgment, and Landau ceased to vilify the Hasidim.

Visiting his friend R. Wolf Zbarasz in Tiberias in 1792, R. Jacob Samson saw the Rabbi's wife washing linen in the courtyard. When he commiserated with her, she replied proudly: 'These clothes are not mine. I am washing them for others and I am being paid for the task. But I feel no regrets. No sacrifice is too great for the privilege of living in Eretz Yisrael.'

After the death of Dov Baer in 1773, Elimelech, son of Eliezer Lipa of Lyshansk (1717-94), became the leader of the Hasidim. He was supported by most of Dov Baer's disciples, among them R. Jacob Isaac Horowitz, known as 'the Seer of Lublin', whom R. Elimelech called 'the Messiah ben Joseph'. R. Elimelech's home town of Lyshansk became the Jerusalem of Hasidism. His most important book, *Noam Elimelech*, a commentary on the weekly Torah reading, first published in Lvov in 1798 and reprinted many times, is one of the classics of Hasidic literature. It was instantly acclaimed for its power and profundity.

Like many Hasidic leaders R. Elimelech wanted to settle in the Holy Land but was dissuaded by his followers. However, his son-in-law R. Israel did settle there. Elimelech and his brother Zusya of Annopol had gone into voluntary exile to atone for their misdeeds, to bring others to repentance and, above all, to bring about the Redemption. Wandering incognito for three years, they suffered many hardships. Often they were weary and hungry. Often their lives were in danger. R. Elimelech would rise before dawn and lament over the exile of the *Shechinah*. Paramount was the need for faith, not only faith in God, but also faith in the zaddik. The zaddik was a central figure in the Redemption process.[23] Elimelech combined his golden vision of Israel's greatness with a realistic attitude towards the present, counselling patience and resignation.[24]

When R. Hayyim of Krasny (d.1793), a relative of R. Zeev Wolf of Zhitomir, was shipwrecked en route to the Holy Land, he regarded the misfortune as a mark of Divine displeasure and forbade the engraving of an inscription on his tombstone, because 'I have not been deemed worthy to visit Eretz Yisrael!' However, he was highly esteemed by his contemporaries. The

Besht said: 'The numerical value of the Hebrew name *Hayyim* (68) and that of his wife *Hayah* (23) totals 91, which is identical to the numerical value of the name of God (*Havayah Adonai*).'

It was said of R. Levi Yitzhak of Berdichev (1740-1809) that he loved God and he loved Judaism, but that he loved his fellow-Jews even more. He was Israel's greatest advocate, tempering justice with mercy. He believed passionately in the inherent goodness of man, quoting 'None hath beheld iniquity in Jacob, neither hath one seen perverseness in Israel' (Num.23:21). He regarded every member of the House of Israel as a letter in a Scroll of the Law, sacred and above reproach. R. Levi Yitzhak communed with God in remarkably intimate terms. He concluded one monologue with the words: 'I will not stir from here until you have brought to an end the sufferings of your people, Israel.' Daily, momentarily, he expected the arrival of the Messiah. In a certificate of betrothal he wrote: 'The wedding will take place in six months' time in Jerusalem and if, God forbid, the Messiah has not arrived by then, it will take place in Berdichev.' When he saw people feasting, he would reproach them gently, saying: 'How can you be so festive when the Temple lies in ruins?'

It is told that once on 9 Av (the day which commemorates the destruction of both the First and Second Temples), the community gathered in the synagogue for the recitation of the Book of Lamentations. The synagogue was plunged into gloom; the lights were dimmed, Ark covers were removed, the worshippers sat on low stools. All waited patiently for the Rabbi. But R. Levi Yitzhak was in no hurry. He stayed in his house, waiting for the Messiah. If the Messiah came on Tishah B'Av, the most sorrowful day in the Jewish calendar would be transformed into a day of joy. How could he join the congregation and weep over the two-fold destruction, when the Messiah was on his way?

Seconds turned into minutes, and minutes into hours, but still the reluctant Rabbi tarried, hoping that his prayers would be answered. Finally, his attendant reminded him of his duty to the long-suffering congregants. 'Rabbi,' he said, 'the time has come for the recitation of the Book of Lamentations.' The Rabbi went sadly to the synagogue. 'The Jews are still in exile. Judaism is still in captivity. The Messiah still has not come,' he cried, and began to recite: 'How doth the city sit solitary, that was full of people! How she is become as a widow' (Lam. 1:1).

In *Kedushat Levi*,[25] his commentary to the Torah, he stressed that Israel is a holy nation, God's peculiar treasure and 'superior to all the worlds', and when they cease to sin, they will be worthy of returning home. Only if they meticulously observed the Torah would the land be restored to the children of Israel.[26]

R. Jacob Isaac Horowitz often spoke of his desire to settle in the Holy Land. Commenting on the verse (Gen. 23:12): 'And Abraham bowed down before the people of the land', he said: 'Abraham paid respect even to the Hittites because they were residing in the Holy Land.' Jacob Isaac grieved when he heard that R. Nahman had returned home: 'His doctrines would have been universally accepted had he stayed in the Holy Land.' Unlike his disciple, R. Elimelech, 'the Seer of Lublin' did not counsel patience and resignation. He urged his fellow-Jews to resettle the land, for only then would Israel be redeemed. Together with R. Menahem Mendel of Rymanov and R. Jacob Isaac of Przysucha, the 'Holy Jew', he was determined to hasten the advent of the Messiah.

R. Simhah Bunam of Przysucha compared the love of the Jews for the Land of Israel with the love of a bride for her bridegroom. When the Messiah came, the marriage would be consummated. Sir Moses Montefiore's first visit to the Holy Land in 1827 fired the imagination of the Hasidim. R. Simhah Bunam expressed surprise that Montefiore did not attempt to purchase the land from the Turks. One of his disciples asked: 'What is the point of purchasing land before the arrival of the Messiah?' 'What would we do with the land if we did acquire it, seeing that the Almighty has not yet ordered us to return there?' 'Let the Jews take over,' replied the pragmatic sage. 'The Messiah will follow.'

In the nineteenth century Hasidim came to the Holy Land as individual settlers or in groups of two and three. Among the new arrivals were R. Zevi of Kaminka and his brother Ben Zion. The journey was not achieved without 'Divine intervention', since R. Zevi could barely earn a living and was far from able to finance the journey. One day a peasant left a pair of boots with him and the Rabbi put them carefully away. A year passed and the peasant did not return to claim his property. On the eve of Passover, while the rabbi was searching for leaven, he came upon the boots and found to his surprise that they were full of coins. 'This good fortune', he told his wife joyfully, 'is the result of Divine intervention to enable us to go to the Holy Land.' There he was highly honoured. His wife saved the life of a Turkish official's wife in a difficult childbirth and as a reward R. Zevi was permitted to visit the cave of Machpelah.

Another settler was R. Issachar Dov Baer of Zloczow, a disciple of R. Dov Baer and a grandson of the Cabbalist R. Naphthali b. Isaac Katz[27] (1645-1719). In what seems to be a prediction of the Nazi holocaust, he wrote: 'The Almighty will set up a ruler whose decrees will be harsher than those of Haman.'[28] Despite his failing health and eyesight, he undertook the journey to the Holy Land. He died shortly after his arrival and was buried in Safed, near the grave of R. Moses b. Hayyim Alshech (1507-1600), a pupil of R. Joseph Caro.

The dynasty of Czernobil was founded by R. Nahum (1730-98).[29] A disciple of the Besht, R. Nahum practised self-denial to an almost unhasidic degree. He lived a life of asceticsm and self-deprivation, his estate consisting of innumerable acts of charity. He would travel from village to village spreading the teachings of the Besht. When he became too frail to continue his journeying, he said sorrowfully: 'Satan has sealed my lips so that I should not reveal the end. To preach the teachings of Rabbi Israel is to hasten the Redemption.'[30]

After the departure of R. Israel of Ruzhin from Russia to Austria, Nahum's son Mordecai (1770-1837) took charge of the funds collected for the Holy Land. The surname 'Twersky' adopted by the descendants of Czernobil means in Russian 'a citizen of Tiberias'.

When the associates and disciples of Dov Baer were no longer alive, R. Abraham Dov Baer of Ovruch (d.1840) revived the Hasidic settlement in the Holy Land. A devoted disciple of both R. Nahum of Czernobil and his son Mordecai,[31] he settled in Safed in 1831 and became the leader of the community. In 1833 R. Menahem Mendel of Kamenetz describes him as 'the head of the Kolel of the Polish Hasidim'.[32] There were many hardships. On 24 May 1834 two earthquakes disrupted Safed. 'The tremors grew in intensity. We were therefore compelled to leave our homes and run outside; for there is no fear in the open but it is death to remain indoors,' writes Menahem Mendel. The walls were rent asunder and fell upon those near them.' A few weeks later came a series of riots among the Arabs and the Druzes and the Arab revolt against Ibrahim Pasha which lasted for thirty-three days. Finally Ibrahim Pasha, son of Muhammad Ali, restored order.

Dr Eliezer (Louis) Loewe, secretary to Sir Moses Montefiore, records that in 1838 the Rabbi invited him home. 'Not only was he acting as Rabbi without drawing any salary from communal funds but he was also dispensing charity. From five to fifteen people would eat at his table every day.'[33]

The troubles of Safed were not over. The Jews were forced to flee their homes and take refuge in an Arab village, Ein Zeitum. Many were robbed or maimed. On 1 January 1837 another earthquake shook the region. Two thousand people died in Safed and Tiberias and a great many people were seriously injured. The Rabbi appealed to Sir Moses for help 'to enable the poor of Safed to till the soil and become shepherds'. In spite of the dangers, he categorically refused to leave. 'We must remain here, no matter what befalls us,' he told his followers, 'in order to maintain this settlement and protect our sacred places.'

The Russian authorities stipulated that unless the Russian and Polish Jews returned to their native land once every six months, they would lose their citizenship. These discarded citizens were protected by the British government, which was the first European power to establish a consulate in Jerusalem and to extend protection to the Jews. In July 1838 William Young was the first vice-consul to be appointed and he was succeeded by James Finn who remained in Palestine for twenty years. The Foreign Office files throw some light on the contemporary scene. 'Most of the Hasidim are Austrians,' recorded the Consul, 'some are British and some Prussians. A few are Wallachians and Moldavians–their number exceeds two hundred families.'[34] The Hasidim were violently opposed to the tuition of Arabic to their children. 'Their motive seems to be the fear that the study of foreign languages would lure away the Israelitish youth from the study of their own sacred literature and imbue them with Gentile ideas, which in turn would interfere with the flow of charitable donations from Europe.'[35] In 1841 Michael Solomon Alexander (1799-1845), bishop of the United Church of England and Ireland at Jerusalem, was sent to organise missionary activities in the Holy Land. On this issue the Jewish community presented a united front and the rabbinic authorities in Jerusalem threatened to excommunicate anyone who visited the missionary establishments.

The British army officer and archaeologist Sir Charles Warren (1840-1927), who conducted excavations at Jerusalem from 1867 to 1870, gives a graphic description of the Jewish community.[36]

There is an irrespressible pride and presumption about this fragile wayward people of Ashkenaz that I could not help admiring; dressed in greasy rags, they stalk about the Holy City with as much dignity as though they were dressed in the richest garments, and give way to no one; years of oppression have in no way quelled their ancient spirit, and if they could only be induced to work and become united, they would be a very formidable race, for their courage and fortitude makes up for the want of stamina.

They are among the most fanatical of mortals and can only believe in their own observances, and look with disgust upon the freedom from ceremony of even the strictest Jews of our own country ... They are in height above the average, but of very slender make–quite fragile–but there is something in their independent walk which tells of a greater strength than at first one is inclined to give them credit for. They have broad foreheads, straight eyebrows–often meeting together–straight noses, full lips, and narrow chins, dark hair and eyelashes, and blue or grey eyes. They wear their hair in long, straggling ringlets, at each side of the face, often twelve inches in length, and they let the hair on their faces grow, but it does not often exceed three inches in length, and frequently the beard is but a few straggly tufts ... They wear a coloured kind of shirt, with a limp collar; over this, a loose cotton, striped robe, gathered in at the waist, like a dressing gown, very similar to what all the natives of the city wear, and over this a cloth great-coat, very loose, with sleeves; this hangs down to their heels. On their heads they wear just anything they can get; any kind of old hat will suit them from a fez to a jim-crow, but the national costume is a cap, fitting close to the head, covered with fur, sometimes so long and thick as to cover the eyes and ears; some wear lambskin caps.

The women are often very beautiful, and do not appear, in comparison, so delicately made as the men. The children, when of three or four years of age, are most lovely; but as they grow up their figures are so slight that it is painful to see them, and difficult to believe that they are not in a decline, so bright is the colour of the eye, and delicate the complexion.

One of the famous Hasidic women was Hannah Rachel (1815-1906), the only daughter of Monesh Werbemacher who became known as 'the Maid of Ludomir' (Vladimir-Volynski). Her mother died when Hannah Rachel was a small child and the lonely girl would spend hours at the grave, meditating and praying there. Once she fainted and became gravely ill. When she recovered, she startled her father with this declaration: 'I have just come from the Heavenly Court and a new and exalted soul was given to me.' Her life changed. Every morning she put on phylacteries and a prayer shawl and spent her days in secluded meditation. A synagogue was built for her, with an adjoining apartment. Every Sabbath at Shalosh Seudot (the third meal), the door of her room would be opened. Heard but not seen, the Maid of Ludomir would deliver erudite discourses to which men of piety listened eagerly and appreciatively.

R. Mordecai of Czernobil said of her: 'We do not know whose soul dwells in her. It is hard for the soul of a zaddik to dwell in the body of a woman.' He persuaded her to get married, and he himself performed the ceremony. The marriage did not last. 'The *Shechinah*', said the Hasidim, 'stands between her and her husband.' She divorced him and emigrated to the Holy Land.

There the Maid entered into a mystical partnership with a Cabbalist and both resolved to hasten the coming of the Messiah. After prolonged and elaborate preparations, a time and place were set for the enactment of the great drama. The Maid of Ludomir arrived punctually at the appointed site, a cave outside Jerusalem, and waited anxiously but in vain. For the Cabbalist collaborator had been detained by a venerable sage, the ubiquitous prophet Elijah in disguise whose role it was to thwart this apocalyptic plot. The Messianic era could not be precipitated by pious stratagems.

Another interesting personality was Meshel (1834-1906), son of R. Zevi Hirsch of Bialystok, a descendant of R. Isaiah Horowitz. For ten years he sat at the feet of Menahem Mendel Morgenstern of Kotzk. Like so many other followers, he felt that 'a fire, a new light, was burning in Tomaszow'. Meshel also followed Menahem Mendel of Lubavitch, Yitzhak Meir Alter of Ger and Yitzhak of Neskhiz. It was R. Jacob Aryeh of Radzymin who encouraged him to live in the Holy Land. 'Go to Jerusalem', the rabbi told him, 'and pray unceasingly for the Messiah.' Meshel took his advice. In 1869 he settled in the Old City near the Western Wall.

Meshel refused to become a Rebbe. His wife ran a small bakery and this sustained them. Like R. Jacob Isaac of Przysucha, Simhah Bunam and R. Menahem Mendel of Kotzk, Meshel did not pray at conventional hours. 'In Kotzk,' said Menahem Mendel, 'we have a soul and not a clock.' Believing that proper preparation was as vital as prayer itself, Meshel rarely commenced the morning service before midday. His close friends were the Cabbalists Simeon Zevi Horowitz and Jacob Ornstein. Meshel instituted regular daily services at the Western Wall and on the eve of the Sabbath he would light candles there.

He was particularly concerned with safeguarding the sanctity of the Temple Mount. He would not permit people even to touch the wall and advocated the reintroduction of *mishmorot*, the watchmen who used to guard the Temple. In 1888 he proposed the building of a Bet Hamidrash near the Wall and enlisted the support of the philanthropist Mendel Rand. Three courtyards were acquired, but the scheme did not materialise.

Another object of veneration was the tomb of Simon the Just (*Shimon Ha-Zaddik*) one of the last survivors of the Great Assembly and a contemporary of Alexander the Great. In a booklet, *Or Zarua Le-Zaddik*, he urged the community to erect a small Bet Hamidrash near the grave. Three times a week he would recite prayers there. Meshel lived in Jerusalem for nearly forty years and rarely left the Old City except to visit Hebron four times a year. A number of his manuscripts were destroyed when the Old City was evacuated in Iyyar 1948. He died while visiting Hebron, and to the very end he prayed for the Redemption of Israel.

VI

CHARITY DELIVERS FROM DEATH

Before the kindling of the Sabbath candles, it was the custom for the mistress of the house to drop a few coins into a collection box known as Kuppat Rabbi Meir Baal Ha-Nes (The Fund of Rabbi Meir the Miracle-Worker). Even the poorest of the poor felt the need to make a contribution. It was regarded as a *mitzvah*, a religious obligation, and in this way the people identified themselves with the Holy Land. R. Meir was a second century Palestinian *tanna* who was a member of the Sanhedrin after the Hadrianic persecution. He distributed one-third of his earnings among needy scholars.[1]

Just as Jews in the Diaspora contributed regularly to the maintenance of the Second Temple, so Jews throughout the ages supported the needy in the Holy Land. It was, in a way, conscience money. Those who were either unable or unwilling to settle in the Holy Land felt that this was the least they could do. A certain amount of self-interest was involved. It was believed that the inhabitants of the Holy Land would intercede on behalf of the Diaspora and make atonement for their sins. 'I am like an Ambassador at the court of the king,' writes R.

Menahem Mendel of Vitebsk, 'and not a day passes without my remembering those I represent.' A similar sentiment is expressed by R. Abraham of Kalisk. 'Our hands are continually raised to heaven,' he writes, 'and we pray for you at all times.'[2]

Supporting the Yishuv, moreover, was tantamount to 'ransoming the prisoners' (*pidyon shevuyim*), a sacred duty which takes precedence over all other obligations. For to be held captive in a foreign land was regarded by rabbis as worse than death.[3] The unstable political conditions in the Holy Land put the Jewish settlers in a very precarious position, virtually in the status of prisoners. 'If there be among you a needy man, one of thy brethren, within any of thy gates, in thy land which the Lord thy God giveth thee, thou shalt not harden thy heart.' So runs the injunction in Deuteronomy (15:7). The *Siphre*, a tannaitic midrash, has this comment on the verse: 'The poor of your own city should be helped before those of another city. One must, however, assist the poor in the Holy Land before helping the poor outside the Holy Land.' Thirteen hundred years later, R. Joseph Caro[4] similarly ruled that 'the poor of the Holy Land take precedence over all the other poor.'

R. Jehiel b. Joseph (d.1267) who defended the Talmud against the charges of Nicholas Donin in the disputation of Paris in 1240, transferred his yeshiva to the Holy Land in 1257. He sent his disciple R. Jacob, probably the first Zionist fundraiser, to enlist the support of French Jewry.

The seventeenth-century Italian scholar Samuel Portaleone[5] records that in Mantua and San Martino there were 'seven charity boxes', one of which was devoted to the Land of Israel. The first authority to refer to the fund of Rabbi Meir the Miracle-Worker is R. Elijah b. Solomon Abraham Ha-Kohen (d.1729). His work *Midrash Talpiyot*, published in Amsterdam in 1698, comprises glosses and commentaries taken from 300 works, and contains 926 (the numerical value of the Hebrew word *talpiyot*) paragraphs in alphabetical order. 'He who loses something,' writes R. Elijah, 'should contribute to Rabbi Meir

Baal Ha-Nes and he will immediately recover the lost object.'
The Besht composed a special prayer: 'O God of Meir, answer
me. And may it be your will, O Lord our God and the God of
our fathers, that just as you heard the prayers of your servant
Meir, and performed miracles and wonders for him, so may you
perform miracles for me, and for all Israel who are in need of
miracles.'

In the seventeenth century, the Jewish community of Venice
decided to subject residents to an annual levy of half a ducat a
head, the total to be sent to the Holy Land. In 1761, the
Ponentine community instituted a proportionate levy of one-
twentieth per cent upon all commercial transactions carried out
by its members.[6]

Under the heading: 'If I forget thee, O Jerusalem, may my
right hand forget its cunning', the Moravian Land Council
by-law, dated 1750, records that the Jews of Moravia undertook
to contribute 50 thalers annually to the poor of Jerusalem.[7]
Money from the Polish communities was sent to the Council of
the Four Lands and to the collectors at Lvov. For thirty years,
Dayyan Joseph (d. 1648) was responsible for this collection, and
even the Chmielnicki massacres did not end this vital expressive
and symbolic activity.[8]

In 1742, the Council of the Four Lands issued a special appeal
on behalf of the inhabitants of Safed. 'They interceded on
behalf of our people, the House of Israel. They risked their lives
to go there, not for the sake of its fruits but to fulfil the *mitzvah*
of dwelling in the Holy Land.'[9]

The newly established Jewish community of England also
lent its support. In 1657 R. Nathan Spira of Jerusalem visited
England to collect funds. The Sephardim had two funds, Terra
Sancta and Cautivos, for ransoming Jewish victims of piracy.[10]
Another emissary, Solomon b. Jacob Ayllon, was offered the
office of *haham* when he reached London, and he accepted the
offer. In the mid-eighteenth century, Hayyim Joseph David
Azulai visited Europe and North Africa on behalf of the four

holy communities, Jerusalem, Hebron, Tiberias and Safed. Gradually the term Halukah became synonymous with funds for the poor in the Holy Land. Those responsible for the collection and for the transfer of the funds were given the title Nesi Eretz Yisrael (Prince of the Land of Israel).

At first, the Sephardim lived harmoniously with the newly arrived Ashkenazim, in marked contrast to their fellow-Sephardim in England who resented the Ashkenazi influence. In fact in the spring of 1682 the Sephardim resolved that needy Ashkenazim who came to England to plead for charity should receive no more than 5 shillings each and should immediately be shipped back to Amsterdam. In the accounts of the congregation for the year 1679-80 there is a special section devoted to 'expenses for sending poor Ashkenazim back to Amsterdam'.[11]

Though the Sephardim in the Holy Land did not adopt so callous an attitude, they soon realised that the newcomers could become a financial liability and they were reluctant to give them an equitable share of the Diaspora benefactions. Simultaneously the Hasidim realised that they could not rely on the compassion of the Sephardim, and they appealed directly to their fellow-Jews in eastern Europe.

Though the Hasidic movement was splintered by now, support for the Yishuv was an issue that united their various groups, even as today support for the state of Israel unites the disparate factions of Jewry. R. Baruch of Miedzyborz, grandson of R. Israel Baal Shem Tov, and Levi Yitzhak of Berdichev, poles apart in temperament, character and outlook, found common ground here. Supported by R. Jacob Samson of Shepetovka and R. Yitzhak of Neskhiz, Levi Yitzhak endorsed the ruling that it was wrong to divert money collected for the poor of the Holy Land to any other charity. Support for the Holy Land became one of the unwritten articles of Hasidism.

R. Abraham of Kalisk, like Menahem Mendel, repeatedly appealed for help. 'We trust that the love of the land will live for ever in the Jewish heart ... Be among those who support the

Torah in the Holy Land.'[12] He urged people to contribute regularly, in addition to donating special offerings at festivities. He even composed a special blessing for those who made such offerings. 'If only the Almighty would help us to sustain ourselves,' wrote R. Abraham, 'our energies would not be diverted by the worries of making a living, we would constantly pray for the well being of the Diaspora.'

Abraham's relations with R. Shneur Zalman were cordial at first. He urged his Hasidim to be guided by Shneur Zalman.[13] 'Go and lead the people,' he wrote to his colleague, 'Sanctify them today and tomorrow.'[14] Shneur Zalman could not forsake his followers, and recalled the words of R. Dov Baer that 'some souls have to live outside the land of Israel'.[15] Though one of the most original of the Hasidic thinkers, Shneur Zalman surprisingly does not throw any new light on the significance of the Holy Land but echoes the views of his teachers and colleagues. He stresses that the love of the Holy Land should be like a burning fire in the heart of man.[16]

Those who reside in the Holy Land take precedence over those who reside outside it.[17] Living in the Holy Land is equivalent to fulfilling all the commandments.[18] The rebuilding of the Holy Land will begin again before the redemption and the rebuilding of Jerusalem will take place before the ingathering of the exiles which will precede the coming of the Messiah.[19]

Repeatedly R. Shneur Zalman urged his followers to make weekly or at least monthly contributions 'to sustain people who are literally without food. They are depending on us and we must help them.' He stressed that God was revealed neither in the Torah nor in prayer but in charity. 'As light springs out of its concealment in dark clouds to flash through the world, so the Divine light emerges through charitable deeds.'[20] Not satisfied with exhortations, R. Shneur Zalman travelled far and wide to raise money. At that time, the Holy

Land was under Turkish rule and Russia was at war with Turkey (1787-92), so R. Shneur Zalman's activities were virtually treason and twice he was arrested.

With the publication in 1797 of *Likkute Amarim*, the bible of Habad Hasidism, the relationship between Shneur Zalman and Abraham of Kalisk began to deteriorate. R. Abraham felt that Shneur Zalman was deviating from the teachings of R. Dov Baer and had 'poured so much oil into the lamp that it might extinguish the light altogether. Hence one must choose one's language very carefully.' To Shneur Zalman, R. Abraham wrote: 'Now I have seen your book. I must admit I do not find it very useful for saving souls.' To the Hasidim, R. Abraham was equally frank. 'I am greatly concerned lest your hearts turn away from the essence of faith and truth . . . Therefore I do not approve the publication of heavenly secrets . . . for not everyone can absorb them.'

Theological differences were intensified by the clash of personalities. R. Abraham felt that his residence in the Holy Land entitled him to precedence[21] and he wanted R. Shneur Zalman to relinquish his stewardship over the funds so that his own emissaries could take over the administration. There were unedifying exchanges. Abraham accused his erstwhile friend of being more concerned with publicity than with the needs of the Yishuv.[22] These accusations were backed by R. Baruch of Miedzyborz and R. Asher of Karlin (1793-1826). 'Awaken in your hearts compassion for the poor. Strengthen the hands of those engaged in the work . . . Be on guard against dissenters . . . who call evil good and deliberately weaken the hands of those who are performing this *mitzvah*.'[23]

R. Abraham had more than long-distance disputes to contend with. In the Holy Land he had to face the antagonism of Eliezer of Disna (near Vilna) who had begun a campaign to discredit him. For two years, R. Shneur Zalman kept back the funds. Eventually the two parties were reconciled but the dispute had lasting repercussions. There was no longer a united Hasidic fund and henceforth Habad took care of its own finances.

R. Abraham Joshua Heshel (d.1825), President of the Kolel of Volhynia and Russia, asked his followers to inscribe upon his tombstone that 'he loved the House of Israel'. 'Rabbi Levi Yitzhak of Berdichev vowed that he would have no peace in the World of Eternity until he had brought about the redemption of his people,' said R. Heshel. 'However, Levi Yitzhak must have forgotten his vow. I am determined to remember mine.'

Collecting for the Holy Land was regarded by the Tsarist authorities as treason. In 1821, the Warsaw censor intercepted two letters from Turkey in which Solomon Polansky, a Hasid of Kotzk, asked his son-in-law for money. He mentioned that in Russia he had met with great success and mentioned Yitzhak Meir Alter of Ger by name. The authorities regarded this innocent and private correspondence as a plot of 'extreme seriousness, threatening the security of the state'. Yitzhak Meir's home was searched. When in December 1821 Polansky returned to Warsaw via Odessa, he was arrested, and died in prison. In the correspondence found on his person, Hasidic rabbis in Jerusalem asked Polish Jews to finance the construction of a synagogue there in which the services would be conducted in accordance with the traditional German Polish ritual.[24]

In the 1830s, Kolelim (groups supported by the communities in their countries of origin) came into being. The immigrants from Germany and Holland formed their own Kolel Hod (abbreviation for Holland Ve-Deutschland). In 1845, Kolel Warsaw was established. By the middle of the nineteenth century the Kolelim were split into twenty-five sections. Among those most prominent were Habad, Karlin, Koidanov, Kossov and Vizhnitz. In 1850, Kolel Polin put up three buildings in the Old City of Jerusalem. In the residential quarter, *Warschawer Heiser* (Warsaw Houses), a number of families lived rent free. More homes were constructed by Jacob Shrage Tenewertzel of Lublin, a relative of the Rabbi of Radoszyce.

Sir Moses Montefiore was not the only Englishman to express active concern. On 18 May 1854 Chief Rabbi Nathan Adler wrote: 'The present condition of our poor bretheren scattered through the four cities, Jerusalem, Safed, Hebron, and Tiberias is absolutely heart-rending.'[25] Another appeal to the Jews of England was made by Elijah Guttmacher and R. Zevi Hirsch Kalischer:[26]

Destruction, epidemics, disease and famine ravage the land this year in the same fearful way that they did last year, and your abundantly flowing gifts and donations are not sufficient to alleviate the misery or to satisfy the hunger. The needy fasten their eyes and their hopes on us. But there is only one way in which the recurrence of such distress can be prevented: colonization, cultivation and improvement of the Palestine soil.

Among the notable Hasidic emissaries was R. Jehiel Fischel Ketilman of Tlumacz (b.1825), Galicia, who in twenty months (1859-61) visited thirty-eight Jewish communities in the Orient.[27] R. Hayyim Jacob Ha-Kohen Feinstein went to Bombay, Calcutta and Arabia in 1866. Some of the emissaries lamented the need for such fund-raising. Visiting Melbourne in 1861 on behalf of the Jerusalem Committee for the Establishment of Battei Mahseh Ve-Hahnasat Orchim (House of Shelter and Hospices), R. Hayyim Zevi Schneersohn (1834-82) declared: 'Behold, we are now realising the profound degradation which systematic dependence on charity must produce and the demoralisation which must be the necessary consequence.'[28] He also travelled to Paris and London, and from there to the United States (1869) in order to gain assistance for the agricultural settlement of the Jews of Tiberias.

Each Kolel had its own President as well as its own Hasidic rabbi in eastern Europe who acted as its guardian angel, and each also devised its own method of distribution and varied in the amounts it gave to its dependants. The controversy between R. Abraham of Kalisk and R. Shneur Zalman was the forerunner of many similar controversies between Hasidic rabbis throughout the second part of the nineteenth century.

In Russia the sons of R. Mordecai of Czernobil established 'courts' in different localities. The eldest son Aaron (d.1872), who became the head of the dynasty and President of the Kolel of Ukraine, resented the fact that the Halukah was supervised by R. Abraham Jacob of Sadagura.

R. Aaron's brother Jacob Israel of Hornistopol openly rebelled against him. He sent out letters requesting that all money should be sent directly to him. In vain, the other brothers, R. Yitzhak (b.1812) of Skvira and R. Johanan (b.1816) of Rachmystrivka, appealed to his sense of family loyalty. R. Jacob Israel was unmoved. 'I have found a *mitzvah* through which I could unite the whole of Israel,' he reasoned. 'Now they wish to rob me of this precious thing on which my spiritual welfare depends.' However, when he realised that the Hasidim were not responding, he revoked his claims. 'I am putting back the sword in its sheath,' he conceded.

In 1866 R. Meir b. Isaac Auerbach (1815-78), rabbi of the Ashkenazi community of Jerusalem, sponsored the establishment of Vaad Klali, a central committee of all Ashkenazi Kolelim, and the records provide a storehouse of information about the settlers. Towards the end of the nineteenth century, the most prominent Hasidic Kolelim were Volhynia, Habad and Karlin.[29] The 'Greater Halukah' was the money collected by the Kolelim in eastern Europe. The 'Minor Halukah' referred to the money collected in western Europe and in the United States. In all, these funds supported 23,616 people with an income of £40,000 per annum,[30] and of these, the Hasidim numbered 2,000 souls.[31]

After the Second Aliyah in 1904, and the expansion of Jewish colonisation, only the residents of the Old Yishuv had to rely on the Halukah.

VII

HASIDISM AND ZIONISM

The great Exodus from eastern Europe began in the late nine-teenth century. By 1887 there were five million Jews in Tsarist Russia, amounting to nearly five per cent of the population. Most of them, some four million, were confined to the Pale of Settlement and all were subjected to punitive taxation. Jews were forbidden to settle in rural areas and were forced to leave the small towns and villages. A *numerus clausus* was imposed on Russian schools and universities. Between 1884 and 1894 the number of Jews unable to earn even a minimum livelihood rose to 27 per cent.

Pobiedonostzev, Procurator of the Holy Synod of Alexander III, had a solution for the 'Jewish problem': 'For one-third emigration; for one-third conversion; and for one-third death.' The May Laws and the pogroms 'laid the foundation of the greatest population shift of the Jews in their entire history.' Three million Jews left Russian territory for Europe and North America between 1882 and 1914.

A sombre analysis of the situation was made by the Odessa physician Leon Pinsker (1821-91): 'To the native-born Russian, the modern Jew is a stranger; to the long settled, a vagabond; to the wealthy, a beggar; to the poor, a millionaire and an exploiter; to the citizen, a man without country.' In his *Auto-Emancipation*, published in Berlin in 1882, Dr. Pinsker came to the conclusion that salvation could be found only in the 'establishment of a unified national body'. Such a home is to be sought, not necessarily in the Holy Land but wherever a fitting soil can be found for the homeless people. Theodor Herzl was so impressed with Pinsker's theories that he told David Wolffsohn: 'Had I known about Pinsker's pamphlet earlier, I might never have written *The Jewish State.*'

Pinsker's work had been preceded by the publication in Lyck of a twenty-two-page tract in 1862, *Derishat Ziyyon Ve-Hevrat Eretz Noshevet (The Quest of Zion)*, the first Hebrew pamphlet to appear in western Europe on the subject of Jewish agricultural settlement. The author was Zevi Hirsch Kalischer (1795-1874), rabbi at Thorn in East Prussia for forty years, who corresponded with Baron Anschel Rothschild and Sir Moses Montefiore. Kalischer stressed that Jews had to help themselves.

Do not imagine that the Almighty will suddenly descend from heaven to blow the great trumpet for the dispersed of Israel and raise a wall of fire round them . . . The redemption will be in a natural manner, set in motion by a human agency and prompted by the willingness of a government to resettle a small portion of Israel's dispersed remnants in the Holy Land.

Kalischer urged the formation of a society of wealthy Jews to finance the colonisation of the Holy Land. He also advocated the formation of a guard of able-bodied young men to protect the settlers from attacks and the establishment of an agricultural school.

Are we inferior to all the nations who sacrificed themselves for the love of their country? Look how the people of Italy, the people of Poland and the people of Hungary risked their lives for their heritage and their land. Should we, the children of Israel, whose inheritance is the glorious land, the 'joy of all the earth', hold our peace and be like men who have no life in them? Surely we shall be contemptible in our own eyes?

Kalischer's efforts were supported by his friend Elijah Gutt-macher (1795-1874), the zaddik of Grätz, the only Hasidic rabbi in nineteenth-century Germany. Elijah was born in Borek, a district of Posen in Russian Poland, on 11 Av 1796, and at nine began to study at the yeshiva of R. Akiva Eger (1761-1837). There he met Kalischer and forged a friendship which lasted throughout his life. Elijah's first rabbinic post was in Pleschen in 1839, and at the age of forty-five he became rabbi at Grätz (now Grodzisk, in Poland), where he remained for thirty-four years. He opposed both the *maskilim* and the Reformers. He distributed amulets, wrote *kamayot* (small parchments containing Cabbalistic or biblical verses) and became known as a 'miracle-worker'. In vain he begged people not to come to see him, even printing such an entreaty in the Hebrew periodical *Ha-Maggid*.[1]

He supported Kalischer and enlisted the aid of his own associates. To R. Abraham Landau of Ciechanow he wrote: 'It is important to acquire land from the Arabs and to fulfil those *mitzvot* that can be fulfilled these days.' Together with Kalischer, he issued a proclamation, in both Hebrew and German, in which he claimed the support of Adolphe Crémieux (1796-1880), President of the Alliance Israélite Universelle, and Sir Moses Montefiore. They were opposed by the Ashkenazi rabbis of Jerusalem, especially R. Meir Auerbach, who feared that the new society would harm the funds of Halukah.

Elijah Guttmacher was anxious to set up Torah institutions in the Holy Land. In a letter dated 1859, he and R. Jacob Ettlinger (1798-1871), Chief Rabbi of Altona and the Province of Schleswig-Holstein (then part of the Kingdom of Denmark), implored the Jews 'to raise the standard of the Torah' by supporting such institutions. The next year Elijah attended a conference of rabbis convened by Kalischer in Thorn to consider practical steps for the establishment of settlements in the Holy Land. He supported R. Jacob Mordecai Hirschen-sohn (1821-88), who settled in Safed in 1848 and established an institution called Sukkat Shalom (The Tabernacle of Peace). A site was acquired near the Bet Hamidrash Yeshurun in Jerusalem and in 1870 was renamed Shnot Eliyahu in honour of Elijah. Kibbutz Sdei Eliyahu in the Bet-Shean Valley also bears his name, and near by is the religious Hapoel Ha-Mizrachi settlement Tirat Zevi founded in 1937 and named after his friend and collaborator, Zevi Hirsch Kalischer.

A number of societies were formed under the banner of Hovevei Zion (Lovers of Zion). Members discussed ways and means of settling in the Holy Land and urged the study of Hebrew as a living language. Dr Karpel Lippe (1830-1913) and Samuel Pineles (1848-1928) were the guiding spirits of the Hibbat Zion in Romania, and Lippe played a major role in the founding in 1882 of Zamarin (later renamed Zichron Yaakov) and Rosh Pina by Romanian Zionist immigrants.

R. Yitzhak Friedman (1805-90) of Bohush, grandson of R. Israel of Ruzhin, gave limited support to the Lovers of Zion. In 1880, he was invited by the communal leaders of Galati to participate in a conference at Jassy, but his reply was non-committal because he felt that the proposed gathering might prejudice the struggle for Jewish civil rights, serving as a pretext for the Russian government to renege on its pledges.

In Elul 1882, when the rabbi of Bohush passed through Czernowitz, a delegation which included Aaron Marcus visited him and urged him to give moral support to the movement. The rabbi pointed out the enormous difficulties, which they would have to overcome, but the Lovers of Zion were not discouraged. In Iyyar 1887 the leaders wrote to the rabbi: 'What can we expect from the mass exodus to America except desecration of the Sabbath and the Festivals? The Land of Israel is the only place where we can live in accordance with the Torah and where we can rear our children in the traditional Jewish way.' They assured him that they had no desire to interfere with the Halukah. 'We want to reawaken in the Jewish heart a great love for our Holy Land and to gather under our banner as many adherents as possible.' On 7 Iyyar Abraham Mordecai Segal, the rabbi's *gabbai*, wrote that the rabbi was willing to encourage the purchase of *etrogim* from the Holy Land. This concession did not satisfy the Lovers of Zion. Five days later they wrote back bluntly pointing out that *etrogim* by themselves would not solve any problem and that those who had settled in the Holy Land were faithful to the covenant and even those Jews who had 'thrown off the yoke of the Torah' in Europe had returned to the fold in the Holy Land.

In 1887 R. Yitzhak made it clear that he did not oppose agricultural settlements in the Holy Land. However, he felt that it was wrong to raise false hopes among Romanian Jewry, since mass immigration to the Holy Land was not feasible in view of the political conditions. He maintained that the best policy was gradual resettlement and slow integration. He urged them to consult experts.[2] Beril Soref, one of the rabbi's followers, was sent to explore the possibility of settling fifty Romanian families in the Holy Land.

R. Hayyim Israel Morgenstern (1840-1906) of Pulawy, son of R. David Kotzk, adopted the 'all or nothing' credo of Kotzk. The founder of the Kotzk dynasty, R. Menahem Mendel (1787-1859), supported the Polish revolt of 1830 but had little faith in the emancipation of the Jews as a solution to the Jewish problem. 'While we are in exile and dwell in a foreign land, it is better to be regarded as foreigners rather than as citizens,' he maintained. He did not believe that legislative enactments could effectively or permanently eradicate anti-semitism. His son-in-law R. Abraham Bornstein supported the Yishuv and encouraged the use of *etrogim* from the Holy Land.[3] 'It would be a great *mitzvah*', he wrote, 'if the authorities were to permit a group of people to settle in the Holy Land. It is highly praiseworthy to engage actively in the pursuit of these schemes.'

When R. David of Kotzk died in 1873, the Hasidim were divided in their loyalty. Some followed his younger son Zevi Hirsch, but the majority transferred to R. Hayyim Israel who had made his home in Pulawa in 1888. In his fifty-page booklet *Shelom Yerushalayim (Peace of Jerusalem)* which was printed posthumously,[4] he demonstrated by means of biblical texts and Talmudic dicta that it was the duty of every Jew to participate in the rebuilding of the Holy Land. He believed that the time was propitious. The vexing and restrictive Turkish regulations which debarred purchases and settlements had been relaxed and Jews were now permitted to acquire land and were even provided with police protection. For these reasons, he urged the purchase of fields and vineyards. It was essential for large groups to settle there; even if they did so only because they were unable to make a living in the Diaspora. Those who live in the Holy Land must undertake to observe all the laws of Shemitah. It was up to the spiritual leaders in the Holy Land to see that harmony prevailed among the different sections of the community. R. Hayyim Israel forwarded copies of his unpublished manuscript to a number of rabbis. R. Bornstein wrote: 'I enjoyed it very much, for it awakens in the heart of the Jew the love of Zion, and it is moreover a great *mitzvah* to acquire property in the Holy Land.' R. Yehudah Leib Alter of Ger was less positive. 'Certainly,' he conceded, 'any Jew who is religious and willing to observe the laws of Tithes (Maaser) and who has the full co-operation of his family, need not hesitate to make his home in the Holy Land ... One should not, however, take such a step unless one is sure that one can make a living there, and be in a position to fulfil the stringent laws of Shemitah.' He advised R. Hayyim to investigate the economic situation.

R. Hayyim's plans centred on the purchase of enough land to house one thousand settlers. Unhappily he aroused the antagonism of many Hasidim, and within a brief period he suffered a number of personal tragedies. His wife and young daughter both died suddenly and he himself became seriously ill. These calamities discouraged him and none of his schemes came to fruition.

While the Jewish world at large was growing increasingly enthusiastic over the activities of Theodor Herzl (1860-1904), the father of political Zionism, for the possible restoration of the Jewish home in Palestine through political means, Hasidism did not generally share this enthusiasm. For the battle still raged between Hasidism and Haskalah. The Hasidim associated Haskalah with assimilation and even apostasy. And many of the *maskilim* carried the flag of Zionism. Moreover repossession of the promised land at this stage was regarded by many Hasidic rabbis as tantamount to interference with the Divine order of things.

Zionism, originally conceived as a means of escape from persecution in eastern Europe and elsewhere, soon became a movement for national liberation. The first Zionist Congress of 1897 gave a powerful impetus to the movement and many groups associated themselves with the Zionist Organisation.

Herzl was anxious to enlist the support of the Hasidim. His intermediary was the Hebrew scholar, philosopher and linguist Aaron Marcus (1843-1916), a native of Old Hansa in Hamburg. Marcus participated in the first Zionist Congress. He had studied at yeshivot in Boskowitz, Moravia and Galicia, and had been a disciple of R. Shlomoh Ha-Kohen of Radomsk. 'Rabbi Aaron is capable of translating my Hebrew discourses into fluent German,' commented the rabbi of Radomsk. Marcus was also influenced by R. Yitzhak Friedman of Bohush, whom he met in Kattowitz on 4 September 1882, and by the Rebbes of Czortkov and Sadagura. He declined to become a rabbi in Glasgow, preferring to earn a living as a wine merchant.

On 27 April 1896 Marcus wrote to Herzl: 'Your wonderful pamphlet, *The Jewish State*, held me enthralled for hours ... It came like a lightning bolt in the dark of night of both the assimilationists and the Hasidim who are so bitterly opposed to each other.' In all, Marcus wrote forty-three letters to Herzl, but only six have been preserved.[5]

In 1898, Marcus published an eleven-page pamphlet, *Dr Herzls Judenstaat*, in support of Herzl's proposals. 'This Aaron Marcus in Podgorze must know the situation,' writes Herzl, 'himself a Hasid and also a high-minded and spirited author who has composed a remarkable book on the more recent philosophies. But in his civil life he is a merchant. He does not live *from* Judaism but *for* Judaism.'[6]

In a letter dated 7 May 1896 Marcus gives Herzl an illuminating account of the state of Hasidism in eastern Europe.[7]

The three million Hasidim in the area that was formerly Poland are distinguished from other Jews by the fact that they are not merely Jews by race, birth, habit, or confession, but are self-aware and, in so far as this is possible under the pressure of circumstances, to some extent politically organised Jews. These masses are under the guidance of some fifty to sixty Rabbis, on whom the propaganda would have to be concentrated. For six generations now, the house of the founder of this organisation, the Friedman family in Bukovina, has acted as a real silent *negotiorum gestatorius*, after the manner of the old exilarchs ... His nephew Isaac Friedman in Bohush (Moldavia), whose Hasidim founded the first settlement Rosh Pina near Safed in 1881, expounded to the directors of the local Bnei Brith Lodge in Kattowitz on 2 September 1882, during an interview at which I was present, the same programme that is set forth in your memorable pamphlet. At the time, I was acting as interpreter between the three little Prussian gentlemen and the imposing Romanian Rabbi, whose dialect they naturally had difficulty in understanding ... Among their adherents are many millionaires. A certain Naftali Koretzer of Berdichev left $9\frac{1}{2}$ million roubles, 1 million for charitable Jewish purposes, 72,000 for the aforementioned Rabbi, and the rest to be divided among his eight children ... A great deal can be done with them.

Herzl's knowledge of eastern European Jews, especially of Hasidism, was limited, but he soon grasped the great potential of this untapped reservoir. About the Russian delegates to the Zionist Congress, he wrote in 1897:[8]

From Russia they were nearly seventy strong, and we can say without fear of contradiction that they represented the views and feelings of the five million Jews of Russia. It was truly humiliating for us who had believed that in culture we were superior to them! All these professors, medical men, lawyers, engineers, manufacturers and business men, have attained a level of education which is certainly not inferior to that of Western Europe.

Herzl realised that it was from Russian Jewry that his main support would come. 'They possess the inner unity which most European Jews have lost ... They are not tormented by fear of becoming assimilated. They are Ghetto Jews, the only Ghetto Jews of our time. By looking at them we understand what gave our forefathers in the midst of the most difficult times the strength to endure.'[9]

At this stage the assistance of Aaron Marcus was invaluable. In his diary under 8 May 1896 Herzl notes; 'The Hasid Aaron Marcus of Podgorze [Galicia] again writes to me a fine letter, in which he holds out the possibility that the three million Hasidim of Poland will join my movement. I assure him that the participation of the Orthodox will be most welcome but no theocracy will be created.'[10]

The Zionist leader kept in touch with R. Leibish Mendel Halevi Landau of Przemysl (1861-1920), rabbi of Bostani for twenty-three years (1897-1920), who offered to negotiate with the wonder-rabbi Moses David Friedman of Czortkov. 'I invited Friedman to send his son,' records Herzl.[11]

A letter to the Rebbe of Czortkov dated 28 November 1896 was drafted by Michael Berkowitz (1865-1935), Herzl's Hebrew secretary, but it is not clear whether it was ever delivered.[12] An entry in Herzl's diary for 10 November 1896 records: 'A man from Jerusalem named Bak came to see me. He is travelling round Europe in order to found an agrarian bank for Palestine, a vest pocket *Jewish Company*, evidently in his vest pocket. He claims to be under the patronage of the Galician Wonder Rabbi Friedman.'[13]

In December 1897 Herzl met Israel Friedman, the rabbi's son, and Marcus joined them in trying to persuade the rabbi to convene a conference of rabbis to promote the aims of Zionism. In January 1900, Marcus once again travelled to Czortkov where he stayed for three weeks. The rabbi asked him to contact Benjamin Aryeh Weisz (1848-1912), rabbi of the Orthodox community of Czernowitz (1872-1913),[14] with the suggestion that Weisz summon rabbis from Stry, Lvov, Cracow and Bendin in order to negotiate with the Zionist Executive. At first, Weisz insisted on a written communication from the Rebbe. This was obtained and it was urged that Herzl himself participate in the proposed conference to be held at Vilna. However, the conference did not take place and Marcus expressed his disappointment in a letter to Herzl on 23 March 1900.

Marcus, whom Herzl called 'the *Hasidische* philosopher', and whom Max Nordau (1849-1923) regarded as 'the greatest living brain in the First Congress', was lost to Zionism. His interests faded and he devoted himself instead to writing books on philosophy and Hasidism.[15] In Hartmann's philosophy he found allusions to Habad.[16] Marcus lived in Cracow until the outbreak of World War I, when he fled to Frankfurt where he died on 1 Adar 1916.[17]

Marcus had undoubtedly underrated the hostility of the Hasidim towards Zionism. This is demonstrated by letters written by both R. David Moses Friedman and his son Israel. The Rebbe stressed that Jews must not anticipate the Redemption by pursuing the 'Dangerous aims of Zionists', and R. Israel Friedman[18] was afraid that Zionist activities would hamper the civic rights of the Jews.[19] R. Israel told Y.L. Maimon, the Mizrachi leader:

I am not a Zionist because I do not know what methods are going to be employed towards this aim. I am equally opposed to those whose opposition to Zionism is not based on facts but merely because certain Rabbinical authorities or Hasidic Rabbis are opposed to Zionism. No human being is infallible, be he a scholar or a zaddik. Was not the Gaon of Vilna, a vehement opponent of Hasidism, yet today many of his admirers are to be found in the Hasidic camp. Did not Rabbi Hayyim of Sanz who was universally admired for his saint-liness and scholarship, did he not engage in a bitter con-troversy against the family of my grandfather, Rabbi Israel of Ruzhin? We have fully forgiven him. None the less, does this not prove that even a zaddik and a great man can make a mistake?

The rabbi of Czortkov was not Herzl's only contact with the world of Hasidism. Herzl reports on yet another encounter: 'One of the most curious figures I have yet met is Rabbi Horowitz, the son-in-law of the Wonder Rabbi there. He came to see me accompanied by his "secretary" . . . He promised to arouse the interest of all the Wonder Rabbis. I will go there for a conference with these gentlemen.'[20] It is also probable that Herzl met R. Mordecai Joseph Eliezer, the rabbi of Radzyn, for the Rebbe remarked: 'Herzl has the elements of leadership.'[21]

Herzl strove also for the attention of the Hasidim of Poland. Writing to R. Yehudah Aryeh Alter of Ger in 1899, Herzl insisted that Zionism was not opposed to religion.[22]

Our main aim is to work for the welfare of our people. It has been rumoured that your honour, whose utterances are regarded by thousands as sacred, has accused us of blasphem-ing. In the name of tens of thousands of Jews whose condition is continually deteriorating, in the name of tens of thousands who are fleeing from Russia, Romania and Galicia to America, Africa and Australia, whose destiny is assimilation and dis-integration, and especially in the name of Torah and God, I beseech your honour to reprimand us publicly for the sins that we have committed on behalf of Zion.

Herzl's moving appeal remained unanswered. To the Polish Hasidim Herzl was not 'a king in Jerusalem', 'a great eagle' or a 'countenance lit with the light of the Messiah'. Herzl had been brought up in an assimilationist milieu with a very superficial knowledge of Jewish culture. He records that when the Chief Rabbi of Vienna, Moritz Güdemann (1835-1918) dropped in unexpectedly at the Herzl home, he was kindling the lights of a Christmas tree for his children. 'Well, I will not let myself be pressurised! But I don't mind if they call it Hanukah or the winter solstice.'[23] In 1890 it had even occurred to him that baptism might be the ideal solution of the Jewish problem.[24] He told Chief Rabbi Herman Adler in 1895 that the creation of a Jewish state was not the result of a religious impulse.[25] To the editor of the *Jewish Chronicle*, Asher Myers, he remarked: 'I am a free-thinker and our principle in the Jewish State will be "Let everyone seek salvation in his own way." '[26]

Although Herzl did not change his attitude towards religion, he refrained meticulously from offending his fellow-Jews and he refused to desecrate the Sabbath when he arrived in Jerusalem on 27 October 1898.[27] However, he refused to be bound to customs he regarded as illogical and he walked through the Via Dolorosa, a street shunned by Orthodox Jews. 'I would have considered it cowardice not to go, so I walked along the street of the Holy Sepulchre. My friends restrained me from entering the Church itself. It is forbidden to set foot in the Mosque of Omar and the Temple area, otherwise one is subject to excommunication by the Rabbis.'[28] None the less he refrained from smoking on the Sabbath and attended the Sabbath services held at Basle before the first Zionist Congress.[29] Herzl defined Zionism as 'the return to Judaism even before the return to the Jewish land'.[30]

Equally unsuccessful in eliciting Hasidic support was Nahum Sokolow (1859-1936), whose grandfather Ephraim Yitzhak was a follower of R. Elimelech of Lyzhansk. Sokolow, a child prodigy, was, in the words of Sholem Asch, 'a legend among the synagogues in the Polish towns'. He visited the court of Ger but was unable to evoke any positive response.[31]

The Rebbe of Ger could not be persuaded that Zionism would not weaken Orthodoxy. 'A veil blinds the eyes of the leaders of the Zionists; because of their lack of faith they fail to realise the extent of the dangers involved in their promises to the masses of the people among whom we live.' This was the attitude of the overwhelming majority of Hasidic leaders until the outbreak of World War I.

VIII

THE RETURN TO ZION

'The Land of Israel for the people of Israel according to the Torah of Israel' was the motto of the Mizrachi (an abbreviation of *'Merkaz Ruhani'*, 'Spiritual Centre'), which was founded by R. Yitzhak Jacob Reines (1839-1915) in 1902 at a Vilna conference of Russian Zionists. The Mizrachi came into being because the religious Jews were dissatisfied with the resolution of the Fifth Zionist Congress at Basle in 1901 that made the cultivation of Jewish nationalism an important aspect of Zionist activity. By 1937, the Mizrachi in Poland had branches in 900 towns and the Union of Mizrachi Rabbis numbered 270. Under Mizrachi auspices, a network of schools, youth organisation and a rabbinic college were established.

Yet even the Mizrachi did not win the support of all religious Jews, and certainly few Hasidic rabbis were involved. Among notable exceptions were R. Baruch Hager (1899-1942), son of Michael of Horodenka, a descendant of Baruch of Vizhnitz. He was active in Bukovina in Zeire Mizrachi (Young Mizrachi), and contributed to the bi-weekly Hebrew paper *Darkenu (Our Way)*.

Another activist was R. Menahem Mendel Hager (1899-1954), a rabbi in Sosnowiec, and a descendant of Kossov. He belonged to the Polish Mizrachi and to the executive of the Mizrachi Rabbinic Organisation. He was also a delegate to the Zionist Congress and at the suggestion of Menahem Ussishkin he worked for the Keren Kayemet. Prominent among the Mizrachi leaders was Menahem Mendel Hayyim Landau, (1861-1935), grandson of R. Abraham Landau of Ciechanow. He had been ordained by R. Joshua Trunk of Kutno and Hayyim Eleazar Wacks of Kalisz. In his controversial book *Mekitz Nirdamim*[1] he urged religious Jews to combine secular and religious studies and to provide education for girls.

The urgent need to find 'the solution to contemporary problems in the spirit of the Torah' led to the conference at Katowice in Upper Silesia on 27 May 1912, and the birth of the Agudat Yisrael (Union of Israel). Over 200 communal leaders, laymen and rabbis, *mitnagdim* and Hasidim, had gathered at Katowice, drawn there for many different reasons. Jacob Rosenheim, vice president of *Die freie Vereinigung für die Interessen des orthodoxen Judentums* (the Free Union to Safeguard the Interests of Orthodox Judaism) founded by R. Samson Raphael Hirsch in 1883, yearned to unite the unorganised Orthodox masses of eastern Europe. Others felt that only a Torah-entrenched citadel could hold back the tidal waves of assimilation, the militant anti-religious ideology of the secularists, and the nationalism of the Zionists.

No discordant voices were heard at Katowice. Dr Yehudah Leib Franks, leader of the German Mizrachi, welcomed the assembly, and the main Zionist organ *Die Welt* greeted the foundation of the Aguda in most cordial terms as 'an event whose importance in the development of contemporary Judaism must not be underrated'.

Rosenheim, the movement's founder and life-long guide, maintained that this was not 'an organisation like other organisations', and R. Elhanan Wasserman stated that 'Israel is not like any other nation, nor is the Aguda like any other party'; yet ultimately the Aguda adopted the whole familiar complex of organisational accoutrements: constitution, general council, executive committees, a rabbinic council (Moetzet Gedole Ha-Torah), with an executive of eleven members, a Torah fund, and even a press bureau.

The ideologist of the Aguda was Nathan Birnbaum, who became disillusioned with Herzl. To him the Jewish nation was not merely a group of people, held together by a common enemy, whose survival could be secured by political concessions in Palestine. Birnbaum maintained that the vitality of a people depended upon its culture. He saw the weakening of Messianic fervour and feared that the secularisation of the Jewish people would remove its God-given distinctiveness.

There were soon sizeable Aguda groups in Budapest, Amsterdam and Vienna. In 1912 a group was established in the Holy Land under Yitzhak Yerocham Diskin and Joseph Hayyim Sonnenfeld. Moses Blau was elected general secretary to supervise the Netzah Yisrael educational establishments[2] which were set up in the Holy Land. Nominally the headquarters of the Aguda remained in Frankfurt until 1935, but its heart and soul were lodged in Poland. During the inter-war years, one-third of Polish Jewry, most of them Hasidim, were associated with the Aguda.

Not only had the Aguda become 'an organization like other organisations', but also in an intricate and often devious manner it did play party politics. Isaac Breuer (1883-1946) believed, like Birnbaum, that 'political Zionism seeks to exchange the Galut of Israel for the Galut of the nations', a belief that coloured the Aguda attitude. Admittedly anti-Zionist, the Aguda in poignant paradox was passionately pro-Zion. Its constitution stated: 'It shall be the purpose of the *Agudat Yisrael* to resolve all Jewish problems in the spirit of the Torah, both in *Galut* and in *Eretz Yisrael* ... The colonisation of the Holy Land in the spirit of the Torah shall be directed towards creating a source of spirituality for the Jewish people.'

The Aguda did not participate in the negotiations that led to the Balfour Declaration. The British government asked the opinion of Dr Meir Jung, Chief Minister of the Federation of Synagogues in London, and head of the English Aguda, and Dr Jung replied in highly affirmative terms.[3] The Jewish Agency for Palestine agreed to allocate 6 to 7 per cent of its immigration certificates to Aguda members. However, for most Agudists, the love of Zion remained a purely spiritual passion and only a few translated the ideals into action.

While the Zionists were building the National Home, the Aguda was mainly Diaspora-oriented. Their achievements in the inter-war years were negligible in the Holy Land. Vociferous in the political arena, they were almost invisible in the area of colonisation. Their vast resources were concentrated in Poland which was their main reservoir of strength. Aguda influence extended to every sphere of east European Jewish life –political, economic and social. Its representatives sat on parliamentary councils in Poland, Lithuania, Latvia, Hungary and Romania. Indeed, in 1928, no less than 2,500 seats in communal councils were occupied by Agudists. They opposed calendar reform at the League of Nations.

In Poland the Aguda published a daily newspaper (*Yiddishe Togblatt*), established a publishing house (Yeshurun), maintained its own schools' organisation (Tzeire Aguda and Pirche Aguda), women's divisions (Bnot Aguda), and co-operatives. Striving to achieve a dominant role for the Torah in the life of each Jew as well as in the life of the community, the Aguda wrested communal leadership from the assimilationists. Yet the Aguda preferred to collaborate with the assimilationists rather than with the Zionists or Mizrachists and the Aguda members of the Polish Parliament (Seym) rarely co-operated with the other Jewish deputies.

The Aguda even considered an alliance with the Revisionists (the party formed in April 1925 by Vladimir Jabotinsky (1880-1940), who advocated a return to Herzl's original conception of a Jewish state), in the hope of undermining the strength of the Zionists. 'Whether Jabotinsky is a good Jew or not', reasoned Rosenheim, 'is a matter of secondary importance. What matters is whether a pact with him will break up the monopoly of a single party.' 'We must put an end to the criminal monopoly of the Zionists,' declared Harry Goodman, political secretary of the Aguda,[4] 'and we shall join forces with anyone who has the same aim in view.' On 22 July 1937 Jabotinsky and Rosenheim jointly wrote a letter to the President of the Jewish Agency:

While fully aware of the substantial differences of outlook between the undersigned organisations, nevertheless we consider it our common duty to put before the Zionist Organisation, the Jewish Agency, and the Jewish and non-Jewish world at large, our demand that the Jewish attitude regarding the future of Palestine be submitted to the decision of a special gathering, representing all of world Jewry.

In August 1923, at the First World Conference (Knessiya) in Vienna, the Aguda resolved to support the Jewish people spiritually and physically in the holy undertakings, primarily for reconstruction work in Palestine. Among the supporters were R. Israel Meir Kahan, the *Hafetz Hayyim* who contributed fifty million Austrian kronen, and Abraham Mordecai Alter of Ger who collected one hundred million Polish marks. The Aguda established a Palestine Office, a Keren Ha-Yishuv fund, and the 'Land and Building Society'. It set up Hachsharah camps in Poland and acquired some land in Palestine. A number of Agudists and Hasidim were among the 280,000 Jews who emigrated to Palestine between 1918 and 1936.

The British administration gave the Jewish community internal autonomy. At a gathering Asefat Ha-Nivharim on 7 October 1920, 300 delegates elected a Vaad Leumi (National Council), and the Chief Rabbinate.[5] The powers of the local rabbinic courts were set out in Article 53 of the Palestine Order in Council, which gave these courts exclusive jurisdiction in matters of marriage and divorce, alimony and settlement of estates. In 1921, the electoral college met in Jerusalem and elected Rabbis Kook and Yaakov Meir as Chief Rabbis. The Aguda did not co-operate, and would not recognise the Chief Rabbinate. Its leader R. Sonnenfeld demanded that '(1) the National Council should acknowledge the authority of the Holy Torah; (2) that no person desecrating the Sabbath should be eligible for membership; (3) women should not have the right to participate in the election of members; and (4) that it should not subsidise such enterprises as workers' kitchens, which served forbidden food.'[6]

R. Joseph Hayyim Sonnenfeld (1849-1932), who settled in the Holy Land in 1873, regarded the Zionists as 'evil men and ruffians'. Yet he had an unbounded love for the Holy Land. When a member of the Royal Commission asked him if Palestine was big enough to absorb more immigrants, he replied: 'When children return from exile to their mother's house, the mother never says "There is no room for you." ' In vain R. Leo Jung of New York pleaded at the Agudist World Conference in September 1929 for communal unity. The majority of the delegates categorised both the Zionists and the non-Zionists as heretics.

Once again the Conference discussed a number of resolutions instructing its executive to proceed with political, economic and cultural work in the Holy Land.[7] These resolutions were adopted but not implemented.

The negative attitude of the Aguda provoked positive counter-reactions in Austria and in Poland. Among those spurred to action was R. Hayyim Meir Yehiel Shapira of Drohobycz (b.1864). His father was Aviezra Zelig, son of Hayyim Meir Yehiel of Moglienice, a descendant of R. Jacob Isaac, 'the Holy Jew', and R. Israel of Kozienice, son-in-law of R. Abraham Jacob Friedman of Sadagura. R. Shapira was present when Sir Laurence Oliphant (1829-88), the English pro-Zionist, visited R. Friedman and proposed the establishment of the Jewish settlements in the Holy Land.[8]

On 14 November 1878, Sir Laurence wrote to the Marquis of Salisbury, proposing to obtain a land concession from the Porte for twenty-five years in order to form a Palestine Development Company. 'I was convinced', wrote Sir Laurence after his visit to the Rebbe of Sadagura, 'that he could lead and command his people with just the barest gesture.'[9] The Rebbe was not particularly responsive. 'We are looking for a miraculous deliverance,' he told the Englishman, 'not for deliverance through human agency.' R. Hayyim Meir did not endorse his father-in-law's attitude. Together with Nisan Bak of Jerusalem, he conceived the plan of establishing a bank giving credit to prospective settlers. When, however, both the First (1897) and Second (1898) Zionist Congresses decided to establish the Jewish Colonial Trust Ltd to promote Jewish settlement in Palestine, Hayyim Meir, anxious not to duplicate the work, dropped the idea. While living in Vienna for eight years, he encouraged pioneers to settle in the Holy Land: 'You are indeed lucky that you are privileged to achieve your aim. Would that my portion were with you.'

He bought a Zionist Shekel and, together with Shlomoh Friedman, formed Ezrat Yisrael, which was at first confined to a small group of rabbis and their sons, but soon this was absorbed into a society called Yishuv Eretz Yisrael with a less restricted membership. Its manifesto which appeared in the Hebrew periodical *Ha-Zephirah* on 13 Nisan 1918 urged Orthodox Jews to help to rebuild the Holy Land. The authors deplored the non-involvement of religious Jews. 'Our aims are the aims of Ezra and Nehemiah. We are anxious to establish settlements in the Holy Land in the spirit of the Torah.'

Among the signatories to this manifesto were Hayyim Meir, Jacob Joseph Twersky of Stanislav and Shlomoh Hayyim Friedman, and several branches were eventually established in Drohobycz and Stry. The Executive debated whether to co-operate with the Zionists. Hayyim Meir persuaded his colleagues that in communal matters, especially matters that concerned the rebuilding of the Holy Land, it was permissible to co-operate with any one who called himself a Jew. The Society did work with the Zionist Federation, and eventually amalgamated with the Mizrachi. He sent a personal telegram to the Meeting of the Supreme Council of the Paris Peace Conference held on 18-26 April 1920 at San Remo, demanding British trusteeship for the establishment of a Jewish National Home in Palestine. In Adar 1922, thirty people went on Aliyah with R. Hayyim Meir and were bade farewell at Vienna by R. Zevi Hirsch Perez Chajes (1876-1927). In the Holy Land R. Hayyim Meir became ill and returned to Vienna, where he underwent surgery. He knew that his days were numbered and yearned to spend them in the Holy Land. He was told that without medical attention he would not survive the arduous journey, so he returned to Jerusalem accompanied by a physician. Whenever he was called up to the Reading of the Law, he made a donation to Keren Kayemet. His home in Jerusalem was a meeting-place for scholars, and to the end he helped and encouraged Hasidim to settle in the Holy Land. He died on 30 Nisan 1924 and his last words were 'Merciful Father, Jerusalem'. His son was the painter Abraham Jacob Shapira, and his grandson Shin Shalom is a noted Hebrew poet and writer.

The first Hasidic attempt to establish an agricultural settlement in the inter-war years was made in 1925 by R. Ezekiel Taub of Yablona (Jablonow in Galicia), a descendant of R. Ezekiel Taub of Kazimierz. 'I would rather be a labourer in the land of Israel', his father Jacob had remarked, 'than a rabbi in the Diaspora.' In Adar of that year the rabbi of Yablona arrived with twelve families. He landed in Haifa rather than Jaffa, for he was afraid that his followers would be attracted to Tel-Aviv. 'Two thousand years ago,' declared R. Taub, 'Cyrus, king of Persia proclaimed: "whosoever there is among you of all His

people–the Lord his God be with him–let him go up"
[IIChr.36:23]. These days, too, we hear such a proclamation
which calls upon the Jews to rebuild Zion and Jerusalem.'

In his autobiography, Dr Chaim Weizmann (1874-1952)
describes with astonishment and approval a visit to these
unusual pioneers:[10]

On the way to Nahalal, we passed a hill crowned with newly
erected barracks, around which clustered a number of people
who looked like recently arrived refugees. They made a striking
group. We discovered that they were Hasidim who, led by
their Rabbi [the rabbi of Yablona], had landed in Palestine only
a few days before. Many of them had since then been compelled
to sleep in the open which, in spite of the light rains still to be
expected in April, they were finding a wonderful experience.
Balfour [Lord Arthur James, 1848-1930] alighted from the car
and went into the barracks to receive the blessings of the Rabbi.
I told him that if he would come again in a year or two he would
find quite a different picture; he would find these people established on their own land, content and looking like peasants
descended from generations of peasants.

The Jewish National Fund allotted these settlers 6,000
dunams of land near Nahalal, and soon there were 110 families
living there. Their industry and courage[11] aroused general
admiration and served to bridge the wide gap that existed
between new arrivals and older settlers.

The rabbi of Yablona was not the only pioneer, for R. Isaiah
Shapira (1891-1945) was a kindred spirit. Isaiah Shapira was
born on 11 Shevat 1891, the younger twin son of R. Elimelech
of Grodzisk.[12] His father had been bereaved of several children
and had remarried at the age of seventy. His second wife gave
birth to twins, Kalonymus Kalmish and Isaiah. When the
infants became dangerously ill, the doctors gave up hope. 'If
they do not recover,' threatened the anxious father, 'I will stop
being a Rabbi.' The children recovered. The rabbi remarked:
'It sometimes pays to be obstinate.'

After Elimelech's death on 1 Nisan 1892, his followers split into two factions. Some made Meir Yehiel of Ostrowiec their leader, and others followed Yisrael, grandson of the rabbi of Grodzisk. Isaiah was brought up by his grandfather Hayyim Samuel Halevy of Chentishin (Checiny) a town in south-east central Poland, and the love of Zion was bred into him. The house was frequented by emissaries from the Holy Land. When a fire ravaged his home, R. Hayyim Samuel exclaimed: 'Children, let us settle in the Holy Land. Is it permissible to spend any money rebuilding a home in exile?' He encouraged Isaiah to learn to play the violin 'for the service of the Almighty'. Isaiah's brother Kalonymus Kalmish became rabbi at Piaceszna, where he established a Yeshiva Daat Mosheh, and wrote the pedagogic work *Hovat Ha-Talmidim (The Duty of the Disciples)*. He perished on 7 Heshvan 1944, in the Warsaw ghetto.

Isaiah married Hayah Sara, daughter of Nathan Ha-Kohen Rabinowicz, a descendant of Radomsk. Although elected rabbi of Mokotow, he did not accept the position, for he was reluctant to become either a rabbi or a rebbe.

For a time he was licensed to sell liquor. He visited the Holy Land for the first time in 1914, but, because of the war, returned to Poland. He participated in the establishment of the Mizrachi in Poland in 1917, and worked with the religious Zionist leader Isaac Nissenbaum (1868-1943). Three years later, Isaiah settled in Jerusalem and became head of the Mizrachi Immigration and Labour Department, organising the construction of the Rosh Pina-Tabgah road. In 1924 he visited Poland and urged the rabbis of Yablona and Kozienice to follow his footsteps. In 1933, Isaiah managed the co-operative Bank Zebulun in Tel-Aviv, and ten years later he settled in Kfar Pines. He died in Jerusalem on 5 Sivan 1945, and was buried on the Mount of Olives.[13]

Another active Hasidic lover of Israel was R. Israel Eliezer Hofstein, son of R. Yerachmiel Moses (1860-1909) of

Kozienice. Israel inherited his love for the Holy Land from his father, who expected every visitor to make a contribution to the resettlement. Encouraged by Isaiah Shapira, Israel formed a colonisation society, Avodat Yisrael (Service of Israel), named after the book of R. Israel ben Shabbetai Hofstein (1733-1814), the Maggid of Kozienice. Another society, Nahlat Jacob, was formed by R. Ezekiel Taub of Yablona.

Israel Eliezer, Hayyim Bornstein and Meir Speizer formed a delegation to visit the Holy Land, staying at the home of R. Shapira of Drohobycz. After acquiring a plot 10 kilometres from Haifa, they returned to Poland.

In Nisan 1925 the rabbi of Kozienice arrived with fifty Hasidim and began to cultivate the soil in Emek Yisrael. They faced overwhelming odds. There were no roads and drainage, and water was in short supply. The Arabs called the swampy, malaria-ridden soil 'the place of the Angel of Death'. Israel, who was known as 'Nasi', worked as a farmer during the week, but turned rabbi on the Sabbath. Unlike his father, he did not deliver Talmudic discourses, but inspirational exhortations in fluent Hebrew. Not only did the colonists have to struggle against the inhospitable environment, but they were also threatened with attack by their Arab neighbours. They lived in tents or crude huts, in extremely primitive conditions. Some aid came from Yagur (founded in 1923), members of the Gedud Avodah who had come in the Third Aliyah.

The colonies were heavily in debt, and at the suggestion of Menahem Mendel Ussishkin (1863-1941), Chairman of the Executive Committee of the Jewish National Fund, the struggling Hasidic settlements of Nahlat Jacob (Yablona) and Avodat Yisrael joined forces in 1927 with a group of Poale Mizrachi (established in October 1926) under the name Kfar Hasidim.

The Keren Kayemet and Baron Edmond James de Rothschild gave them every assistance. The Jewish National Fund allocated additional land. The poet Shin Shalom who taught in the newly established colony gives a vivid description of the enthusiasm of the rabbis and their Hasidim. In 1929 R. Israel Eliezer successfully drove off an Arab attack on Kfar Ata. In the course of time, the settlers succeeded in establishing prosperous dairy farms and some of them engaged in handicraft. They set up a workers' co-operative and a small holding settlement (Moshav Ovdim). Today Yeshiva Knesset Hezkeyahu established in Kfar Hasidim in 1948 in memory of Hezkeyahu Joseph Mishkovsky, rabbi of Krinki in Poland, has 200 students and thirty young men studying in the Kolel. In 1950 a second village, Kfar Hasidim Bet, was set up. By 1968 both settlements together had 675 people and were affiliated to the Hapoel Mizrachi Moshavim Association. A religious youth institute, Kfar Hanoar Hadati, is situated nearby.

Though Kfar Hasidim was founded by the Hasidim, it has lost its Hasidic character and only the name perpetuates its origin. The atmosphere changed when both the founders left the settlement. R. Israel Eliezer's health deteriorated and the doctors advised him to seek a more salubrious climate. In 1930 he returned to Poland to urge his followers to support his ventures, and after four years he became rabbi in Paris, succeeding R. Joel Leib Herzog (1865-1933). In 1942 he found refuge in the United States where he worked with the Union of Rabbis. He returned to the Holy Land after the war and died in 1966. The rabbi of Yablona no longer pursued his rabbinic calling and found work as an insurance agent in the United States.

In 1928 a Hasidic rabbi inadvertently caused a dangerous incident in Jerusalem. Aaron Menahem Gutterman (1860-1934), rabbi of Radzymin since 1903, headed the Rabbi Meir Baal Ha-Nes fund in Poland. In Elul 1928 he visited Jerusalem for several weeks, and at the Western Wall he set up a screen to separate the men and the women (as is customary among Orthodox Jews). However, it was forbidden to erect such structures, and Police Inspector Douglas Duff ordered the congregants to dismantle the screen. When the order was ignored, the police removed the screen. Enraged congregants tried to prevent its removal and several people were injured in the ensuing mêlée.

Jewry observed 26 October 1928 as a fast day in protest, and a complaint was submitted to the League of Nations by the Zionist Organisation. A White Paper issued by the British government on 19 November 1928 stated: 'The Government considers that the removal of the screen was necessary.' A commission appointed in 1930 by the League of Nations under Eliel Lofgren, formerly a Swedish Minister for Foreign Affairs, ruled that the ownership of the Western Wall was vested in Moslem authorities and subject to certain restrictions. For example, the use of benches, chairs, curtains, and screen was forbidden. The British government reaffirmed the Turkish *status quo* in a White Paper.

PART TWO

IX

THE POWER OF GER

Ger or Gura Kalwaria (Ger in Yiddish and Gur in Hebrew), a small town near Warsaw, became the Jerusalem of the greatest Hasidic dynasty in Poland. At one time more than 100,000 Jews owed allegiance to the Rabbi of Ger and there was hardly a town without a Gerer *shtiebel*. Ger controlled the Aguda and the Bet Jacob schools, and its influence was far reaching. In Israel even today over 4,000 families owe allegiance to Ger.

I visited R. Israel Alter one Friday evening in December 1971. Inside the spacious modern Bet Hamidrash in Rehov Malche Yisrael in the Geula district of Jerusalem there were nearly 400 Hasidim. Some were studying the Talmud, others were discussing the weekly portion of the Law or the *Sefat Emet* by R. Yehuda Aryeh Alter of Ger.

At about 10 pm, four hours after the beginning of the Sabbath, the small side door suddenly opened and Israel Alter, the rabbi of Ger, entered. Instantly the atmosphere changed and a hushed silence enveloped the entire gathering. The Hasidim rose to greet him and made a path for him through their midst. Briskly he strode to the centre table. The Hasidim on both sides formed a cordon. He looked at them and they looked at him. No words were spoken. To be near him was in itself an experience, and to catch his eye was an honour. By a sign known only to the initiated, he indicated those who were to join him at the table, a selection process called *homot*, 'the ceremony of the walls', by the followers of Ger. The Rabbi and some forty selected followers took their seats. The young Hasidim, known in Poland as 'the Cossacks of Ger', pushed forward. The others leaned over one another and stood on tip-toe to observe every gesture of their revered leader. After the singing of one or two melodies, the rabbi commented briefly on the weekly portion of the Law. A rather retiring man, he is very sparing with words and scorns rhetorical devices. He speaks quickly and quietly, yet the ideas are almost telepathic-ally transmitted from Hasid to Hasid. I could not hear his words, as I was at the far side of the Bet Hamidrash, but a young Hasid near him courteously and clearly repeated the discourse as though he had heard every word.

Commenting on the verse, 'And they told him all the words of Joseph' (Gen.45:27), the Midrash states that Joseph identi-fied himself by reminding his father that the last subject they had studied together was the section on the heifer (Deut.21:6). The heifer is killed in expiation of an unsolved murder, symbolising that the community is not responsible for a crime perpetrated in its midst. Similarly, the brothers of Joseph could not be blamed for selling him, for the act was destined by Providence.

After the discourse, the *gabbai*, Chanina Schiff, announced the names and places of origin of the Hasidim who were supplying wine for the congregation that evening. 'Moshe Hayyim David of Lodz gives wine', he cried. 'Aaron Shohet of Bne Brak, Moshe Keshenover, Shmuel Yitzhak of Sokolow'. As they were named, the Hasidim arose and the Rebbe wished them *'Le-Hayyim'* ('To Life!'). After partaking of the wine and fruit *(peirot)* which had been brought in, the Rebbe gave *shirayim* to his Hasidim. Sabbath table melodies were chanted by Jacob Kaminer, Leibel Goldknoff and Hayyim Moshe Knoff. With the recitation of Grace After Meals, the *tish* came to an end and the Rebbe disappeared as abruptly as he had come.

Every morning at 11.15 am (earlier on Sundays), the Rebbe was 'at home' to Hasidim and visitors. In conformity with the traditions of Ger, women were not admitted to his presence, nor did he accept *pidyonot*.

The founder of the dynasty was R. Isaac Meir Rothenburg (Alter) (1789-1866), known as the *Hiddushe Ha-Rim* ('Novellae of R. Isaac Meir'). He studied in the yeshiva of his relative R. Aryeh Leib Zinz, later rabbi of Plock and author of ten important works. With single-minded passion, R. Isaac Meir devoted himself to his studies, spending some eighteen hours a day at his books. Like his father, R. Isaac Meir was a follower of R. Israel Hofstein, the Maggid of Kozienice, R. Simhah Bunem of Przysucha and R. Menahem Mendel Morgenstern of Kotzk.

R. Isaac Meir's personal life was beset with tragedies. He had thirteen children and outlived them all. In 1834, his sole surviving son R. Abraham Mordecai died at the age of forty. R. Mendel of Kotzk died in 1859, and reluctantly R. Isaac Meir became a Hasidic Rebbe, first in Warsaw and later in Ger. In simple terms he set forth his objective. 'I am not a Rebbe. I do not want money. I do not care for honour. All I want is to spend my years bringing the children of Israel nearer to their Father in Heaven.'

The doctrines of Prsysucha and Kotzk were combined in Ger. There was neither emphasis on miracles nor acceptance of *pidyonot*. Like his teachers, the rabbis Israel of Kozienice, Menahem Mendel of Kotzk and Simhah Bunem of Przysucha, he revered the Holy Land and through strenuous efforts 40,000 roubles were raised for the Yishuv between 1838 and 1840. During the Polish rebellion of 1863 he commented pointedly: 'We see how the Poles are sacrificing themselves to liberate their country from foreigners, but what are we doing to regain our land?'

In 1866, a serious injury brought him increasing and continu-
ous pain, but with calm fortitude he continued his normal way of
life. He died on 23 Adar that year. His last words, 'Leibele
Kaddish', were interpreted to mean that his grandson R. Yehudah
Leib should recite Kaddish after him and be his successor.

His grandson, R. Phinehas Menahem Eliezer Justman (1849-
1921) of Pulawy,[1] yearned to settle in the Holy Land, but his
dream was not fulfilled. 'Wherever Phinehas Menahem is,' said
R. Abraham Mordecai Alter, 'there you sense the sanctity of the
Holy Land.'

After seven years of leadership, which the Hasidim call 'the
seven years of plenty', Isaac Meir was succeeded by his grandson, Yehudah Leib (1847-1905), known as *Sefat Emet* (from the
verse in Prov. 12:19: 'the lip of truth shall be established for ever'),
his literary pseudonym. In 1888 he took part in a conference of
rabbis convened to discuss the imminent compulsory secular
education of Jewish children in Russia. His colleagues called him
'the King of Israel'. 'Just as the Jews need the Holy Land,' wrote
the Rabbi, 'so the Holy Land needs the Jews to bring out its
intrinsic holiness. The bond, pre-ordained and divinely forged
between the land and the people, has not been broken despite the
fact that the Jews have been driven from its soil.' In one Respon-
sum he tells of a Hasid who sent a cargo of *etrogim* for the Festival
of Tabernacles to the United States *via* Beirut instead of Jaffa.
The cargo did not arrive until after Hanukah, four months later,
which led the rabbi to conclude: 'A man must carry out his
business with integrity and not employ devious means. It was
wrong to divert the cargo from Jaffa to Beirut.'[2]

In a letter to R. Hayyim Morgenstern of Pulawy (1870-1906),
the author of a booklet *Shelom Yerushalayim* in which he demonstrated that every Jew was duty bound to participate in the
building of the Holy Land, R. Yehudah Leib wrote: 'Certainly,
it will be reckoned as a *mitzvah* to settle in the Holy Land.' Like R.
Hayyim Eliezer Wacks of Kalisz, the rabbi urged the Hasidim to
import Palestinian *etrogim*.

R. Yehudah Aryeh participated in a conference convened in 1888 by R. Shapiro of Grodzisk to discuss ways of strengthening the traditional educational system. He volunteered to raise 100,000 roubles for this purpose. The dark clouds of persecution were gathering in Tsarist Russia. In April 1881 there were pogroms in forty-eight towns. Jews who were conscripted into the Russian army suffered unspeakable hardship. The unfortunate youths thronged the rabbi's court for counsel and spiritual consolation. The rabbi worried over the thirty thousand Jewish soldiers who were fighting the Japanese (1904-5). All who wrote to him from the battlefield received personal letters expressing sympathy and encouragement.

His son and successor, R. Abraham Mordecai Alter (1866-1948), was an unassertive diffident man who acted with courage and resolution in times of crisis. He cultivated the virtue of *zerizut* (extreme diligence), and it was his habit to 'interrupt' the Sabbath services with study periods.

'I received your cheque', he wrote to one of his overseas Hasidim, 'and have already allotted half to the completion of our building; with the rest I will establish a fund to publish the work of my revered father, the *Sefat Emet*, who left many manuscripts.' R. Abraham Mordecai participated at a conference under the leadership of Dr Isaac Breuer in 1909 at Bad Homburg (a German summer resort), which paved the way for the founding of the Aguda, and he also attended the three Agudist world conferences (Knesiya Gedola) in 1923, 1929 and 1937.

During World War I, the German authorities sent rabbis Pinchas Kohn (1867-1942) and Emanuel Carlebach (1874-1927) to Poland, where they established the Warsaw orphanage under the aegis of the War Orphans' Fund of Agudat Yisrael. They tried to persuade the Jewish population to support Germany. The rabbi of Ger was unconvinced, saying: 'I believe that the Germans are descendants of the Amalekites.'

On 14 November 1916 the preliminary meeting of the Agudat Ha-Orthodoxim took place, and within a short time the new party had enrolled some 17,000 members. The rabbi encouraged the publication of *Dos Yiddishe Vort (The Jewish Word)*, which first appeared on 1 February 1917 under the editorship of N.L. Weingott.

The Aguda conference at Marienbad in 1937 discussed the proposal of the Peel Commission (set up by the British government in 1936 under Viscount Peel) that the Holy Land be partitioned into two sovereign states, one Jewish and the other Arab, with historic and strategic sites remaining under British jurisdiction. In forceful opposition, R. Abraham Mordecai quoted the prophet Joel (4:2): 'I will gather all nations, and will bring them down into the valley of Jehoshaphat; and I will enter into judgment with them there for My people and for My heritage Israel, whom they have scattered among the nations, and divided My land.'

'Just as a Hasid must visit his Rabbi from time to time,' said R. Abraham Mordecai, 'so must I visit the land of Israel periodically.' On his first visit for twenty-eight days in 1921, he left a day after Purim and travelled via Vienna, Trieste and Jaffa. When he arrived in Jerusalem he made his way to the Wall, where he tore his coat as a sign of mourning. He described the Chief Rabbi of the Holy Land, R. Abraham Yitzhak Kook (1865-1935), in the rabbinic idiom as *Ish Ha-Eshkolot*, 'a man in whom all is contained'. When R. Abraham Mordecai expressed concern over irreligious pioneers, R. Kook told him: 'The Holy of Holies was very sacred. Only the High Priest was permitted to enter there once a year and this annual visit was preceded by special preparations. But when the Holy of Holies was being built, all kinds of workmen went casually in and out. Similarly at this stage the land of Israel is being rebuilt, and we should not worry about the practices of those who are engaged in the rebuilding.'

On board ship on his way home on 7 Iyyar, he wrote down his impressions.

I visited the Institutions, the yeshivot and the Talmud Torah schools and I was very pleased with what I saw. However, they all need financial help from the Diaspora. It reassured me to observe that it is possible to conduct oneself in the way of our fathers and forefathers. Those whom God favours can undoubtedly make a living there and lead a true Torah life without difficulty or restraint. Those who are either unwilling or unable to settle there should support those who go. They should either set aside a fixed sum of money or invest it there. It will yield rich dividends. I myself have acquired land in Jaffa for commercial development ... I visited the High Commissioner, Eliezer Samuel [later Viscount Samuel, 1870-1963], and he has assured me that he would give every assistance to religious settlers.

The rabbi was convinced that a friendly relationship could be established with the Arabs.

I noticed that the Arabs, riding their camels, cleared the way for our entourage. If only our neighbours in Europe showed a little of this respect. It is my opinion that we can live together with the Arabs in brotherhood ... You have undoubtedly heard that at the last conference of the Aguda all the zaddikim and scholars unanimously promised to assist in a concrete manner every aspect of the yishuv.

He was in contact with the Agudist leaders Rabbis Sonnenfeld and Yitzhak Yerocham Diskin, and tried to make peace between them and the Jerusalem Rabbinate. He endorsed the resolution adopted by the Council of Rabbis in Vienna that the Aguda should take practical steps to rebuild the National Home.

Three years later, in Shevat 1924, he again visited the Holy Land, accompanied by R. Isaac Zelig Morgenstern of Sokolow, his brother-in-law, Heinoch Levin, rabbi of Bendin, his son-in-law Yizhak Meir Levin and a number of followers from Lodz. This time he stayed six weeks. 'If 500 wealthy Hasidim would emigrate to the Holy Land,' he said on his return to Poland, 'they could take over the country economically and spiritually.'

In 1925 a delegation of Ger Hasidim purchased 400 dunams in Hadar Ramatayim. That year Yeshivat Sefat Emet was established in Jerusalem. The rabbi of Ger believed that 'the existing yeshivot were inadequate, and their methods unsuitable for Polish Hasidim.'

The rabbi spent a fortnight in the home of an affluent industrialist, Jacob Wichliski. Every evening he summoned people urging them to invest capital in the Yishuv, and as a result, a number of Hasidim participated in the Fourth Aliyah. On 23 Elul, however, he advised Hasidim not to contribute to the Zionist funds, 'for they support settlements which desecrate the Sabbath.' Nor did he approve of the Aliyah of R. Ezekiel Taub of Yablona to the Holy Land, for he 'associated with non-religious elements'.

On his third visit in 1927, the rabbi travelled via Trieste and Alexandria, accompanied by his brother-in-law Hirsch Heinoch Levin of Bendin and his son Phinehas Levin. At the cave of Machpelah the guard was willing to allow the venerable visitor to descend into the cave (at that time the Jews were allowed no further than the first few steps), but the rabbi declined to take advantage of such a concession: 'All the children of Israel are the children of the king. I do not desire special privileges.'

The rabbi's friendship with R. Kook aroused the antagonism of the Orthodox extremists, and a zealot, Meir Heller Semnitzer, wrote a scurrilous pamphlet which was published by Joseph Simeon Pollack of Satmar, entitled *Bet Vaad Le-Hachamim (A Meeting-Place for the Wise)*. The Agudat Ha-Rabbanim (Rabbinic Association) of Poland excommunicated both the author and the printer.

The rabbi's fourth visit took place five years later in the winter of 1932, and this time he travelled overland through Vienna and Sofia and Istanbul, an itinerary that aroused the interest of Hasidic Jewry. 'I want to explore the different ways that lead to the Holy Land', he explained to his followers. He was accompanied by his brother Menahem Mendel, Rabbi of Pabianice. On his return journey there was a violent storm at sea. 'This is because we are leaving the Holy Land,' commented the rabbi. R. Meir Berlin, the Mizrachi leader, visited him to enlist his support for the Yishuv. R. Abraham Mordecai proposed that a world conference of rabbis should be convened to decide whether to support the Aguda or the Mizrachi, but this did not materialise.

When Hitler came to power in January 1933, the rabbi said: 'For 150 years our German brethren have not known the meaning of the word exile. Now they will probably find refuge in the Holy Land. I am afraid of one thing: they will take with them their assimilated customs and will adversely influence the vitality of the religious life.'

The fifth pilgrimage, the longest and the last, took place just before Rosh Hashanah 1935, and lasted eight months until Rosh Hodesh Iyyar 1936. By then the rabbi regarded himself as a resident of the Holy Land, and no longer observed Yom Tov Sheni (the Second Day of a Festival observed in the Diaspora). He was reluctant to return home, but a Bet Din consisting of Rabbis Jacob Meir Bidermann, Heinoch Levin and Abraham David Eizner counselled him not to desert his 'great multitude' in Poland.

With the outbreak of World War II on 1 September 1939, the fate of eastern European Jewry was sealed. The rabbi urged his followers to subscribe generously to the Polish Air Defence Loan, for 'the destiny of Jewry is bound up with the destiny of the Polish state'.

Within a week the Nazis had reached Warsaw and within a fortnight the Polish government itself had left the country to take refuge in Romania. On 17 September the Russians moved in to claim their part of the country, and eastern Poland was annexed to the Soviet Union. After twenty-seven days of bombing and nineteen of shell-fire, Warsaw capitulated on 27 September and the Jewish Community Council was dissolved on 4 October. A Judenrat (Jewish Council) was set up instead and the wheels of destruction were set in motion. On the Day of Atonement 1940, the Germans announced the setting up of a ghetto in Warsaw. Soon most Polish Jews were confined to ghettos which were run by elected or appointed Jewish councils responsible to the Nazis, and by 1941 their segregation was almost complete.

At the outbreak of the war, the rabbi moved to Warsaw and kept changing his residence to evade the Nazis, who spared no efforts to locate the 'wonder rabbi'. Periodical pogroms gave way to remorseless organised annihilation, and Poland soon became the central cemetery of the great Jewish communities in Europe.

An energetic committee in the United States headed by Rabbis Menahem Mendel Kasher and Eliezer Silver, and supported by Justice Louis Dembitz Brandeis (1865-1941) and the Democratic congressman from New York, Sol Bloom (1870-1949), managed to get him an entry visa to Palestine. To obtain an exit visa from the Nazis, the Hasidim bribed the manager of the Iranian Shipping Line. He left Poland and journeyed through Austria and Italy, arriving in Jerusalem in early Nisan 1940 accompanied by his wife, his sons Phinehas Menahem, Israel and Simhah Bunam and his son-in-law Yizhak Meir Levin. Some Hasidim were anxious for him to settle in the United States, but the rabbi declined: 'I cannot go back into exile again.'

Fearful reports arrived from Poland. The first death factory, complete with gas chambers, was set up near the Polish town of Chelmno, late in 1941. Five others also in Poland at Belzec, Sobibor, Treblinka, Auschwitz and Maidanek were completing 'the final solution of the Jewish problem', as the Nazis euphemistically called it. The rabbi participated in a special service of intercession for Polish Jewry held in the 'Hurvah of Rabbi Judah Hasid' in Kislev 1942.

'It is a time of trouble for Jacob,' he lamented. 'Repentance, Prayer and Charity can avert the evil decree. We must pray that wickedness may pass from the world and evil be consumed like smoke. May we be worthy of consolation; may we live to see the time when all will be well with Israel.'

The rabbi died on Shavuot (Pentecost) 1948, and Dr Herzog declared in his eulogy: 'On Shavuot the Torah was given, and on Shavuot the Torah was taken away.' He was buried in the courtyard of Yeshiva Sefat Emet in Jerusalem. More than two decades have passed. Jerusalem has been reunited and the Mount of Olives cemetery is once again in Jewish hands, yet the rabbi's remains still repose in their temporary burial-place because the present rabbi has not yet authorised their re-interment on the Mount of Olives.

R. Abraham Mordecai was succeeded by his son R. Israel. He was born in Ger on 24 Tishri 1892, and was named after the father of the *Hiddushei Ha-Rim* who was Rabbi of Ger. On 4 Nisan 1910, R. Israel married Hayyah Sarah, daughter of R. Jacob Meir Biderman (son-in-law of the *Sefat Emet*). During World War I, R. Israel lived in Warsaw in Twarda 29. When his father returned after the war to Ger, R. Israel remained in Warsaw, where he prayed in a *shtiebel* in the home of R. Leibel Schochet. His wife had died during the war. In 1940 R. Israel managed to escape from Poland together with his father, and reached the Holy Land. There he married Perl, daughter of R. David Weidenfeld and sister-in-law of R. Abraham Weinberg of Slonim who lived in Tel-Aviv. They had no children. In accordance with the Last Will and Testament of R. Abraham Mordecai, R. Israel succeeded his father as Rebbe of Ger on Shavuot 1948.

It was said of R. Israel that although time was precious to him, he had time for everybody. Twice daily he would receive people in private audience. He was able to grasp the most complicated problem with almost lightning speed. People of all shades of religious observance sought his advice on a wide range of matters. His home in Rehov Geula and his heart were open to everyone in need. His discourses were of rare brevity, seldom lasting more than a few moments. The brevity did not diminish their depth and there was original thought in every one. He took an active interest in the work of the Aguda, which he endearingly called 'the Agudat Israel of my father', and was one of the prominent leaders of the Moazei Gedolei Ha-Torah. He expanded the Yeshiva Sefat Emet in Jerusalem and encouraged the building of the vast Yeshiva Hiddushei Ha-Rim in Tel-Aviv and other educational institutions. He died on 2 Adar 1977 and was buried on the Mount of Olives in Helkat Poilin near the graves of R. Itze Fishel Heine (d.1944) and R. Simon Alter (d.1974).

R. Israel was succeeded by his brother R. Simhah Bunem, who was born in Ger in 1889. His mother was the daughter of Noah Shahor of Biala. Simhah Bunem married Ita, daughter of R. Nehemiah Alter (the third son of the *Sefat Emet*) who was *dayyan* in Lodz. Together with his father-in-law he visited the Holy Land in 1923 and stayed there for a few years. On returning to Poland, he lived in Ger, Lodz and Warsaw. As a Palestinian citizen, he, together with his family, was able in 1940 to leave Poland for the Holy Land. His father R. Abraham Mordecai called him 'the wise one'. He has two children. Though a renowned scholar, he made a livelihood in property both in Poland and in Israel.

The Rabbi's younger brother R. Phinehas Menahem (b. 1926) has seven children. He heads the Hasidic institutions (*mosdot*) of Ger.

While the rabbis of Vizhnitz, Belz and Lubavitch were establishing networks of educational institutions, Ger could not lag behind. Attached to the yeshiva is a Kolel, a Talmud Torah and a Yeshiva Ketana, while the most recent addition is Yeshiva Le-Zeirim, which was founded in 1967 with sixteen students. The Hotel Babad was converted to a yeshiva for fifty students between the ages of thirteen and seventeen.

In Tel-Aviv there is a Yeshiva Hiddushe Ha-Rim with an enrolment of 150. Its five floors on a 5-dunam site in Ramat Ha-Hayil, a garden suburb of Tel-Aviv, will accommodate 600 students, and its synagogue–seating 100 worshippers–entailed a capital expenditure of nearly three million Israeli pounds. The foundation stone was laid in Elul 1952, the building was consecrated on 9 Sivan 1969. Apart from the Yeshiva of Ponovezh, in Bne Brak, this is the most ambitious Hasidic yeshiva project in Israel.

Tel-Aviv in the 1950s was not well equipped with Hasidic centres of learning, for most of the Hasidim settled in near-by Bne Brak. To fill this gap, Ger Hasidim established Bet Hamidrash L'Hora'ah at Nahlat Binyamin in Iyyar 1954. By 1972 it had nearly fifty students, and moved to more spacious accommodation in the Bet Haknesset of Yavneh. One of the aims of the Institute is to publish the second volume of the letters of Abraham Mordecai as well as *Hiddushe Ha-Rim* on *Yoreh Deah* by R. Yitzhak Meir, a manuscript which was rescued from the Holocaust. The Memorial Foundation of Jewish Culture in New York is helping to defray the cost of publication.

Yitzhak Meir Levin, who died in 1971 at the age of seventy-seven, was the spokesman of the Aguda, and one of the first Hasidic politicians to emerge in inter-war Poland. He was born on 19 Tevet 1894, the son of R. Zevi Hanoch Ha-Kohen formerly rabbi of Bendin, and son-in-law of Yehudah Leib, the *Sefat Emet*. Yitzhak Meir married Matil, daughter of R. Abraham Mordecai. As a young man, he helped his father-in-law to establish the Aguda. Kiryat Ha-Rim Levin in northern Tel-Aviv is named after him.

For half a century he fought fearlessly, first in his native Poland and after 1940 in Israel, to strengthen Torah Judaism. 'Every day', said R. Abraham Mordecai, 'Yitzhak Meir studies the Tractate of the Agudat Yisrael.' One of the signatories to the Declaration of Independence, he became a member of the Knesset in 1949, and he served in the Israeli Provisional Government (1948-9) and as Minister for Social Welfare in the Coalition Government (1940-52). On 22 January 1948 he informed the United Nations Working Committee at Lake

Success that the Agudat Yisrael was united with all Jewry on the political future of Palestine. 'The Land of Israel and the people of Israel form one complete entity, forever inseparable.' 'Let us be frank for a moment,' he told the Knesset in 1966. 'Can country, language, or army be sufficient in themselves to safeguard our future in the spiritual sense? Surely all these have no meaning and no value unless there is a real soul in the centre of our activity.' Even his opponents admired his courage and forthrightness. 'The words of Rabbi Levin came from an aching heart,' said Prime Minister Levi Eshkol in 1967, 'and showed a deep concern for the historic continuation of the Jewish people.'

R. Abraham Mordecai Alter of Ger

R. Hayyim Meir and R. Moses Hager of Vizhnitz (Bne Brak)

R. Moses Hager of Vizhnitz

R. Berele Rokeah of Belz

*R. Jekutiel Judah Halberstam of Klausenburg
(Kiryat Sanz, Netanyah)*

A diamond factory in Kiryat Sanz, Netanyah

R. Yehiel Joshua Rabinowicz, Rebbe of Biala (Jerusalem)

R. Abraham Hayyim Roth (Jerusalem)

R. Shlomoh Friedman (Tel-Aviv)

*R. Mordecai Shalom Joseph Friedman of Sadagura-Przemysl
(Tel-Aviv)*

Four generations of rabbis of Nadvorna

R. Moses Mordecai Biderman of Lelov (Bne Brak)

R. Israel Alter, Rebbe of Ger (Jerusalem)

*President Zalman Shazar on a visit to the printing school
in Kfar Habad, 1957*

Music lesson at Bet Rivkah (Kfar Habad)

The yeshiva in Kfar Habad

R. Joel Teitelbaum of Satmar

R. Solomon Halberstam of Bobow

*R. Hananiah Yom Tov Lipa Teitelbaum lays the
foundation stone of Kiryat Yismah Mosheh, 1963*

Knessiya Gedola, Agudat Israel World Conference,
Jerusalem, 1954

Children studying in a Talmud Torah (Jerusalem)

A Hasid studying in a Kolel (Jerusalem)

Hasidic farmers in Israel

X

KIRYAT VIZHNITZ

Adjoining Ramat Gan, north-east of Tel-Aviv, is the flourishing township of Bne Brak which has a large autonomous Hasidic settlement, Kiryat Vizhnitz, named after the townlet of Vizhnitsa (Vijnita in Romania), home of the rabbis of Vizhnitz, a dynasty that has produced in the last two centuries eight generations of Hasidic leaders.

The Kossov-Vizhnitz dynasty was founded by the Cabbalist Jacob Kopul (d. 1787) of Kolomyja in Galicia. He was a descendant of R. Obadiah Bertinoro (1450-1510), who settled in the Holy Land in 1486. When R. Israel Baal Shem Tov visited Kolomyja, he recognised the presence of a sage whom he identified as Jacob Kopul, a shopkeeper. Kopul became a devoted follower of the Besht and frequently acted as Reader in his Bet Hamidrash. He often declared that Kopul's prayers ascended directly to the Throne of Glory and caused rejoicing in the celestial spheres. As a legacy, he made Kopul responsible for the spiritual welfare of the Jews of Marmaros and the Carpathian region. 'I am giving you a beautiful garden,' the Besht told him. 'Look after it.'

His son Menahem Mendel (1768-1826) settled in Kossov, eastern Galicia, not far from Stanislav near the Hungarian border. He came under the influence of R. Elimelech of Lyshansk, author of *Noam Elimelech*. 'Only one who is able to revive the dead is able to understand this book,' was the comment of Menahem Mendel. He was also a disciple of R. Zevi Hirsch of Nadvorna (d.1801), R. Zeev Wolf of Tscharny-Ostrog and R. Moses Leib of Sassov (1745-1807). Like the Besht, Menahem Mendel lived by three principles: love of God, love of Israel and love of the Torah. He maintained that his three-fold ideal could be achieved through music, his melodies echoing through Hungary, Romania, and Czechoslovakia. His discourses are preserved in three books.[1]

The traditions of Menahem Mendel were continued by his son, R. Hayyim (1795-1854).[2] Commenting on the verse: 'so that I come back to my father's house in peace, then shall the Lord be my God' (Gen.28:21), R. Hayyim said: 'If I return in peace to the house of my fathers, then the Lord will be my God, for the Talmud states: "If a man dwells in the Diaspora, it is as if he has no God." ' His second son, R. Joseph Alter Hager of Radovitzy, settled in Safed in 1873, but died in Haifa fifty-four years later, on 8 Tammuz, and was buried near the third-century Palestinian scholar, Abdimi (Dimi) of Haifa.

R. Hayyim's youngest son Menahem Mendel (1830-85) settled in Vizhnitz (which then belonged to Austria), and married Miriam, the daughter of R. Israel Friedman, founder of the Ruzhin-Sadagura dynasty. Modelling himself after his father-in-law, Menahem Mendel, head of the Kolel of Vizhnitz and Marmaros, built a palatial residence with a large Bet Hamidrash surrounded by gardens and orchards. He employed a man whose sole duty was to distribute money anonymously to charitable causes. Such vast sums were involved that his brother-in-law R. Nahum of Stefanesti remarked: 'If the rabbi of Vizhnitz had kept for himself all the money he has given away to charity, he would have been richer than Rothschild.'

R. Menahem Mendel's son Baruch (1845-93) also made his home in Vizhnitz, where he published his father's writings,[3] and works on the Pentateuch entitled *Imre Baruch*.[4] He died at the age of forty-eight, leaving twelve children. The most outstanding of R. Baruch's progeny was R. Israel (1860-1935), known among the Hasidim as Ohev Yisrael ('Lover of Israel'). According to legend, the Besht had once said: 'My soul will return to this earth after one hundred years.' The Hasidim of Vizhnitz believe that this did in fact happen and that his soul found a new home in Israel of Vizhnitz. He was born in Vizhnitz on 2 Elul 1860, and at the age of fifteen married the daughter of R. Meir Horowitz (d.1878) of Dzikov,[5] a grandson of R. Naphtali of Ropszyce. R. Israel lived with his father-in-law for three years, studying with his brother-in-law, R. Joshua of Dzikov. He succeeded his father as rabbi of Vizhnitz when he was thirty-three, and was particularly interested in education, setting up a Talmud Torah and a Yeshiva Bet Yisrael.

With the outbreak of World War I, he found refuge in Grosswardein (Nagyvarad in Hungarian) in Transylvania. At first the mitnagdic community gave him an unfriendly, if not hostile, reception, but gradually he won their affection. He attended the communal synagogue and listened to the German discourses of R. Benjamin Fuchs. He recited *piyyutim* (Hebrew liturgical poetry), a custom his Hasidim adopted. 'I will continue to love my enemies until they become my friends,' vowed this patient, even-tempered sage.

After the war he did not return to Vizhnitz, for he yearned to settle in the Land of Israel, and his son Eliezer became rabbi in his place. He was involved in a bitter dispute with R. Hayyim Zevi Teitelbaum over the Presidency of the Kolel, a fund for the needy in the Holy Land. Since they were unable to settle their differences, they were made jointly responsible for the fund. A staunch supporter of the Aguda, R. Israel often urged his followers to vote for the 'right' candidates at elections. Many zaddikim were among his disciples, and from these distinguished followers he refused to accept money. 'A coachman does not charge a fellow-coachman,' he said with a smile. Fourteen years after R. Israel's death, he was reburied in Bne Brak on the Fast of Esther, 1949. His son welcomed the coffin with the Vizhnitz melody 'Shalom Aleichem' ('Welcome Ye Ministering Angels').

R. Israel's discourses are to be found in *Ahavat Yisrael*.[6] 'The phrase "the sanctity of the Land" is numerically equal to the Hebrew phrase, "the Holy Sabbath",' said the rabbi. 'This can be interpreted as meaning that only through observance of the Sabbath will the land be restored to us.'[7]

Three of R. Israel's five sons settled in the Holy Land. Hayyim Meir Hager, founder of Kiryat Vizhnitz was born on 14 Kislev 1888 in Vizhnitz, and was ordained by R. Shalom Mordecai of Brezany and R. Benjamin Aryeh Weiss of Czernowitz. At seventeen, he married his cousin Margalit, daughter of R. Mordecai Zeev of Rahmastrivka, a descendant of Czernobil, who at the outbreak of the Russian Revolution settled in the Holy Land, where he died on 20 Sivan 1937 and was buried on the Mount of Olives. R. Hayyim Meir divided his time between Vizhnitz and Vilcovitz, his first rabbinic post. In 1935 Hayyim Meir visited the Holy Land accompanied by his brothers, R. Baruch and R. Eliezer. In 1940, the yeshiva at Vizhnitz was closed and in the same year the Russians occupied Bukovina. In September, Grosswardein was overrun by the Hungarians, and a ghetto was established in 1944 for 35,000 Jewish inhabitants.

Miraculously, the rabbi's family survived the Holocaust. His home was open to all who were homeless and destitute. Although it was dangerous, he visited the communities of Vilcovitz and Marmaros and conducted clandestine services. When transports to Auschwitz began, the rabbi escaped with only his *tallit* and *tephillin*. For a time he chopped wood in a labour camp and eventually after an arduous journey, he made his way to Budapest. At the end of the war, he returned to Grosswardein and tried to rebuild the shattered community. His brother Eliezer (1891-1946) found refuge in the Holy Land in 1944. Eliezer was R. Israel's favourite son. 'I have five books of Moses,' said R. Israel of his five sons. 'The third is Eliezer. When the doors of Paradise are closed to me, I will state I am Eliezer's father and all the gates will open.' R. Eliezer was the author of *Damesek Eliezer*.[8] As soon as he arrived in Israel, he set up a Bet Hamidrash and a yeshiva in Jerusalem. Two years later he fell ill. Although in pain, he would not permit the doctors to hush the Hasidim who were singing and dancing in the near-by synagogue. 'They do not disturb me,' said the rabbi to the doctor. 'On the contrary, their songs and dances give me new strength.' He died on 2 Elul 1946 and was buried on the Mount of Olives.

R. Hayyim Meir had little success in post-war Grosswardein, and decided to emigrate. After a short stay in Antwerp, he settled in 1947 in Tel-Aviv, where he had so many followers that a hall had to be rented to accommodate them on the High Holydays. After three years he was ready to found his own settlement. 'Because only by building and establishing new centres of Torah here can one effectively strengthen the faith.' Acquiring 33 dunams in Bne Brak, he established the first Hasidic Shikun since the establishment of the state of Israel.

The foundation-stone was laid on the site of an abandoned orange-grove near Zichron Meir on 2 Sivan 1950, the anniversary of his father's death. Two years later, when only two houses were ready, the rabbi moved in. The Shikun grew rapidly and problems were resolved with despatch and ingenuity. By 1973 it housed over 350 families, a population of nearly 3,000.

The street names tell the story of the dynasty of Kossov and Vizhnitz. Rehov Torat Hayyim, Rehov Imre Baruch, Rehov Ahavat Shalom, Rehov Zemah Zaddik and Givat Phinehas (named after R. Phinehas of Borsa).

Predictably, the chief building is the magnificent yeshiva Bet Yisrael V-Damesek Eliezer, modelled after the far-famed yeshiva that had been destroyed in Bukovina, and 250 students study there. It houses the library of the late R. Meir Meiri, author of *Humash Torah Meiri*.[9] After completing their studies at the yeshiva, students progress to the Kolel Damesek Eliezer, and graduates of the Kolel have been appointed to rabbinic posts in different parts of the world. The forty-five students there receive monthly stipends, in addition to a family allowance for each child. Exceptionally gifted students receive extra money. These stipends are augmented by parents or by the salaries that the young wives earn as teachers.

The Kirya is virtually self-sufficient, particularly with regard to its educational facilities. Young children attend kindergarten, then up to the age of fourteen three hundred children attend the Talmud Torah, where there are an additional fifty places in dormitories for non-resident children of the Kirya. After fourteen, the boys attend the Yeshiva Ketana, while the girls are enrolled at the Bet Jacob schools, and many of them go on to the teachers' seminary at Zichron Meir. Adult education is not neglected. There are regular classes after the morning service and at the end of the working day.

Kiryat Vizhnitz is well equipped with social welfare organisations. Bet Shalom houses 100 elderly people. The Gemilat Hesed fund grants interest-free loans to the needy; Ezrat Nashim provides financial aid for indigent students; the Bikkur Holim (Society for Visiting the Sick) fund takes care of the ailing, and a permanent building fund enables people to acquire apartments relatively cheaply. In the central banquet hall, residents and even non-residents celebrate their festivities, while a sixty-eight-room hotel caters for the many visitors to the Kirya.

'Where there is no food, there is no Torah,' says the Mishnah.[10] R. Hayyim Meir realised that one of his first responsibilities was to provide his Hasidim with means of earning a living. The settlement has its own diamond factory, bakery, printing-press, a butcher shop, a greengrocery, and a special bakery where unleavened bread is baked by hand. Its twelve ritual baths open at 3 am and are visited by more than 1,500 people a day. The Kirya has its own generator, the maintenance of which does not require a Jew to work on the Sabbath.

Every Sabbath the rabbi would conduct three public meals, and Friday night was the highlight of the week's activities. He would enter the Bet Hamidrash with the words, '*Gut Shabbos, Gut Shabbos, Heilige Shabbos, Teiyre Shabbos, Shreit Yiddlech, Gut Shabbos*' ('Good Sabbath, holy Sabbath, dear Sabbath, let us Jews welcome the Sabbath'). The meal rarely terminated before 2 am. His discourses were interwoven with *gematrias* (a method of Biblical exegesis based on interpreting words according to the numerical value of the letters in the Hebrew alphabet), and a *notarikon* (the abbreviation of Hebrew words or phrases). Commenting on the verse (Gen.4:15): 'And the Lord set a sign for Cain', the rabbi explained that the Hebrew word for 'sign' stands for Torah, love and reverence. The rabbi published his father's discourse under the title *Ahavat Yisrael*.[12]

The rabbi believed that joy was one of the basic tenets of Judaism. A man should rejoice in his day-to-day life as well as when he seeks communion with his Creator. How should a man rejoice? By means of concentration and fervour. It was a touching experience to hear him sing 'Nishmat' ('The Breath of Every Living Being', part of the morning service for the Sabbath) or 'Hallel' (Hymns of Praise, recited on the New Moon and Festivals), and to hear him sing such Sabbath melodies as 'Kol Mekadesh' ('All who Sanctify the Sabbath') or 'Bene Hechale' ('Members of the Palace').

Every day petitioners came to the rabbi and each was greeted with the utmost tact and lovingkindness. There was nothing stereotyped about these interviews. Some lasted a few minutes, others for hours. Each visitor was important and the children were treated with particular tenderness, being addressed in endearing diminutives. Israel was Israelniu, Mendel Mendele, Nahum Nahumnieu.

The Kirya is proud of its high birthrate, and is known as 'the university for child-bearing'. The average family has six or seven children and ten or twelve is not unusual. The marriages are arranged by shadchanim, and couples are matched according to cultural backgrounds and compatibility. The Hasidim point out that those who are quick to 'fall in love' can just as quickly 'fall out of love', and that the love that follows marriage is more lasting. Arranged marriages are essential in settings where the sexes are segregated from infancy. Boys and girls play separately; young men and young women pray separately, and at festivities there is no casual mingling. As a result, promiscuity, as well as juvenile delinquency, is virtually unknown among the Hasidim.

Contrary to popular misconception, the Hasidim do not avoid military service, and many members of the Kirya are on the army reserve list. The rabbi encouraged them to participate in the Six-Day War, which he called 'the beginning of the Redemption'. He was a staunch Agudist and he himself led the way to the polling booths at election time. In 1961 he and his brother Baruch in a joint public proclamation urged 'All those who have any association with Vizhnitz to participate in the coming election and to vote only for the Aguda.'

R. Hayyim Meir died at the age of eighty-four on 9 Nisan (22 March) 1972. Fifty thousand people from all over Israel attended his funeral. At the yeshiva *hakkaphot* (Circuits) were made around the coffin. He was succeeded by his son Moses Yehoshua Hager (b.1916), son-in-law of R. Hayyim Menahem Panet of Dej in Transylvania. Moses Yehoshua was ordained by R. Phinehas Zimetbaum, head of the Bet Din of Grosswardein, and R. Mordecai b. Joseph Briszk (1884-1944), founder and head of the yeshiva at Tasnad. The rabbi visited London twice in 1966 and in 1972 on behalf of the Kirya. He has four daughters and two sons, and his brother R. Mordecai is the spiritual leader of the Hasidim of Vizhnitz in the United States. One son is R. Israel who was born on Israel's Independence Day. He was ordained by R. Phinehas Epstein and David Jungreiss, and married the daughter of R. Zusya Twersky of Ben Brak.

In addition to Kiryat Vizhnitz in Bne Brak, there are groups of Vizhnitz Hasidim in Jerusalem, where the centre has a Bet Hamidrash, a Talmud Torah (Imre Hayyim) and a yeshiva. There is another Bet Hamidrash in Netanyah under Naphthali Hayyim Adler, son-in-law of R. Hayyim Meir and step-son of R. Baruch of Sereth. Like the Hasidim of Klausenburg, Vizhnitz too is planning to establish an agricultural settlement in the Negev.

RAMAT VIZHNITZ

On the heights of Mount Carmel overlooking the blue waters of the Mediterranean and the Bay of Haifa, where the road twists and turns before it reaches the wooded plateau, stands Ramat Vizhnitz, a Hasidic centre established by Baruch Hager.

R. Baruch, the fourth son of R. Israel, was born in Vizhnitz in 1895 and named after R. Baruch of Visha (Felsoviso). R. Israel called him 'the Wise One', and he was ordained by R. Meir b. Aaron Judah Arik (1855-1926) of Buczacz and Abraham Menahem b. Meir Halevi Steinberg (1847-1928) of Brody.[11] He married the daughter of R. Issachar Dov of Belz, a union that ended in divorce. His second wife Tzyril was the daughter of R. Eliezer Nisan Horowitz, a descendant of Dzikov. From 1928 he occupied rabbinic positions in Rizkova, Kotzman (Kitsman) in Bukovina and became rabbi in 1934 in Sereth-Vizhnitz where he established a yeshiva. Like his father and brothers he was active in the Aguda and advocated the establishment of agricultural centres for the training of religious *halutzim*. A courteous and considerate man, he listened thoughtfully to the opinion of others, presenting his own views with a gentle persuasiveness that often carried the day.

After suffering great hardships during the war, R. Baruch arrived in Israel in Sivan 1947. While his brother planned to establish a shikun in Bne Brak, R. Baruch founded his settlement in Haifa on 3 Tammuz 1954. Many religious Jews were attracted to Hadar Har-Carmel, and its illustrious Yeshiva Yehel Yisrael. In the realm of education, the rabbi was uncompromising. 'Nadab and Abihu [sons of Aaron] offered strange fire before the Lord [Lev.10:1], and they were punished by death. Why did they deserve such a fate? Because they failed to realise that only consecrated fire was permitted,' explained the rabbi. 'Only by ensuring that our children are grounded in traditional Judaism can we ensure the survival of Israel.'

The shikun's large synagogue Mekor Baruch seats some five hundred. There is a Talmud Torah for 120 children, an elementary school recognised by the Ministry of Education, a home for 100 elderly people, and many social welfare organisations. It accommodates nearly 100 families. The rabbi was pleased with the progress of settlement. 'Red Haifa is getting whiter and whiter' he remarked; meaning of course that the Labour-controlled teeming city was becoming more and more observant. He died on 2 Heshvan 1963 at the age of sixty-eight and was buried in Bne Brak, and is survived by three sons and a daughter. Two of his sons, Eliezer and Moses divided their father's patrimony; R. Eliezer became Rebbe, his brother head of the yeshiva. 'My aim is to maintain and expand the glorious path of my ancestors,' stated the Rebbe. A publishing house has been added to the settlement, and recently it issued a commentary on the Sabbath table melodies by the rabbi of Kossov-Vizhnitz. [13]

In January 1973 a new building, Zeev Hesed Ve-Eliezer David Halevi, was consecrated. It provides additional facilities for the students of the yeshiva and for research into the history of Vizhnitz.

XI

THE SABRA RABBI

'The sun also ariseth, and the sun goeth down', says Ecclesiastes (1:5). This biblical verse comes to mind when one enters the magnificent Bet Hamidrash in Jerusalem (behind the Sharei Zedek Hospital) where the Israeli-born R. Issachar Dov popularly known as 'Rabbi Berele', or 'the Belzer Rov' (as the Hasidim call him) maintains the traditions of Belz. The founder of the dynasty of Belz (a town in eastern Galicia, now part of the Soviet Ukraine), was R. Shalom b. Eliezer Rokeah (1799-1855), a militant opponent of haskalah. Through R. Solomon of Lutsk (d.1813), a disciple of R. Dov Baer, the Maggid of Mezeritz R. Shalom was drawn to Hasidism. The high incidence of apostasy among the Maskilim convinced R. Shalom that haskalah represented a danger to Judaism. He refused to temporize with the Reformers, categorising as rank heresy the slightest deviation from the traditional path.

In defence of traditional Judaism, his son and successor R. Joshua (1825-94) formed Mahzikei Ha-Dat (Upholders of the Faith) in 1878 and a year later issued a publication of that name.[1] The rabbi was the unofficial spokesman of Galician

Jewry and the appointment of rabbis, ritual slaughterers and other communal functionaries required the tacit *imprimatur* of Belz.

The second son of R. Joshua, Issachar Dov (1854-1927), extended the power of the dynasty and Belz became for Galicia what Ger was to Poland. 'The entire world', Hasidim used to say, 'journeys to Belz.' Large groups of Hasidim of Belz were soon to be found in Czechoslovakia, Hungary and Romania.

The poet Jiri Langer (1894-1943), 'the bachelor Hasid from Prague' and author of *Nine Gates* visited Belz in 1913, 1914 and 1918. He describes his reception in these graphic terms:[2]

Once again he shakes my hand, this time lingeringly, and regards me kindly. He looks at me with only one eye. The other is blind. It seems to me that a ray of light shines from his seeing eye and pierces me to the heart.

He is a sturdy tall old man with broad shoulders and an unusual patriarchal appearance, dressed in a caftan of fine silk. Like all the other men he wears on his head a *shtreimel*, a round fur Sabbath hat, around which hang thirteen short dark-brown sable tails (on weekdays he wears a *spodek*, which is a tall heavy velvet cap, worn by Rabbis, similar to a grenadier's cap.) . . . The crowd, which till now has been completely quiet, almost cowed, suddenly bursts forth in a wild shout. No one stays in his place. The tall black figures run hither and thither round the synagogue, flashing past the lights of the Sabbath candles. Gesticulating wildly and throwing their whole bodies about, they shout out the words of the Psalms. They knock into each other without concern or consideration, for all their cares have been cast aside; everything has ceased to exist for them. They are seized by an indescribable ecstasy.

To Langer, Belz was 'the Jewish Rome'. He records:

On weekdays, at Belz, we do not recite the morning prayers until noon, when the Rabbi enters the House of Study with his sons. We pray at the synagogue only on the Sabbath. The weekday service, which in other places lasts nearly an hour, is completed with miraculous speed at Belz in fifteen or twenty minutes. This speed is very important for no sinful thoughts can steal into prayers, if the words are spoken quickly and without any pauses. A person who cannot say a thousand words with one breath has no right to be called a saint.

'My brother did not come back from Belz,' said Frantisek Langer (1894-1943). 'He had brought Belz back with him.'[3] The symbolism in the writings of Franz Kafka (1883-1924) owes much to the inspiration and influence of Belz on the writings of Jiri Langer.

On 22 Heshvan 1927 R. Aaron Rokeah (b.1878) succeeded his father. Like his ancestors he was both a man of many interests and a man of action, and his influence was far-reaching. He participated in the 1931 delegation led by R. Israel Meir Kahan, the *Haphetz Hayyim* (1838-1933), to the Polish Prime Minister Bartel, seeking support for Orthodox education. When Hitler became German Chancellor on 30 January 1933, R. Aaron declared: 'Hitler is the very personification of the devil. He is worse than Amalek or Haman.' When Prince Peter of Greece, a relative of the British royal family, visited him early in 1937, the rabbi urged the prince to persuade Britain to suppress Arab terrorism in the Holy Land.[4]

The rabbi supported a number of men known as *yoshevim*, who devoted their whole time to prayer and study, and every Hasid who visited the rabbi was required to make a contribution towards their maintenance. On the Day of Atonement he told his worshippers that it was forbidden to associate with either the Zionists or the Mizrachi.[5] Despite the efforts of many rabbis, including the rabbi of Ger, R. Aaron declined to participate in the Aguda.

For four perilous years (1940-4) the rabbi lived precariously in Nazi Europe, travelling from Sokal to Przemysl, to Vizhnitz to the ghettos of Bochnia, Cracow and Budapest. He withstood unspeakable hardships. He changed his name first to 'Aaron Singer', then to 'Aaron Twersky', in order to confuse the Nazis who pursued him relentlessly.

A concerted effort to rescue him was set in motion by his followers. In the Holy Land his Hasid, Berish Urtner, interceded with Chief Rabbi Herzog, Moses Shapira the Mizrachi leader, and Yitzhak Meir Levin. R. Joseph Isaac Schneersohn of Lubavitch in New York supported these rescue efforts and the necessary certificates were issued. The rabbi arrived in the Holy Land on 9 Shevat 1944, and the anniversary of his arrival is a holiday for the Hasidim of Belz. After a brief stay in Haifa, he settled in Tel-Aviv with his brother and 'Foreign Secretary', R. Mordecai Rokeah, formerly rabbi of Bilgoraj in Poland. Upon his arrival, the Hasidim offered R. Aaron the white caftan, the traditional garb worn by the pious of Jerusalem, but the rabbi declined: 'It is the custom of Belz not to adopt new customs.' He refused to make his permanent home in Jerusalem: 'The sanctity of Jerusalem is so great that I am not able to live there. Besides, I would like to dwell in a town which is inhabited entirely by Jews.' Consequently, from 11 Nisan 1944, he made his home at 63 Ahad Ha-Am in Tel-Aviv, where he lived for thirteen and a half years.

R. Aaron did not forget his fellow-Jews in Nazi Europe. On 25 Adar, a Fast Day was proclaimed by the rabbi of Belz, R. Abraham Mordecai Alter of Ger and R. Mordecai Rokeah. Another Fast Day was fixed for 14 Sivan 1944. R. Aaron broke the tradition of Belz neutrality when he urged his followers, at the first election to the Knesset in 1949, to support the United Religious Front which comprised the Mizrachi, Ha-Poel Ha-Mizrachi, Aguda and Poale Agudat Yisrael.

In the Holocaust the rabbi lost his wife, three sons, four daughters and twenty-six grandchildren. He remarried in Israel, but the marriage ended in divorce. His third wife was the daughter of R. Yehiel Labin of Makow, but they had no children.

A number of Hasidim followed their rabbi's example and settled in Israel or made periodic pilgrimages to see him. He divided his time between Tel-Aviv and Jerusalem, where he spent the summer months. On one occasion when the Jordanians complained to the United Nations Armistice Commission about the heavy military traffic in Israeli territory, it transpired that the large 'military convoy' consisted of an escort of civilian vehicles filled with Hasidim of the rabbi of Belz, accompanying him to Jerusalem.

Despite the rabbi's lack of interest in politics, he participated on 10 Av 1953 in the rabbinic conference convened in Jerusalem to protest against the proposed conscription of girls. 'The conscription contravenes a Biblical prohibition', declared the rabbi, and in 1956 he signed a manifesto supporting the aims of the Aguda. 'These days the Aguda does what the Mahzikei Ha-Dat did in the time of my grandfather.'

During the Sinai campaign (28 October to 3 November 1956), he fasted for three days in ceaseless prayer for an Israeli victory. Alone in his room, he pleaded for 'the tiny Israeli army fighting against seven armies'. When he finally emerged, he declared: 'My sons, we have won with the help of the Almighty.'

Here is a typical Sabbath as celebrated in Tel-Aviv. The year is 1957, hundreds of Hasidim gather on Friday evening to welcome the Sabbath in the presence of their rabbi. According to the custom of Belz, the rabbi dons a *tallit* before Minchah (the Afternoon Service) and wears it throughout the Evening Service, even though he does not officiate at the Reader's desk.

After the Afternoon Service, he retires to his study for an hour or two and then he rejoins his followers for the Evening Service. Having welcomed the Sabbath, he welcomes his followers, greeting them individually. At midnight he returns to the Bet Hamidrash to recite 'Shalom Aleichem'. After Kiddush he removes the *tallit*. At the meal that follows, he distributes *shirayim* to those who sit at his table, while the *gabbai* (beadle) hands morsels to the Hasidim in the Bet Hamidrash. Sabbath songs are sung and then there is another intermission. It is not until 1 or even 2 in the morning that the rabbi finally emerges to complete the meal. He then wishes his followers 'L'Hayyim Tovim' ('A good life'), and adds in Yiddish, 'Lozen mir yidden hoben a yeshiyeh' ('May we be granted salvation, health and contentment. May peace be granted to all Israel and to the whole world.')

The Sabbath morning service is also unconventional. The preliminaries (*Pesuke D'Zimra*) are recited at about 10 am, and then the rabbi retires again to his study, often leaving the door open so that he can listen to the Reading of the Law. Following the tradition among Hasidic rabbis, he is called up for the Reading of the Law, for Shishi (the sixth portion of the Sidra), which the Cabbalists regard as particularly significant because the sixth sephirah is called *Yesod* (foundation) and also because the zaddik in the Book of Proverbs (10:25) is called *Yesod*, for 'the righteous is an everlasting foundation.'

On those rare occasions when the rabbi officiates, such as on Sabbath Shirah (when the Song of Moses is read out), the main service does not end before 3 pm. At the Kiddush on Sabbath afternoon, the rabbi pays special attention to the children, personally distributing sweets and cakes and kind words.

The month is June, and the Sabbath is due to end just before 7 pm. Tel-Aviv's innumerable cafés, restaurants, cinemas and bars are already opening, already thronged by pleasure-seekers; but a different atmosphere pervades 63 Rehov Ahad Ha-am, the two-storey house of the rabbi. Although 'three stars' (indicating that the Sabbath has ended) have already appeared in the sky, the rabbi is preparing for his first Sabbath meal! 'Those who have clocks,' as R. Menahem Mendel Morgernstern of Kotzk once remarked, 'have no souls.' In its disregard for the conventional prayer times, Belz has followed Kotzk. 'That evil man has enveloped the earth in darkness,' the rabbi of Belz said of Hitler. 'There is neither day nor night. He has deprived me of all sense of time.' The biblical verse (Gen.8:22): 'day and night shall not cease', was taken to mean that time had been suspended with the advent of Nazism, evil incarnate.

It is a hot evening, and the Bet Hamidrash is crowded, the windows are shut and the rabbi is dressed in heavy garments, with a *shtreimel* and a very heavy Turkish *tallit*. He looks emaciated, all soul and very little body. He delivers a terse discourse in a low voice, audible only to those who sit next to him, but even those who cannot hear are impressed and awed by his mere presence. He leaves the table for the traditional *hafsakah* (interval) which lasts more than an hour, and he returns at about 9 pm. Four large candles are kindled by a follower who has already recited Havdalah, the prayer that signals the conclusion of the Sabbath. The rabbi and his followers partake of a single fish dish which the Hasidim call *der lichtige fish* ('the luminous fish'), for the lights have now been lit. Then there is another interval. It is Sunday morning, about 2 am, before the rabbi finally recites Havdalah, having extended the Sabbath for eight hours or so.

His very last discourse was based on the verse in the *Shema* (Deut.11:21): 'that your days may be multiplied, and the days of your children, upon the land which the Lord swore unto your fathers to give them, as the days of the heavens above the earth.' The rabbi stressed the importance of education, and told his followers that they must strive to make a bridge between heaven and earth.

The rabbi ate little and kept highly irregular hours, three attendants caring for him in eight-hour shifts. His asceticism may have been rooted in a childhood incident. Hasidim relate that when he was a small boy his grandfather R. Joshua found him eating with great relish and administered a stern rebuke. 'Have you come down to earth merely for this?'

The New Year's Day was the greatest day in the calendar of Belz. Before the blowing of the *shophar* the rabbi would recite six verses forming an acrostic, 'Kera Satan' ('Tear Satan').[6] He would weep as he chanted and the entire congregation would weep with him at this poignant moment of prayer.

R. Aaron died on 21 Av 1957, at the age of seventy-nine in the Shaarei Zedek Hospital, Jerusalem. Following the ruling of

R. Dov Berish Weidenfeld, he was interred on Har Ha-Menuhot in Jerusalem and not near his brother Mordecai Rokeah in Tiberias. Twenty thousand people attended his funeral, and the rabbi of Ger (who was then in Safed) returned to Jerusalem to pay his last respects. Some of his followers wished to appoint R. Jacob Joseph Twersky (1900-68) of Skvira, then resident in the United States, as his successor. He had married the daughter of R. Phinehas Twersky, the Rebbe of Ostilla, son-in-law of the Belzer Rebbe, and for two years Jacob Joseph lived in Belz. The majority, however, were willing to wait until Issachar Dov, known as Berele, the young nephew of R. Aaron, reached maturity.

Berele was born on 8 Shevat 1948 in Tel-Aviv. His father Mordecai (1902-49), Rabbi of Bilgoraj, had accompanied his brother Aaron to Israel and his mother Miriam was the daughter of R. Zevi Hayyim Glick of Huszt, a relative of R. Moses Grünwald (1853-1910), the author of erudite works.[7] R. Mordecai was indefatigable in his efforts to arouse the Yishuv to the plight of the Jews in Europe. 'The Germans are more concerned with destroying Jewry than with vanquishing the Allies,' he reiterated to gatherings large and small. In 1948 he visited England, Belgium and France on behalf of Belz institutions.

When R. Mordecai died on 24 Heshvan 1949, his son was barely one year old, and for the next eight years his uncle, R. Aaron, took care of the boy. When R. Aaron died, the Hasidim regarded Berele as his heir and they called him 'Ha-Yenuka' ('the Child'), a designation given to Israel (1873-1921), son of R. Asher the second of Karlin, who was four years old when his father died.

Berele's education was supervised by R. Joshua Feder and R. Shalom Brander, and on 15 Adar 1965 the youthful Rebbe was married at Bne Brak to Sarah, daughter of R. Moses Hager of Vizhnitz. Just as the wedding at Ostilla in the early nineteenth century between the son of R. Dov b. Isaac of Radziwill and the daughter of R. Joseph b. Mordecai of Neskhiz had fired the imagination of the Hasidim, so the Belzer-Vizhnitz wedding was the most publicised and most picturesque Jewish wedding of the year. Thirty thousand Hasidim from all over the world were participants or spectators. Over 5,000 *halot* (loaves) were consumed. On Monday evening (the wedding was on Wednesday), the rabbi of Vizhnitz gave a traditional 'beggars' banquet' to which all the poor of Bne Brak and surrounding areas were invited. A lavish repast was served and each guest received 5 Israeli pounds. The young couple had met briefly for the first time at their betrothal ten months before the wedding. They saw each other for the second time when the bridegroom lowered the veil over the face of the bride before they were led to the bridal canopy which had been set up in the courtyard in front of the fort-like towers of Vizhnitz Yeshiva. The entire quarter was illuminated by coloured lights and later 3,000 people attended the wedding banquet. On his wedding day, R. Berele was showered with quitlech (petitions) by the Hasidim of Belz.

Following the wedding, Berele and his wife, a graduate of the Bet Jacob seminary, continued to live in Bne Brak, and the young husband continued his studies under R. Moses Weiss, a Hasid of Belz. After his ordination by R. Dov Berish Weidenfeld and R. Moses Grünwald (now in the United States), Berele was encouraged by R. Hayyim Meir Hager of Vizhnitz, R. Israel Alter of Ger and R. Judah Jekutiel Halberstam of Klausenburg to take over the leadership of Belz. Berele's mother thought it was too big a burden for her son, and urged his wife to dissuade him from accepting, but Sarah refused to interfere.

On Sabbath Nachamu (the Sabbath of Comfort, when the prophetic portion begins with the words 'Comfort ye, comfort ye my people') R. Berele became the Rebbe of Belz and from then on made his home in Jerusalem. He had stepped into the shoes of a living legend. Unlike his uncle, the present rabbi is highly organised and services are held at appointed times. Some of the older Hasidim are discontented, maintaining that 'the countenance of Rabbi Aaron was like the sun and the face of Rabbi Berele is like the moon',[8] but R. Berele has generally been accepted as a worthy occupant of the throne of Belz. The dissidents under Isaiah Jacob Klapholtz are mainly limited to Bne Brak.

In the five-storey yeshiva at Rehov Agrippas in Jerusalem, there are now over 200 students, including some from the United States and different parts of Europe. It was established by R. Aaron in 1952. 'I lay the foundation-stone to enable Jewish children to acquire Torah and the fear of Heaven,' he had said. 'It is my wish that they should be able to eat, drink and sleep there and have all their needs taken care of.' He was anxious that time should be devoted to the study of *Kedushat Levi* by Levi Yitzhak of Berdichev and *Maaseh Rokeah* by R. Eleazar Rokeah of Amsterdam.[9] Berele has expanded the yeshiva and it now has a nucleus of advanced students as well. Additionally the rabbi also has his own Kolel, attached to his home.

Belz institutions in Tel-Aviv include a Talmud Torah, Mahzikei Ha-Dat, a Yeshiva Ketanah and a small Kolel. The activities of Belz Hasidim in Bne Brak started in 1954, with the establishment of a *shtiebel*, and today 250 Hasidim worship there every Sabbath in the large Bet Hamidrash in Bne Brak. Among the Mosdot Haside Belz there is a Talmud Torah for 300 children, a Yeshiva Ketanah and a Kolel for 50 students, but so far no Belz Yeshiva has been established outside Jerusalem. Haifa has a Belz shtiebel and a Kolel.

Berele visited Belgium, Switzerland and the United States in 1972, paying a special courtesy call on R. Joel Teitelbaum of Satmar. 'I regard myself as a disciple of Satmar,' R. Berele remarked. 'I studied in the Talmud Torah of Satmar in Katamon, Jerusalem.' He insisted on taking *shirayim* from the Rebbe and gave him a petition. R. Berele is anxious to build a new quarter, Kiryat Belz, on the outskirts of Jerusalem. Ambitious plans have been drawn up for the erection of 700 apartments, two separate kindergartens for boys and girls, a Talmud Torah and a home for the elderly. The Rabbi said: 'We have to do it to enable our children to be reared in the spirit of Belz.'

The flame of Jewish life was cruelly extinguished in Belz, Galicia, but the fires of Belz are burning brightly in the state of Israel. Under the Sabra Rabbi, Belz remains a bright star in the Hasidic constellation.

HE DREAMED A DREAM AND BUILT A CITY

Twenty minutes' walk from Netanyah, a cosmopolitan Mediterranean resort with 80,000 inhabitants and over sixty fashionable hotels, stands Kiryat Sanz, the home of 300 families and the greatest Hasidic settlement in Israel outside Bne Brak and Jerusalem. It was founded by Jekutiel Judah Halberstam of Klausenburg.

The dynasty of Sanz (Nowy Sacz) began in a small town of that name in western Galicia with Hayyim b. Leibish Halberstam (1793-1876), a descendant of R. Zevi Hirsch Ashkenazi who was known as *Haham Zevi* (1660-1718). It is said that soon after he arrived in Nowy Sacz the Hasidim changed the name of the town to Sanz, spelling it with a *zaddik* (literary 'righteous') indicating that a zaddik, or one of the perfectly righteous, had come to the city.

During his forty-six years in Sanz, R. Hayyim attained a reputation as the leader of the entire Hasidic community of Galicia. He wrote extensively, publishing *halachic* works and a Bible commentary, all under the name of *Divre Hayyim*. His first work on the correct spelling of Hebrew names in divorce bills and the laws of ritual purity was published with characteristic modesty, anonymously in Zolkiew in 1864. His Responsa[1] reflect the social and religious life of Galician Jews in the mid-nineteenth century, and through his erudite writings and his personal piety, he refuted the allegations of both the *mitnagdim* and *maskilim* that Hasidism was synonymous with ignorance. R. Joseph Saul Nathanson (1810-75) of Lvov called him 'Holy Gaon, the Light of the Exile'.

From such great Hasidic masters as R. Naphtali of Ropszyce, R. Zevi Hirsch of Zhydachov and R. Shalom of Belz, the young R. Hayyim had learnt to pray with impassioned abandon. When 'the Light of the Exile' stood in prayer, light seemed to radiate from him, and he was so caught up in the liturgy that he would completely forget his surroundings. He even forgot his ailing and badly ulcerated leg, stamping it until it bled as he poured out his heart before his Father in Heaven.

Like many of the greatest Hasidic leaders, R. Hayyim was the founder of an important dynasty. Unlike other dynasties, however, that of Sanz was not dominated by a single leader, but spread forth in many branches. The sons of R. Hayyim established their own 'courts' in different parts of eastern Europe, and influenced such diverse dynasties as Bobow and Satmar. One son, R. Ezekiel Shraga of Sieniawa (1811-99),[2] was responsible for the publication of the commentary by R. Abraham b. Mordecai Azulai (1570-1643) on the Zohar and R. Hayyim Vital's *Sepher Ha-Gilgulim*.

Another of R. Hayyim's sons, R. Baruch of Gorlice (1826-1906), married the daughter of R. Jekutiel Judah Teitelbaum (1808-83).[3] He founded a Hasidic dynasty in his own right, giving rise to the houses of both Sighet and Satmar. R. Baruch in turn had a son, Zevi Hirsch (1851-1918), who was rabbi first in Niske for two years and then assumed the leadership at Rudnick, a town where both his father and grandfather had briefly served as rabbis. R. Zevi married Hayah Mindel, daughter of R. Meir Meshullam of Lancut. R. Zevi was exceedingly, perhaps excessively, humble. 'When the Messiah comes, no one will pay any attention to me,' he said. 'Now in this world of false values, some even regard me as a zaddik. Hasidim come to me, honour me, and give me money. But when the truth becomes known, they will all forsake me.' Unlike his father, R. Zevi Hirsch prayed quietly and punctually. Acting as a Reader only for a brief part of the service, the preliminary Psalms (the Pesuke de-Zimrah that open the Sabbath Morning Service). Later he became the spiritual leader of the Hasidic community (the Sephardi Kehilla) in Klausenburg (Cluj) in Transylvania, now part of Romania.

Jekutiel Judah, who was later to become the Klausenburger Rebbe, was born in 1904 in Rudnick and named after his maternal grandfather. When his father died at Kleinwardein at the age of forty-four, the fourteen-year-old Jekutiel Judah delivered the eulogy. He was brought up by his grand-uncle R. Sholem Eliezer of Ratzfert, and he soon attained a reputation as an outstanding genius. One of the projects he completed as a young man was a comprehensive study of all the halachic opinions involving sunset Bein Hashmashot which determines when one day ends and another begins. This would have been a major contribution for a mature scholar, and the fact that its author was still an unbearded youth created a profound impression on the entire community and he was ordained by R. Meir Yehiel Halstock of Ostrowiec and R. Meir Arik.

R. Hayyim Hirsch Teitelbaum of Sighet (1882-1926)[4] sought out the young scholar as a son-in-law, and the houses of Halberstam and Teitelbaum were once again united. After living with his father-in-law for a year, he accepted at the age of twenty, the position of rabbi to the Hasidic community of Klausenburg.

With his extraordinary talent and capacity for work, Jekutiel Judah earned a reputation as a dynamic rabbi, working hard and inspiring others to work equally hard. He was an exacting and at the same time, a stimulating and considerate teacher. Unlike R. Moses Samuel Glasner, (1856-1925) a leader of the

Mizrachi movement in Hungary, and his son Akiva Glasner (d.1944) who both sought a more liberal approach, R. Jekutiel Judah was firm and uncompromising, especially when it came to challenging the nascent Reform community of Klausenburg. The rabbi's twenty years in Klausenburg were fruitful and fulfilling, and during this period he gained renown as a rabbinic leader. This period, however, was to come to an abrupt and tragic end with the German 'New Order' which brought destruction to the Jews of south-eastern Europe. Two-thirds of Romanian Jews perished during the war in one way or another. After the Hungarian annexation in 1940, anti-Jewish measures were imposed and in 1942 most men of military age were conscripted for forced labour and were transported to the Russian-German front. In 1944 the Jews of Cluj, numbering 16,763, were confined to a ghetto. The rabbi saw his community scattered and deported before the Nazi hordes. He himself was interned in a number of labour camps in Hungary and transferred to the ghetto of Nagy Banya. For a time he was forced to work in the ruins of the Warsaw ghetto, where conditions were cruel and the labour virtually beyond human strength, starting at 4 am and finishing late at night. In 1944 he was taken to the hell that was Auschwitz.

During the Nazi domination the rabbi's wife and ten children were murdered in Auschwitz, and an eleventh child died of typhus. Such tragedy would have broken a lesser man and caused him to lose faith, but R. Jekutiel Judah emerged with a fiery determination to rebuild a Hasidic community that had been completely demoralised.

Immediately after the liberation he went from camp to camp nourishing the broken shards of humanity with the teachings of their fathers. His once flowing beard had been shaved off in the concentration camps, and, with little more than stubble on his chin, he dedicated himself to the rehabilitation of these broken remnants of Jewry. He established kosher kitchens, yeshivot, religious schools for girls, and Bate Midrashim (study centres) for adult study. Desperately he attempted to sort through the pathetic human wreckage; children without parents, parents without children, husbands without wives, and wives without husbands. He listened, talked, counselled, comforted, publicised the plight of these unfortunates, and exerted every influence humanly possible. Working in the Friedenwald displaced persons' camp he soon gained a wide reputation as 'the wonder Rabbi'.

General Dwight D. Eisenhower, who was then commander-in-chief of the European theatre of operations, visited the Friedenwald camp, and was especially interested in meeting this 'wonder Rabbi'. It was the Day of Atonement and the arrival of the general did not disturb the rabbi's devotions. Afterwards, he told Eisenhower, 'I was praying before the General of Generals, the King of Kings, the Holy One blessed be He.' The earthly general had to wait. Eisenhower was so impressed by this man, for here was no cowering refugee, but a leader of men, working to rebuild a community. He asked if there was anything he could do to help. 'Yes,' replied the rabbi. 'The Festival of Tabernacles is soon coming, and it is impossible to procure the "Four Species" here in the Camp.' This might have seemed like a trivial request, but the rabbi stressed the importance of every element of spiritual rehabilitation in this forlorn camp. The general to his credit acceded to his request and even sent a special aeroplane to Italy to procure an ample supply of the 'Four Species' in time for the festival.

In order to mobilise the conscience of Jewry, the rabbi travelled to the United States and spoke widely in different communities. He returned to Germany after a few months, but soon realised the futility of remaining in Europe, the valley of the shadow of death. In 1947 he settled in the Williamsburg section of Brooklyn, founding Yeshiva She'erith Ha-Pletah, which over the years expanded rapidly, and eventually the Bet Moses Hospital was purchased and transformed into a large and vibrant yeshiva. In order to accommodate the growing Sanz community, the Marcy Theatre was acquired and converted into a beautiful and spacious synagogue. Branches of the Sanz Yeshiva were also established both in Montreal and Mexico City.

Shortly after his arrival in New York, the rabbi married Hayah Nehamah, a daughter of R. Samuel David Ha-Levi Ungar (1886-1944). They had two daughters and five sons. R. Ungar had succeeded R. Abraham Aaron Katz as rabbi of Nitra, a community of 500 families. He opened the Aguda World Conference on 10 Elul 1937 at Marienbad with the recitation of Psalm 10:1: 'Why standest Thou afar off, O Lord? Why hidest Thou Thyself in times of trouble?' His manuscripts were preserved in Hungary by a Gentile woman who kept them in safe custody until after the war.

At first R. Jekutiel Judah followed his father-in-law's political ideology and associated with the Aguda and anti-Zionist factions. When in October 1951 Dr Nahum Goldman, President of the World Jewish Congress, invited a number of Jewish organizations to establish the Conference on Jewish material claims against Germany, R. Jekutiel Judah was one of the few rabbis who urged Orthodox Jewry to participate in the negotiations.[5] Under the treaty between Germany and Israel concluded in 1952, the State of Israel received payments in the form of goods worth three milliard marks to be made within twelve years and many Orthodox institutions and individual victims of Nazi persecution benefited from this agreement.

Even though R. Jekutiel Judah was establishing his roots in the United States, his heart was in Israel. He constantly spoke of the miracles of its rebirth and counselled many of his followers to settle there. He quoted his grand-uncle R. Ezekiel of Sieniawa who visited the Holy Land in 1869, and later remarked: 'If a man loves the Land of Israel, it becomes his friend–the best friend a man can ever have.' The rabbi constantly spoke of the close links between Sanz and the Holy Land.

R. Hayyim Halberstam himself longed all his life to settle in the Holy Land, but was unable to do so, and six years before he died he had raised enough money to build a synagogue which still stands in Safed. His son-in-law R. Moses Ungar of Dombrova settled in Safed and he was soon joined by another son-in-law, R. Naphtali Hayyim Horowitz, son of R. Meir of Dzikov, author of *Imre Noam*. In 1923 Abraham Zevi Hirsprung prepared an elaborate genealogical tree of the Sanz dynasty and this is prominently displayed in the Safed synagogue.

R. Jekutiel Judah first visited Israel in 1954 and for seven weeks he searched for a site that would be suitable for his Hasidim. Jerusalem was the obvious choice, almost too obvious. 'Jerusalem is already steeped in holiness,' the rabbi explained. 'I want to add to the holiness of the rest of the land of Israel.' It was for a similar reason that he rejected Safed and Bne Brak which had been suggested by the Israeli government.

During his visit the rabbi met David Ben Gurion who had in December 1953 resigned as Prime Minister and was living in Sedeh Boker in the Negev. Expressing his love for this southern region, Ben Gurion urged him to settle in the Negev. But the rabbi was not convinced. 'The Torah states',[6] he said, 'that Abraham journeyed, constantly going toward the south'; i.e. the Negev, as southern Judah was called. He did not begin in the Negev, but eventually reached there. Similarly the rabbi felt that he also should not initially settle in the Negev.

The rabbi's travels finally led him to Netanyah where he met its mayor, Oved Ben Ami. At the mayor's suggestion, he acquired the 300 dunams of land that would become the setting for his community. The site, which had originally belonged to a group of Belgian Jews, had many advantages; the climate was idyllic, the panorama pleasing and it was close enough to a major growing seaport to provide industry and employment to its inhabitants.

There was little question what this settlement would be called. The rabbi closely identified with his great-grandfather, founder of the Sanz dynasty, and this community would be the resurrection of the town made famous by his ancestor. The new settlement would henceforth be known as Kiryat Sanz. The date for its dedication was chosen with equal care. R. Elimelech of Lyshansk, 'the Rebbe Reb Melech', was one of the pioneers of Hasidism in Poland and another great individual whom the rabbi considered his spiritual ancestor. The dedication therefore took place on his *Yahrzeit*, the anniversary of his passing from this world. The foundation stone was thus laid on Sunday, 4 March 1956 (21 Adar 5716) and was attended by many Hasidim from all over Israel.

A year later the rabbi arrived in Israel with a Scroll of the Law and a nucleus of fifty American immigrants. Other rabbis followed his example; R. Hananiah Yom Tov Lipa established Yismah Mosheh and R. Menahem Mendel Taub founded Kiryat Kalev, and within a decade a number of Hasidic settlements had sprung up in the Holy Land. From one quarter, however, the rabbi met with opposition. His cousin and uncle by marriage, R. Joel Teitelbaum, the Satmar Rabbi, viewed this move as being tainted with secular Zionism. The rabbi of Klausenburg retorted to this censure:

How absurd to suggest that I am following in the footsteps of the secular Zionists. On the contrary, I am following the paths of the disciples of Rabbi Israel Baal Shem Tov and of Elijah, the Gaon of Vilna, and of the great medieval sages like Nahmanides who either visited Israel or settled in the Holy Land. I am not afraid of the secularist government which is transitory and can very suddenly pass away. One must not detract from the sanctity of the Land of Israel which does not depend on the government in power or on the conduct of the inhabitants. Even in the time of Abraham our father, when the Cannanites lived in the land, the Land of Israel was still selected and sanctified over all other countries in the world. We might reasonably draw the analogy of a Scroll of the Law which had fallen into the hands of a heretic. It does not lose its sanctity, but on the contrary it is our sacred duty to retrieve it and maintain its sanctity. The Land of Israel will likewise always be holy, even though it may be temporarily contaminated by non-religious elements.

Religious Jews, especially those in the western world, were urged by the rabbi to settle in Israel because 'an influx of Orthodox Jews would transform the state into a veritable wall of fire which would render it indestructible. The achievements of Torah-true Jews, imbued with a spirit of self-sacrifice, would amaze the entire world.'

The rabbi remained in the forefront of negotiations with architects, building contractors and engineers and was involved in every detail of the development. Plans were based on an optimistic projection of growth and the key buildings were designed to cater for an expanding community. An ultimate population of up to 20,000 was provided for, and the master-plan included a total of forty-three major buildings.

Under the rabbi's expert direction the dream was rapidly translated into reality. The city was built entirely according to Jewish law and custom. Its most impressive building is the 'Great Synagogue', built at a cost of over one million Israeli pounds. The centrepiece of this synagogue is a 300-year-old Italian Ark constructed of beautiful red veined wood and ornately covered. The synagogue, which seats over 500 people, is used mainly on High Holydays and other special occasions.

Directly opposite the Great Synagogue is the small Bet Hamidrash, which is in constant use for prayer and study. In the evening after work the men of Kiryat Sanz gather together to study Talmud and the Codes. The rabbi sets a standard of scholarship for his followers, quoting the Talmudic dictum: 'An ignorant man cannot be truly pious.'[7] 'To me,' he declared, 'a Hasid is not one who just comes to my weekly discourse or sits at my table, but one who studies eighteen hours a day, and studies eighteen pages of the Talmud or recites eighteen chapters of the Psalms.'

Diverse Torah institutions cater for every age. The primary school with its attractive layout and modern equipment, includes a kindergarten, a clinic and a gymnasium. There is a Talmud Torah for 150 pupils, a yeshiva ketana for 60 students, and a boarding-school where 100 girls receive elementary education. Ninth, tenth and eleventh grades were added to enable graduates to complete their education and qualify as teachers. The dormitory is open to girls outside Kiryat Sanz and free education is provided for boys. The language of instruction is Yiddish (not Hebrew), although Hebrew is, of course, a key subject. The Sanz educational establishments are not part of the Hinuch Atzmai.

The pride of the community is the main yeshiva which also reflects the rabbi's high standards of scholarship and has had a strong impact on the general Israeli yeshiva community. A student who mastered only 300 pages of the Talmud qualifies for the title of 'Zurvah Mirabbanan' (a young student of Rabbinic lore). A student who has committed to memory 600 pages of the Talmud together with its commentaries is given the title of 'Haver' (Associate), while the mastery of 1,000 pages entitles him to the coveted degree of 'Morenu' ('Our Teacher'). The highest degree, that of 'More Morenu' ('Revered Master'), is reserved for those who have mastered the entire Talmud. Older Talmudic sages who visit the yeshiva are virtually awe-stricken by the sight of teenage students who can *recite* half the Talmud from memory. Over 150 students are enrolled in the yeshiva with its comfortable and contemporary dormitory in the southwest of the Kirya.

Thirty advanced students, all of them married, continue their studies in a Kolel, where every Monday the rabbi delivers an intensive Torah discourse. A number of its graduates hold rabbinic and educational posts in Israel and other countries. Every Kolel student receives a free apartment and a monthly stipend. This is supplemented by the parents and the young working wives of the students.

The rabbi's efforts are not confined exclusively to his Hasidim. He is particularly concerned with the status of Israel's Yemenite and North African citizens and becomes incensed when he hears of discrimination or intolerance towards the Sephardim. 'How can we have anything but admiration', he declares, 'for a community that produced the Golden Age of Spain, and such luminaries as Isaac Alfasi, Moses Maimonides, Joseph Caro, Hayyim Ibn Atar, Shalom Sharabi and Abraham Azulai?' For Oriental Jews the rabbi has established Yeshivat Maharshad, named in memory of his father-in-law, R. Samuel David Ungar. Kiryat Sanz also contains an orphanage for Sephardi children ('the story of every child here is a tragedy'), and a synagogue where they can follow their own traditional liturgy and where the style of worship is oriental. 'Let us show that all Jews, whatever their origin, can live together in harmony,' says the rabbi.

Fifty people, many of them retired Americans, live in Bet Avot (Home of the Fathers), in pleasant self-contained flats. There is a diamond factory which employs thirty people. The Kirya has its own shopping centre, post office, bank and *mikva* (ritual bath). Nearly 50 per cent of the Kirya's inhabitants are of American origin. Not all are Hasidim, but all are observant Jews, for only religious Jews are admitted as residents. Television is not allowed, but radios are permitted. The Kirya has an air-conditioned 100-room hotel, Galei Sanz, with such unique features as its own handsomely appointed synagogue, three *sukkot* (booths), one a dining-room, one a lounge, and the third a dormitory. Bathing facilities for men and women are provided on the beach on different days. The Kirya employs a ritual slaughterer for poultry, but meat is provided from Bne Brak.

The most interesting building in the Kirya is probably the Laniado Hospital, the first religious hospital to be built for eighty years. It accommodates 145 patients and, in the words of the Mayor of Netanyah, helps 'to solve a most important hospitalisation problem in the area'. In a region where there are over 200,000 people, there is no municipal hospital. The total cost of the hospital will be nine million Israeli pounds.

Recently the American government contributed four hundred thousand dollars towards the project, the first time that it has made such a contribution to a religious hospital. The staff of the hospital number about 185 and the doctors assembled by Professor Y. C. Richie, the hospital's Medical Director, include physicians and surgeons from the United States and Israel. The hospital is under the supervision of the Israeli Minister of Health but has an international Board of Directors drawn from Europe, Canada, the United States and Israel. Eventually a school for nurses will be attached. Like most countries, Israel suffers from an acute shortage of qualified nurses, since Orthodox girls are reluctant to become nurses because of the lack of a suitable religious environment. In the proposed school, Hebraic studies will be combined with the nursing curriculum.

Life in the Kirya revolves round the person and personality of the rabbi. It is he who supervises all the religious spiritual activities. The fruit and vegetables are not sold until the tithe has been taken, and special rules are observed during the Seventh Year (Shemitah). Every Friday the entire Kirya is examined to ensure that the *eruv* (the symbolic boundary within which people may carry things on the Sabbath) is intact. The Kirya has a Hevrah Kadisha (Burial Society) and its own plot at the Netanyah cemetery. In the Sanz tradition, they follow the view of Rabbenu Tam (1100-71), the French Tosaphist, in terminating the Sabbath one hour later than anywhere else in Israel.

The high point of the week is the Sabbath, which to a large extent is dominated by the Rabbi's *tish*, the Friday night ceremonial meal. Quite late in the evening, about 11 pm, some five hours after the inception of the Sabbath, the rabbi enters the small Bet Hamidrash which adjoins his beautiful home. With his eyes closed, he chants the traditional greeting to the Sabbath Angels, 'Shalom Aleichem', 'Peace be with you, ministering angels, Angels of the Most High, coming from the King who rules over kings, the Holy One blessed be He.'

At the table, he is flanked by his two oldest sons, Hirsch Melech and Samuel David, as well as his two sons-in-law, Solomon Goldman son of Mordecai, Rebbe of Zewill in Jerusalem, and Dov Berish Weiss. After the recitation of the Kiddush, the sanctification over wine, he breaks one of the twelve loaves, representing the twelve tribes of Israel, which are arrayed before him. The traditional courses are interspersed with Sabbath melodies handed down from the Hasidic masters. The rabbi only tastes each dish, while the remainder is passed around as *shirayim*, for the Hasidim believe that the rabbi sanctifies everything he touches. Imprisoned sparks, they believe, are released and restored to their original source. The Hasidim eat and sing, but most of all, they watch and listen, for every gesture of the rabbi is significant.

The climax is reached around midnight when the rabbi begins a lengthy unrehearsed discourse, usually on the weekly Torah portion. The entire vast spectrum of Talmudic, rabbinic, Hasidic and Cabbalist literature is at his fingertips, and he quotes freely and extensively. Many of his followers are major Talmudic scholars in their own right, and he often pauses for their comments or corroboration: most are content to nod approvingly, others finish his quotations.

Another Sabbath highlight is Shalosh Seudot, the Third Sabbath Meal. The lights are out and in the gathering dusk, the rabbi speaks in illuminating phrases and the Hasidim sing mystical melodies of R. Isaac Luria, such as 'Bene Hechala' ('The Children of the Heavenly Palace') and 'Askinu Seudata' ('I Shall Arrange the Meal'). The meal rarely ends before midnight. This kind of service requires great physical stamina, and it is not surprising that only a very small number of Hasidim attend the rabbi's services and meals during the Sabbath.

The rabbi leads an ascetic life, rising every morning at five and spending the early hours immersed in study. Like many other Hasidic masters, he starts the morning service quite late. A special rota of students provide him with a quorum (*minyan*). The Afternoon Service rarely starts before 7 pm, and the Evening Service may take place at midnight. The rabbi himself acts as Baal Keriah (Reader of the Law) on Sabbath and Festivals, a practice not unusual among Hasidic rabbis. He reads simultaneously from the printed text and the Scroll of the Law, and the service on Sabbath mornings rarely terminates before 2 pm.

On Monday mornings the rabbi lectures to the more advanced married students, and at various other times delivers discourses on Talmudic and *halachic* topics. Every Tuesday from 11 am to 2 pm the Rabbi is 'At Home' to his followers. Scores of people from the Kirya, from all over Israel as well as from abroad, come to him with petitions. These relate to the entire spectrum of human problems–recovery from sickness, longing for a child, the need for finding a suitable mate for one's child, the difficulty of earning a living. The Hasid writes his name and that of his mother on the petition (*quittel*), but not that of his father–a custom traced by the Zohar to King David, who prayed: 'Save the son of thy handmaid.' Accompanying the petition is a *pidyon* (Redemption money) which varies according to the finances of the petitioner, and it is usual to give a sum that corresponds with numerical value of the Hebrew word *Hai* (Life) i.e. eighteen. Although he receives everyone kindly, the rabbi appears to be somewhat aloof. Strangers are often given preference over the natives of the Kirya. The rabbi hates hypocrisy and mere convention.

He follows the traditions of R. Hayyim Halberstam, who published very little during his life, but wrote many Responsa and discourses. Many of his expositions have appeared in the monthly *Yisrael Saba* published in the Kirya and in the Sanz periodical *Ha-Midrash* published in Bne Brak. He delivers a major two-hour discourse once a month on the Sabbath on which the Blessing for the New Moon is recited and also preaches on key occasions during the year, such as on the Sabbath before Passover (Shabbat Hagadol) and on the Sabbath between New Year and the Day of Atonement (Shabbat Shuva). On New Year and the Day of Atonement, he joins his community in the large communal synagogue for worship. He delivers a one-and-a-half-hour discourse before the blowing of the *shophar* (ram's horn) on New Year and before the opening prayer on the eve of the Day of Atonement.

To the rabbi, Israel is a spiritual Eden, a foretaste of the Golden Age to Come. He faces daily disillusionment, for it grieves him to witness an ungodly act in the Holy Land. He is fond of explaining the Talmudic passage[8] which relates how R. Jose b. Hananiah used to kiss the stones of Acre. 'Why', asks the rabbi, 'did he kiss the stones of Acre in particular? The reason is because the traditional border of the Holy Land runs through the city, half of which lies within Israel while half is technically outside. When Rabbi Jose stood at Acre, he could appreciate the difference between the sanctity of the Holy Land and the secular nature of other countries. As a mark of this appreciation, he would kiss those stones of Acre which were part of the Land of Israel'.

The rabbi's life in Israel is not devoid of problems, technical as well as spiritual. Once, when construction of the Kirya was in full swing, a severe shortage of cement blocks developed. In response to this urgent need, a factory had to be set up. Religious and national issues were not quite so easy to resolve. At one point in 1963, such an issue almost brought about the rabbi's departure from Israel and only the personal intervention of President Zalman Shazar dissuaded him from taking this drastic step.

The rabbi has many ideas for expanding the Kirya and for encouraging fellow-Jews to observe the Commandments. One example of such concern was when he sent out young scribes to examine *mezuzot* (the parchments which are enclosed in a metal or wooden case and attached to doorposts) and *tephillin* throughout the land. 'It is not important just to observe the commandments,' he said, 'but they must also be observed correctly.' It is vital that the phylacteries one wears should be without defect. The rabbi is confident that the spiritual influence of his community will have far-reaching effects, and that eventually people will not say 'Kiryat Sanz near Netanyah' but 'Netanyah near Kiryat Sanz'.

Encouraged by the success of the Kirya, he established a *shikun* of fifty dunams to the north-west of Jerusalem near Shikun Habad at Tel Arza. It has 500 housing units and nearly 300 families have already settled there. The *shikun* has a synagogue, a Kolel and a Talmud Torah (Darke Avot). There is even a Bet Hamidrash in which services are conducted in the non-Hasidic ritual (*Nusah Ashkenaz*) rather than the liturgy of the Cabbalist Rabbi Isaac Luria (*Nusah Ari*) adopted by Hasidim since the eighteenth century.

Among the Sanz institutions in Bne Brak are a Kolel for thirty students, a school for girls, a kingergarten, a ritual bath, a home for older people, factories, a commercial centre and a public park. Small Sanz groups flourish in Petah Tikvah, in Tiberias (Kiryat Shmuel) and in Safed, and a large tract of land has been acquired in Beersheba for a new Kiryat Sanz.

R. Halberstam does not believe in courting publicity. He shuns every artifice and gimmick that might in any way colour the dry facts of what he is trying to accomplish. 'Actions not words' seems to be his favourite maxim, and his ambition is nothing less than 'to establish Torah institutions in every town in Israel'. R. Halberstam now resides in Union City, New Jersey, but maintains a close link with his Kirya.

XIII

THE KOTEL AND THE REBBE

Today the Holy City is a thriving centre of Hasidism, the home of a number of Hasidic rabbis and academies. Yet until recently few Hasidic leaders resided in Jerusalem. It was asserted that Jerusalem did not need a Hasidic rabbi, for Jerusalem had the Kotel, the Western Wall, 'the greatest Rebbe'. 'Why give a *quittel* to the Rebbe when there is the Kotel, and it does not even take *pidyonot*?'

The early Hasidic pioneers lived in either Safed or Tiberias. R. Nahman of Braclav did not even visit Jerusalem, the explanation for this seeming neglect of the Holy City being in the realm of Hasidic eschatology.

An early Hasidic pioneer who did settle in the Holy City was R. Moses (1776-1850), son of R. David b. Solomon of Lelov (1746-1813), a disciple of R. Jacob Isaac Horowitz, 'the Seer of Lublin'. When Moses was thirteen, his father exhorted him to make his home in the Holy Land. 'I have not been worthy to do so,' said the father, 'but you should go there and hasten the Redemption.' His father-in-law Isaac Jacob, 'the Holy Jew' of Przysucha, also encouraged the young man to undertake the journey. R. David bequeathed property to his sons Avigdor and Nehemiah but left nothing to Moses, because 'a house is already for you in Jerusalem.' Moses needed little urging. 'When with the help of the Almighty I arrive safely in the Holy Land, I will go directly to the Western Wall in Jerusalem. There I will lift up my voice like a trumpet and I will hasten the advent of the Messiah.'

The path to the Holy Land was far from smooth; problems, personal and financial had to be overcome. His wife Rebeccah Rachel strongly opposed her husband's journey and could not be won over. Summoned to a special meeting to discuss the matter, she stood in the doorway and cried: 'Show some respect for the daughter of the Holy Jew.' Other voices were also raised in opposition. 'The Polish Jews are foolish', said R. Israel of Ruzhin, 'to let such a zaddik leave their midst.'

R. Moses was not to be dissuaded, and his faithful disciple R. Solomon of Radomsk helped to raise funds. 'Devout Jews have a moral obligation to help the rabbi on his journey,' he asserted. R. Moses left Poland in 1850, accompanied by his two sons and ten followers, but not by his wife. The rabbi celebrated the High Holydays at sea and a *sukkah* ('booth') was erected on the boat. Arriving in Acre, he stayed for a short time in Safed and Tiberias, but Jerusalem drew him like a magnet. 'The Lord has chosen Zion for his habitation,' he replied, 'and so have I.'

The journey from Poland to Jerusalem had taken two months. When he arrived in the Holy City, he was exhausted and in rapidly failing health. He could not even walk to the Western Wall and implored his sons to carry him there. 'It is important that I visit the Western Wall this very day.' On the way to the Old City, Arabs attacked the little group and R. Moses did not reach his destination. He died on 13 Tevet 1850 in his seventy-fourth year, seventy-four days after arriving in the Holy Land. One of his last wishes was, however, fulfilled. He was interred near the grave of the prophet Zechariah in Jerusalem.

The descendants of R. Moses left their impact on the Yishuv. For thirty-two years his son Eliezer Menahem Mendel (1827-83) lived a life of hardship and penury in Jerusalem, but his sufferings did not lessen his ardour. 'The *Seder* conducted by Rabbi Menahem Mendel', remarked R. Hayyim Halberstam, 'is superior to the *Sedarim* of all the zaddikim.' Every day, regardless of the weather and the risk of attack by marauding Arabs, he made his way to the Western Wall to spend three hours reciting the Afternoon and Evening Prayers. He died on Purim and R. Jacob Saul Eliashar (1817-1906) said in eulogy: 'Alas, the festival of Purim has become like Tisha B'Av [the Ninth of Av] for us.'

His son David Zevi Solomon (1844-1918) was educated in the home of R. Aaron of Karlin, author of *Bet Aaron*. R. Jerahmiel Isaac Dancyger (1863-1910) called him 'a Scroll of the Torah whose ecstasy in prayer causes others to repent'. Like Sir Moses Montefiore before him, the rabbi encouraged Jews to settle outside the Old City. He was instrumental in obtaining large sums of money for building Bate Warshaw in Jerusalem. Fifty homes were erected on this site. Since he was the head of the Warsaw Kolel, he was careful to avoid preferential treatment for his family. He was responsible for the finances of the Kolel. Once when it was heavily in debt, he was arrested by the Turks and was released only through the intervention of R. Yehudah Aryeh Alter of Ger and R. Abraham of Sochaczew.

The rabbi's kindliness was proverbial. During World War I a Turkish officer provided him with food, which was in short supply. The rabbi promptly distributed it among the needy. 'I am old. I have lived. I must strengthen those whose life is just beginning.' R. Mordecai Twersky of Rahmastrivka said in tribute: 'When Rabbi David died, half the Jewishness in Jerusalem died too.'

The traditions of the family were maintained by his second son Simon Nathan Nata (1870-1929). A native of Safed, he studied in the yeshivot of eastern Europe for fifteen years and returned to the Holy Land in 1926. Today the torch of Lelov is carried by R. Moses Mordecai Biderman who lived in Tel-Aviv for two decades and now resides in Bne Brak.

Another nineteenth-century Hasidic establishment was the synagogue Tiferet Yisrael or Bet Ha-Knesset Nisan Bak which was associated with R. Israel of Ruzhin (1797-1851), who had yearned to settle in the Holy Land. He became a Turkish citizen and his passport was stamped 'Native of Jerusalem'. 'There will come a time when nations will drive us out of their lands,' he predicted. 'How strange that after such a long-drawn-out Exile, the Redemption should take place under such humiliating circumstances.'

One hundred years before the Balfour Declaration, the rabbi prophesied: 'As in the time of Ezra, a government will arise which will permit the Jews to return to the land of their fathers. The nations will realise that, despite all persecutions and massacres, the only way to get rid of us will be to send us to the land of Israel.'

Like Maimonides and Nahmanides, R. Israel believed that the Redemption would take a natural course and would be neither miraculous nor supernatural. He realised that only mass aliyah could transform the country. 'If I alone settle in the Holy Land, they will ask me, "Why did you not bring your followers with you?" What answer can I give to such a question?' He maintained that the deliverance of Israel would take place even before Israel's repentance and regarded R. Menahem Mendel of Vitebsk and R. Abraham of Kalisk as trail-blazers.

Between 1577 and 1587 six books were printed in Safed by Abraham b. Isaac Ashkenazi, a resident of Safed, and Eliezer b. Yitzhak Ashkenazi, a native of Prague. After this, however, for more than two centuries the Holy Land was without a printing-press. Then the Bak family, Hasidim of Ruzhin, became pioneers in Hebrew printing. Israel Bak (1797-1875), son of a bookseller, traced his lineage to printers in Prague and Leghorn.

One of his ancestors died a martyr's death and the family adopted the surname Bak, which stands for the first letters of the Hebrew words Ben Kedoshim (Son of Martyrs). He acquired his printing skill at the Hasidic printing-press of Slavuta.

After printing twenty-six books in Berdichev (1815-21), he settled in Safed in 1831. The first book he printed there was *Siddur Sefat Emet*, a prayer-book endorsed by the Safed Rabbinate. After two years he was joined by his wife and five daughters and his son Nisan, as well as by other families from Berdichev and Odessa. His printing-press grew, and soon he had a staff of thirty.[1] He became friendly with Sir Moses Montefiore who acted as *sandek* (godfather) to his grandson Samuel in 1839. Dr Louis Loewe (1809-88), secretary and travelling companion of Sir Moses, records: 'They attended divine service in the German synagogue and were present at the naming of a child, the son of a distinguished member of the community, for whom they had been requested to act as godparents.'[2]

During the peasant revolt against Muhammad Ali in 1834, his printing-press was destroyed. Three years later his son-in-law perished in the earthquake that rent Safed on 24 Tevet 1837, and after the Druze revolt of 1838 when he was attacked physically, he moved to Jerusalem where he enjoyed a monopoly of printing Hebrew books for twenty-two years. By 1883, nearly 130 Hebrew books had been printed by Bak. Sir Moses Montefiore sent him a new printing-press in 1843, and the printer records: 'the gift of Sir Moses and Judith'. The first book printed in Jerusalem in 1841 was *Avodat Ha-Kodesh* by the Cabbalist Hayyim Joseph David Azulai (1724-1807), known by his Hebrew acronym *Hida*. In 1844-6 he printed the Zohar, with a frontispiece of an engraving of the Western Wall, the Temple Mount and the Mount of Olives. It became the traditional printer's mark for all Israel Bak's books printed in Jerusalem.

When competitors published a Hebrew periodical, *Ha-Levanon*, in March 1863, Bak, five months later, with the help of his son-in-law, Israel Dov Frumkin (1850-1914), began to publish a monthly periodical, *Havazzelet*. The last page had the words 'printed by the printing-press of Sir Moses Montefiore and his wife, Lady Judith'. After six or seven issues, the Turkish authorities closed both journals, and Bak went to Instanbul to appeal for the ban to be lifted. In 1870 *Havazzelet* resumed publication, but five years later his son Nisan Bak sold his printing-press to Samuel b. Jacob Halevi Zuckerman (1856-1929) and his brother-in-law Israel Dov Frumkin, who became editor-in-chief, continuing in that position for forty years.

Printing was only one facet of Israel Bak's activities. In 1837 he acquired land on Mount Yarmak and farmed it. He recorded:[3]

It had springs around it and it was only half an hour from the village of Meron. Formerly there were gardens and orchards in that village, but at the time there were only forest trees and rocks, and all vegetation was in the clefts between rocks. Then on 1 January 1837 came the great earthquake ... I was compelled to go to the village given me by the Pasha. I built dwelling-houses there, made gardens and sowed fields, and already in that year I ate plentifully of the produce of the land. Next year I had cattle, sheep and goats ... and with God's help I obseved the Sabbath in all particulars. I carried out the precepts connected with the soil, and my house was wide open. The blessing of God was upon all my doings, in house and field. Although the place was not suitable for sowing, since many stones were there, yet I fared well, and God prospered me, except for the many tribulations that came upon us in 1839, owing to the fearful war between our Lord the Sultan and the Pasha of Egypt, which forced me to leave this lovely village and come to Jerusalem.

Bak inspired Montefiore and other European philanthropists to found agricultural colonies. Two years later, Nisan Bak visited for the first time R. Israel of Ruzhin who sent him to London to urge Sir Moses to persuade the Tsarist government to permit fund-raising in Russia for the Holy Land.

In 1845, Sir Moses sent Nisan, together with Mordecai b. Zalman (1805-65) and Yitzhak Rozenthal of Danzig to Caterham near Preston, to study the art of weaving. When Sir Moses subsequently opened a weaving workshop in Jerusalem, there was friction between the Gentile expert and the local Jewish workmen. Sir Moses replaced the Gentile expert by a Jew, Shlomoh Elbo, but change of personnel did not improve the situation and in 1858 the weaving venture came to an end.[4]

In 1843 Nisan Bak (1815-89) had told R. Israel that the Tsar was planning to buy a site near the Western Wall to erect a monastery. Quickly the rabbi raised the money which enabled Bak to acquire this strategic piece of land. Legend has it that when Tsar Nicholas I (1796-1855) heard that he had been outmanoeuvred by the rabbi, he exclaimed: 'That Jew always blocks my path!' But the difficulties were not over: the grave of a Sheik Abu Shush was discovered and it took delicate diplomacy, including the intervention of the Austrian Consul, to have the remains re-interred in another locality. No wonder that R. Israel dreamed that he was not destined to see the erection of a synagogue, and that his son would have to build a house 'for My name' (II Sam.7:13).

Meanwhile the synagogue Hurvah Judah Hasid, which had stood in ruins for nearly 150 years, was being rebuilt. The foundation stone was laid on 17 Nisan 1857 and the synagogue was dedicated on 24 Elul 1864. It took over eight years to build, and became the foremost synagogue of Jerusalem. The completion of the Hurvah, or Bet Jacob as it was also called, inspired Bak to persevere in his efforts to erect the Hasidic synagogue. In a public proclamation, he pleaded that 'it is already twelve years since we have acquired the site to erect a magnificent structure.' He was backed by R. Abraham Jacob of Sadagura, and by the family of Ezekiel Reuben Sassoon. When the Emperor Franz Joseph I (1830-1916), who was present at the dedication of the Suez Canal, visited Jerusalem on 14 November 1869, he noticed the unfinished building. 'Where is the roof of the synagogue?' asked the Emperor. 'Your Excellency,' replied Nisan, 'even the synagogue is happy to welcome you and has taken off its cap in deference to your Majesty.' The Emperor took the hint and donated 100 francs to complete the structure.

The beautiful synagogue, with thirty windows facing the Temple Mount, and a twelve-windowed dome designed by a Russian architect, was consecrated on Sabbath Nahamu (the Sabbath of Comfort) 1870. It was known as Tiferet Yisrael (in honour of R. Israel of Rhuzin), or Bet Ha-Knesset Nisan Bak (Nisan's *shul*), for Nisan was the first *gabbai* (warden). Together with fifty-seven other historic synagogues, it was destroyed by the Jordanians in 1948.

For a time, the spiritual leader of Tiferet Yisrael was R. Akiva Joshua Schlesinger. In 1879, Nisan Bak and Mordecai Warshavsky helped to build the Kirya Neemanah project (or Bate Nisan Bak) in Jerusalem, to provide homes for new immigrants.

Today, the Yeshiva Metivta Tiferet Yisrael of Ruzhin in Jerusalem attracts students from the United States and England, and of 125 students, 40 are in residence and 28 advanced students attend the Kolel. Among its supporters is Israel Friedman, son of R. Moses Heschel, the rabbi of Kopycienice. R. Shlomoh Friedman of Tel-Aviv formed an association to support the yeshiva, and the appeal which was launched was signed by nine rabbis of the Ruzhin dynasty.

In his Bet Hamidrash at Rehov Joseph ben Mattiyahu, R. Yehiel Joshua Rabinowicz (b.1900) carries on the traditions of Biala. The rabbi is the sixth direct descendant of R. Jacob Isaac, 'the Holy Jew' of Przysucha. His father, R. Jerahmiel Zevi (1880-1906) was the son of R. Isaac Jacob of Biala (1847-1905), the third son of R. Nathan David of Szydlowiec. Isaac Jacob married the only daughter of R. Joshua of Ostrow and after the death of his father-in-law in 1873, he became Rebbe. He settled in Biala which became known as 'the Ruzhin of Poland'. The Rebbe of Biala followed the doctrine of Przysucha. Protestations of piety

were discouraged. Action and service, charity and lovingkindness were encouraged as the true measure of a man's sincerity.
The Rebbe was known far and wide for his warm heart and
open house. A special kitchen at his 'court' provided meals for
visiting Hasidim and poor townsfolk. In his deep concern that
standards of preparation should be high and that the poor
should be treated as members of his own household, the rabbi
himself regularly tasted the dishes.

In the true traditions of Biala, R. Jacob Isaac left a Will of
high spiritual import, which yet underlines the essential humility of the man. He implored his Hasidim to 'notify' his saintly
ancestors, his father, his father-in-law and the Holy Jew of his
death, that they might intercede on his behalf. 'I pray you to
publicise by means of placards and through newspapers the fact
that I beseech forgiveness of those people who brought me gifts
while I was alive. They gave me money because they regarded
me as a zaddik. But verily I am unworthy.' He died in Warsaw
in 1905. His father-in-law had written in his Will that no one
should be buried next to him, but a specially convened Bet Din
decided that the son-in-law could be buried at his side.

His gifted son, Jerahmiel Zevi, excelled as Reader for the
congregation and a choir accompanied him. Once, when he was
ill, his anxious mother urged his father to dissuade Jerahmiel
Zevi from officiating at the Reader's desk, but the father refused
to interfere. 'The entire heavenly host waits to hear the prayers
of my son. How dare I stop him?' R. Zevi became rabbi on 8
Iyyar, the anniversary of the death of his grandfather, R.
Jerahmiel, but he was a rabbi for barely six months. He died
aged only twenty-six, on 7 Heshvan 1906, the anniversary of
the death of his grandfather Nathan David, leaving six
children.

The eldest son, Nathan David (1899-1947), arrived in London in 1928 and became the centre of a growing group of
adherents. He was an interesting and unusual man with a
brilliant mind, a warm personality and an engaging sense of

humour. He treated his Hasidim with understanding and sensitivity, often quoting the verses: 'For the vineyard of the Lord of hosts is the house of Israel' (Isa.5:7), and 'Who am I that I should disparage or condemn the house of Israel?' During his brief illness, he wrote an 'Ethical Will' for the guidance and comfort of his friends and family, a remarkable statement of faith and courage and serenity in the face of death, reflecting Hasidism at its loftiest level. 'Make Kiddush (sanctification) over the Sabbath wine', he demanded of his wife a few days before he died. In awe and anguish she complied. And he bequeathed her in loving legacy 'an equal share in all the Torah that I have learned and in all the precepts, however few, which I have performed.'

In 1917 Yehiel Joshua Rabinowicz was married, in Wlodawa, to the daughter of Eliezer Barenholtz and at twenty-three he became rabbi at Siedlice, his father's home town. In 1940, during the Ten Days of Penitence, he was arrested by the Russians but managed to escape. For three days he hid in the loft in the home of one of his Hasidim and he fasted for that period, refusing to take bread because he had no water to wash his hands. Eventually he and his five children found refuge for ten months with his brother-in-law R. Alter Perlow, the Koidonover Rebbe of Baranowicze, husband of Perele, who later became famous in the Vilna ghetto as the founder of a religious institute for women. From the valiant Perele, the women of the ghetto drew comfort and strength in those black hours.

From Baranowicze, the rabbi and his family were taken to Siberia in 1941. Even under the most perilous conditions the rabbi would not modify his practices.[5] In the absence of *mikva* (ritual bath), he would break the ice on a pond or stream with an axe and immerse himself in the icy waters. Only the resourcefulness of his wife, Hannah, enabled the family to survive. After the war the rabbi returned to Poland and with the help of R. Dr Solomon Schonfeld, who directed the Chief Rabbi's

Emergency Council of London, he travelled to France and then to the Holy Land where he arrived just after Passover 1947. For eight years he lived in Tel-Aviv and in 1955 moved to Jerusalem.

Ger may have its 'ten thousands and Belz its thousands', but the rabbi of Biala ministers to a hand-picked few. The ardour of the frail sage is legendary and has earned for him the title 'Servant of the Lord'. With every ounce of his strength he prays, sings and delivers his discourses. Here is no 'still small voice', but 'fire and thunder'. On the Sabbath he acts as a Baal Keriah (Reader of the Law). Every Thursday young people are encouraged to visit him and during the summer months he studies the 'Ethics of the Fathers' with them. Like R. Jacob of Radzymin, the rabbi of Biala has a reputation as a 'Wonder-Worker'. There are few Biala Hasidim in the Holy Land, but men and women from all the Hasidic denominations visit him for guidance. His friend and neighbour R. Israel Alter of Ger occasionally referred Hasidim to R. Yehiel.

The Rabbi has a number of unusual liturgical customs, such as reciting 'Aleinu' ('It is our Duty to Praise') after the Shaharit Service on the Sabbath, in addition to repeating it after the Musaph (the Additional Service). After the Sabbath service he recites five chapters of the Psalms. A small Kolel is attached to his Bet Hamidrash and in 1965 he established Yeshiva Or Kedoshim (the Light of the Holy Ones), and a Biala *shtiebel* in Bne Brak. It is unfortunate that the establishment of a dissenting Biala *shtiebel* near his home in Jerusalem caused this man of peace unnecessary grief.

Rehov Geula is the home of R. Ezekiel Shraga Lipshitz Halberstam, a direct descendant of R. Hayyim of Sanz. A native of Stropkov, where he was born in 1908, he studied with his father Issachar Dov, rabbi in Ungvar, Czechoslovakia. During the war, the rabbi was imprisoned in Auschwitz and after the liberation he became rabbi in Bamberg, Germany. In 1949 he settled in Jerusalem and when his uncle Menahem

Mendel Halberstam, rabbi of Stropkov, died in New York on 7 Iyyar 1954 Ezekiel Shraga became rabbi. That same year his Hasidim dedicated his Bet Hamidrash Divre Menahem in Meah Shearim.

A prolific author, the rabbi published *Divre Ezekiel Shraga*, a selection of his Responsa and discourses, and he also edited and reprinted some of the works of his ancestors. An eloquent speaker, he delivers discourse in Hebrew as well as in Yiddish. His well-ordered library reflects a well-ordered mind. One of his treasured possessions is *Avodat Kodesh* (printed in 1857), a book which was used by R. Hayyim Halberstam, his son Ezekiel, and by R. Shalom Halberstam, and bears their signatures.

R. Jerahmiel Judah Meir (1901-27 Iyyar 1976), son of R. Simon Shalom of Amshinov, lived in Bayit Vegan. The founder of the dynasty was R. Israel Isaac of Warka (1779-1848), known as 'the lover of Israel', one of the most community-minded of the Polish rabbis. He was concerned with every facet of Jewish life as well as with the economic plight of the Jews in the Holy Land, for whom he assiduously collected funds.

On the death of his father, R. Menahem Mendel, on 15 Sivan 1868 at the age of forty-nine, R. Simhah Bunam (1851-1907) became rabbi. The 1880s saw a resurgence of interest in the Holy Land among the down-trodden Jewish masses in Russia.

After the pogroms of 1881, the publicist Moses Leib Lilienblum (1843-1910), concluded that 'the Jews would always be regarded as aliens everywhere', and that 'the rebirth of the Jewish people is possible only on the historic soil of their forebears in Palestine.' The Hebrew writer Perez Smolenskin (1842-85), too, dreamed of 'a spiritual and political rebirth of the Jewish people on the soil of Palestine', and he conducted a correspondence on this subject with the English Palestinophile, Laurence Oliphant.

Religious Jews were caught up in the fervour. R. Hayyim Eleazar Wacks (d. 1881) of Kalisz, author of the Responsa *Nefesh Hayyah*, sponsored the acquisition of land in Kfar Hittin,

Galilee, for the cultivation of *etrogim*. Accompanied by his son-in-law, Israel Elijah Joshua Trunk of Kutno (1820-1893), Hayyim Eleazar visited the Holy Land in 1876 and R. Simhah Bunam yearned to follow him.

Obstacle was piled on obstacle. In 1887 and 1889 Sultan Abdul Hamid (1876-1909) put a general ban on Jewish immigration. Permission to settle was granted only after a special application and even a permit to visit was only grudgingly given. A 'Red Card' allowed a maximum stay of three months. All this bureaucracy had the desired effect and decreased the flow of immigrants. But Simhah Bunam was not deterred. In the winter of 1887, accompanied by his wife, three sons, two daughters and two beadles, the rabbi set out for the Holy Land. Like all Russian tourists, the party was given leave to stay for thirty days. Overstaying this period, R. Simhah Bunam was arrested and spent five days in Acre prison. He was freed on medical grounds and allowed to remain in Tiberias. After three months he went back to Poland. His sixteen-year-old daughter Rachel fell ill en route and died soon after their return.

The rabbi settled in Otwock but could find no peace. 'If you can make a living in the Holy Land without being dependent on charity, then by all means settle there,' R. Abraham of Socha-szew advised him. 'Do not be concerned about leaving your Hasidim behind. Poland is not short of rabbis.'

Yet it was not until the winter of 1906 that he returned to Palestine. At first he stayed with R. David of Lelov. Then he settled in the *Deitsche* quarter (German section) of the Old City. 'When I left Poland,' he protested, 'I threw the Rebbe overboard. I am no Rebbe here.' But in spite of his protestations, Hasidim flocked to him. 'Pray for me,' he implored them. For the last year and a half of his life he lived in Tiberias, where he died on 2 Shevat 1907, at the age of fifty-six. He was buried near R. Menahem Mendel of Vitebsk.

His son, Simeon Shalom Kalisz, spent 1934 in the Holy Land, but his plans for settling there were disrupted by the outbreak of World War II. His wanderings took him to Vilna, Kovno, Japan and New York, where he died in 1954. Rebbe Jerahmiel Yehudah Meir was born in Przysucha in 1901. After living for some time in Holon, he established a yeshiva in Jerusalem called Shem Olam after his father R. Simon Shalom, and he also published his father's discourses. He died on 27 Iyyar 1976, and his grandson R. Jacob Milikovsky succeeded him as Rebbe. R. Hayyim Milikovsky, the late Rebbe's son-in-law, heads the yeshiva.

A neighbour of the rabbi of Amshinov in Bayit Vegan is the rabbi of Talno, Johanan Twersky, a descendant of R. David of Talno (1808-82), son of R. Mordecai of Czernobil.

Born on 2 October 1906, he was seven years old when his father David Mordecai emigrated to New York, one of the first Hasidic rabbis to settle there. 'In the old country,' said young Johanan at his Bar Mitzvah celebration, 'my greatest wish would have been for material things. Here in the United States, my most fervent desire is that I remain a Jew.' When he was seventeen he travelled to the Holy Land where he became a follower of R. Aaron Roth and was ordained by R. Joseph Hayyim Sonnenfeld.

In 1927 his father David Mordecai visited the Holy Land and took his son back to the United States. After his marriage in 1928 to Pearl, a descendant of the Rebbe of Stretyn, he became the Rebbe of Talno in Montreal, where in 1933 he set up a yeshiva. The war brought many refugees to Canada and all were made welcome at the rabbi's house. He interceded with the authorities on behalf of the Jewish internees and took care of their religious needs.

In 1950 he visited Israel and three years later settled there. After living in Rehavia for seven years he settled in 1960 in Bayit Vegam, where he published two of R. David of Talno's works.

XIV

A DYNASTY IN THE MAKING

R. Abraham Hayyim Roth, the rabbi of Beregszaz, is building a centre in the Meah Shearim area of Jerusalem known as Shomre Emunim. The 30-dunam (about 7½ acres) site was acquired by him about twenty-five years ago for a mere one hundred thousand Israeli pounds. Here he plans to erect a yeshiva, a Talmud Torah, a synagogue, apartment houses, a school for girls, a home for elderly people, a hotel and an industrial centre. So far only a few apartments have been completed and the rabbi maintains a small Kolel in the Old Bet Hamidrash in Meah Shearim.

The highlight of R. Roth's activity is his public meal on Friday night. He enters the Bet Hamidrash late in the evening, accompanied by his son and his son-in-law. The songs are melodious, the discourses erudite and the dancing joyful. When the Grace After Meals has been recited, the rabbi distributes fruit, and with Nishmat ('The Breath of Every Living Thing shall Bless Thy Name') the dance begins. Hands as well as feet are caught up in the passion of the dance. It becomes a form of self-expression even to the point of self-oblivion.

Redemption tends to be the main motif of his discourses. He quotes the Zohar to the effect that the Redemption will come after domination by alien and irreligious elements. His comments are illuminating and his opinions are expressed with precision and wit. He is a friendly, unpretentious man who welcomes all his visitors with warmth and spontaneity. Scholarly wisdom is, moreover, combined with considerable business acumen.

The founder of the dynasty, R. Aaron Roth (1894-1947) or Reb Arele, was born in Ungvar. His father Samuel Jacob was a merchant who traced his descent from Sabbatai b. Meir Ha-Kohen, known as the *Shack* (1621-62), and R. Isaiah Horowitz, known as the *Sheloh*. As a young boy Aaron studied in the yeshivot in Galicia and in Waitzen in central Hungary, which was under the direction of R. Isaiah Silberstein (1857-1930), author of *Maasei le-Melech* (2 vols, 1913-30), on the *Mishneh Torah* of Maimonides.

During World War I he became acquainted with many of the rabbis who found refuge in Budapest, among them Engel of Radomysl, Issachar Dov of Belz and Zevi Elimelech Shapira of Blazowa (d.1924). In 1916, Aaron married the daughter of Yitzhak Katz of Budapest. Two years later, when R. Zevi Elimelech settled in Rzeszow in Galicia, Aaron followed him there.

R. Aaron rejected easy answers and tried to solve problems in depth. Although he was frail and ailing, the moment he started to pray he was transformed. Prayer was more than 'service of the heart'. It was an act of ecstasy, of spiritual elevation. Wherever he went, he attracted kindred spirits. His own Rebbe called him 'the Good Jew', and his associates idolised him. When R. Zevi Elimelech died in 1924, Aaron went to the Holy Land, but, on the advice of his doctors, left for Beregszaz and Satmar five years later. In 1939 he journeyed back to the Holy Land almost on the last boat from Romania. Even the usually belligerent R. Hayyim Eleazar Shapira spoke in laudatory terms about Aaron, saying 'A man of such qualities and attributes would have been a novelty even in the time of the Rabbi Israel Baal Shem Tov.' Aaron suffered even fools gladly. On one occasion, when a shoemaker abused and ridiculed him, R. Aaron listened without a word. Before the Day of Atonement, he went to the shoemaker. 'I have come to apologise to you,' he said. R. Aaron died on 6 Nisan 1947, and was buried on the Mount of Olives.

In his Last Will, he urged his family not to become involved in politics: 'Do not be among those Hasidim who slander others. Do not associate with such people. The aim of Rabbi Israel Baal Shem Tov was to establish harmony and unity.' He urged his son-in-law Abraham Yitzhak and his son Abraham Hayyim to stay on good terms and 'be submissive to one another'.

R. Aaron begged his followers to lead disciplined lives. He bade women cut their hair after marriage and keep their heads covered with a kerchief, to wear thick black stockings and long skirts. 'Sleep for five hours, you do not need more,' he wrote to his followers. 'After prayers, study for half an hour and recite a few Psalms . . . Eat enough to satisfy yourself, but from time to time stop in the middle of a meal and do not eat any more, for this is also counted as fasting. Each week you should fast for one day until noon and the best day for this is Friday. During the month of Elul, and during the winter days, fast three times a week until noon.' Strict regulations governed the community's way of life. Men were not allowed to shave their beards or cut off their side locks. Non-conforming strangers were allowed little leeway, but if they habitually attended the synagogue they used to be exhorted to adopt the community's life-style and become permanent members.

Abraham Yitzhak Kahn was born in 1917 in Safed, a descendant on his mother's side of the bibliographer R. Samuel Heller, who amassed one of the greatest private libraries in the Old Yishuv. He also traces his lineage from R. Michael of

Zloczow and Elimelech of Lyshansk. Abraham Yitzhak studied for seven years in Satmar and under R. Aaron Roth. 'I looked everywhere for a suitable son-in-law,' said R. Aaron, 'Nowhere could I find a young man as God-fearing as you.'

After the death of R. Aaron, Abraham Yitzhak became Rebbe, and his brother-in-law became principal of the yeshiva, a dual leadership which did not endure for long. When they separated, the overwhelming majority followed the son-in-law. His adherents maintain that a vote decided the 'succession'. R. Aaron Rokeah of Belz and R. Friedman of Husiatyn, on the other hand, urged Abraham Hayyim to succeed his father. Twenty-five years of co-existence have shown that there is ample scope for both of them to maintain and expand the community founded by R. Aaron.

While R. Abraham Hayyim was concerned with ambitious plans for his future, his brother-in-law Abraham Yitzhak was busy creating an independent community. He established a Talmud Torah, a large yeshiva, and a Kolel for thirty students. He is an extremist, closely associated with the Edah Ha-Haredit, and a sympathiser of Amram Blau, leader of the Neture Karta. It is not surprising that a number of his yeshiva students participate in violent demonstrations sponsored by the militants. The young students of the Talmud Torah are familiar with intricate passages of the Talmud but are totally ignorant of Jewish history.

Despite a budget of nearly £32,000 per month, the rabbi refuses to accept contributions from the Vaad Ha-Yeshivot. Nor does he appear to approve of the Agudist Hinuch Atzmai. The girls attend the Old Yishuv institution Bnot Yerushalayim. Abraham Yitzhak is the author of *Divre Emunah* – Yiddish discourses – and has published his father-in-law's book *Shomer Emunim*, which consists of homilies concerning faith, reward, and punishment, redemption, confidence and providence.

Apart from Ger, no other rabbi in Jerusalem attracts so many followers on Friday night when more than 300 people crowd into the large Bet Hamidrash. The rabbi's labours are bearing fruit. He has already raised a generation of diligent disciples.

XV

SLONIM IN JERUSALEM

The Hasidic dynasty of Slonim is represented in Israel by the frail and aged R. Abraham Weinberg of Jerusalem.

The founder of the dynasty was Abraham Weinberg (1804-84) a disciple of Rabbi Noah of Lachowicze (1774-1832), whose Hasidim were primarily concerned with self-discipline. Each one was charged with perfecting himself and giving of his best to God and man. In 1821 he appealed on behalf of the Haisidim in the Holy Land. 'All his life my revered father not only preached but also performed this *mitzvah* [of supporting the Jewish settlers in the Holy Land],' wrote R. Noah.[1]

Day and night he did not cease or rest from awakening men's hearts to accustom them and strengthen them in the performance of his *mitzvah* ... He implanted this *mitzvah* in their hearts ... and appointed regular times for them to bring their contributions to the prayerhouse ... that no one should miss a single Sabbath in the regular weekly payment of his contribution. And even those who had a mere pittance – he would exhort them to make their contribution before the Kiddush on the Sabbath eve.

After the death of R. Noah, most of the Hasidim of Slonim turned to R. Moses of Kobryn (1784-1858). Son of a baker, he was never oblivious of his humble origin. 'Why have you come to me,' he once asked a Hasid, 'when you have already been to your own Rebbe? Your Rebbe is a zaddik, the son of a zaddik, whereas my father was just a villager.'[2] He was no author. 'I have written my books', he said, 'on the hearts of Israel.'[3]

With the death of R. Moses, many Hasidim transferred their allegiance to R. Abraham Weinberg of Slonim. He was a prolific author and left thirty-two manuscripts, of which only two have so far been published. A number of his followers settled in the Holy Land and R. Abraham wrote them warm encouraging letters. 'The Diaspora is a temporary resting-place, a mere lodging-place,' he wrote, 'but the Holy Land is the House of the Lord. You do not realise how grateful you should all be that you are residing there.'

R. Abraham died at the age of eighty (11 Heshvan 1884). The principle of hereditary leadership, so firmly rooted in Polish Hasidic life, had no guaranteed place in Slonim, and R. Abraham's son, Michael Aaron (d.1894) did not succeed his father, but he encouraged his grandson Samuel (1850-1916) to become Rebbe instead. R. Samuel maintained the traditions of his grandfather, publishing his works and collecting funds for the Holy Land, and helping to establish there the Or Torah (Light of the Law) Yeshiva beside the tomb of R. Meir Baal Ha-Nes, and a soup kitchen for the poor.

R. Samuel was succeeded by his son Abraham the Second (1884-1933) who in 1918 established Yeshiva Torat Hesed in Baranowicze. He visited the Holy Land in 1929 and 1933 and established *shtieblech* in Tel-Aviv and Bne Brak. He died at the age of forty-nine (1 Iyyar 1933) and his brother Shlomo David Joshua (1912-43) succeeded him. Shlomo died on 6 Heshvan 1943.

A grandson of R. Abraham and a brother of R. Samuel, Noah emigrated to the Holy Land in 1880 and settled in

Tiberias. He refused to become a Rebbe but studied in the Kolel of R. Meir Baal Ha-Nes. For nearly half a century,Slonim Hasidim in the Holy Land had no official Rebbe. R. Abraham Weinberg, son of R. Noah, was born in 1890 in Tiberias and ordained by R. Moses Kliers of Tiberias. He too visited Poland and studied together with his relatives, Samuel and Shlomoh David Joshua (d.1942). He married the daughter of a Slonim Hasid in Tiberias, and participated in the civic life of the town. Elected a member of the municipality, this rabbinic scion became associate mayor in 1938. In 1929 one of his four sons was killed in Tiberias by Arab terrorists.

R. Abraham refused resolutely to become Rebbe and regarded himself as a follower of R. Mordecai (Motel) Hayyim Kislintz (1868-1954), a disciple of the first R. Abraham, who lived in the Holy Land. R. Motel too, found it irksome to wield authority. 'If you call me Rebbe,' he told his adherents, 'I will not forgive you either in this world or in the next.' He did not deliver discourses but simply told Hasidic stories. It was not until after the war, in which all his relatives perished, and after the death of R. Motel in 1954, that R. Abraham two years later reluctantly assumed the leadership of the Hasidim of Slonim.

The unpretentious rabbi conducts a public meal on a Friday evening. The married Hasidim sit at his table while the younger ones stand, and during each meal he delivers several brief discourses. He is highly respected for his diligence and his learning. He spends his days in scholarship, completing the study of the whole Talmud twice a year, on the anniversary of his father's death in Elul, and his mother's in Adar. He does not accept petitions, but an exception is made before New Year when he accepts a composite 'petition' drawn up by his Hasidim. He is active in the Aguda and is a member of its Council of Sages. He has not entirely recovered from a car accident in which he was involved a few years ago.

The attractive modern five-storey yeshiva Bet Avraham established in 1942 now accommodates two hundred students

and there are forty graduates in its Kolel. Slonim stresses
comprehension and depth rather than the accumulation of facts
– a legacy of the Lithuanian mitnaged Rabbi Hayyim
Soloveichik. The yeshiva is directed by the rabbi's son-in-law,
Shalom Noah Brosovsky (b.1911), formerly head of Habad
Yeshiva in Tel-Aviv. Again and again he stresses: 'The Torah
was given in fire and must be studied with fiery enthusiasm.'
The yeshiva houses an excellent library of over 5,000 volumes
and its Gemilut Hasadim (free loan society) has distributed
nearly 850,000 Israeli pounds since 1971. The Hasidim are now
planning to build a Bet Hamidrash for 500 worshippers.

XVI

REBBES IN THE ALL-JEWISH CITY

A stretch of desert dunes in 1910, Tel-Aviv is today the largest city in the state of Israel, its polyglot half-million population reflecting 'the Ingathering of the Exiles'. It has more than 700 synagogues and there are few Hasidic dynasties which do not have a *shtiebel* in Tel-Aviv.

Before the outbreak of World War II, Tel-Aviv became the refuge of the descendants of R. Israel Friedman of Ruzhin (Rijin), many of whom had been living in Vienna in the inter-war years. His six sons, 'the Six Orders of the Mishnah' or 'the six wings of the Angel' (Isa.6:2), established their courts in Sadagura, Czortkov, Husiatyn, Stefanesti, Leovo and later in Kopycienice, Bohush and Vaslui.

Today there are few rabbis of Ruzhin in Israel. R. Shlomo Friedman, son of R. Israel of Sadagura, died in August 1972. He was born in Sadagura on 18 May 1887, and at the age of fourteen he wrote articles for the *Mahzike Ha-Dat*, a Zionist Orthodox weekly. Together with his family, he found refuge in Vienna in 1914. With Hayyim Meir Shapira of Drohobycz, he formed an association called Yishuv Eretz Yisrael, and was active in the Mizrachi. A witty and trenchant polemicist on a variety of current issues, he was much in demand as a writer and speaker. He married the daughter of the wealthy Samuel Ha-Kohen Hornstein of Radomysl. R. Shlomo attended the 1920 Zionist Conference in London, as well as the Zionist Congresses in Carlsbad in 1923, and in Lucerne in 1935, which discussed the establishment of the Jewish Agency. The Nazi annexation of Austria on 12 March 1938 led to unprecedented persecution of the Jews. Some Zionist leaders were arrested and taken to Buchenwald concentration camp. When the Gestapo came to his home in Vienna, it was the Gentile caretaker who defended him like a 'pillar of fire'.

Shlomo settled in Tel-Aviv in 1938. His five brothers became Rebbes but he refused to do so. A dedicated scholar who elected to live a secluded life with his books and his memories, he was selective and restrained in his speech, preferring to say that something was 'not good', rather than that it was bad. He wrote fluently in Hebrew, Yiddish and German and contributed frequently to the Mizrachi daily *Hatzofeh*. Shlomo was a man of many interests; Albert Einstein's theory of relativity, for instance, had a special fascination for him.

In 1949 he went to Switzerland, concerned about the number of Jewish children who were still in monasteries, and enlisted the help of R. Hayyim Zevi Taubes (1900-66) in rescue efforts, which he continued in New York from 1950 to 1953. He was always genuinely interested in people and their problems. Sedulously he shunned public appearances, but from time to time, as on 12 Tishri, the anniversary of his father's death, he would deliver a discourse. After the Six-Day War, Shlomo asked to meet Zalman Shazar, President of Israel, but the reason for the meeting was never divulged. He was anxious that the name of Ruzhin should be perpetuated, and encouraged the Hasidim to support the Ruzhin Yeshiva in the Holy City. He used to spend the summer months in London where he died. He was buried at Nahlat Yitzhak in Tel-Aviv.

One of the first Rebbes of the House of Ruzhin to settle in Tel-Aviv was R. Israel of Husiatyn (1858-1949), son of Mordecai Shraga Feivish (1834-94), who arrived with his son-in-law R. Jacob of Bohush in 1937.

R. Israel married the daughter of R. Aviezer Zelig of Moglienice. When his father-in-law died in 1894, he became Rebbe and in 1914 moved to Vienna. It was a matter of great pride to him that his ninetieth birthday (16 Kislev) coincided with the day (29 November 1947) that the United Nations passed the Partition Resolution recommending the establishment of both a Jewish and an Arab state in Palestine. When Field Marshal Rommel was threatening Alexandria before the battle of El Alamein, R. Israel prayed for hours at the grave of R. Hayyim ibn Attar on the Mount of Olives. When he finished, he said: 'Rommel will advance no further.'

The Rebbe regularly paid the Zionist *shekel* (a small levy which entitled one to participate in the elections to the World Zionist Congress). 'To redeem the Holy Land from the hands of the gentiles is a great mitzvah,' he said. 'Would that the air of the Holy Land made all the inhabitants wise, so that they might join forces to serve the Lord with a perfect heart.' He had cordial relations with Chief Rabbi Herzog and in 1943 visited the religious settlements. In his Will dated 23 Nisan 1939 he wrote: 'I would like to be buried on the Mount of Olives in Jerusalem. If this is not possible, then bury me either in Safed or Tiberias.' He died at the age of ninety-one on 29 Kislev 1949, and was buried in Tiberias.

His son-in-law R. Jacob Friedman of Husiatyn (1878-1953) was the son of R. Yitzhak of Bohush. In 1895, at the age of seventeen, he married Hayah Sarah, daughter of R. Israel, but did not become Rebbe. He supported the settlers of Rosh Pinah, a village in northern Israel, which was founded in 1878 by immigrants from Romania and Russia. In Vienna he supported the Yishuv Eretz Yisrael association and acted as Chairman of the Mizrachi. He maintained that nationalism and religion were closely interwoven and attempted to organise religious Jewry to ensure that the Torah influenced all aspects of life. 'Can a Jew have a more noble objective?' he asked. Like Shlomo Friedman, he wrote articles and gave lectures.

If only religious Jewry had worked to rebuild the land, our position here would have been entirely different ... We observe that even irreligious Jews are moved by the spirit of nationalism and love of the country and gradually accept the Torah. To those who say that Zionism has a secular connotation, I maintain that the opposite is true. Let us divert these energies into religious channels.

He used to conduct a celebration meal on Israel's Independence Day.

With the death of his father-in-law in 1949, he became Rebbe, and during the next few years frequently visited religious settlements. He believed that 'the religious labourer not only cleanses the soil from its uncleanness, but also purifies his soul from the stains of the exile.' R. Jacob led a protest demonstration in Tel-Aviv against Sabbath desecration. 'A man should be prepared to give up his life for the Sabbath.' he said. He felt that the role of the Rebbe was to 'purify' the hearts of those who came to him and 'to illumine their souls with the light of holiness'.

It was the custom of Husiatyn to start the Sabbath meal without donning the *gartel* (girdle). 'When we commence the festive meal,' he explained, 'we are not yet worthy to wear it.' Before he died, on 18 Heshvan 1953, he said, 'I am not concerned with my own pain. The main thing is that it should be well with my people.' He was buried next to his father-in-law.

In 1914, seven and a half years after becoming Rebbe, Abraham Jacob, brother-in-law of R. Shlomo and son of R. Israel of Sadagura, moved to Vienna, and after the war refused to return to his native city. 'It is our tradition not to go back,' he said. 'This is the gate to the land of Israel.' In 1938 the Nazis rounded up bearded Jews and forcibly shaved them. Abraham Jacob bent his head, 'Cut off my head,' he declared, 'but leave my beard alone.' The Nazis laughed and let him go. 'We can use a bearded Jew', they jeered, and forced him to wash the streets of Vienna and perform other menial tasks, sights which photographs duly recorded for posterity. He vowed that when he arrived in the Holy Land he would clean the streets there, and he was punctilious about the fulfilment of this vow. Every morning in Tel-Aviv he would sweep the steps near his home.

The rabbi was active in the work of the Aguda. At the Fourth Kenesiyah in 1954, he urged religious Jews to settle in the Holy Land and not to heed leaders who discouraged them. He told religious settlers, 'I can study *Zeraim* [the Order of the Mishnah which deals with agricultural laws], but you can actually fulfil the Commandments by putting them into practice. You can demonstrate to the whole world that it is possible to be an agricultural worker and an observer of the Torah.' He loved to visit Haifa, which he called 'the Mountain of Elijah' in view of the close association of the ancient prophet with Mount Carmel. When he was asked in 1961 whether Israel should have diplomatic relations with Germany, he replied: 'We are a state. A state has obligations. We are not in a position to settle our account with Germany. We can never settle it. Only the Almighty, God of Justice and of Vengeance, can do that.'

'I believe that Hasidism can bring about a much-needed spiritual revival', said the Rebbe.

The Hasidic atmosphere, with its concomitant joy expressed in song and dance should be introduced into every home. We know well that many young people today are seeking something. Their lives lack spiritual content and are void of aim and purpose. If we could show them religion in its true light, if we could bring the great light of Hasidism to the confused and straying younger generation, I am convinced that they would be attracted. Youth needs overwhelmingly joy, ecstasy and devotion that transcends the normal tenor of everyday existence. All this and more can be obtained from Hasidism.

R. Abraham died in 1961.

THE ROYAL RABBI

The rabbis of Ruzhin and Sadagura were virtually the Exilarchs of Hasidism. They dressed elegantly, their residences were palatial, their coaches were drawn by four horses, and they employed a large retinue of servants.

In the north of Tel-Aviv, above his newly built and handsomely appointed synagogue, was the home of R. Mordecai (Motel) Shalom Joseph Friedman of Sadagura-Przemysl. One by one, the Rebbes of Sadagura and Czortkov passed away and R. Motel was the last great survivor of a notable dynasty. He was the possessor of a valuable library of 15,000 volumes, including rare works, and letters of R. Israel of Ruzhin.

As is customary in Ruzhin, R. Motel prayed by himself in a room attached to the synagogue. Whilst he was hidden from the congregation, he could hear each word of the service. Every Saturday he was honoured with a different aliyah, which he himself selected. 'Every section of the Torah is equally holy,' he said, 'but some sections are more tasty than others.'

R. Motel was born on 21 November 1897 in Sadagura. When his father, R. Aaron (1850-1912), author of *Kedushat Aharon*,[1] died on Hol Hamoed Sukkot, Motel at the age of sixteen became Rebbe in Vienna, which had the third largest Jewish community in Europe after Warsaw and Budapest. To keep in touch with his scattered followers, he travelled regularly to Przemysl. The outbreak of World War I found him there and he hastened to return home; but to avoid desecrating the Sabbath, he broke his journey at Oswiecin. The train continued without him, and was wrecked on the way.

The rabbi hated his brief sojourn in Oswiecin. He relates that when the voluntary exiles R. Elimelech and his brother Zusya of Annopol arrived there, Zusya said to his brother: 'We cannot stay here, Jewish blood is being spilt. I sense it. I feel it.' This was in 1773. Nearly 170 years later, Oswiecin (Auschwitz), 30 miles west of Cracow, became the site of the largest Nazi concentration camp, where approximately one and a half million Jews perished.

When Dollfuss became Chancellor of Austria in 1932, the rabbi realised that nothing could halt the Nazi infiltration and he moved to Przemysl where as many as 1,500 Hasidim would turn up on Friday night to listen to his discourses. An additional attraction was the cantorial rendering of Cantor Levi Rosenblatt, brother of Josele. The rabbi saw the writing on the wall, and it was not difficult to read. The Nuremberg Laws and the economic boycott were sinister auguries of what was to come. Urgently he implored his Hasidim to settle in the Holy Land. But of the three hundred followers to whom he specifically addressed himself, only thirty took his advice, among them Joel Lieber, who became a noted chocolate manufacturer in the Holy Land. A number settled in Shechinat Zevi near Netanyah. The rabbi himself visited the Holy Land in 1933, and began the erection of Kiryat Sadagura. The rabbi's foreboding regarding the fate of his Austrian followers was soon proved to be justified. By September 1938 some 60,000 of the 190,000 Jews of Vienna were dependent on communal help, and Hermann Göring announced the avowed Nazi policy of making Vienna 'Jew-free within four years'.

On 10 Adar 1939 the rabbi settled in Tel-Aviv. He was active in the Aguda, in the Mo'atzei Gedolei Ha-Torah (Council of Sages), and in Hinuch Atzmai. Yet, despite his identification with the Aguda, he disliked political machinations. 'I am here', he told an Aguda gathering, 'to see that there are no party politics.' He was one of the few Hasidic rabbis present at the induction of R. Isser Yehuda Unterman as Ashkenazi Chief

Rabbi of Israel in 1964. Unlike many of his rabbinic colleagues, he celebrated Yom Ha-Atzmaut, Israel's Independence Day, each year.

The rabbi disliked long-winded discourses. 'He who gives us the ability to speak also gives us the ability to refrain from speaking.' His comments have sparks of originality. On the fourth benediction of the Amida for the Sabbath morning service, Yismah Mosheh (Moses Rejoiced), where it says: 'In his hand, he brought down the two tables of stone on which was written the observance of the Sabbath', the Rabbi comments:

The Decalogue [Exod.20:1-26] contained ten precepts, so why is the reference merely to the 'Observance of the Sabbath'? Because when Moses returned to the camp after forty days and beheld the people worshipping the Golden Calf, he felt they were unworthy of the Divine Tables of the Law. The Tables fell and were shattered [Exod. 32:19], with only one fragment remaining intact, the fourth Commandment which stresses observance of the Sabbath.

The rabbi has not fulfilled his dream of establishing a Kirya to perpetuate Sadagura. His two sons, Yisrael Aaron and Abraham Jacob, live in New York. 'The rabbi of Klausenburg has an easier task,' said the rabbi. 'Most of his followers in the United States settled there after World War II, and their roots are shallower. It is comparatively easier for them to resettle in the Holy Land. My Hasidim, however, have lived in the New World for many years. It is hard for them to uproot themselves.' To maintain contact with his followers, he travelled to the United States and England. 'This generation is doubly orphaned. Both the shepherd and his sheep have perished,' laments the rabbi. 'It is not good for sheep to be without a shepherd. It is equally bad for a shepherd to be without sheep.' He died on 29 Nisan 1979 and was succeeded by his son Abraham Isaac.

'Ahad Ha-Am' was the pen-name for Asher Ginzberg, the essayist and philosopher who believed in the establishment of a 'National Spiritual Centre' in the Holy Land which would influence the Jews in the Diaspora. Born in the Ukraine and educated in the traditional Jewish manner, he was taken in his boyhood to the Rebbe of Sadagura. Even at that early age, he adopted a critical attitude and he never developed much sympathy for Hasidism. Yet Rehov Ahad Ha-Am in Tel-Aviv has become 'the Street of the Rabbis'. Here lived the rabbi of Belz, R. Mordecai Shalom Friedman, R. Abraham Jacob, R. Shlomo and R. Nahum Mordecai Friedman (1875-1946), the son of R. Israel of Czortkow, who settled in the Holy Land in 1939.

Nahum Mordecai's father, R. Israel, was one of the first Hasidic leaders to advocate the establishment of vocational schools. When he was asked to return to Czortkow after the war, he replied: 'Vienna is nearer to the land of Israel.' He urged R. Abraham Mordecai of Ger to encourage his followers to emigrate. 'I do encourage them,' replied the rabbi of Ger, 'but they do not listen to me.' R. Nahum Mordecai died on 18 Adar 1946, and was buried on the Mount of Olives.

His son, Shlomo Mordecai (1894-1959), made his home a centre of Jewish life and took an active part in communal affairs. When the Neture Karta asked him to withdraw his support from the Aguda and Hinuch Atzmai, 'since they accept financial support from the Zionists,' the rabbi refused. 'I am interested in hearing only good reports about the state of Israel. I will not listen to malicious censure.' He died on 15 Heshvan 1959, at the age of sixty-five, surviving his eighty-four-year-old mother, Havah Leah, by just a few days.

The son-in-law of R. Israel of Czortkow was R. Zevi Aryeh Twersky (1897-1968), son of Mordecai Joseph, Rabbi of Zlatopole-Czortkow. R. Zevi, or 'Hershelle' as he was popularly known, was educated by his father, who said: 'He is fit to be a Rebbe of Rebbes.' Like so many rabbis he found refuge at the beginning of World War I in Vienna, where he became rabbi in 1929. He was taken by the Nazis to the Dachau concentration camp, but managed to smuggle into the camp a pair of *tephillin* which were used extensively by the Jewish inmates. On his release from the camp he settled in Tel-Aviv in 1939. The author of the Hasidic work *Ha-Tov Ve-Ha-Tachlit*,[2] he was interested in philosophy and ascribed to Hasidism a significant place in mystical speculation. He died on 18 Av 1968, and Kolel Czortkow Zlatopole has been established in his memory by his son-in-law, R. Phinehas Biberfeld (b.1915). A native of Berlin and son of a physician, Biberfeld studied in the Berlin Rabbinic Seminary under R. Yehiel Jacob Weinberg and subsequently in the Hebron yeshiva in Jerusalem.

From 1925, R. Mordecai Shlomo Friedman of Boyan (1891-1971) lived in New York, but frequently visited the Holy Land. He supported the Yeshiva Tiferet Yisrael in Jerusalem and participated in the annual pilgrimage on Lag Ba-Omer to the little town of Meron in Upper Galilee, near Safed. On this day, men and women, Ashkenazim and Sephardim, Hasidim and *mitnagdim*, sabras and Yemenites converge on the white-domed tomb of R. Simon b. Yochai and his son Eliezer. On the elevated pillar stands a large stone basin filled with olive oil. Devout pilgrims immerse kerchiefs of silk and pieces of embroidered cloth in the oil. At the stroke of twelve, the *hadlakah* (bonfire) is lit as a signal that the celebrations have begun. By tradition, the honour of kindling the bonfire belonged to R. Mordecai Shlomo of Boyan. He died on 5 Adar 1971 and was buried on the Mount of Olives.

R. Isaac Friedman of Bohush was born in Spikov in Russia in 1903, the son of R. Shalom Joseph Friedman, a descendant of Ruzhin. Isaac married the daughter of R. Mendel Friedman of Bohush. After the Russian revolution, the family endured the assaults of Simon Petlura, the Ukrainian leader who instigated many pogroms. In 1920, Isaac succeeded his father-in-law and settled in Bucharest. During World War II, his home in the capital of Romania was a haven for refugees, and the rabbi saved many lives.

In 1959 he moved to Tel-Aviv. He has a large following among the many settlers from Romania who came there after the war. He is the people's Rebbe rather than the scholars' Rebbe. 'I regard him as a friend,' said one woman who was waiting to see him, 'rather than as a Rebbe.' 'My surname is Friedman,' he points out, ' "A man of peace." The Psalm [128:5] says: "Mayest thou see the good of Jerusalem all the days of thy life", which indicates that it is a man's duty not to behold iniquity in Jacob, nor perverseness in Israel. To be capable of such positive vision, a man must cultivate humility and humanity. He must remember that every Jew is "a prince and the son of a prince".'

The rabbi maintains a small Kolel of six students. On the Sabbath he sings a number of wordless melodies which according to tradition were sung in the Temple in Jerusalem. Unlike other sons of Hasidic rabbis who remain for years studying in the Kolelim preparing to become Rebbes, the Rebbe's son is an accountant and his son-in-law is an educationist. This tendency seems to be prevalent among the descendants of Ruzhin and Sadagura, whose Rebbes are too tolerant to force their children to follow in their footsteps. Hence many of the descendants of Ruzhin are engaged in other professions in Israel, the United States and England. So it is not surprising that, after three decades, this many-sided family has not enlarged its Hasidic domain. Over thirty rabbis of Ruzhin perished in the Holocaust. Most of the rabbis who found refuge in the Holy Land have died, and their children have pursued other careers.

The most prolific of the contemporary Hasidic rabbis was Moses Yehiel Epstein (1890-1971), Rebbe of Ozarow, Poland, whose father was Abraham Shlomoh (1865-1918), son of R. Aryeh Yehuda Leibish of Ozarow. His mother was a granddaughter of R. Hayyim Samuel of Checiny, a descendant of Jacob Isaac Horowitz, 'the Seer of Lublin'. Moses Yehiel, a child prodigy, received his Rabbinic Diploma at the age of eighteen. At twenty-four, he became rabbi of Radom, declining an invitation to become *dayyan* of the large Jewish community of Lodz, and two years later, he became rabbi in Ozarow. In 1921 he visited the United States as a member of the Aguda delegation, and seven years later settled in New York. In 1949 his only son Abraham Shalom died at the age of twenty-one. After twenty-five years in New York, he settled in Tel-Aviv in 1953. He often addressed large gatherings, participating in the deliberations of the Mo'atzei Gedolei Ha-Torah and was concerned with Hinuch Atzmai.

The last eighteen years of his life were devoted to his great works *Esh Dat* (eleven volumes) and *Be'er Mosheh* (seven volumes), a total of over 10,000 printed pages. His output was colossal and his works are encyclopaedic in scope, full of insights and new ideas. The first three volumes were published in New York, the remainder in Israel. Like the *tanna* Eliezer ben Hyrcanus, he was 'a cemented cistern that does not lose a drop'.[3] For the last three decades of his life he was severely handicapped by failing eyesight, yet he persevered. He was honoured with many awards by the civic authorities of Tel-Aviv and Jerusalem. 'His books give me a spiritual uplift', said Chief Rabbi Isser Yeduda Unterman. When he died on Rosh Hodesh Shevat 1971 at the age of eighty-one, he was, on the advice of R. Israel of Ger, buried in Bne Brak, near the grave of R. Abraham Yeshayahu Karlitz, the *Hazon Ish*. His grandson R. Tanhum Becker, who came from the United States, and R. David Gross of Ponevezh direct the Kolel Esh Dat.

Modzhitz occupies a high place in the history of Hasidic musicology. What Habad did for the philosophy of Hasidism, Modzhitz did for its music. The founder of the dynasty was R. Ezekiel Taub of Kazirmierz (1806-56). The family tradition was maintained by Samuel Elijah of Zwolen (1818-88), who was gifted with a fine voice as well as a fine mind. All five sons of R. Samuel Elijah were music-lovers. The successor of R. Ezekiel, was however, R. Israel (b.1848). In his work *Divre Yisrael (Words of Israel)*, R. Israel devotes a lengthy excursus to music. 'They say that the Temple of Song is adjacent to the Temple of Repentance,' he writes. 'I maintain that the Temple of Music is the Temple of Repentance.'

For two decades R. Israel lived in Modzhitz, attracting followers from far and wide. In 1913 he fell dangerously ill, and one of his legs was amputated in Berlin. Pain did not extinguish his fiery spirit nor crush the music of his soul. On the operating table he composed a soaring song, consisting of thirty stanzas, called 'Ezkerah Elohim ve-Ehemayah' ('I will remember and pour out my heart within me').

The next Modzhitzer melody-maker was R. Israel's son, Saul Yedidiah Eleazar Taub, who was born in 1886 at Ozarow. R. Taub received no formal grounding in the rudiments of musical theory, yet there was music in his veins. After living in Rakow and Karzew, he moved to Otwock near Warsaw in 1929. Music-loving *maskilim* as well as Hasidim from all over Poland, Jewish and Gentile, flocked to Otwock to listen to the compositions of the untutored genius. What other rabbis achieved through scholarship, R. Taub achieved through music. He is said to have composed more than 700 melodies.

Narrowly escaping the Nazi clutches, he journeyed via Siberia and Japan to the United States. He visited the Holy Land in 1925, 1935 and 1938, and during his first visit was received by the British High Commissioner, Herbert Samuel. He settled there in 1947, but died several months later on 29 November (16 Kislev) 1947, the day on which the United Nations recommended the establishment of a Jewish state. He was the last person to be buried on the Mount of Olives before it was taken over by the Jordanians. There was not even time to put a tombstone on his grave; this was not done until after the Six-Day War, when the Old City was captured by the Israelis.

R. Saul Yedidiah Eliezer's son, Samuel Eliyahu Taub, lives at the Bet Modzhitz in Tel-Aviv. He was born in Lublin in 1906, and was ordained by the Warsaw Rabbinate. In 1935, he accompanied his father to the Holy Land and decided to settle there. He is the composer of many melodies and creates fifteen new tunes every year. He is a fine Baal Tephillah (Reader) in the style of Vizhnitz and Kossov. He collected the discourses of his father and published them under the title *Imre Sha'ul (The Words of Saul)*. He became Rebbe in 1948.

Though an Israeli, the rabbi observes some of the customs of the Diaspora, such as the *hakaffot* (circuits) on the night of Shemini Atzeret. 'If our fellow-Jews outside the Holy Land are celebrating', said the rabbi, 'we should, nay we must, partici-pate in their joy.' He dedicates the sixth circuit of the *hakaffot* ('Ozer Dalim' – 'Who Supports the Poor'), to the memory of the six million Jews. The lights of the synagogue are dimmed, and mournful melodies are chanted. The rabbis refuses to despair over the state of religion in Israel. 'Conditions today', he says, 'are much better than they used to be.' The heir-apparent of Modzhitz is his son, Israel Dan.

The Karlin-Koidanov dynasty was represented by R. Hanoh Heinoch Dov Silberfarb of Koidanov, born in 1891 at Toporov. His father, Meshullam Zalman Joseph, was a descendant of the rabbi of Karlin and ordained by R. Hayyim Soloveichik, and lived in Stropkov for forty years. Hanoch was also a descendant of R. Hanoch Alesker, author of *Lev Sameah* on Genesis and Exodus, who was known as 'a miracle-worker'. Together with his younger son Elimelech he perished in Belzec concentration camp during World War II.

R. Silberfarb studied under his father at Toporov and later under the rabbi of Belz. During the war he was interned for nineteen months in Romania. The rabbi, who was losing his sight, spent his days in prayer and study. He died on 8 Av 1978 and was succeeded by his son R. Aaron.

An interesting personality was R. Yehuda Zevi Brandwein of Stretyn (1903-69), a descendant of R. Yehuda Zevi (d.1830), a disciple of Uri of Strelisk. Yehuda Zevi was born in Safed and studied in the yeshiva of Satmar. On his return to the Holy Land, he continued his studies at the Yeshiva Hayye Olam and

Shar Hashamayim and was ordained by R. Joseph Hayyim Sonnenfeld and R. Kook. In 1957 he began to work in the Religious Department of the Histradut (General Federation of Workers in Israel).

The Department helped to erect over 350 synagogues throughout the country, assisted in the construction of sixteen ritual baths, opened 130 libraries and supplied countless Scrolls of Law to immigrant centres. It also assisted needy members to acquire a complete set of the Talmud under an easy-payment plan. Yehuda Zevi's communal preoccupations did not deter him from making a notable contribution to the study of mysticism and in 1958 he completed Ashlag's commentary, *Ma'alot Ha-Sullam*, on the Zohar.

XVII

THE LONELY RABBI

'There is no town without a Rebbe of Nadvorna,' say the Hasidim. R. Hayyim Mordecai lives in Bne Brak, R. Asher in Haderah, R. Issachar Baer and R. Yitzhak Eizig in the United States; R. Abraham Abba Leifer lives in Ashdod, R. Joseph Leifer in Petah Tikvah, R. Yehiel Leifer in Jerusalem, R. Menahem Eliezer Zeev in Rehovot, R. Israel Nisan in Kiryat Gat, R. Eliezer Zeev in Ramat Gan and R. Zevi in Kfar Ata.

The head of the dynasty whose branches have spread far and wide was R. Ithamar Rosenbaum of Yad Eliyahu in Tel-Aviv. The progenitor of a large family, he lived alone in a flat attached to his Bet Hamidrash, attended by his faithful warden. Ailing and frail, he was a cheerful friendly man who made every visitor feel at home. Ithamar was born in 1886 in Mihaileni in Romania, and is a descendant of R. Meir of Przemyslany and R. Zevi Hirsch (d. 1802) of Nadvornaya (Nadvorna), a disciple of R. Dov Baer and R. Mordecai (d. 1895) of Nadvorna.

R. Mordecai was an ascetic: 'I must train my body to be satisfied with whatever I eat.' He would pray for hours on end. 'I am sorry to keep you waiting,' he once told his followers, 'but you know that I was not playing cards or visiting the theatre.'

'There were no Hasidic yeshivot in Romania in my day,' explained R. Ithamar. He studied under his father, R. Meir of Kretshnov (Craciunesti), and under private tutors when such were available. His father was very concerned about the lack of suitable tutors, and fervently prayed on New Year's Day for Divine help in this matter. His prayer was answered with Divine promptness. After the service he was told that a new tutor had arrived. 'Are you the teacher for whom I have been praying all the morning? Has the Almighty answered my prayer so quickly?,' asked R. Meir. 'Would that all your prayers might be fulfilled even as this one has been,' replied the teacher.

In 1900, at the age of fourteen, Ithamar married the daughter of R. Asher Isaiah of Kolbiesov (near Rzeszow), a descendant of Komarno and Ropszyce. R. Meir died in 1902, and was succeeded by his brother Eliezer Leib. Ithamar, after living during World War I in Vienna and Marmaros, settled in Czernowitz, which he describes as a 'Golden City'. All were welcome in his home, and other Hasidic rabbis visited him regularly. He liked to drop in on his colleagues without fanfare. 'When I long to see someone, I do not wait for an invitation.' The local rabbi remarked: 'Your home is a model not only for Czernowitz but for the whole of Bukovina.' Even the *mitnagdic* Rabbi Benzion Katz encouraged people to consult Ithamar: 'Listen to him. He does not speak empty words.'

He was a proud and loving father. 'If you have such children, you need never sigh,' a rabbi told Ithamar. As a rabbi, he was very conscientious:

Contrary to popular opinion, being a rabbi is not the easiest way to make a living. First of all, even a rabbi has a Jewish heart. It is difficult to listen day after day to tales of woe. Furthermore, to give advice is a tremendous and onerous responsibility. Often the problem is a question of life and death. It is no less difficult to advise people on monetary matters when a man's life savings depend on the advice. A rabbi's position is less defined than a doctor's. The physician knows the patient's symptoms but the Rebbe has only the patient's petition [*quittel*] in front of him. He truly needs the *Urim* and *Tummim* to provide the right guidance.

Romania was Germany's ally, and by the middle of the 1942 almost half of the Jews of Romania had been murdered. The Nazis entered Czernowitz on 5 July 1941, and between 2,000 and 3,000 Jews were slaughtered during the first twenty-four hours after the entry of the German army. The victims included the Chief Rabbi of Bukovina, R. Abraham Mark, and the leaders of the community. Ithamar and his family survived. He wanted to settle in the Holy Land but could not obtain the necessary permits from the British authorities.

After the war he settled in Washington Heights in New York, where he attracted many followers. He often officiated at the Reader's desk and read the Law. 'I read it,' said R. Ithamar with a twinkle in his eye, 'like all other Hasidic Rebbes, neither in correct Hebrew nor in accordance with the musical notations. We do not fast as often as the Lelover Rebbe nor do we sing like the Rebbe of Modzhitz, but we do our best to be Jews.' He did not approve of rabbis who become involved in politics. 'I belong to the party to which my father of revered memory belonged – the party of the Lord.' He deplored R. Joel Teitelbaum's anti-Israel activities. When a Hasid of Satmar recently told Ithamar that R. Joel was 'a Messiah', he retorted: 'If you were to say that Rabbi Joel is a great scholar, I would agree. I would also endorse the view that he is a zaddik, a giant among men, but to assert that he is the Messiah! That is ridiculous and preposterous. How could we face the world with him as the Messiah?' He attributed to luck the influence that R. Joel now wields over large masses of Hasidim. 'The owner of a Fifth Avenue store is not necessarily superior intellectually to a shopkeeper in the Bronx. The former was just lucky; Fortune smiled upon him.' He found it incomprehensible that the rabbi of Satmar forbade his followers to visit the Western Wall. 'If he lived here,' said R. Ithamar, 'he would visit the Wall.

Only in heaven is it known who is a genuine Rabbi.' However, he endorsed the Satmar Hasid's view that television is 'Satan's domain' when watched excessively and indiscriminately. The radio did not appeal to him either. 'Bad news I do not want to hear. Good news I will know in any case.'

Naturally he would have liked to see a revival of religion in the Holy Land. 'A Torah true city would be an ornament for the entire world.' He was not optimistic about the revival of interest in Hasidism in Israel and in the Diaspora. 'In bygone days, most people were observant; now it is only a tiny minority. They are the exceptions. It is unlikely that a tiny minority will transform the lives of the majority.'

Ithamar found it hard to explain the dissension and disputes among the Hasidic Rabbis before the Holocaust:

There was once a rabbi who cried bitterly when told that his opponent had died. The informant expressed surprise. 'But, Rabbi, while he was alive, you criticised him, rebuked him and even excommunicated him. Why do you weep, now that he is no longer alive?' 'How little you understand,' lamented the rabbi. 'My opponent had a haughty soul and only my attacks sustained him, acting as an antidote to his pride. Were it not for me, he would have died a long time ago.'

Death had no terrors for the Rabbi, as he advanced in years. 'I am not afraid of death, but I do not like the preliminary lodging arrangements.' His greatest joy was the fact that he had lived to see 'children, grandchildren, and great-grandchildren studying the Torah'. On 22 Sivan 1973, surrounded by his children, his grandchildren and his great-grandchildren, R. Ithamar was gathered to his fathers. His son R. Yitzhak Eizig, known as 'the rabbi of Zutzke', left Boro Park where he had lived for the previous sixteen years to take over his father's Beth Hamidrash in Tel-Aviv.

XVIII

THE TORAH CITADEL OF BNE BRAK

The greatest concentration of Hasidim in the Holy Land is to be found in Bne Brak, three miles north-east of Tel-Aviv, a Torah state in miniature. In addition to Kiryat Vizhnitz and Shikun Joel, it houses many Hasidic rabbis and their *shtieblech*. This is one of the few towns in Israel where all roads are closed to traffic on the Sabbath and on Holy Days. The yeshiva of Ponevezh, founded by R. Joseph Kahaneman (1888-1969) in 1944, now covers an area of 200,000 square feet, accommodating 1,200 students in its many buildings. In addition there are twenty-two other yeshivot, thirteen Kolelim, eleven schools of Hinuch Atzmai, a Bet Jacob seminary and over 200 synagogues.

Bne Brak, an industrial town of 60,000 people, was founded in 1924 by thirteen Polish Orthodox families led by R. Yitzhak Gerstenkorn (1891-1967). Born in Warsaw, and coming under the influence of R. Isaac Jacob Reines, he began to advocate the establishment of a Hasidic settlement in the Holy Land and formed a society, 'Bet V'Nahlah' ('Home and Inheritance'), for this purpose. Encouragement came from R. Menahem Mendel

Gutterman of Radzymin and R. Abraham Mordecai Alter of
Ger, and from both the Mizrachi and the Aguda. On 7 Adar
1922 he put a £900 deposit on 1944 dunams in Bne Brak. The
foundation-stone for the new town was laid on 11 Tammuz
1924. By 1937, there were 4,000 inhabitants, and Gerstenkorn
was appointed first mayor of Bne Brak. He wrote an eight-
volume work on the Psalms *(Ne'im Zemirot Yisrael)*, as well as
memoirs.

At the invitation of R. Gerstenkorn, R. Joseph Zevi Kalish
(1885-1957) became spiritual leader of the new settlement. R.
Kalish was the son of R. Simon of Skierniewice (1857-1927),
known as 'Rabbi Simon the Merciful'. A descendant of R.
Yitzhak of Warka, R. Kalish was the son-in-law of R. Jacob
Isaac of Biala. At first he was rabbi in Kurzuz, but when his
father died on 20 Tishri 1927, he became rabbi in Skierniewice
and in 1934 settled in Bne Brak. A tall handsome man with a
flowing white beard, he endeared himself to Hasidim of all
denominations. It was one of his customs to kindle two lights on
the eve of Sabbath, a duty most Jews delegate to their wives.

R. Gerstenkorn was succeeded as mayor by Reuven Aharon-
owitz (1903-75), a Hasid of Ger who came to the Holy Land in
1934, and by Simon Siroka of the Aguda. The Chief Rabbi of
Bne Brak, R. Jacob Landau (b.1893) was a graduate of the
Yeshiva Tomchei Temimim and a friend of R. Joseph Isaac
Schneershon of Lubavitch.

A century earlier, the town of Alexander (or Alesandrow)
had become the home of the Dancyger family, the rabbis of
Alexander. Only Ger had a larger Hasidic following in Poland,
and there were few Polish towns without one or two Alexander
shtieblech. Whilst Ger lured the scholars, Alexander drew the
baale batim (householders), the merchants and the masses. A
number of Alexander Hasidim were closely associated with the
Mizrachi.

The founder was Shraga Feivel (d.1849), but the dynasty
grew in influence and prestige under the sixteen-year

leadership of Yehiel Dancyger (1828-94) and Jerahmiel Isaac (1836-1910), author of *Yismah Yisrael*, a homiletical work on the Pentateuch. His son Isaac Menahem Mendel (1880-1943) stood at the helm for eighteen years, founding yeshivot in both Alexander and Lodz. Just as Warsaw was the stronghold of Ger, Lodz, 'the Manchester of Poland', was a centre for Alexander Hasidim and it had some thirty-five Alexander *shtieblech*. The emphasis was on good deeds, and each *shtiebel* had a fund for the needy. The rabbi kept in touch with Yitzhak David and Eleazer Mendel Biderman in Jerusalem. In his Will, he requested: 'My household effects are to be sold and the money used for charitable causes in the land of Israel.' He perished in Treblinka on 23 Elul 1943 at the age of sixty-three.

'Everything needs luck, even a Scroll of the Law in the Ark',[1] runs an adage that can be applied to the present rabbi in Bne Brak. While Ger is rebuilding its empire, Alexander remains a mere shadow of its former glory. The Hasidim of Alexander are numbered in hundreds, not thousands. There are two *shtieblech* in Tel-Aviv, one in Jerusalem, and a small yeshiva and Kolel in Bne Brak.

The rabbi of Alexander, Yehudah Moses Dancyger (1893-1973), was born in Plavna in 1893. He was the son-in-law of Bezalel Hayyim, son of R. Yehiel of Alexander. On his maternal side he was descended from R. David Dov Taub, author of commentaries on the Talmud.

Yehudah Moses studied under Yehiel Dancyger and received his Rabbinical Diploma from R. Meir Yehiel Halevi Holstock (1851-1928) of Ostrowiec, who described him as 'a great Talmudist, as well versed in the law as one of the experienced sages'. He was known as the *Ilui* ('Talmudic prodigy') of Lodz. His work *Hashuvah Le-Tovah* was acclaimed by his colleagues, and R. Kook praised his reasoning and understanding.

In 1934, with the blessing of the rabbi of Alexander, Yehudah Moses settled in Jerusalem. At first he refused to become a Rebbe and worked as a diamond-cutter. Later he was persuaded by Abraham Zevi Shur of Jerusalem to join the Hasidic Bet Din. It was not until 1947, that he agreed to assume leadership of the Hasidim at Alexander. He settled in Bne Brak and travelled to the United States to raise funds for his institutions. Commenting on the Mishnah, 'Wander forth to a home of the Torah,'[2] the rabbi said: 'Travel abroad to collect money, so that you may be able to establish in your home a home for the Torah.' The rabbi aimed at establishing charitable as well as educational institutions. Considerable rivalry had existed between the followers of Ger and Alexander in Poland. In Israel, however, there is none. 'After the Holocaust," said the rabbi, 'dissension disappeared.' His only son Abraham Menahem has succeeded him.

The dynasty of Nadvorna was represented in Bne Brak by R. Hayyim Mordecai Rosenbaum (1904–22 Tevet 1978). Born in Romania, he came to the Holy Land in 1947 and for ten years lived in Tel-Aviv. In 1960 he settled in Bne Brak, where he established a small Yeshiva Maamar Mordecai. 'Politics are lies,' said the Rebbe. 'There is no point in protesting against the lack of religion here. The most effective form of protest is to create new yeshivot.' One of the Rabbi's sons, Eizig, was killed in 1946 at the age of seventeen, when he attempted to enter as an 'illegal' immigrant on the boat *Knesset Yisrael*. The Rebbe himself spent three years in Nazi concentration camps. He was succeeded by his son R. Jacob Issachar Baer. The Rebbe's sons-in-law R. Zevi of Kfar Ata and R. Eliezer Zeev live in Ramat Gan.

Although Hasidism is generally opposed to asceticism, there have been ascetics among the zaddikim. A present-day example is R. Moses Mordecai Biderman of Lelov. He was born in 1904 in Jerusalem, and lived for two decades in Tel-Aviv before he finally made his home in Bne Brak. A descendant of the 'Holy Jew', he follows the Przysucha custom of praying late in the day. The Morning Service is rarely finished before evening. On the Sabbath he combines the midday meal with Shalosh Seudot (the third meal).

On the day that I visited him in December 1972, the large clock in his small Bet Hamidrash in Bne Brak had stopped at 4.15 pm. It was, however, already ten minutes past six, and the Sabbath was officially over. Yet the rabbi of Lelov was just emerging from his study, as he had just completed the Morning Service (Shaharit). Nine students were waiting for him. The rabbi took out a Scroll of Law. He himself was 'called up' to the Reading of the Law and made the set benedictions. In view of the lateness of the hour, he used a shortened form: 'May He who blessed our Fathers bless our young men.' He keeps on crying 'Mamme' (Mother), which the Hasidim take to mean 'the King of kings, the Holy One blessed be He.'

On 13 Heshvan (the traditional anniversary of the death of Rachel) he visits her grave at Bethlehem and then the graves of the Patriarchs at Hebron. 'When one is in trouble, one first goes to the mother and then to the father,' explained the rabbi. He has a small following, for it is difficult for people to adjust to his way of life. He spends most of the day preparing himself for prayer, praying that he should be able to pray.

R. David of Lelov, the ancestor of Moses Mordecai, used to officiate as Baal Makre (the guide for the officiant who sounds the *shophar*) on Rosh Hashanah. Hasidic legend maintains that he performs this role even after death. Moses Mordecai carries on the tradition of his family. At the Sabbath morning meal, he pays particular attention to the children.

It is sad that this gentle sage is the target of criticism from the followers of Karlin. The controversy is linked with the future of the Karlin dynasty. R. Elimelech Perlow of Karlin, perished in the Pinsk ghetto on 14 Heshvan 1942. The only surviving member of the family, the youngest son of R. Israel (d. 1921), R. Johanan escaped with partisan fighters to Russia, where his wife and elder daughter died. He and his surviving daughter Zipporah reached Palestine in 1946 and lived for a short time in Haifa. In 1948 he settled in New York where he published *Siddur Bet Aharon ve-Yisrael*,[3] a liturgical compendium of the rites and customs of Karlin. After his third visit to Israel, he died on 21 Kislev 1955 in New York and his remains were interred in Tiberias. His only male survivor was his grandson Baruch Jacob Meir Shochet, who was born in 1954. Orphaned of their spiritual leader, many Hasidim of Karlin persuaded R. Moses Mordecai Biderman to become their rabbi and to assume the title of Zaddik of the Lelov-Karlin Hasidim. They declared on 15 Av 1962:

With the help of God, and on behalf of the Karlin Hasidim in the Holy City of Jerusalem and all the cities of our Holy Land and the Diaspora, we hereby undertake to regard you as our Master, Teacher and Rebbe – our appointed leader. We trust that you will guide the holy congregation in the way of the holy forefathers of the Karlin-Stolin dynasty. We pray to Him that dwells on high that we may all be granted to advance, together with our Rebbe, to meet our righteous Messiah.

A large section of Karlin Hasidim, however, pledged their allegiance to the *yenuka* (child), and were prepared to wait for him to grow in years and wisdom. R. Moses Feinstein in New York sided with the dissidents.

Shikun Naveh Ahiezer is the home of R. Abraham Eger of Lublin. He was born in 1915, a descendant of R. Shlomo (1786-1852), who was the son of R. Akiva Eger (1761-1837), one of the foremost rabbinic authorities in Europe. In 1839, R. Shlomo succeeded his father as rabbi of Poznan. Meeting Nathan Marcus Adler (1803-90), the Chief Rabbi of British Jewry in Hanover, he tried to engage Adler in his struggle against the Reform movement.

R. Shlomo was in charge of the charitable collections for the Holy Land. From 1821 onwards, almost every synagogue in Poland had a collection-box for this purpose. R. Shlomo urged that the money should be forwarded directly to Poznan and not sent through emissaries, since overheads devoured half the money: 'Why should we deprive the poor?' Influenced by

R. Menahem Mendel of Kotzk and R. Mordecai Joseph Leiner of Izbice, his son Judah Leib (1816-88) became a Hasid and in 1852, a Rebbe. But he did not completely discard his *mitnagdic* ancestry. He would not accept *pidyonot* and lived on the income derived from a small business carried on by his wife.

A British emigré was R. Aryeh Leib Twersky, who lived in London for more than thirty years and had a small Bet Hamidrash in Bne Brak.

The son of Mordecai Zusya, Rabbi of Jassy in Romania, R. Twersky was born in 1895 in Turisk. For six years (1917-23) he lived under Soviet rule in Odessa and in Kamieniec Podolsk. He lived briefly in Warsaw, in Vienna and, on the advice of R. Israel of Czortkow, in Berlin. He said, however: 'My heart told me not to stay there.' In 1923 he became the first Hasidic rabbi to settle in England. He opened a Bet Hamidrash in the East End of London and later transferred it to North London. At that time there was no Orthodox Jewish school in London, and his three sons and his two daughters were educated by private tutors. So he had pressing personal reasons for encouraging R. Victor Schonfeld (1880-1930), head of the Union of Orthodox Congregations, to establish a Jewish Day School in North London. The rabbi's melodious services and his kindliness attracted even the indifferent and irreligious to his Bet Hamidrash.

He lived a comparatively retired life in Bne Brak. 'Everyone is a Rabbi here,' he said. 'We are not short of Rabbis, but we could do with more Hasidim.' He died on 21 Tishri 1979.

A Kolel in Bne Brak commemorates R. Shlomoh Menahem Bornstein (born in 1936), leader of the Hasidim of Sochaczew and Radomsk.

Shlomoh Menahem was a descendant of R. Abraham Bornstein (1829-1910), the author of learned Responsa. R. Abraham was steadfast in his support of the Holy Land and urged his Hasidim to settle there, provided that they were able to make a living and would not be dependent on charity. He commended

R. Israel of Pulawy on his tract *Sha'ali Shelom Yerushalayim*: 'I have examined the contents of your work and have derived much pleasure from it.' In 1898 he sent his son and son-in-law to purchase land from the Turkish overlords. The mission was abortive. However, his grandson David (b.1876) did acquire property in the Holy Land in 1938. At an Agudist Conference on 20 Tevet 1934, R. David urged the assembly to support the Yishuv. 'Only in the Holy Land,' he said, 'will the revival of Judaism take place.'

He visited Palestine, accompanied by R. Aryeh Leib Frumer. They made plans to settle there, but these were nullified by World War II. He died in Warsaw in 1942 and only one of his manuscripts survived, a commentary on the Passover Haggadah that was published posthumously in the Holy Land.

On his mother's side, R. Shlomoh Menahem was descended from R. Shlomoh Henoch Ha-Kohen Rabinowicz, rabbi of Radomsk. In the latter's book, *Tiferet Shlomoh*, he writes: 'Why should the children of Israel be impoverished and afflicted and down-trodden more than all other nations? Must the descendants of the patriarchs be subject to the despicable Egyptians?' The spiritual leaders are criticised for their apathy: 'How does it comfort a father who is languishing in prison, when his son visits him and tells him that he is making progress in Talmudic studies. Surely the father would ask, "What steps are you taking to have me released from prison?" ' Shlomoh Hanoch was a man of substance who owned a glass factory as well as properties in Sosnowiec, Cracow and Berlin. He established Yeshiva Keter Torah, which soon had thirty-six branches scattered through Poland and Galicia. When the Gestapo broke into his home, he greeted them with defiance. 'I know you are going to kill me. I prefer to die in my own home and not on a cattle wagon.' He was reciting the *Shema* when they shot him. Shlomoh Menahem's father, R. Hanoch, a brother of David of Sochaczew, was born in 1897 and at the age of twenty-eight settled in the Holy Land, where his brother-in-law R. Isaiah

Shapira lived. His son Shlomoh Menahem studied in the Yeshiva Knesset Hezkeyahu, Kfar Hasidim and in the Hebron Yeshiva Jerusalem, and married a relative of R. Joseph Ber Soloveichik. At one time he worked in an office and edited the periodical *Haod* published by the Keren Kayemet. In 1969 he became rabbi of Yad Eliyahu, Tel-Aviv. While he was on his way to visit a sick Hasid on 26 Av that year, he was killed in a road accident, leaving five children.

'The Redemption will begin when we are permitted to rebuild the Temple,' wrote R. Gershon Heinoch Leiner (1839-90). 'If we prove worthy, permission will be granted even before the Ingathering of the Exiles.' In 1887, he published a study of *Ptil Techelet* (the blue thread in the ritual fringes prescribed in the Torah, Num.15:38). The blue dye was derived from a mollusc called *halozon* in the Talmud,[4] but so complex was the process of obtaining the dye that for two thousand years Jews had ceased to include the prescribed coloured strand. R. Gershon studied the Italian seashore, became an expert on marine life and claimed to have rediscovered the *halozon (Sepia officinalis)*. A workshop for the manufacture of ritual fringes was established at the rabbi's court in Radzyn.

The last rabbi of Radzyn, R. Solomon, urged Hasidim in the ghetto of Wlodawa (near Lublin) to fight back, to escape to the forests and to join the partisans. Vehemently he denounced the collaborators: 'Whoever crosses the threshold of the *Judenrat* [the Jewish Council appointed by the Nazis], will forfeit this world and the World to Come, for they are helping to murder their fellow-Jews.' The poet Isaac Katznelson (1866-1944) wrote in tribute 'The Song concerning the Rabbi of Radzyn'. The rabbi perished at the age of thirty-four on Rosh Hodesh Sivan 1942.

The present representative of the Radzyn dynasty is R. Abraham Issachar, who married the daughter of R. Mordecai Joseph Eliezer (1865-1929). R. Abraham, whose father Israel

Engelard was the rabbi of Sosnowiec, became a partisan during World War II and after living in the United States for a number of years, settled in Bne Brak in 1968.

Near the Ponevezh yeshiva lives R. Zusya Twersky, the Rebbe of Czernobil, who was born in 1917 near Kiev in Russia. His father was R. Hayyim Yitzhak, a descendant of R. Nahum of Czernobil. He emigrated to the Holy Land before World War II, and married the daughter of R. Jacob Mordecai Brandwein. His father was exiled to a labour camp in Siberia, where he died. His mother was killed by the Nazis. For eighteen years (1941-59) he lived in Jerusalem and then settled in Bne Brak. In accordance with the tradition of Czernobil, he rarely gives discourses but maintains a Kolel of fifteen students.

One of the last rabbis to leave the Soviet Union was R. Abraham Joshua Heshel Twersky, the rabbi of Machnovka. He was born in Skvira in 1885, and is a descendant of R. Nahum of Czernobil (d.1795). His father Joseph Meir was born in 1876 and died on 29 Av 1917. The rabbi of Machnovka was persecuted by the Yevsektsiya (Jewish branch of the Russian Communist Party), and was exiled to Siberia. From 1958 to 1964 he lived in Moscow.

Like R. Baruch Rabinowicz of Holon, the rabbi claims to have a Scroll of the Torah which belonged to R. Israel Baal Shem Tov, and which had been written by his scribe Zevi Hirsch Sopher. This Scroll is used once a month. Unlike most Hasidim, the rabbi does not chant 'Lechah Dodi' ('Come, My Beloved') or 'El Adon' (God, the Lord over All Works'), but merely recites the poems. He is greatly concerned with the plight of the new immigrants from eastern Europe and does not hesitate to demand help for them. Today many Russian immigrants visit 'the Rebbe of the Proletariat' in Bne Brak.

XIX

THE LION OF THE TWENTIETH CENTURY

The two Ashlag brothers live in Bne Brak. R. Solomon Benjamin Ashlag was born in Warsaw in 1906, and is the principal of a small Kolel Ateret Ha-Talmud. In 1943 he became *dayyan* in Haifa, moving to Bne Brak in 1960. Not much love is lost between him and his elder brother Baruch Shalom. Each claims to be heir to the succession, and two decades have not healed the rift between them. Baruch lived in Manchester until 1962, and was one of the tutors of R. Solomon David Sassoon.

Head of the Ashlag family was the colourful Cabbalist Yehudah Leib Halevi Ashlag (1886-1955), a disciple of R. Meir Shalom Rabinowicz (d.1903) of Kalushin, and of his son Joshua Asher Rabinowicz (d.1938) of Porissov. He also visited R. Issachar Dov of Belz, but attributed his vast knowledge of Cabbalah to an unidentified tutor. In his youth he wrote a number of esoteric religious poems which have never been published. He also composed songs on the Psalms.[1] He was so poor that the compositions were written on scraps of paper. He was particularly concerned with the observance of the

Festival of Tabernacles and on one occasion, when the necessary 'four species' were scarce and costly, his wife sold her jewellery to obtain them.

In 1920 Yehudah Leib emigrated to the Holy Land and then for two years lived in London, first in the home of R. Joseph Lew and then in the house of Joseph Margulies.[2] During this time he studied the large collection of Cabbalist manuscripts in the British Museum. Many of these priceless documents have never appeared in print, a fact so distressing to R. Ashlag that he resolved never to write a new book unless it was sure of publication.

In 1936 he began to publish a periodical in Tel-Aviv called *Kuntres Matan Torah*, but only a few issues appeared. In these he propounded the daring theory that there was no contradiction between Judaism and socialism. It is not clear whether the publication was shut down because of its revolutionary views or because it lacked an official licence.

Ashlag became rabbi in Givat Shaul, a suburb of Jerusalem, where he established a small study circle of Cabbalists. Among his disciples were David Minzberg (now in Hayye Olam Yeshiva), Moses Jair Weinstock and Joseph Weinstock. Each student paid a small fee and the money subsidised publications. Students who could not afford the minimal sum were expected to help to sell the publications. Lessons began one hour after midnight, and lasted throughout the night. From 1940, owing to failing health, he restricted his lectures to one a week, and six years later he moved to Tel-Aviv.

R. Ashlag felt that Cabbalah was a neglected subject. Just as Gershom Scholem introduced Jewish mysticism to the secular world, so R. Ashlag reintroduced it to Jewish scholars. Like R. Isaac Judah Jehiel Safrin of Komarno (1806-74), Ashlag believed that the survival of Israel depended on the study of the Zohar, and felt that Israel's troubles were due to its neglect. 'To study Hasidic works without the Zohar is like studying the commentary of Rashi without the Pentateuch.' The study of

Cabbalah should not be restricted to an elite, but was for young and old, scholar and unlearned. Even at the tender age of nine, a child could begin to study mysticism.[3] A teacher was an asset, but not indispensable. Indeed it was better to study Cabbalah without a teacher than not to study at all. 'For with the Book of the Zohar the children of Israel will go out of exile.'[4]

He began work on his twenty-one-volume magnum opus *Ha-Sullam (The Ladder)* in Heshvan 1943 and finished it in 1954. Many attempted to dissuade him, crying: 'We are in the midst of a terrible war. The Nazis are battering at the gates of Egypt. There are shortages of food. What relevance has such a work these days?' R. Ashlag had a ready reply: 'Sword and slaughter come to the world because people fail to study the Zohar.'

The Ladder is a running commentary as well as a translation of the Zohar. It received high praise from Rabbis Joseph Hayyim Sonnenfeld, Abraham Mordecai Alter of Ger, Mordecai Rokeah, brother of the Rabbi of Belz, Jacob Friedman of Husiatyn, Nahum Mordecai Friedman of Czortkow and R. Kook.

He celebrated the conclusion of his work on 18 Iyyar 1954 at Meron, the burial-place of Simon Bar Yohai. 'I am incapable of finding the right words with which to thank God for enabling me to conclude this task,' he said. A steady stream of books testify to his industry and meticulous scholarship.[5] R. Joseph Shapotsnik, a self-styled Chief Rabbi of London, published a twenty-nine page Ashlag exposition of the *Etz Hayyim*. *The Ladder*, for all its undeniable strength, lacks Hasidic fervour. There is greater insight and moral warmth in *Tifereth Hanochi* by R. Gershon Hanoch Leiner (1829-91) of Radzyn.

R. Ashlag died on the Day of Atonement in 1955. His last words were: 'With long life will I satisfy him, and make him to behold My salvation, (Ps.91:16). He was buried on Har Ha-Menuhot in Jerusalem. At the suggestion of David Ben Gurion, an *ohel* (stone canopy) was erected over his grave. R. Ashlag's voluminous works gave an impetus to the study of Cabbalah and his works have been reprinted both in Israel and in England.

XX

HABAD IN ISRAEL

Notable among the Hasidic settlements is Kfar Habad. Situated in the Lod Valley, on the main road from Bet Dagon to Sarafand, 5 miles from Tel-Aviv, it was founded in 1949 by the rabbi of Lubavitch, Joseph Isaac Schneersohn of New York.

Habad is the acronym of the three Hebrew words *Hochmah* (Wisdom), *Binah* (Understanding) and *Da'at* (Knowledge), three kindred faculties. *Hochmah* is the initial idea, *Binah* is the development of the idea, and *Da'at* is its logical conclusion. Habad believes that the mind has domination over the heart, that faith must be allied to understanding. Lubavitch, named after a small town Lybavichi in Belorussia where the *Mittler* Rabbi (the Middle Rabbi), son of R. Shneur Zalman, made his home, has a long history of association with the Holy Land. R. Shneur Zalman, 'the Old Rebbe' (1745-1813) and the founder of Habad, believed that 'the rebuilding of the land will commence before the coming of the Messiah, and the rebuilding of Jerusalem will take place before the ingathering of the exiles.' He constantly and consistently urged his followers to support the Yishuv, 'for they who dwell in the Holy Land are zaddikim, pious men, amongst whom there is neither jealousy nor hatred, and they spend their time in study and service ... Salvation emanates from the charity we give to the Holy Land, which is the gateway to Heaven.'

Shneur Zalman himself was tempted to follow in the footsteps of R. Menahem Mendel of Vitebsk and settle in the Holy Land. He and his family, accompanied by his brothers and their families and disciples, left Liozna for Mohilev on the Dniester. For three months he wavered and could not make up his mind. According to Hasidic legend, R. Dov Baer, the Maggid of Mezeritz, appeared to R. Shneur Zalman in a dream, urging him not to leave his followers without a leader. 'I wish to inform you that I would like to settle in the Holy Land,' R. Shneur Zalman wrote in 1776 to R. Israel of Polotsk, 'but for a number of reasons it is not possible. The main obstacle is that I have no one with whom to leave my followers.'

Having denied himself the privilege of living in the Holy Land, he did his utmost to support those who settled there. He urged his Hasidim to contribute at least once a week to this deserving cause, for 'charity hastens the Redemption'. He made this point in no fewer than forty letters, and five sections in the fourth part of the Tanya deal with the subject. His letters stress four major themes: the importance of living in the Holy Land, the supremacy there of the religious leader, the need to provide financial aid, and the belief that such support hastens the Redemption. Among the ten virtues with which his followers endow him is listed his 'support for the Holy Land'.

Not content with writing letters, he travelled extensively, personally soliciting contributions. 'This is our duty and this is our life and our portion for all our labours ... We have to maintain the Yishuv in the Holy Land.' On two occasions he was imprisoned by the Russian authorities for sending large sums of money to Palestine, then under the jurisdiction of

Turkey, Russia's enemy. His ordeals in prison did not discourage him. Indeed, he believed that his exertions for the Holy Land helped to save his life.

R. Shneur Zalman's son and successor, Dov Baer of Lubavitch (1773-1827), took a similar attitude and warned those responsible for the funds not to divert the money for any other cause. He recommended placing the collection-boxes in every home and had one in his own house. Like his father, he too was accused by the Tsarist authorities of sending money to the Holy Land, 'a highly subversive act'. Like his father he too wished to settle in Hebron, site of the Cave of Machpelah. Prayers recited there were particularly praiseworthy, for tradition maintained that this was the gateway to Paradise. He quoted the views of Rabbinic authorities to the effect that a man who owned land in Hebron is saved from 'the tribulations of the grave'. He encouraged his son-in-law, R. Jacob Slonim, to settle there and the rabbi himself acquired a small plot in Hebron.

The Habad Kolel of Hebron sent Yitzhak b. Shlomoh Ashkenazi to Iran in 1830, and the Sephardim and Hasidim issued a joint appeal.[1] Emissaries from Hebron went to the East for support, and often appealed to Sir Moses Montefiore for help. The Habad group, however, sent their own emissaries, a gesture much resented by the Ashkenazim. As early as 1821, R. Moses b. Zevi Hayyim had published a five-page pamphlet in Venice, chastising Habad for breaking 'the united front'. In 1833 the traveller Menahem Mendel of Kamieniec noted in *Korot Ha-Ittem*[2] that 'the Habad Kolel in Hebron consisted of worthy people who are charitable and hospitable'.

The third rabbi of Lubavitch, R. Menahem Mendel (1789-1866), known as the *Zemah Zeddek*, actively supported the Yishuv during his thirty-five years of leadership. He sent money to establish synagogues in Safed, Hebron, Tiberias and Jerusalem. By 1872, there were 489 people living in Hebron. They had their own Hevrah Kadisha, Hevrat Bikkur Holim (Society for Visiting the Sick) and Hahnasat Kallah to assist the poor and the orphaned in their marriage preparations, including the provision of dowries. Sir Moses Montefiore contributed £5 a year towards the funds of the society. An interesting group was Ole Regalim, headed by R. Zalman Slonim. It enabled ten members of the community to visit Jerusalem at the Festivals. Lots were drawn to select the people, and each pilgrim received £2 sterling to help to defray their expenses.

It is not certain whether the present Habad Synagogue in the Old City of Jerusalem stands on the site of the original Habad Synagogue which was established in 1848 and administered by R. Elijah Joseph Rivlin, author of *Ohole Yoseph*. The Habad community consisted of fifty families. It was at first called Das Mosheh Vi-Yehudit but in 1866 the name was changed to Bet Menahem V'Knesset Eliyahu. By then there was also a ritual bath, a small Talmud Torah and such ancillary bodies as a Society for Visiting the Sick. The synagogue was financed by the contributions of Sir Albert (Abdullah) Sassoon (1818-96), first Baronet of Kensington Gore, Elias Sassoon (1820-90) and Reuben Sassoon (1835-1905). The Hebrew periodical *Havazzelet* (18 Tammuz 1879) records that Elias gave £200 pounds sterling in memory of his wife Leah Farhi, and the synagogue was renamed Knesset Eliyahu. Habad Hasidim lived in Baron Street and Habad Street in the Old Jewish Quarter of Jerusalem until it was occupied by the Arab Legion in 1948. The Habad Synagogue in the Old City was the first synagogue to be renovated after the Six-Day War.

R. Shalom Dov Baer (1860-1920), the fifth Rabbi of Lubavitch, was antagonistic to Zionism and criticised Herzl for 'desecrating the Torah' by entering Jerusalem with his head uncovered and for visiting the Temple Mount. He believed that Herzl was interested primarily in 'a State anywhere', not necessarily in the Holy Land, since Herzl had at first permitted discussion about the settlement of Jews in other parts of the world. In 1881 when pogroms broke out in the southern provinces of Russia and the police stood by watching the murder and pillage, the Rabbi of Lubavitch remarked:

If they had listened to me, a great many Jewish lives could have been saved. I wanted to say to them [the representatives of the Russian government], if you do not improve your attitude towards the Jews, I will settle in the land of Israel, and will take hundreds of thousands of Jewish families with me. And I would have done it. But at that point, Bilu was established. If only they had been motivated by religious ideals, I would have joined them.

In 1911 a relative of R. Shalom Dov Baer, Shneur Zalman (son of Levi Yitzhak), settled in Haderah and married the daughter of the wealthy philanthropist Joseph Hindin. During World War I, his son-in-law Levi Yitzhak joined *Nili* (Hebrew initials of 'The Glory of Israel will not lie'–I Sam.15:29), the pro-British and anti-Turkish underground organisation headed by Aaron Aaronsohn. In 1912 Yeshivat Torat Emet under the leadership of R. Shlomoh Zalman Havlin was established in Hebron. Fifteen disciples were sent by the rabbi to study there, but with the outbreak of war in 1914 they had to return to Russia.

R. Joseph Isaac Schneersohn (1880-1950) visited the Holy Land for seventeen days in Av 1929, meeting the religious leaders Rabbis Sonnenfeld, Kook and Meir, and the Chief Justice of the High Court, Mr Gad Frumkin. 'During the twelve days that I have been in Jerusalem,' said the rabbi, 'I have gained a lot and I have achieved a lot. I visited every place. I leave Jerusalem, taking with me the tremendous impression it has made on me. May God grant that the Messiah should be revealed soon so that the passing of time should not cool the feelings I have.' It was his wish that a Hasidic settlement be established in the Holy Land and many years later this wish was fulfilled.

In Kfar Habad, on the ruins of a former Arab village, Safariya, there are nearly 400 families, most of them engaged in farming. The settlement began with seventy-four families in 1949 and they were soon joined by another fifteen from Morocco and by Russian immigrants. Conditions were extremely primitive, but with the Rabbi's encouragement the pioneers persisted.

In the Kfar Habad Talmud Torah (established in 1954) the timetable is evenly divided between Talmudic and secular studies. The pride of the settlement is Yeshivat Tomhe Temimim, where 200 students between the ages of seventeen and twenty-five are enrolled. Every morning before the service and every evening after dinner, there are lectures on Habad. On the Sabbath, at the Third Meal, a student recites one of the rabbi's discourses which he has learnt by heart. Special departments cater for students from Morocco and Yemen, for students who wish to qualify for the Rabbinical Diploma, and for those who wish to become ritual slaughterers. Attached to the Yeshiva is a Kolel (also established in 1954) for advanced students of Rabbinics. 'An excellent thing is the study of the Torah combined with some worldly occupation', says the Mishnah,[3] and Kfar Habad also offers vocational training which makes it a rarity among yeshivot, both *mitnagdic* and Hasidic, where the ideal is the study of the Torah for its own sake.

With the help of the Joint (American Jewish Joint Distribution Committee), and ORT (Organisation for Rehabilitation through Training), Kfar Habad has set up a printing press. Much of the machinery was provided by the Jewish Master Printers and the Jewish Aid Committee in London. There is also an agricultural school, carpentry, locksmith and tool-shops, and facilities for training in electronics and motor mechanics. R. Joshua's Talmudic dictum:[4] 'Give half to God and keep half yourselves', is taken literally in Kfar Habad. Students devote fifty-eight hours a week to intensive study of the Bible, Talmud, Laws, Hasidism and secular subjects; the rest of the time is allotted to vocational training.

Two hundred girls attend the Bet Rivka school set up in 1959 and the teacher training seminary. The comprehensive curriculum provides the students with a broad education according to the requirements of the Ministry of Education. Graduates of the seminary have become teachers at Habad schools in the USA, France and Italy. In the words of the rabbi, 'The Bet Rivka schools must become a spiritual centre not only for Kfar Habad, not even only for Israel, but for the whole world.'

The Vocational Departments, too, provide the students with extensive religious training as well as the general education required by the Ministry of Education. The latest addition to the village is a youth centre known as Bet Shazar (House of Shazar), in honour of President Zalman Shazar who was named after the first rabbi of Habad.

On 2 Iyyar 1955 five students and a teacher were reciting the Evening Service when they were murdered by Arab terrorists. The rabbi exhorted the inhabitants not to panic, and a special institute called Yad Ha-Hamishah (Memorial of the Five) School of Printing and Graphic Arts was set up in their memory. To strengthen the village, Georgian families were encouraged to settle there, and a piece of the Soviet Union has now been transplanted to Kfar Habad.

Many young people visit Kfar Habad on the Sabbath, on Festivals, on the High Holydays and on other occasions, when Habad Hasidim celebrate in characteristic fashion. At regular *Farbrengen* (get-togethers), they study the Tanya and *Likkute Torah*, a series of mystical commentaries on the Pentateuch by R. Shneur Zalman, as well as the discourses of the present rabbi. They analyse the doctrines of Habad, intellectual contemplation fused with emotion and *hitlahavut* (ardour), the twin rich legacies of Hasidism.

Yeshiva students are exempted by law from military service, but during the Sinai campaign of 1956, a number of Kfar Habad students waived their right and joined the army. After the war, members of the settlement set up a programme headed by Mrs Shifra Golopowitz, herself a war widow, for the families of the bereaved. The orphans receive special care and their education is carefully supervised. Periodically a group of boys are gathered together to celebrate their Bar Mitzvah. Every guest family is boarded with a Kfar Habad family which has children of a similar age, and close friendships have resulted from these groupings.[5]

'U-faratzta' ('And thou shalt spread abroad,' Gen.28:14) is the theme of a lively melody popular with Lubavitch Hasidim and this is the motto of the present rabbi of Lubavitch, Menahem Mendel Schneerson, who celebrated his seventieth birthday on 11 Nisan (March 1973). From his headquarters at 770 Eastern Parkway in Brooklyn, the rabbi directs his spiritual empire and expands the already far-reaching manifold activities of the movement. Some 3,000 people a year consult him on personal matters. There are fourteen Lubavitch day schools in the USA with a roll of 4,000 students, and all over the world there are Lubavitch institutions.

Religious Jews are often charged with living in self-made ghettos, indifferent to their less observant co-religionists. But such charges cannot be made against Lubavitch. The main strength of Lubavitch was in Tsarist Russia, and the 1917 Revolution was a death-blow to Lubavitch Hasidim. When R. Joseph Isaac left the Soviet Union he had almost to create a new movement.

In the nineteenth century and in the first decade of the twentieth century, Lubavitch emissaries had spread Hasidic fervour to remote villages throughout Russia. In this tradition their modern counterparts carry the message to the campuses of universities in the western world. The rabbi is anxious to expand his activities in Israel. A second Habad village has been established near the first one. The corner-stone was laid in March 1969, on the rabbi's sixty-seventh birthday, and the new village will eventually accommodate 5,000 people, mainly immigrants from the Soviet Union. The first building will be a vocational high school for girls.

After Kfar Habad, the largest Habad settlement is Nahlat Har Habad, near Kiryat Malachi, established in 1969, where there are now over 400 families, including many recent immigrants from Georgia. It has an industrial school, a diamond-polishing factory and even a Kolel, established in 1969.

Shikun Habad, established in 1961 in the north-west of Jerusalem, has modern apartments for 116 families, a Talmud Torah for 200 children, a kindergarten, Gan Hannah for 80 children, and a girls' school (Bet Hannah), named after the rabbi's mother, for 180 children. Yeshiva Torah Emet is now the main centre for Habad learning in the Holy City. Another Habad Shikun is rising rapidly in Lod.

Educational Lubavitch establishments in Israel include Yeshiva Torah Emet in Meah Shearim, as well as small branches in various other regions. There are twenty Ohole Yoseph Yitzhak schools and kindergartens in the United States. In 1968 a small group of pioneers headed by a young rabbi, Levinger, settled in Hebron against the will of the Israeli government, and the rabbi of Lubavitch was asked by settlers to help with the revival of the town. He promised to send 100 yeshiva students from Habad institutions in Italy, but the decision of the Israeli authorities is still pending.

Unlike other Hasidic institutions which were created primarily to cater for their own followers, Lubavitch aims towards a wider community. Its objective is to create new Hasidim. In all, 8,000 pupils are educated under the auspices of Lubavitch. Nor are the adults ignored. Lubavitch stresses that however estranged a Jew may be from Torah-true Judaism, he can be made conscious of his heritage, provided that the right approach is used.

The Ze'ire Agudat Habad (Young Habad) is charged with many activist missions designed to bring Judaism to Jews. They blow the *shophar* at the New Year for patients in hospitals, and have for many years carried out 'Operation *tephillin*'. Thousands of visitors to the Western Wall are urged to put on phylacteries and recite the appropriate benedictions. 'The commandment of *tephillin*', says the rabbi of Lubavitch 'unites mind and heart, intellect and emotion'.

The rabbi has recently intensified his attacks on the state of religion in Israel. He has accused the Ministers of the National Religious Party of displaying insufficient zeal, and he is dissatisfied with the separation of religion and state in Israel, since it is inappropriate for a people who are 'destined to be a kingdom of priests, and a holy nation'. He believes that the Torah encompasses the universe: every new invention, theory, piece of knowledge, thought and action. Everything that happens now must be interpreted from the point of view of the Torah.

The rabbi opposes mass meetings and public protests against the Soviet authorities on behalf of Russian Jews. His own approach is based on *shtadlanut* persuasion at diplomatic level. He called upon the Orthodox ministers of the Israel government to show 'the same courage in protecting the honour of the Torah as the soldiers on the Suez Canal are showing in protecting Israel's frontiers.' In 1972 he secured the release of a number of yeshiva students arrested on a charge of arson. He persuaded the aged Chief Rabbi Unterman to stand for re-election in 1973 and attacked Chief Rabbi Goren's ruling on the Langer case, and even told him to resign.

So far the rabbi has not set foot inside Israel. However, lengthy discourses are relayed by telephone throughout the world. 'I have not left Brooklyn since my father-in-law's death,' he told Baroness Birk in 1972. Contrary to popular belief and despite the glare of publicity and elaborate public relations, Lubavitch in Israel is not very numerous; Ger, Belz and Vizhnitz have a greater following. But the fervour, dedication and intense loyalty of the adherents more than compensate for lack of numbers.

XXI

A HASIDIC ISLAND IN A SECULAR SEA

It was a young shepherd's lovesong that caught the fancy of R. Yitzhak Eizig (1751-1821) of Kalev (Nagy Kallo) in northern Hungary: 'Royz, royz, vi vayt biztu? Vald, vald, vi groyz biztu? Volt di royz nisht azoy vayt geven, volt der vald nicht azoy groys geven.' ('Rose, rose , how far away are you? Forest, forest, how vast are you? If the rose were not so far away, the forest would not seem so vast.') He substituted *'Shechinah'* (Divine Presence) for 'rose' and *'Galut'* (Exile) for 'forest', and created a song that inspired and consoled generations of Hasidim. He sang the tune to the following words: 'Holy Spirit, how far away are you? Exile, Exile, how long are you? If the Holy Spirit were not so distant, then the Exile would not seem so long.'

'Father in Heaven,' he once said, 'You must be my father, I have no other God beside You. Show me the green pasture where I may feed my flock.' The simple faith of this untutored shepherd impressed R. Leib Sarahs, a contemporary of R. Israel Baal Shem Tov, and he made him a shepherd of men. He took the youth for guidance to R. Shmelke Horowitz of

Nikolsburg and R. Elimelech of Lyshansk. Later Yitzhak Eizig established his court in Kalev, in his native Hungary, where he lived for forty years. He never lost the common touch and would often interject Hungarian words into his dialogues with the Almighty. Thousands of Hungarian Hasidim sing his song 'Szol a kakas mar' ('The Cock Crows'), and according to R. Hayyim Halberstam, the Ministering Angels joined in the refrain. Yitzhak Eizig's contemporaries held him in high esteem: 'The light that emanates from his *Seder*', remarked the Seer of Lublin, 'illumines the whole world.'

The rabbi's melodies often expressed longing for Zion and the Redemption. Once, on the Second Day of the Festival of Passover, he approached the Reader's desk for the Evening Service without first donning the *tallit*. His son approached him and handed his father the prayer-shawl. The rabbi accepted it with reluctance, saying: 'My children, I was completely absorbed in the atmosphere of the Holy Land, where the Second Day is not observed. Hence I approached the Reader's desk without a prayer-shawl, as I did not feel the sanctity of the Festival.'

R. Yitzhak Eizig died at the age of seventy on 7 Adar 1821. His burial-place at Nagy Kallo became the Meron of Hungary, a place of pilgrimage for his Hasidim. 'From the synagogue to the cemetery where the zaddik is buried,' said R. Naphtali of Ropszyce, 'you feel the atmosphere of Jerusalem.' The Hebrew spelling of the place-name 'Kalev' was taken as an acrostic of Psalm 145:18: 'The Lord is nigh unto all them that call upon Him, to all that call upon Him in truth.'

The songs of Kalev are now heard in Kiryat Kalev near Rishon L'Ziyyon, a town in the Judean coastal plain founded in 1882 by Russian Bilu pioneers. Kiryat Kalev was established on 7 Adar 1967 by R. Menahem Mendel Taub, a sixth-generation descendant of R. Yitzhak Eizig, and these songs are now becoming familiar to the 33,000 inhabitants of Rishon L'Ziyyon.

The Kirya has one of the most beautiful synagogues in the State of Israel. The five chandeliers are made up of 613 lamps – equivalent to the 613 commandments listed in the Pentateuch. Each lamp has been fashioned like a miniature Scroll of the Torah. As a visible reminder of the glory that was Kalev, two bricks of the original synagogue in Hungary have been placed in a prominent position on the eastern wall.

Hasidic *shtieblech* are generally devoid of artistic embellishments, relying for their atmosphere on the ardour of the worshippers rather than on the artistry of the décor. Kiryat Kalev synagogue is a noteworthy exception. 'This is my God, and I will glorify Him' (Exod. 15:2) – a verse that is interpreted to mean that precepts should be observed in a manner that is aesthetically pleasing – was taken literally by the rabbi of Kalev.

The four walls of the synagogue present a pictorial history of Judaism. The southern wall depicts the tent of Abraham, the binding of Isaac, the dream of Jacob, the giving of the Ten Commandments, Aaron the High Priest and the city of Hebron. These are flanked by David's citadel and a symbolic representation of six tribes, Dan, Naphthali, Gad, Asher, Joseph and Benjamin.

On the western wall are scenes showing the life of Jonah, the prophet Elijah, the exploits of Samson, the division of the Red Sea, the crossing of the River Jordan, the sun standing still at Gibeon and Daniel's exploits. The lower panel illustrates the Six Days of Creation.

The northern wall features the burning bush, King David and his harp, Isaac musing in the field and the fiery furnace of the Book of Daniel. The lower panel shows the tribes of Reuben, Simeon, Levi, Judah, Issachar and Zebulun. The eastern Wall, with its impressive Ark, has representations of the Western Wall of the Temple and Hebron. The painter was a local artist, Jacob Epstein, whose sheer inventive resourcefulness more than compensates for lack of creative originality.

R. Menahem Mendel, the present rabbi, was born in Mar-
ghita in Romania in 1918. His father, Yehuda Yehiel, rabbi in
Rosla, died when his son was twenty. Two weeks before World
War II, Menahem Mendel married Hannah Sarah Shiphra,
daughter of R. Phinehas Shapira, Rabbi of Kechinev, a descendant of the Rabbi of Nadvorna. He was barely twenty-one
when the war broke out and, to use his own expression, went
through 'the seven fires of Gehenna'. He was imprisoned in
several concentration camps, including Belsen, and together
with the Rabbi of Klausenburg was taken to Warsaw after the
liquidation of the ghetto. Every day, every hour, he faced a
fearful death. On one occasion, death was so imminent that he
made his confession and prepared to die. At the very last instant
an SS officer drove up to conscript workers, and the rabbi was
taken to a labour group. He was liberated on the last day of the
war. His wife had been sent to a different concentration camp,
but they were eventually reunited. His father-in-law, however,
perished on 3 Sivan 1944.

The intervention of his brother-in-law enabled the rabbi to
emigrate to the United States, and he settled in Cleveland,
Ohio. He believed that he had been spared for a very special
reason – to revive Judaism in the free world. In the home town
of R. Hillel Silver, a centre of Reform Judaism, the rabbi set up
a yeshiva for fifty students. Later he moved to New York,
where he published *Zophnat Paneah*[1] (discourses on the Torah
and Festivals) by his father-in-law.

After seventeen years in the United States, the rabbi longed
to settle in the Holy Land. On the verse of Isaiah 40:3: 'Hark!
one calleth: "Clear ye in the wilderness the way of the Lord",'
he commented: 'Now that eastern Europe has been turned to a
wilderness, and the soil drenched with the blood of six million
Jewish dead, Jews are summoned to return home and rehabili-
tate the Holy Land.' Carefully he searched for the right site.
The Torah environment of Bne Brak impressed him. 'But if I
settle in Bne Brak, what will happen to the rest of Israel?' he

asked. In 1967 he planned a project at Toheret (near Kfar
Habad) with a thousand housing units. R. Aaron of Belz told
him encouragingly: 'Rabbi of Kalev, Rishon L'Ziyyon is waiting for you . . . You are destined to achieve great things here.'

The rabbi has also launched a number of educational projects. From time to time he and his entourage leave Rishon
L'Ziyyon and spend the Sabbath in different parts of Israel. 'I
hate political parties,' he says, 'but I love Jews.' He has a
missionary spirit and feels he has the ability to redeem people.
'Together we dance, we pray, we sing, we partake of the
Sabbath meals, we give discourses. Then everybody is bound
to feel the sanctity of the Sabbath which I call "Der Lebedige
Tog" ("the Living Day"). He is a spellbinding story-teller, a
man of great charm and phenomenal energy.

He does not approve of Orthodox Jews creating their own
ghettos. He maintains that the Torah is the heritage of the
entire congregation of Israel. Every Jew has a part in it and no
Jew is exempt from studying it. He has launched an education
drive, 'Bar B'rav d'had Yoma' ('One Day Scholar scheme') to
provide every area with facilities for adult Torah education.

The rabbi maintains a Kolel where the students are expected
to help him to further his educational schemes. Some of them
are engaged in examining *mezuzot* and have discovered that
many of them are not valid, as they contain printed not hand-
written texts of the first two paragraphs of the *Shema*. Some
mezuzot even contain the priestly benediction or assorted
prayers.

Recently the rabbi dedicated a new centre, Mishkan Kalev in
Tiberias (near Kiryat Shmuel), a town which has a special
importance for the Hasidim of Kalev. They believe that
Yitzhak Eizig miraculously used to immerse himself in the
legendary 'well of Miriam' which accompanied the children of
Israel through their wanderings in the wilderness and was
ultimately absorbed into the waters of Lake Tiberias. The rabbi
hopes that Mishkan Kalev will eventually attract tourists. He is

also planning a centre in Jerusalem and the establishment of a Bet Hamidrash near the grave of Simon Bar Yohai. Kalev is hardly a mass movement. The rabbi's success lies in his individualistic approach and his creativity. Almost every day he comes up with new ideas for strengthening religion in the State of Israel.

XXII

THE LOVE-HATE SYNDROME OF SATMAR

Perhaps no Hasidic rabbi of the twentieth century provoked as much veneration and as much antagonism as R. Joel Teitelbaum of Satmar (Satu Mare in north-west Romania), which belonged, until World War I, and between 1940 and 1944, to Hungary. Idolised by some, and vilified by others, his entire career has been engulfed in fierce controversies.

Founder of the dynasty was R. Moses Teitelbaum (1759-1841), author of *Yismah Mosheh*, a homiletical commentary on the Pentateuch. R. Moses was born in Przemysl in Galicia, and was a disciple of R. Jacob Isaac of Lublin. At the age of twenty-six he became rabbi in Sianawa, where he lived for twenty-three years and later he settled in Ujhely (Ohel). It was his learned son-in-law, R. Aryeh Lipshitz, who converted him to Hasidism. He had visions of R. Yitzhak Luria and R. Hayyim Vital, and he believed that he had had three previous incarnations on earth. In one of his dreams he revisited the Paradise of the *tannaim*, and marvelled when he saw one of the masters studying the tractate Bava Kamma ('The First Gate'). He was told, 'You seem to think that the *tannaim* are in Paradise, but that is not so. Paradise is in the *tannaim*.'

R. Moses lived in daily expectation of the coming of the Messiah. Each night before he went to sleep he would prepare his Sabbath clothes, and remind his beadle to wake him the moment the Messiah arrived. Like R. Levi Yitzhak of Berdichev, R. Moses would hold 'public dialogues' with the Almighty. Once on the eve of the Day of Atonement, when he was eighty-two, he exclaimed: 'Master of the Universe, had I known in my youth that I would grow old before the coming of the Messiah, I would not have been able to survive all these years. I would have died in anguish. Only faith and hope kept me alive to this day.' He lived in an old decrepit house and refused to let his Hasidim provide him with a more suitable home. 'Why should I build a home here in the land of the Gentiles? Surely the Messiah will come soon, and I will return to the land of my forefathers.' The Messianic yearning became an obsession. When he heard a noise, he would ask, 'Has he arrived?' Once he remarked, 'I cannot understand why the zaddikim in the World of Eternity are not trying to hasten the coming of the Messiah. They should turn heaven and earth upside down. Perhaps when they enter Eden, they become oblivious to what happens to mortal man.' On another occasion, he cried out, 'Lord of the Universe, grant my request and let the Messiah come. I am not concerned for my own welfare. My main concern is that the Divine Presence should suffer no longer.' Hasidim attributed to R. Moses the soul of Jeremiah, the prophet who lamented the destruction of Judea and Jerusalem.

His grandson Yekutiel Zalman Judah Teitelbaum (1808-83), son of R. Eleazar Nisan of Drohobycz, was rabbi in a number of communities – Stropkov, Ohel, Gorlice, Drohobycz and Sighet. He was the author of the Responsa collections *Avne Zedek* and *Yitev Lev*[2] on the Pentateuch and the Festivals. His son Hananiah Yom Tov Lipa (1836-1904) succeeded his father as rabbi in Sighet. He engaged in a fiery controversy with the Rabbi of Vizhnitz over responsibility for the charitable collections for the Holy Land (Rabbi Meir Baal Ha-Nes). A court of five rabbis under R. Moses Grünwald (1853-1910), Rabbi of Huszt in Carpatho-Russia, decided to divide the collections into two parts, one under the Rabbi of Vizhnitz and the other under the Rabbi of Sighet.

R. Joel Teitelbaum was born in Sighet in 1888 and studied under his father and with a private teacher, Jacob Hirsch Turner. He was ordained by R. Moses ben Aaron Greenwald and in 1904 married Havah, the daughter of R. Abraham Hayyim Horowitz, rabbi of Plantsheh in Galicia, a descendant of Ropszyce and Dzikov. As a wedding-present, R. Joel asked his father for a pair of Rabbenu Tam phylacteries. (Rabbenu Tam, a twelfth-century authority, differed from Rashi as to the order of the texts on the four parchments, and some pious people put on two pairs of *tephillin* according to the two versions.) 'Do not worry,' his father assured him. 'You will have mine.' Hananiah Yom Tov Lipa's premonition came true, as he died a few days after his son's wedding, on 29 Shevat 1904. R. Joel's elder brother Hayyim Hirsch (1881-1926), the author of *Atzei Hayyim*[3] on the Torah and the Festivals, was appointed rabbi in Sighet, an appointment opposed by R. Joel. However, the Rabbis of Vizhnitz, Munkacs and Spinka supported the elder brother.

When R. Joel visited the court of R. Issachar Dov Rokeah of Belz, he was asked to officiate at the Additional Service for the Sabbath. After the service, the rabbi of Belz whispered in his ear, 'You should get yourself a *tilip*' (coat, the traditional mantle worn by rabbis). From 1906 he lived privately in Satmar, where he established a yeshiva. When the Rabbi of Satmar, R. Judah Grünwald (1845-1920), was asked whether he had any objection to R. Joel living in the town, he replied, 'Unworthy and selfish people settle here all the time without asking my permission. A saintly man moves here and I am asked whether I object. I am delighted to have him.'

R. Joel chose the ascetic path. Most weekdays he would fast and sleep on a hard bench. Only on the Sabbath would he eat normal meals, and sleep in a bed. His first rabbinic post was in Orsova, in the Hungarian district of Ugoca. Subsequently in 1926 he became rabbi in Krolleh (Carei or Nagy Karoly). It was there that he became a vehement opponent of Zionism, and issued instructions that no one who contemplated aliyah to the Holy Land should be called up to the Reading of the Law. On one occasion when his ruling was ignored, he closed the synagogue. R. Joel participated with R. Hayyim Eleazar Shapira in the anti-Zionist conference convened at Csap (Cop) on 3 Tammuz 1923. Although he regarded Zionism as 'a child of the devil', he did not, unlike Hayyim Eleazar, indulge in curses or excommunications.

In 1926 R. Joel's brother Hayyim Hirsch died at Kleinwardein at the age of forty-five, after being rabbi in Sighet for twenty-two years. R. Joel at first would not permit Hayyim Hirsch's son, R. Zalman Leib, to succeed to his father's post. Eventually peace was made and Zalman Leib became both the Rabbi of Sighet and also R. Joel's son-in-law.

R. Joel was continually embroiled in controversies. He urged the appointment of R. Samuel Gross as his successor in Krolleh, while others favoured R. Abraham Abish Horowitz, the son of the Melitzer Rebbe and the son-in-law of Yitzhak Eizig Weiss of Spinka. The community was divided, and even the civic authorities were involved in this unseemly quarrel.

Satmar had a Jewish population of 15,000, half of whom were Hasidim. For fifty years R. Zeev Mandelbaum (d.1896) had led the community. His successors were R. Judah Grünwald, who was rabbi in Satmar for twenty-two years and established a large yeshiva, and R. David Grünwald (d.1928). It also had a non-Orthodox community of 300 families under the leadership of Dr Samuel Zangwill Jordan. Satmar also had the first Hebrew kindergarten in Hungary.

The death of R. Grünwald started a bitter quarrel lasting for nearly four years over the appointment of a suitable successor. Hebrew tracts were published by the supporters of R. Joel's

candidature as well as by his vehement opponents. This con-
troversy ended in a decisive victory for R. Joel, who became the
Rabbi of Satmar in 1934. He appointed his son-in-law Hananiah
Yom Tov Lipa of Sassov as head of the Satmar Bet Din.

R. Joel devoted himself from 1934 to 1939 with unsparing
energy to converting Satmar into a stronghold of Orthodoxy.
With his keen mind and sharp wit he would go straight to the root
of any problem. After the Sabbath service he would visit stores
that were open for business, pleading with the owners to close for
the day, often succeeding in persuading them. His yeshiva soon
catered for nearly 400 students. Concerned not only with high
standards of scholarship but also with the material needs of his
charges, he set up a Bet Tavshil (soup-kitchen) nicknamed
'Minza', to provide hot midday meals. In addition, each student
received 1 kilo of bread every morning. To supervise these
activities, he organised the Tomhe Dal (Supporters of the Poor)
committee.

Taharat Mishpacha (family purity), the laws of ritual clean-
liness, became one of his main preoccupations. The *mikva* at
Satmar was constructed according to his detailed specifications.
The water had to be either natural spring water, rainwater, or
water obtained from melting ice. The Supervisor kept a register
to make sure that no one evaded this religious duty. The rabbi
would not permit a wedding to take place unless he was assured
that no non-Orthodox practice, such as mixed dancing, would be
allowed.

R. Joel's personal life was beset with tragedy. Of his three
daughters, two died before World War II, another died after it
and his wife died in Satmar in 1936. 'This happens to a sinner',
said the rabbi, resigning himself to the will of God. Two years
later he married Feige Rachel from Czenstochowa, a descendant
of Sanz and Kozienice.

From 1938 to 1941 Hungary received territorial gains at the
expense of Czechoslovakia, Romania and Yugoslavia. These
added 300,000 Jews to Hungary's Jewish community of

500,000. By mid-1941, Hungary was called upon to deliver supplies to Germany and had to force the population into the war effort. Jews aged twenty-one to forty-five were mobilised into labour battalions, building roads, digging canals and working in factories and quarries. R. Joel advised his followers to evade conscription and not to co-operate with the authorities.

On 8 August 1941 the Nuremberg Laws were enforced in Hungary, and thousands of Jews who were unable to produce proof of Hungarian nationality were deported. In January 1943 a Zionist Committee for Mutual Assistance – the Vaada (Vaad Ezra V-Hazzalah B'Budapest) – was set up in Budapest under Otto Komoly, Dr Rezso Kasztner, Samuel Springmann and Joel Brand. On 19 March 1944 German forces occupied Hungary, and Adolf Eichmann and his assistants Krumey, Hunsche, Dannecker and Wisliceny began the 'Final Solution' of the Jewish problem. Within three months of Eichmann's arrival in Budapest, a total of 437,402 Hungarian Jews had been deported to Auschwitz. R. Joel, together with his wife and the beadle Joseph Ashkenazi, escaped to Klausenburg in a Red Cross ambulance. On 3 May 1944 they were arrested and taken to Bergen-Belsen where they remained until December. One potato a day was their only source of sustenance.

Dr Kasztner, vice-president of the Zionist Organisation in Budapest, together with his assistant Joel Brand, began to negotiate with Eichmann for 'Blut für Ware' (blood for goods). The Nazis were willing to spare the lives of the 350,000 Hungarian Jews and even let them leave the country if the Allies would send Germany important war stocks including 10,000 army lorries – an offer which the Allies refused to consider. Kasztner also began to negotiate for a special 'test convoy' to enable 1,684 people to reach a neutral country. He enlisted the help of Sally Mayer, the director of the American Joint Distribution Committee, and Dr Chaim Posner of the Palestinian Office at Geneva. Himmler demanded 20,000,000 Swiss francs and 5,000,000 francs were paid. At first Josef Fischer, Kasztner's father-in-law, was against the inclusion of the anti-Zionist rabbi. His mother, however, appeared to Fischer in a dream and urged him to include the rabbi. R. Joel refused to curtail his denunciations of Zionism. The train left Budapest on 20 June and stopped for three days at Moson-Magyarovar, and also made short stops at Vienna and Linz, and on 8 July it reached Bergen-Belsen near Hanover, where R. Joel joined them. Among R. Joel's companions on the 'Noah's Ark' (as the train was called) were Philipp von Freudiger, President of the Budapest Orthodox community, Councillor Samuel Stern, Chairman of the Progressive Jewish community, Dr Szondi, a psychologist of world-wide renown, a number of rabbis, extreme right-wing revisionists and many orphans. The dire threat of the train being diverted to Auschwitz was always with them, and it was only after protracted negotiations that the train reached the Swiss border on 8 December 1944 (21 Kislev, a day now celebrated by the Hasidim of Satmar as a festive day). The rabbi arrived in Geneva and stayed for several months in the home of a Hasid, Moses Gross.

It was through the efforts of Chief Rabbi Herzog that he was allowed to travel to Palestine. He arrived in 1945, but soon decided to settle in Williamsburg, in Brooklyn, where he arrived in the autumn of 1946. He revisited Israel in 1952, 1956 and 1965, went to England in 1952 and 1965, and to Vienna in 1955. When in Israel he visited the Rabbi of Belz in Katamon, and urged him not to associate himself with the election manifesto of the Knesset. On this occasion R. Joel's effort proved to be fruitless. 'In the United States,' he remarked, 'they give me money and I give advice. Here in Israel I give money and others give me advice.'

With the influx of refugees from Hungary, Czechoslovakia and Romania, many Hasidic families settled in Williamsburg. The Satmar community (Kehal Yitev Lev D'Satmar), a self-sufficient and cohesive entity, was headed by R. Joel, who had a remarkable flair for organisation. Satmar issues periodicals and a weekly newspaper (*Der Yid*); it has its own welfare organisations, a holiday fund for orphaned children, insurance and pensions schemes, an emergency rescue service and a burial society. It operates its own butcher-shops and supervises a variety of processed foods. It maintains *mikvaot*, a *Shatnez* laboratory, a kindergarten, a Bet Rachel school for girls, and a bakery where hand-made matzot are prepared.

The yeshiva building, a converted naval yard, acquired by the property magnate, Getzel Berger of London, is the biggest yeshiva in the world with 850 students. It includes dormitories and *mikvaot*, and has an annual budget of three million dollars. It is not unusual to find 700 worshippers on a weekday in the large synagogue. In all, the Satmar community is responsible for the education of 4,000 children, and thirty-two buses transport them to and from the Satmar establishments. After finishing at the Talmud Torah, they continue their studies in the yeshiva and eventually in the Kolel. The girls can choose between commercial courses and studying for a teaching diploma. With the exception of Yeshiva University, Satmar has the largest Jewish educational organisation in the western world.

In order to cover its mounting budget, Satmar relies on tuition fees, with state aid for transport, textbooks and luncheons. To become a member of the Satmar community, a man must undertake to observe the Sabbath, and bring up his children in the Orthodox tradition. A committee of three investigates the religious and moral suitability of every applicant. In all, there are more than 5,000 member families, numbering approximately 35,000 to 40,000 in all.

R. Joel was the author of a number of learned works,[4] and was regarded as the senior Rebbe of this generation. Rabbis and Rebbes gathered round his Sabbath table, and there were days when as many as 120 people sought his counsel. He had a complex personality, uncompromising in the realm of religion, yet kindly and considerate, with a keen sense of humour, and generous to a fault. Many a Hasid of Satmar owes his financial success to the money that the rabbi gave him. These acts of kindness have always been imaginative and always inconspicuous.

His services were remarkable experiences. In his active days he used to officiate at the Sabbath morning service, and on Sabbath Rosh Hodesh he would recite Hallel and Musaph (the Additional Service). Every Sabbath three public *tisch* (meals) were held. He would also read the Megillah in public. The rabbi insisted that his Hasidim should work for a living and exhorted them to be honest in their business dealings. 'Here [in the United States] we live under a merciful government, and it is our duty to observe scrupulously the ethical precepts of Judaism.'

In 1968 the rabbi suffered a stroke, and thenceforth lived in Belle Harbor, Long Island, in semi-isolation. Population changes and the influx of underprivileged and unruly elements caused many Hasidim to abandon Williamsburg for newer and more salubrious areas. R. Joel at first vehemently opposed this mass exodus, but later decided to establish an additional new community in up-state New York.

The years did not diminish R. Joel's virulence towards the Jewish state. He believed that a Jewish state was 'an abomination'. To him, Zionism was an evil creed, and to co-operate with the Zionists was a major sin.[5] Nationalism was 'an imitation of the Gentiles'.[6]

'The kingdom of Ben Koziba [Bar Cochba] was meticulously observant and righteous but was nevertheless destroyed. Its chief sin was that it attempted to hasten the redemption.' R. Joel took literally the Talmudic statement[7] that God adjured Israel not to rebel against the nations of the world, or to use force in a mass return to the land of Israel. God alone would redeem Israel in a supernatural and miraculous manner.[8] The precept of Yishuv Ha-Aretz (settling in the Holy Land) applied only to the period of the Temple, and was not binding today, he said.[9]

Once, before Kol Nidre, he emerged from his study in New York with a Scroll of the Law in his arms, and solemnly declared: 'If there is any Jew here who believes that the land of Israel is "the beginning of the Redemption", let him leave this synagogue. Even if I had to remain here all alone, I still would not worship with him.' After the Six-Day War, he issued a booklet denouncing Israel. He regarded the State of Israel as a satanic kingdom controlled by Samael, the Prince of Demons. He maintained that even if the people and the leaders of the state were to observe the law, they would have forfeited everything by establishing a state before the advent of the Messiah.[10]

At the time of the uprising in Hungary, he advised a number of followers not to settle in Israel. His followers are not permitted to visit the Western Wall. In vain R. Aaron Kotler (1892-1962), one of the leaders of the Aguda in the United States, urged R. Joel to change his attitude. 'That is not possible,' affirmed the rabbi. 'I am already the sixteenth generation of those who meticulously observe the Covenant (Notre Ha-Berit).' Satmar followers picketed the United Nations, carrying placards with such slogans as 'Israel cannot represent authentic Judaism', 'The State of Israel is a defilement of the Jewish faith', and 'Zionism has brainwashed American News.' There were slogans condemning Israel's raid on Beirut International Airport. But there were no references to the attacks on El Al aircraft at Athens, in which an Israeli was killed, two days before the Beirut operation. Rabbi Joel died on 19 August 1979, and was succeeded by R. Moses Teitelbaum of Sighet.

After the death of R. Selig Reuben Bengis (1864-1953), the Rabbi of Satmar became the spiritual head of the Edah Ha-Haredit which also comprises the Neture Karta (literally 'Guardians of the City' – a Talmudic phrase[11]), a group of about 300 Jews led by Amram Blau. They live mainly in the Meah Shearim area of Jerusalem which was built in 1860 and

is virtually enclosed by six large iron gates. In the winding
alleys of Meah Shearim the men are bearded and wear long
caftans and round felt hats, while the women and girls wear
long-sleeved high-necked dresses.

Under the British administration, the Jewish community had
internal autonomy. Every Jew over the age of eighteen years
was a member of the Knesset Yisrael. Its executive branch was
the Vaad Leumi, and the Rabbinic Council was composed of
two Chief Rabbis, one for the Sephardim and one for the
Ashkenazim. They exercised authority in religious matters and
formed the Rabbinic Tribunal which had jurisdiction in
matters of personal status of members of the community. In
February 1921 the Assembly elected R. Abraham Yitzhak
Kook as Ashkenazi Chief Rabbi, and R. Yaacov Meir as
Sephardi Chief Rabbi. The Rabbinic courts were given exclusive jurisdiction in matters of marriage, alimony, confirmation
of wills, and other matters of personal status. However, the Old
Yishuv in the Holy City refused to associate itself with Knesset
Yisrael. When the founding conference of the Rabbinate was
convened in February 1921, they declared a fast day.

They have contracted out of the community in accordance
with enabling powers in the legislation, and are not subject to
the Rabbinic Council for purposes of jurisdiction in matters of
personal status. The Aguda supported these separatist tenden-
cies and eventually obtained the right to establish the Edah
Ha-Haredit (Orthodox community) with its own Bet Din.

Yet complete harmony did not prevail even within the Edah.
An extremist group, Hevrat Hayyim ('The Society of
Hayyim') named after R. Joseph Hayyim Sonnenfeld, led a
venomous campaign against Chief Rabbi Kook, with Meah
Shearim living up to its reputation as a cauldron of extremism.

On 19 March 1880 the London *Jewish Chronicle* reported:
'Joseph Blank, a teacher of Arabic, was set on in the streets of
Jerusalem and beaten up by some of the Hungarians, who are
the most fanatical.' In the 1930s the Hevrat Hayyim group

vilified R. Zevi Pesah Frank and R. Jacob Moses Harlap. In spring 1933, rabbis and leaders of the Yishuv issued a public statement condemning the group (Knufio) for its infamous conduct.

In 1936 the Aguda leaders Isaac Breuer (1883-1946) and Dr P. Kohn settled in the Holy Land. When the Aguda began undertaking practical tasks in the Holy Land, they were castigated by the ultra-Orthodox. 'The Aguda was founded with one aim, namely as a defence against Zionist heresy. Today it has become the most dangerous adversary of religious Jewry.' When Arab riots swept the country in 1936, the national institutions set up a defence fund under the name 'Kopher Ha-Yishuv' in order to finance the activities of the Haganah. For once, the Aguda co-operated with the Jewish Agency and the Jewish National Council. It was this act that led the extremist group to break away from the Aguda and form an independent group under the title Neture Karta. Its avowed purpose was to strengthen religious life and arrange evening classes to study the Torah and to supervise religious observance of the Torah both as regards the public and the individual.

During the lifetime of R. Abraham Blau there was some semblance of unity between the warring sections of the Edah Ha-Haredit community. Following his death in 1948 at the age of sixty-one, the last links were broken. In 1971 R. Yitzhak Jacob Weiss of Manchester, author of the Responsa collection *Minhat Yitzhak*,[12] was appointed to succeed R. David Jungreiss as head of the Bet Din. The community has a yeshiva for 150 students, a Talmud Torah for 250 pupils, a school for 150 girls, and a Kolel for 30 students. About 7,000 people are connected with the community.

The militant arm of the Edah Ha-Haredit is the Neture Karta, which implored Britain before the proclamation of the State of Israel: 'take mercy upon us and rescind your decision to relinquish your rule over our land.'

In 1948 Meah Shearim was under heavy shell-fire, but Amram Blau refused to abandon the area and was wounded. There is no foundation for the report that, during the siege of Jerusalem, the leaders of the Neture Karta hoisted a white flag, signifying surrender to the Jordanian forces. It is known, however, that they pleaded with Count Bernadotte (1895-1948) the United Nations mediator in the Jewish-Arab conflict, for Jerusalem to be declared an international city.

The Neture Karta regards Zionism as a product of false Messianism founded on assimilationist ideologies. The Zionist ideal of an independent Jewish state is regarded as a threefold denial of God, of Israel, and of Torah. They are convinced that the holocaust represents divine retribution for the aims of Zionism.

Dr Stewart, Bishop of the Anglican Church, declared at the special United Nations Commission on Palestine in June 1947, that he had been asked to present the view of 'a certain group of independent Jews'. They claim, said Dr Stewart, 'to have 25,000 people and could have 50,000 if they were allowed to organise'.[13]

When the State of Israel was established, the Neture Karta refused *de jure* or *de facto* recognition. They also refused to be registered as citizens. Instead, Blau issued certificates for his followers which bore the verse from Esther (3:2): 'But Mordecai bowed not down nor prostrated himself.' Their theme-song is a poem: 'The Lord is our king. We are His servants. We do not recognise the State of the Heretics.' They boycott all local and national elections and they refuse to pay taxes. Their sons and daughters do not register for national service. They publish a monthly paper, *Ha-Homah* (now *Homatenu*). This small group uses contemporary publicity techniques with some skill. They are vociferous, well organised and well financed. They believe that they are the conscience of Judaism and must impress their own interpretations of the Torah upon all Jews. Frequently demonstrations by the Neture Karta result in violent confrontations between the demonstrators and the police, with neither

acting with restraint. The Neture Karta now form a state
within a state. Amram was supported by his sons-in-law, R.
Yeshaya Schoenberger and R. Aaron Katzenellenbogen. There
is a Talmud Torah for 100 children, a yeshiva for 15 students
and a Kolel for 30 scholars, but they are reticent about their
budget and refuse to publish a balance sheet. 'We supply copies
to our members only, and not to our supporters.' They have
Israeli passports but oppose the use of Hebrew in daily life.
They have even organised anti-Israel demonstrations in New
York, accusing the state of 'conducting an Inquisition against
religion'. 'The members of Neture Karta are not only senseless',
declared the Mizrachi leader Mordecai Nurock (1885-1962),
'they are wilful criminals who betray themselves and their
country in this historic, fateful hour, true to their age-old blind
hatred of Zionism, the movement to liberate the country.'

Against the advice of his own Bet Din, Amram Blau (1890-
1978) married a French proselyte. He lived in the Bate
Hungarian ('Hungarian Houses') in Jerusalem and on his door
there was a plaque which read in Hebrew, English and Arabic:
'I am a Jew and not a Zionist.' He was arrested 153 times for
disrupting the Sabbath traffic.[14]

There are few Hasidim among the Neture Karta. 'The
Hasidim', said a Hasidic rabbi, 'are incapable of harbouring
such a poisonous hatred.' The overwhelming majority of
Hasidim dissociate themselves from the excesses and doctrines
of this extremist fringe. Of the 20,000 people who live in Meah
Shearim, only about 300 are avowed followers of the Neture
Karta. Yet R. Joel's opposition to the existence of the State of
Israel did not prevent him from building two settlements, in
Bne Brak and in Jerusalem.

Shikun Joel in Bne Brak, established in 1954, will eventually
comprise twenty-eight buildings. By 1972 it had seven modern
blocks of flats, each accommodating six families, as well as a
school for 350 girls (Bet Ha-Sepher Livnot Eretz Yisrael). It has
a Talmud Torah for 250 children, a yeshiva for 100 students

and a Kolel for 25 scholars. The *shikun* has a home for 50 elderly people. In all, it houses 125 families, most of whom are employed there in either the diamond workshop or in other industries.

The leader of the *shikun* is R. Benzion Jacobovitz, author of works on the Codes. In the eighteen years of its existence, there has not been a single divorce or Halitzah. No newspaper, apart from *Der Yid* (published in New York) and *Ha-Homah* (published in Jerusalem), enters the *shikun*.

The Satmar Yeshiva in Jerusalem has 200 students and a site has been acquired for additional construction. Dormitories are provided for the students. The Kolel in Jerusalem, which was established in 1952, has eighty-five students, graduates of the Satmar Yeshivot in New York, Bne Brak or Jerusalem.

The Talmud Torah attended by 800 children is independent and has no connection with the Aguda educational system. The girls attend Bnot Yerushalayim, Bnot Esther or Bnot Eretz Yisrael. A unique Satmar institution is a Kolel for laymen in Jerusalem. Men study for half the day, then engage in their secular occupations. Satmar Shikun in Katamon, Jerusalem, houses fifty families. On the Sabbath they do not turn on the electricity provided by the municipality but use their own generator and also special water-tanks.

Although the aged rabbi lived in the United States, he had a great deal of influence over his Hasidim in the Holy Land. These, however, have little effect on the moral or cultural climate of the State of Israel. It is a pity that members of the Neture Karta do not heed the words of R. Kook: 'Israel was destroyed through *sinat hinam* [hatred without a cause] but never through *ahavat hinam* [disinterested love].' The attitude of Satmar perpetuates and widens the gulf between the religious and non-religious sections of the community.

XXIII

FROM DAN TO BEERSHEBA

In the eighteenth and early nineteenth century, many Hasidic rabbis settled in Safed, one of the 'Four Holy Cities' that the Cabbalah endows with mystical significance. The Cabbalist Hayyim Joseph David Azulai maintained that the inhabitants of Safed were more fitted to fathom the depths of the Torah and to penetrate its secrets than the inhabitants of any other city in the Holy Land.[1] The numerical value (570) of the Hebrew for Safed was equivalent to the Hebrew *Teka*, from the prayer, 'Sound the great horn for our freedom'.

In the fifteenth century Safed became a centre for the manufacture of woollens. R. Jacob Berab, who settled in about 1533, attempted to revive there the ordination of rabbis according to the ancient procedure, so as to 'accelerate the Redemption'. Here also Joseph Caro (1488-1575) wrote the *Shulhan Aruch*, which regulates the daily life of the Jew. And it was in Safed that the first Hebrew printing-press in the Holy Land was established about 1577. Here the 'Holy Lion', the '*Ari*', R. Yitzhak Luria, lived and died. Near his resting-place is the grave of his master Moses ben Jacob Cordovero (1522-70), and

243

his disciple Solomon Ben Moses Alkabetz (*c.*1505-84), the author of the Sabbath hymn 'Lechah Dodi', ('Come, My Beloved'). Surrounded by breathtaking views of Mount Meron and the Sea of Galilee, the city has inspired James Michener and Leon Uris, even as it inspired the mystics of the Cabbalah.

In 1837 an earthquake almost destroyed the community. Two years later Sir Moses Montefiore paid his second visit to the Holy Land and had a census taken. There were 273 Hasidim, 69 per cent of the total Jewish population. Among the notable Hasidim was R. Kopel Horowitz (d.1856), son of R. Jacob Isaac, the 'Seer of Lublin'. However, in later years, Safed did not attract Hasidim in large numbers. Of the twenty-two synagogues in the Old City of Safed only ten are Hasidic, including *shtieblech* of Czortkow, Vizhnitz, Czernobil, Karlin, Kossov, Habad, Trisk and Sanz. Near the tomb of R. Simon bar Yochai there is a small yeshiva, directed by R. Johanan Twersky of Jerusalem.

'The flame of my soul will burn until the coming of the Messiah,' said R. Nahman of Braclav in the first decade of the nineteenth century. 'Safed is a town', said R. Abraham Steinhartz (a descendant of R. Nathan of Nemirov), 'where one can do much for Judaism.' Inspired by Solomon Aryeh Gottlieb, an ex-follower of Satmar, the Hasidim of Braclav have undertaken to build a settlement in Safed. The 'Toite Hasidim' ('dead Hasidim'),as the followers of R. Nahman are known, are coming to life. The entrepreneurs call themselves 'The Society for the Revival of the Religious Settlement of Upper Galilee'. There are blueprints for homes, schools, welfare institutions and local printing and diamond industries, which will be expanded to provide work for the growing population. The first stage of the building operation requires two million Israeli pounds. Plans have already been approved by the Ministry of the Interior and Land Authority, and the project is endorsed by many rabbis as well as by the Jewish Agency.

'From Tiberias the Israelites will be redeemed,' says the Talmud.[2] 'The King Messiah', declares the Zohar, 'will appear in Tiberias.' During the second half of the sixteenth century the Turkish statesman Don Joseph Ha-Nasi (1524-79) and his mother-in-law, Dona Gracia Mendes (1510-69), obtained a charter from Suleiman the Magnificent granting them Tiberias and seven surrounding villages, with permission to rebuild the walls of the city and to settle the town and the land with Jews, whether immigrant or native. Don Joseph planted mulberry trees to encourage a silk industry, and imported the finest wools from Spain for weaving. With the death of Don Joseph, the scheme to establish an autonomous Jewish settlement in Tiberias was abandoned.

In the eighteenth century the city attracted the Hasidic leaders R. Menahem Mendel of Vitebsk and R. Abraham of Kalisk. In the middle of the nineteenth century, a group of Karlin Hasidim opened a synagogue there. In 1866 R. Aaron, son of R. Baruch Mordecai of Karlin, wrote:

We have received several letters from the Holy Land and from our Kolel in the holy city of Tiberias ... informing us of hardships ... The epidemic is growing steadily worse all the time, until we are obliged to place guards over the houses and courtyards. Let none of our followers lessen his contributions. Every couple should give one gold piece. Let the poor not give less than that, in addition to the regular yearly contributions to the Holy Land.

It was in Tiberias that R. Moses Kliers, together with the followers of R. Samuel Weinberg of Slonim, founded soup-kitchens for the needy, and the Or Torah Yeshiva beside the tomb of Rabbi Meir Baal Ha-Nes. Now an all-Jewish city of more than 23,000 inhabitants, Tiberias has relatively few Hasidim.

The founding of Kiryat Sanz and Kiryat Vizhnitz encouraged other Hasidic rabbis to establish settlements. Bat Yam, on the coast south of Tel-Aviv, founded in 1926 by twenty-four religious families, now has a population of 62,000. This was the home of the Yiddish writer Scholem Asch. And it was in Bat Yam that R. Solomon Halberstam of Bobow founded Kiryat Bobow.

The dynasty of Bobow (Bobowa in western Galicia) was founded by R. Solomon (1847-1905), a grandson of R. Hayyim of Sanz, and was expanded and developed by his son Benzion (1874-1941). Bobow was next in importance to Belz. A melodious singer as well as a noted scholar, R. Benzion combined the erudition of Sanz with the music of Modzhitz. He maintained that Hasidim without a melody were like a body without a soul. When the famous cantor Josef Rosenblatt (1882-1933) heard R. Benzion sing 'By the Waters of Babylon', he exclaimed: 'Without the Holy Spirit it is impossible to compose such a melody.' R. Benzion established forty-three yeshivot (Etz Hayyim) throughout Galicia. He was one of the first Hasidic rabbis to pay special attention to young people, whom he treated with great consideration.

Like the rabbi of Belz, the Rabbi of Bobow did not associate with the Aguda, but he did participate in communal affairs and often intervened successfully with government departments. In 1938 he took part in the Rabbinic Conference in Warsaw when *shehitah* was threatened by the so-called Humane Slaughter Bill, introduced into the Seym (Parliament) by Janine Prystor. At a meeting of 300 rabbis, a 'fortnight without meat' was proclaimed. From 14 to 30 March 1938, Jews were required to refrain from eating meat (poultry was permissible as it was not affected by the Bill), even on the Sabbath.

On 28 October 1938 over 15,000 Polish Jews, some of whom had spent practically all their lives in Germany, were aroused from their beds by the Nazis and driven without money or possessions of any kind across the frontiers of Poland. Among them were old people, invalids and infants. The train stopped four miles from the Polish frontier, and the passengers were ordered to leave the carriages. Five thousand were virtually kept prisoner in a camp at Zbaszyn, a small Polish township, where they lived under the most pitiful and unhealthy conditions. 'Let everyone contribute according to his ability,' appealed the rabbi. 'For the practice of charity is one of the three pillars on which the world stands.'

R. Benzion, his younger son Moses Aaron, his three sons-in-law, Ezekiel Shraga Halberstam, Moses Stempel and Shlomoh Rubin, were killed in Lvov on 4 Av (25 July) 1941. This was the Black Friday on which 12,000 Jews were murdered by the Nazis and Ukrainians to commemorate the death of the Ukrainian pogromist Petlura who was killed by Shalom Schwartzbard. Death held no terror for the rabbi: 'How can we hide from the pangs of the Messiah?' He met death dressed in his Sabbath garments and his *shtreimel*. His commentary on the Pentateuch 'Kedushat Zion' was published posthumously in New York in 1967.

R. Solomon, the present Rebbe of Bobow, was born on 1 Kislev 1907 in Bobow. He studied under his father and was ordained by R. Samuel Führer and R. Jehiel Nebentzhal of Stanislav. At the age of eighteen, Solomon married his cousin, the daughter of R. Hayyim Jacob Teitelbaum of Leminov, a descendant of R. Moses Teitelbaum. From 1931, while his father Benzion was away for five years, living in Trzebin, R. Solomon became rabbi in Bobow and principal of the Yeshiva Etz Hayyim.

At the outbreak of World War II, R. Solomon lived with his parents in Lvov, which was under Russian domination. His brother Hayyim Joshua and his family escaped to Siberia. Solomon remained in close touch with him, and on one occasion sent him not only a ram's horn (*shophar*), but one thousand gold coins hidden in a jar of honey. Hayyim Joshua acknowledged receipt in a cryptic message, 'The honey has a thousand tastes.'

After the German invasion of Russia, R. Solomon and his family returned to Bobow and were soon confined to the labour camp at Bochnia, near Cracow. The rabbi escaped the massive Nazi purges in August and from 10 November 1942 he was the organiser of an underground escape-route which enabled many people to get away to Hungary and Czechoslovakia. In the camp itself, moreover, under the leadership of Baruch Koning-isser, a 'secret' yeshiva was established accommodating forty-six students. On one occasion the rabbi's wife and two of their children were caught by the Gestapo, and he himself with his eldest son Naphtali was arrested. With only a small piece of bread to sustain him, he did not despair. 'In Bobow we fulfil every precept with joy,' he told his son. 'Similarly, let us be courageous and sanctify God's name with joy.' His Hungarian citizenship stood him in good stead, as he was permitted to return to Bochnia. His wife and two children, however, were taken to Auschwitz.

Solomon's narrow escape did not deter him from resuming his rescue operations. To deceive the Germans, a coal-truck was utilised. Eight people and three children were piled into it and covered with coal. The driver and local farmers were bribed, and many people owe their lives to these clandestine operations. The rabbi, his mother and his son escaped first to Grosswardein and from there to Romania. After the war he made his way to Italy, but he could not obtain a permit there to enter Palestine. He came to London and in a moving address in the Conway Hall urged British Jews to rescue the remnants of European Jewry. He settled in New York, first in Manhattan, then in Crown Heights, and subsequently in Boro Park, Brooklyn. In 1947 he married his second wife, Freda, the daughter of R. Rubin of Ciechanow, by whom he has had five daughters and one son. He founded a network of educational establishments, and, like his father, he pays great attention to young people. The Bobow holiday camp gives many children the opportunity of spending summer in a traditional atmosphere.

The rabbi does not hesitate to break new ground. He introduced a scheme whereby courses leading to jobs in industry are taught in his yeshiva trade school. At one time he planned to build a twenty-million-dollar housing project for 200 families at Parsons Boulevard in Long Island, and the foundation-stone was laid on 27 June 1965. Because of the opposition of local residents, however, the scheme was abandoned. In 1966 a Bobow yeshiva was established in London. The foundation-stone of Kiryat Bobow in Bat Yam was laid on 20 Kislev (2 November) 1958, and R. Joseph Kahaneman, the founder of the Ponevezh Yeshiva, declared: 'In my mind I can already envisage Kiryat Bobow as a traditional Jewish city.' Today there are nearly 100 families living in the Kirya's modern flats. The magnificent Yeshiva Kedushat Zion and the synagogue Bet Joshua, the gift of the rabbi's brother-in-law Osias Freshwater, were founded in 1963. Two-thirds of the students are Israelis, and the rest come from the United States.

The yeshiva is justifiably proud of the excellent accommodation and efficient medical services that are provided for the students. The Talmud Torah (Kol Aryeh) is named after R. Aryeh Leib Rubin, rabbi of Tomaszow, the martyred father of the rabbi's wife. 'The most effective answer to the problem [of religion in Israel] lies in education,' declared the Rebbe. 'If we increase Torah Hinuch in Israel, if we are able to bring up more and more children to lead a truly traditional life, we shall succeed in our struggle for the national recognition of Torah in Israel's public life.'

Forty-eight elderly people live in a pleasant comfortable home called 'Segullah', which was opened in 1963. The rabbi's plans for the expansion of the Kiryah include the establishment of a store, a bakery, a carpet-manufacturing plant, and a knitting mill. An Israeli Credit Corporation was established in 1961. The bank issued shares, half held by the Hasidim of Bobow and the rest by immigrants from Iran. The rabbi maintains a flat in the Kirya and frequently stays there, accompanied by his son Naphtali. The Kirya's development has been hindered by technical and financial problems, as it is difficult to create a new Kirya by remote control from New York.

R. Solomon is approachable, very lucid, and illustrates his points by rabbinic maxims or parables. When asked why he did not influence his wealthy followers and his millionaire relatives to erect flats for the yeshiva students in Israel, he replied:

There was once a simple villager who had a very small shop in the village. He was always harassed by his creditors. One day he visited a big city and stood gazing for a long time outside a huge store. 'What are you doing here?' he was asked, 'and what are you thinking?' 'I have a tiny shop in a village,' replied the man, 'and I have many debts. I am wondering how much money the owner of this great store must owe to his creditors.'

'Similarly,' said the rabbi, 'I have tremendous problems to balance the budget of my educational establishments both in the United States and Israel, and it is not easy for me to take up new financial commitments.'

'Love peace and pursue peace, love your fellow creatures and draw them near to the Torah.'[3] This Mishnaic maxim aptly describes the life and work of R. Hananiah Yom Tov Lipa Teitelbaum (1906-66), founder of Kiryat Yismah Mosheh, near Ramat Gan, and Kiryat Ono. R. Teitelbaum's father was R. Hanoch Heinoch of Sassov, a descendant of Belz, Sassov and Alisk. On his mother's side he was a grandson of R. Hananiah Yom Tov Lipa Teitelbaum, author of *Kedushat Yom Tov*.[4]

The rabbi was born in 1906. At seventeen he married Hayah Rusa, daughter of R. Joel Teitelbaum, and later he became head of the Bet Din at Satmar. Then he became rabbi in Samiah, where he was also principal of the yeshiva. During the war, disguised as a beggar and sometimes as a soldier, he escaped to Romania. From 1944 to 1947 he lived in Jerusalem where he established Yeshiva Yitev Lev and a girls' school, Or Ha-Hayyim, in Bne Brak. He settled in New York, but visited Israel frequently.

His wife died in 1954, and he remarried in Israel. In Adar 1963 he laid the foundation of the new 260-dunam Kirya. 'In

the Diaspora, the dangers of spiritual disintegration and assimilation loom large, even in the main centres of Jewish population,' declared the rabbi. 'There is no bulwark against the
onslaught of assimilation. It is my fervent aim and cherished
desire to rescue these Jews.' Unlike his kinsman R. Joel, the
rabbi sought the support of David Ben Gurion and the Mizrachi
leader Shlomoh Zalman Shraga for his new project. 'If you
want an up-to-date apartment in a pleasant environment, then
come make your home at Yismah Mosheh', he urged his followers in the United States.

'If a man comes here,' remarked the rabbi, 'then his heart will
rejoice.' Aesthetic considerations were important. He insisted
on flower-beds and even chose the plants himself. 'Whenever a
woman looks out of the window, let the fragrance of the flowers
delight her.' He was a perfectionist, and amazed the architects
with his knowledge of technical details. His familiarity with
building matters, his tolerance and readiness to listen to diver-
gent opinions, his relaxed generosity and courtesy endeared
him to many, but the strain undermined his health. In the
summer of 1963 he became very ill, and, was forced to spend
the next eighteen months in hospital. From his bed, he planned
and directed new projects for the Kirya. When R. Joel Teitelbaum visited him in hospital, the ailing rabbi summoned his last
ounce of strength in order to greet the father of his first wife.
Both patient and visitor wept bitterly, knowing that this was
probably their last meeting on this earth. The rabbi died on 11
Adar 1966, leaving one daughter and four young sons. After the
funeral the eldest boy, Joseph David (b. 1954), was proclaimed
Rebbe, the Yenuka of Sassov. He studied at the yeshiva of the
rabbi of Klausenburg and under R. Rosner of Bne Brak.

After the death of the Rebbe, the Kirya was faced with
tremendous financial problems. In August 1972 the rabbi's wife
sold 200 dunams to African-Israeli Investment Limited, one of
Israel's foremost property and development companies. This
company plans to build a new garden suburb called Givat

Savyon which will contain 1,300 residential units in addition to shopping facilities and public services and has undertaken to give priority to religious settlers. At the moment there is no Hasidic yeshiva there, because the yeshiva in the Kirya has been 'lent' to a Lithuanian group. There are four houses of worship, two kindergartens, and a Bet Jacob school. R. Joel advised the rabbi's family not to leave Israel during the Six-Day War, but has, however, shown no interest in the Kirya.

Rehovot, home of the Weizmann Research Institute, was also the residence of David Moses Rosenbaum (1925-69), the Rebbe of Kretschnov, a descendant of R. Meir of Przemyslan and R. Mordecai of Nadvorna (d. 1880). David Moses' grandfather Meir (d.1908), son of R. Mordecai, settled in Craciunesti, in Romania. His son Eliezer was murdered in Auschwitz.

After the war, R. David Moses returned to Romania. Sixteen members of his family had perished in the Nazi terror, and only one sister survived. In 1946 he married in Bucharest Esther Rachel, daughter of the rabbi of Nadvorna. In 1948 he settled in Israel. 'Stay in Rehovot,' R. Aaron Rokeah of Belz advised him. 'It is a pleasant town.' R. David Moses took this advice and his home in Rehovot attracted many followers. He set up a Talmud Torah, a yeshiva, a Kolel, and an Old People's Home, and he urged religious Jews to present a united front at the municipal elections. 'Only through unity,' declared the rabbi, 'will we be able to strengthen the religious life of the Yishuv.'

The rabbi's father was an accomplished violin player. 'I myself have fashioned it,' he said of his violin. 'It is as sacred as a Scroll of the Law, and if fire breaks out it must be rescued together with all other religious objects.' Similarly, the son played the violin during highlights of the religious year. 'Hell has no terror for me,' he said. 'I have been in Auschwitz, what can be worse than that?' The Rabbi died on 26 Sivan 1969, while visiting Sighet in Romania to pray at the grave of his ancestors. He was buried in Rehovot and left seven sons and seven daughters. R. Menahem Eliezer Zeev in Rehovot and R. Israel Nisan in Kiryat Gan maintain the traditions of the family.

For a Rebbe to abdicate in the prime of his life in favour of his sons is a rare phenomenon. Yet this is the story of the most versatile of the Hasidic personalities in the Holy Land, R. Baruch Joseph Yerahmiel Rabinowicz, Chief Rabbi of Holon, a town 2 miles south of Tel-Aviv-Jaffa. The rabbi gave up the leadership of the turbulent Hasidic movement of Munkacs for the equally demanding but less rewarding office of rabbi of Holon, a community of nearly 70,000 people not known for their religious fervour. Many Hasidim are grieved that he has not re-established Munkacs in Israel. They disapprove of his strong leanings towards Mizrachi, his discourses in fluent modern Hebrew, his modernity (he drives his own car) and, above all things, his marriage to a commoner.

Baruch was born in Parczew in Poland, on 13 September 1914. His father was R. Nathan David Rabinowicz, son of R. Jacob Isaac of Biala, a descendant of the Yehudi, 'the Holy Jew of Przysucha'. The four sons of the Biala Rebbe branched out and established their own courts in different parts of Poland. The eldest, Nathan David of Parczew (1866-1930), married Leah, daughter of R. Yehiel Jacob of Kozienice. At the outbreak of World War I, his father left Parczew for Retzitz and from 1918 onwards lived in Siedlice. Baruch obtained his rabbinic diploma from R. Ezekiel Michelson of Warsaw and R. Yehiel Meir Blumenfeld, head of the Mizrachi Rabbinic Seminary Tachkemoni of Warsaw, as well as from R. Joseph Elimelech Grünwald of Ungvar. His marriage in 1933 to Frima, only daughter of the Rebbe of Munkacs, made him heir-apparent of Munkacs.

The dynasty of Munkacs had been founded by R. Solomon Shapira (1832-93). It was under his son, R. Zevi Hirsch (1850-1914), that Munkacs became an important Hasidic centre. He ranked with R. Abraham Bornstein and R. Yitzhak Meir Alter of Ger as the pre-eminent *halachic* authority of the late nineteenth century, and his monumental work *Darke Teshuvah*[5] is an indispensable adjunct to Talmudic studies. He opposed the Hungarian demand that children be taught secular studies, even opposing the establishment of Jewish schools in which the curriculum included secular subjects.

His son, R. Hayyim Eleazar (1872-1937), was a prolific writer, best known for his work *Minhat Eleazar* (1902-30) which was published in four parts. He also wrote *Ot Hayyim V'Shalom*,[6] an essay on the laws of *tephillin* and circumcision. A bibliophile who collected a valuable library, his language could acquire apocalyptic fire. Because of his mercurial temperament, he was often unable to curb his violent emotions. As a staunch champion of tradition, he was prepared to clash headlong with those who opposed him. R. Hayyim Eleazar disapproved of both political Zionism and the Aguda, and the *herem* (excommunication ban) was widely used, and even more widely misused, by the rabbi of Munkacs.

In the Middle Ages, the *herem* was the most powerful weapon that the Jewish authorities possessed, as it enabled them to maintain law and order within the community; in those days the mere threat of the *herem* would often subdue unruly elements. The weird ceremony, complete with wax candles and *shophar*, was designed to strike terror into the heart, and the words fell on the victim like a sentence of death. When R. Hayyim Eleazar was engaged in a dispute with R. Issachar Dov Rokeah of Belz, who lived in Munkacs from 1918 to 1921, the rabbi of Munkacs excommunicated his opponent. 'He and I', said R. Hayyim Eleazar, 'cannot live in the same city.'

In his opposition to Zionism, he was backed by R. Joel Teitelbaum and R. Schneerson of Lubavitch. In fact there were many undertakings that the rabbi of Munkacs opposed, among them the first Hebrew elementary schools that were established in Munkacs by Elijah Rubin, the high school founded in 1924, and the four Yiddish papers that appeared in the town. He called an immigration certificate to Palestine 'a passport to apostasy'.

Like his father R. Zevi Hirsch, Hayyim Eleazar was in charge of fund-raising for the poor of the Holy Land (Rabbi Meir Baal Ha-Nes), and he was President of the Kolel Munkacs V'Aseret Gelilot. He maintained not only that it was forbidden to associate with the Mizrachi, but also that the Aguda was to be condemned for its vote in Zurich in 1919 in favour of resettlement in the Holy Land. Even during World War I he was able to send money to the Holy Land. The rabbi kept in touch with the Cabbalists of Jerusalem and Safed, particularly with R. Saul Ha-Kohen Duwaik, one of the outstanding Cabbalists of the Sephardi community, and with Solomon b. Jacob Alfandari (1829-1930), who held rabbinic posts in Istanbul, Damascus and Safed. Alfandari settled in the Holy City in 1926. R. Hayyim Eleazar endearingly called him 'The Holy Grandfather' and visited him in 1929. After Alfandari's death on 27 Iyyar, the Hasidim of Munkacs dedicated a hymn to his memory.

'A man of war who sows righteousness' is the phrase that the Hasidim of Munkacs applied to their Rebbe. Fiery and uncompromising in his public utterances, Hayyim Eleazar was in private life a loving and thoughtful father. He subjected his future son-in-law to a searching examination in Talmudics. When the young man passed the test, the Rebbe declared: 'Thou art my son, this day have I begotten thee' (Ps.2:7). In his Last Will, R. Hayyim Eleazar wrote: 'I am not sorry that I cannot bequeath you material possessions. Wealth by itself does not bring happiness.' When he died on 2 Sivan 1937, R. Baruch Rabinowicz became Rebbe and later was elected rabbi of Munkacs. He expanded the Yeshiva Darke Teshuvah, where, by 1939, 400 students were in attendance.

In 1941 Baruch, together with his wife and four children, escaped to Budapest, where they lived until 1944. Many Jews were sheltered in his home and he saved many from death. In that year he and his family were permitted to enter the Holy Land, where he lived in Tel-Aviv. His wife died on 25 Nisan 1945. Subsequently he accepted a rabbinic post in São Paulo, Brazil, where he received the degree of Master of Philosophy for a thesis on 'The Conflict between Contradictory Ethical Principles'. R. Baruch 'abdicated' in favour of his sons, R. Moses Yehuda Leib and R. Jacob, who have established the Darke Teshuvah and Minhat Eleazar yeshivot in New York and show a spiritual affinity with R. Joel Teitelbaum of Satmar.

R. Baruch became Chief Rabbi of Holon in 1963, and faced the dual challenge of eliciting the co-operation of the civic authorities and overcoming the hostility of the local rabbis. While his scholarship is outstanding, his diplomacy is less so. His adherence to the Mizrachi has alienated the ultra-Orthodox factions.

He delights in his father-in-law's library of over 5,000 books, including an incunabulum of R. Moses b. Jacob of Coucy's work *Sepher Mitzvot Gadol* (known as *Semag*), printed in 1488 at Soncino, and many sixteenth-century rareties. He possesses a Scroll of the Law said to have belonged to R. Israel Baal Shem Tov and to have been written by his scribe Hirsch Sopher. He also has a pair of phylacteries that belonged to R. Elimelech of Lyshansk, a Scroll of Esther written by R. Zevi Elimelech of Dinov (author of *Bne Issachar*), a chair that belonged to R. Jacob Isaac, 'the Holy Jew' of Przysucha, as well as circumcision knives that belonged to his forebears.

In 1968 R. Baruch founded Darke Teshuvah, the Institute for Rabbinic Education and Training in Tel-Aviv. It accepts students who have completed their basic yeshiva studies and are ready for advanced theoretical and practical studies in a three-year course which prepares candidates for the Rabbinate. 'There is a dearth of trained experienced rabbis,' says the rabbi. 'Everyday life in the State of Israel confronts them with new problems.'

XXIV

THE REBBES OF SPINKA

The Hebrew spelling of the name of the town of Spinka (Marmaros, Carpathian Russia) is equivalent to the Hebrew for *Esh* (fire), say the Hasidim. Before World War II, many scholars belonged to the dynasty of Spinka which combined the mysticism of Zhydachov with the scholarship of Sanz and the ardent services of R. Uri b. Phinehas of Strelisk (d.1826), known as *Ha-Saraph* ('the Seraph'). After Belz it had the largest following in Hungary. Today there are many Spinka Hasidim in Israel and also three rabbis of Spinka.

Spinka is a comparative latecomer among the Hasidic constellations. The founder R. Joseph Meir Weiss (1838-1909), son of Samuel Zevi, *dayyan* of Munkacs, was influenced by the Cabbalist R. Yitzhak Eizig Eichenstein. R. Joseph Meir himself was the author of six profound books on mysticism and homiletics known as *Imre Yoseph*.[1] He corresponded with the leading rabbinic authorities of his time, R. Yitzhak Elhanan Spector of Kovno and R. Shalom Mordecai Ha-Kohen Schwadron (1835-1911). After Joseph Meir's marriage to Perl, daughter of R. Jacob Bash, he settled in Spinka, on the river Tissa. With the death of his teacher, Yitzhak Eizig, the disciple took over most of his followers.

His only son, Yitzhak Eizig (1875-1944), named after the Rebbe of Zhydachov, established a Yeshiva Bet Joseph. During World War I, he lived for a time in Budapest and Munkacs, but to avoid the antagonism of R. Hayyim Eleazar, moved to Selische, near the Czechoslovak border. Yitzhak Eizig was known as a *matmid par excellence*. The Talmud was his constant companion. His love of learning was an all-consuming passion and his life was an act of worship. 'Holy Creator,' the rabbi would often exclaim, 'have compassion on me. My only desire is to serve you.' He was known for his kindliness and he would not begin his prayers before he had distributed charity. When he had no alms to distribute, he would borrow money for this purpose. 'First I study the laws relating to loans,' he remarked, 'then the laws pertaining to charity.' At the age of fifteen he married Miriam, daughter of R. Issachar Dov of Verecke. 'I need not be ashamed of my son-in-law,' said Issachar Dov. 'He can hold his own among all the rabbis.'

Though Selische was now his residence, Yitzhak Eizig did not sever his links with Spinka. Twice a year, on the *Yahrzeit* of his father and mother, he would make the pilgrimage to his home town to renew his ties with his followers. It was there that a Yeshiva Bet Joseph was established under his son Naphtali. Selische was only 50 kilometres from the Polish border, and after the outbreak of World War II many Polish Jews, escaping the Nazi inferno, found refuge in the rabbi's home. To accommodate the ever-increasing flow, he built a bunker where they could hide in comparative safety. The Hungarian authorities soon became aware of what was happening. The rabbi was arrested and reprimanded for harbouring aliens. 'I cannot ask a fellow-Jew for his passport,' was his answer. He was released, and his prison experience did not deter him from continuing his rescue operations.

The rabbi had many opportunities to leave eastern Europe. He was offered a certificate to enter the Holy Land; a relative, R. Dov Bergman of New York, procured an American visa for him, and he received a permit to enter England. But the aged rabbi could not bear to abandon his followers and family. Conditions rapidly deteriorated. The day after Passover 1943, 12,000 Jews were crammed into a ghetto. On Rosh Hodesh Sivan, the rabbi and his eldest son, Israel Hayyim, and his family were taken to Auschwitz. A Jew implored him: 'Rabbi, pray for a miracle. We are travelling to our death.' 'Don't be afraid,' the rabbi comforted him. 'We are going to welcome the Messiah. Surely the Messiah is in chains; it is our duty to redeem him.' Throughout the fearful journey he sang: 'Purify our hearts that we may serve Thee in truth and in love and fervour.' With the words, 'Fire shall be kept burning upon the altar continually' (Lev. 6:6), he met his Maker on 13 Nisan 1944, and thirty members of his family perished with him.

R. Jacob Joseph, son of Israel Hayyim, the eldest son of Yitzhak Eizig, was the only member of the family to survive the war. He was born in 1915 in Spinka, and was brought up by both his father and his grandfather. He was transferred from camp to camp, each time narrowly missing death, but his wife and three children perished. One Saturday evening he left his hut in order to 'Sanctify the Moon'. At that moment the camp was attacked by Allied bombers, and the entire hut was destroyed. He was captured by the Russians, who refused to believe he was fleeing from the Nazis and prepared to execute him. A Russian officer who happened to be passing by asked him the meaning of a Mishnah in the Tractate Berachot. The rabbi's ready explanation established his identity and saved his life.

After the liberation he returned to Selische, where he found a manuscript of Yitzhak Eizig which contained Responsa on the Four Orders of the *Shulhan Aruch*, and discourses. He named it *Hakal Yitzhak*, since the Hebrew word *Hakal* is equivalent to 138, the numerical value of Eizig.

For a time Jacob Joseph lived in Borsa, in Transylvania. In 1945 he married the daughter of Abish Horowitz, rabbi of Carei Mari, the successor of R. Joel Teitelbaum. A year later, he settled in Crown Heights, New York, where he established a Bet Hamidrash and a yeshiva. Despite his growing popularity, his dream was to live in Israel–which he visited frequently– and in 1955 he settled in Bne Brak. He keeps in touch with his American Hasidim and, just as his grandfather visited Spinka, so he regularly visits New York.

The rabbi feels that spiritual improvement must precede material improvement. On Friday night he does not deliver discourses, because rabbis of Zhydachov believed 'that no one should give a discourse, unless he has heard it directly from the Almighty. The discourse should be for edification of the speaker as well as the listeners.' Instead, the Rebbe tells tales of the zaddikim, choosing those the anniversary of whose death falls in the course of that week. His father (who did deliver discourses) would precede each one with a modest disclaimer: 'How dare I, a lowly creature, expound the words of the Torah before this holy nation?'

The rabbi is very selective in his choice of students for his yeshiva in Bne Brak. He also maintains a yeshiva in Jerusalem and a school in Acre and has set up a number of welfare agencies.

In 1969 the rabbi acquired 25 dunams in Petah Tikvah and made elaborate plans to erect a Kirya. Because of technical and administrative problems, these plans have still not left the drawing-board. The crowning catastrophe was the death in 1972 of the rabbi's son, Abraham Abish, at the age of twenty-five leaving two young daughters. To perpetuate his son's memory, a Kolel Ner Avraham (The Light of Abraham) was established in Elul 1972. That same month, the rabbi brought the remains of his great-grandfather, R. Joseph Meir, from Romania to be interred next to his son in Petah Tikvah.

In Bne Brak lived another Spinka Rebbe, R. Nahman Cahane who was born in Spinka on 2 Heshvan (11 October) 1904. Until his wedding-day he studied with his father R. Zevi Cahane,[2] son-in-law of R. Yitzhak Eizig. In 1924 Nahman married the daughter of the rabbi of Szasregen in Transylvania. He received his Rabbinic Diploma from R. Jacob Gottlieb of Miskolc in Hungary and R. Zevi Hirsch Kunstlicher, rabbi in Hermannstadt in Transylvania, who became rabbi of Spinka in 1928. During World War II he lived in different Romanian ghettos and afterwards became rabbi at Cluj (Klausenburg). He sent his four children as 'illegal immigrants' to the Holy Land, where he joined them in 1950. For a time he lived in Bne Re'em, the first Moshav of the Poale Agudat Yisrael, named after R. Abraham Mordecai Alter. In 1955 he settled in Bne Brak, where he had a Bet Hamidrash and a small Kolel. On Friday evening the rabbi gave three discourses, two before the meal and one after it. He did not belong to any political party, but nevertheless participated in the protest demonstration against Chief Rabbi Goren's *halachic* ruling on the Langer case. He died on 17 Tishri 1976. He is survived by two daughters and five sons, and was succeeded by his son, R. Moses Eliakim Briah.

Nahman's brother, Joseph Meir Cahane, lived in Jerusalem. He was born in 1910, also in Spinka, and studied under his maternal grandfather R. Baruch Rubin of Gerela, being ordained by R. Joseph Elimelech Cahane of Ungvar, R. Joel Wolf Glattstein of Kiralyhelmecz and R. Joab Adler of Hanusfalva. In 1930 he married the daughter of R. Yitzhak Teitelbaum of Husakov, near Przemysl, and for the first three years he lived in the house of his father-in-law. Then he became rabbi of Seredna, near Munkacs, and two years later moved to Radwanka, a suburb of Ungvar, where he too became known as the Spinka Rebbe. He was the first of the Spinka dynasty to reach the Holy Land and in 1941 made his home in Jerusalem, where he established a Kolel for thirty students. He died on 22 Tevet 1978. His aim was to reconcile the teachings of Zhydachov with the doctrines of the

Cabbalah. His son-in-law R. Mordecai David Teitelbaum, the Husakover Rebbe is Beersheba, in the only Hasidic rabbi in the Negev.

XXV

THE HASIDIC COMMUNITY

Most Hasidic children attend the schools of the Hinuch Atzmai, which was founded in 1953. Twenty years later it was operating 231 schools with an enrolment of 30,000. In these schools a thorough study of Jewish subjects goes hand in hand with the secular curriculum. The language of instruction is Hebrew, and the sexes are segregated. Though nominally Hinuch Atzmai is independent and free from party influence, it is guided by the Aguda and such Hasidic rabbis as Abraham Jacob Friedman, Baruch Hager, Israel Alter of Ger, Hayyim Meir Hager of Vizhnitz and Mordecai Shalom Joseph Friedman of Sadagura, who have identified themselves with its aims and activities. 'The Hinuch Atzmai network of schools is a vital necessity,' wrote these rabbis. 'We appeal to every Jew to strengthen and help to maintain the Hinuch Atzmai to enable it to fulfil its aim of safeguarding Jewish education.'

In 1932, control of Jewish education was transferred from the Jewish Agency to the Vaad Leumi (1932-48). The Aguda, remaining outside the national system, established schools in Jerusalem, Tel-Aviv and Tiberias. In 1936 there were 200 independent schools with 19,064 pupils.[1] By 1948 it had nearly 40,000 pupils. With the establishment of the State of Israel, there were three educational systems: general, Mizrachi and Labour, and soon recognition was accorded to the fourth system, Hinuch Atzmai. The State Education Bill was passed on 8 August 1953 by thirty-nine votes to sixteen. In the 1953 Act, 'the Agudat Yisrael schools are recognised as educational establishments'. The Ministry of Education insists, however, that the formal qualifications of Aguda teachers be equivalent to those required in other institutions, and that the language of instruction must be Hebrew, not Yiddish. The state pays 85 per cent of the salaries of the teachers, an increase of 25 per cent since 1953.[2]

With the establishment in Poland during the inter-war years of schools for girls, such as Tarbut under Zionist auspices and Zisho, the Central Yiddish School Organisation, the Hasidim also established their own girls' schools. The first Bet Jacob school for girls was founded in Cracow by Sarah Schenierer in 1917. The name Bet Jacob comes from the verse: 'O House of Jacob, come ye, and let us walk in the light of the Lord' (Isa: 2:5). By 1937-8, there were 248 Bet Jacob schools in Poland with a total of 35,586 pupils.

The Bet Jacob schools were acknowledged by the Knessiya Gedolah (The Great Assembly) of the Aguda to be 'the best solution for the education of girls'. Moral support came from the Rabbis of Belz and Ger. 'It is a sacred duty to work nowadays for the Bet Jacob movement,' wrote the rabbi of Ger. ' ... The future mothers of Israel are being educated there in the true traditional spirit of the Torah and are receiving a sound all-round schooling.'

In the Holy Land the first Orthodox girls' school was established by R. Benzion Yedler and named Bet Hinuch Livnot al Yedei Darke Yisrael Saba, popularly called 'Benzion Yedler Heder'. In 1921 the first Bet Jacob school was established in Jerusalem. Another was founded three years later in Tiberias and one in 1933 in Tel-Aviv. By 1972, there were eighty-three Bet Jacob institutions.

In the nineteenth century the Hasidim in eastern Europe did not establish their own yeshivot, and their young men would study in Bate Midrashim. But in the last quarter of the nineteenth century and in the first four decades of the twentieth, Hasidim did establish yeshivot such as the Metivta founded in 1919 under R. Meir Dan Plotzki of Ostrova (1867-1928). R. Joseph Isaac Schneersohn founded a number of Tomchei Temimim ('Supporters of the Perfect') yeshivot and R. Solomon Hanoch Ha-Kohen Rabinowicz (b.1882) of Radomsk directed thirty-six yeshivot Keter Torah in Poland and Galicia. There was also the famous Yeshiva Hachmei Lublin founded by R. Meir Shapira (1887-1934), the Hasid of Czortkow, which was consecrated on 28 Nisan 1930, and was one of the finest buildings in pre-war Poland. 'I hope to establish a yeshiva in Jerusalem which will put to shame the buildings of the Hebrew University,' proclaimed this rabbinic builder. Three years later he died at the age of forty-six.

The growth of yeshivot has been phenomenal. In 1929-30 there were sixteen large ones with 2,873 students, thirty-two smaller ones with 1,735 students in eastern Europe, and by 1937 there were seventy-eight yeshivot.[3] In the United States there are today 250 yeshivot with 40,000 students.

In Israel the establishment of yeshivot is part of the Hasidic way of life. Almost every Rebbe has, or wishes to have, his own academy. In 1971 there were 300 different yeshivot with 20,000 students. Of the 120 educational institutions enumerated in the Directory of Recognised Agencies (published by the Ministry of Social Welfare, 1970-1), nearly one-third are Hasidic. Of the 158 Israeli yeshivot, half of them are Hasidic and associated with the Vaad Ha-Yeshivot (Yeshivot Committee), which provides food and clothing for students and their dependants. The Ministry of Education exerts no supervision over the yeshivot, but the Ministry of Religious Affairs provides subsidies for them and their students. The ultra-Orthodox have their Ihud Ha-Yeshivot (Union of Yeshivot) which supports fifteen institutions in Jerusalem. The voice of the Torah is heard by day and night, not only in the Israeli *mitnagdic* yeshivot of Mir and Slabodka, but also in the Hasidic citadels. In eastern Europe few yeshivot made provisions for the maintenance of their students. According to the prevailing system of 'essen tag' (literally 'eating days'), local residents undertook to feed at least one yeshiva student for one day in the week, and a student had to make the round of seven homes each week. On days when he had no dinner invitation, the yeshiva would supply him with bread or a small sum of money.

This humiliating system had been gradually dying out in eastern Europe, and in the inter-war years the yeshiva authorities were beginning to recognise their responsibilites for the physical welfare of the students. In Israel, most yeshivot now provide dormitories and kitchens.

The Hasidic yeshivot in Israel, like their forerunners in eastern Europe, are not training-schools for professional rabbis, and students have no immediate vocational objective. 'We eat, drink, sleep; and the rest of the time we study,' said R. Hayyim of Volozhin (1802-92), and conditions are still the same in 1973. Yiddish is still the primary language of the yeshivot and the overriding concern is to produce learned laymen rather than spiritual leaders, for few students wish to qualify for the Rabbinical Diploma. Apart from Lubavitch, the Hasidic yeshivot frown upon yeshiva-cum-technical college institutions.

To support a student son-in-law was customary among Hasidim in eastern Europe. After marriage, a young man would live in the home of his bride's father, whose support enabled him to devote himself full-time to study. The Kolel, which subsidised the studies of married students, was hardly known in Poland. In the last three decades there has been an extensive growth of Kolelim in Israel, where students continue their studies at a higher level from five to ten years after marriage. The institution owes much to R. Abraham Yeshayahu Karlitz, who established a Kolel in Bne Brak. 'The

Torah is not like secular knowledge,' he maintained. 'The Torah is acquired only by those who labour all their lives.'[4] Conditions vary from one Kolel to another. To maintain their ever-growing families, a number of students attend two Kolelim, one in the morning and the other in the afternoon or evening.

The birthrate among Jews geneally is declining. The average young Jewish family in Israel has three or four children, and the number of families with six children has decreased from 20.7 per cent in 1961 to 18 per cent in 1970.[5] The average Hasidic family has five or six children and most of their wives work. Aid from in-laws, salaries of wives and supplementary social service benefits enable them to support their growing families. They regard birth-control as contrary to *Halachah*, and in the aftermath of the Holocaust they also consider it as the sacred duty of every Jew to increase the birthrate. Though many of them were born in Israel, Hasidim all speak Yiddish, because 'A Yid redt Yiddish' (' Jew speaks Yiddish').

Hasidim have been represented on the Aguda Council of Sages by Rabbis Baruch Hager of Haifa, Dov Berish Weidenfeld, Hayyim Meir Hager, Mordecai Shalom Friedman and Moses Yehiel Halevi Epstein. They read the daily newpaper, *Ha-Modia*, published by the Aguda in Jerusalem, *She'arim*, published by the Poale Aguda, *Bet Jacob*, a monthly literary journal, *Diglenu*, the organ of Ze'ire Aguda, the *Niv Ha-Moreh* of the Aguda Teachers' Union.

A small number of Hasidim live on Aguda and Poale Aguda settlements: in Nahal Sorek (which is called 'the country of the Torah'), in Bet Helkiya (established in 1954), Kfar Eliyahu, Hafetz Hayyim and Kfar Gideon. They operate their farms efficiently and observe such Torah injunctions as the non-mixture of plants, and the prohibition of seed grafting. The Poale Aguda's Institute of Agricultural Research, according to the Torah, worked out schedules of agricultural work for the year of the Shemitah, so that work is carried out by hydroponics (growing plants without soil in a manner which is permissible in the Shemitah year). The Hasidim have their own workers' organisation, youth groups (Ze'ire Aguda) and womens' organisations (Bnot Aguda).

There is a letter to the Aguda dated 19 June 1947,[6] signed by David Ben Gurion, then Chairman of the Jewish Agency, Judah Leib Maimon (Fishman), representative of the Mizrachi, and Yitzhak Gruenbaum on behalf of the General Zionists. It indicated a willingness to accede to the religious camp's desires in regard to marriage, the Sabbath, education and the dietary laws in the Jewish state, 'when it is established in our own days', but also pointed out 'that it is not the intention to establish a theocratic state'. The letter states:

(a)　It is agreed that the legal day of rest in the Jewish state should be the Sabbath.
(b)　All necessary measures shall be taken to guarantee that every state kitchen intended for Jews will be kosher.
(c)　Everything possible will be done to satisfy in this respect the profound need for adherence to the faith so as to prevent the division of the House of Israel into two parts.
(d)　The full autonomy of every 'trend' in education will be guaranteed. There will be no interference on the part of the Government with the religious conviction and the religious conscience of any section in Israel. The state will naturally determine minimal compulsory studies, the Hebrew language, history, science etc., and supervise the fulfilment of this minimum, but will give full freedom to every group to draw up its own curriculum.

Although the Aguda proclaimed that 'the Torah was the soul of their organisation',[7] and believed that religion was a collective responsibility which had to be enforced by the state, it participated in the Provisional Government from 14 May 1948 to 10 February 1949, and joined the United Religious Front from 10 March 1949 to 19 December 1952. A member of the Aguda held the post of Minister of Social Welfare.

Under the Law of Return, every Jew has the right to come to Israel unless he has been guilty of offences against the Jewish people, or is liable to endanger public health or security. From the establishment of the State of Israel till the end of 1951, 648,000 Jews arrived.

Many immigrants from Poland and the Soviet Union have non-Jewish spouses, and sons who have not been circumcised. A Bet Din was set up by the Immigration Department of the Jewish Agency with the participation of Akiva Eisenberg, the Chief Rabbi of Vienna. They became known as the 'Gere Vienna', 'the proselytes of Vienna', and many felt that these rabbis were not qualified to perform their duties. In Sivan 1971, under the signature of R. Israel Alter of Ger and other leading authorities, it was stressed that the Law of Return, which provides the automatic right of citizenship for those who can prove that they are Jews, should be amended to conform with the strict religious code of *Halachah*, which stipulates a Jewish mother or conversion by an Orthodox rabbi as the sole qualifications.

We strongly appeal to you, and to all who cherish the existence of the Jewish people, and warn those who have attempted to undermine the authority of the Torah, not to disrupt the unity of our people, not to cause a malignant growth, not to attack the very foundation of the Torah and its principles nor to sabotage 'the vineyard of the Lord'.

The Aguda was not satisfied with the 1948 Act which established the Sabbath and the Jewish Festivals as official days of rest. It urged the government to legislate for the cessation of all non-essential services, especially buses and trains, from sundown to sunset on the Sabbath. Nor were they happy with the 1951 Act which ruled that every employee was to have at least thirty-six hours of leisure each week, since it did not specify that those were to include the Sabbath.

In September 1948 the Knesset adopted the Defence Service Law which made women as well as men subject to conscription. The government agreed to exempt Orthodox girls who applied for exemption on religious grounds. It was stipulated that such girls would be assigned agricultural or social welfare tasks. Relief from national service could be administratively granted for a number of reasons, including 'a family's special way of life'. In 1971 the Israeli Cabinet decided to organise a volunteer service for Orthodox girls exempted from military service on religious grounds. Religious Jews assembled at the Wailing Wall, blew the *shophar*, and prayed: 'Our Father, Our King, repeal the evil sentence.' The Cabinet decision has not yet been implemented. The Aguda demanded total exemption without any reservation. It has also demanded the closure of the mission schools, the prohibition of pig-breeding, and major changes in the Anatomy and Pathology Act of 1953 which permits *post mortem* operations without the prior consent of the deceased or his family. As a safeguard, three doctors are required to sign a certificate of necessity before a *post mortem* operation can take place. The Aguda opposes this Act because they consider the mutilation of the dead to be a desecration.

The Aguda is represented on the town councils of Israel, including those of Jerusalem, Tel Aviv, Haifa and Bne Brak, but it is not free from internal dissensions. The Poale Agudat Israel, which was founded in 1923, is now an independent party. In the 1949 elections to the Knesset, Poale Aguda formed a part of the Religious Front, but in 1951 it campaigned independently, obtaining in the fifth, sixth and seventh Knesset elections two seats with an average of 1.9 per cent of the total votes. The Poale Aguda leader, Benjamin Mintz (1903-61), Minister of Posts from 1960 until his death, advocated *haluziut* (Pioneering), and served on the Yishuv's Security Committee. In 1951 he became Deputy Speaker, a position he held until 1960 when he joined the government.

In the 1965 Knesset elections, the Aguda obtained 3.3 per cent of the votes, with four seats in Parliament. In the 1969 elections it polled 42,002 votes and obtained the same number of seats as in 1965. The breach that had existed since 1959 between the Aguda and Poale Aguda was ended by the creation of the Torah Religious Front. In the December 1973 elections the joint list of the Aguda and the Poale Aguda obtained five seats. The refusal of the Poale Aguda in 1969 to join the government, in protest against the official decision to recognise as Jews many whom Jewish Law considered as Gentiles, paved the way to reconciliation. On political issues the Aguda has taken a more moderate line than the National Religious Party, holding that a settlement with the Arab states can be achieved only on the basis of territorial compromise. The Torah Bloc refused in 1974 to join the government. The Mo'atze Gedole Ha-Torah (Council of Sages) ruled that participation was dependent on the Alignment's concession on two points— amendment of the 'Who is a Jew' Law and the abolition of military service for girls.

Apart from the United States, the largest number of Hasidim in the world live in Israel. Most are associated with Ger (about 4,000), Belz, Satmar and Vizhnitz. There are about 3,000 *shtieblech* in the Holy Land. Although no official figures are given, the Hasidim and their dependants probably number well over 150,000.

The Aguda does not support the demonstrations organised by the Neture Karta in London, New York and Washington. It realises that it will take more than posters and propaganda in the Diaspora to generate religious fervour in Israel. Only an increased aliyah of Orthodox Jews will transform the Promised Land into the Holy Land. There is no place for intolerance in Israel, and the freedom of the individual must be respected and guaranteed. Hasidim are gradually coming to terms with this idea.

XXVI

HASIDIC LITERATURE

The fate of the Hasidic book was bound up inextricably with the fate of the Jew; it was banned, censored, mutilated, desecrated and destroyed. In 1939 there were 469 Jewish libraries with a total of 3,307,000 volumes in twenty European countries. In Poland alone there were 251 Jewish libraries with 1,555,000 books, most of which were destroyed in the Holocaust.

The Hasidic books and manuscripts which survived have been gathered together. The valuable library of the bibliophile R. Abraham Mordecai of Ger was lost, but the Rebbes of Ruzhin-Sadagura and the Munkacs dynasties were able to bring many important items with them from Europe.

In a special Hasidic exhibition in Tel-Aviv in the summer of 1960, organised by the late Benjamin Mintz, nearly 200 items were shown.[1] Noteworthy were the candlesticks of R. Levi Yitzhak of Berdichev, the spice-box of R. Phinehas of Koretz, letters from Abraham Mordecai of Ger, Phinehas Menahem of Pulawy, Mordecai Joseph Leiner, Benzion of Bobow, Abraham Joshua Heshel of Opatow and R. Hayyim of Krasni.

Another exhibit was the copy of *Toledot Yaakov Yosef* used by R. Baruch of Medzyborz, grandson of R. Israel Baal Shem Tov.

There are some 250 entries on Hasidism, in the new *Encyclopaedia Judaica* edited by the late Dr Cecil Roth and published in Jerusalem in 1972, the Hasidic section being edited by Dr Abraham Rubinstein, a native of Tomaszow and senior lecturer in Jewish History at Bar Ilan University. The Jewish National and University Library has a large collection of Hasidic works, including the archives of Elijah Gutmacher, autographed letters of Jacob Aryeh Gutterman of Radzymin and R. Hayyim Israel b. David Morgenstern of Pulawy. The Bar Ilan University Library houses the Margaliot collection consisting of about 1,000 books and 700 manuscripts. Mordecai Margaliot was born in Warsaw in 1909, and died in Jerusalem in 1968. He was visiting Professor of Talmudic Literature at the Jewish Institute of Religion from 1947 to 1948 and from 1950 to 1957 was Visiting Professor of Rabbinic Literature at the Hebrew University. In 1948 he received the Warburg Award, and in 1949 the Rabbi Kook Award. One-quarter of the Margaliot manuscripts deal with mysticism, including the works of R. Hayyim Vital and Samson Ostropol,[2] and Hasidic discourses.[3] Bar Ilan has a recently endowed Chair in Hasidic Studies. The Ramban Library of Tel-Aviv has a comprehensive collection of Hasidic works, and contains a number that originally belonged to the Rebbe of Czortkow and to the library of Yeshivat Hachmei Lublin. The largest Hasidic collection, apart from the items in the Jewish National and University Library, is at Mosad Ha-Rav Kook.

In recent years, scholars have been increasingly attracted to Hasidism, and the public appetite for books on this subject seems insatiable, but no one has so far attempted a comprehensive history of the movement. We are left with a plethora of monographs which spotlight various personalities or dynasties, but rarely seek to relate their themes to the picture as a whole. More than 3,000 works of Hasidic literature have enriched the minds of men, yet Hasidism still has no standard bibliography. An attempt was made some years ago by the YIVO Institute in New York to collect source material, but little has as yet emerged.

When the news of R. Kook's death reached the World Zionist Congress in session at Lucerne in 1935, it was decided to establish an institute in his memory. In 1958 this institute merged with the Talmudic Research Institute of New York, and it was endowed with the valuable library of Rabbis Maimon and Uzziel. Under the dynamic drive of Yitzhak Raphael, a small centre for Hasidic studies has been established at the Institute. The centre is preparing a lexicon of Hasidic rabbis, writers and scholars, a total of some 1,500 biographies, from R. Israel Baal Shem Tov to our own time, as well as a six-volume encyclopaedia which will deal with bibliography, Hasidic concepts, and cities which became Hasidic centres. In 1967 the Memorial Foundation of Jewish Culture contributed 10,000 Israeli pounds for the first volume of the encyclopaedia. The Hasidic Department is staffed by the scholars Menahem Porush and R. M.I. Gutman. Shortage of funds, however, is delaying the work. So far, only the sixth letter of the Hebrew alphabet, vav, has been reached in the area of bibliography, and only 900 Hasidic authors have been indexed. Meanwhile the Institute has published a number of Hasidic studies in its periodical, *Sinai*. It is steadily increasing its holding of Hasidic literature, and it now has over a thousand works, including forty manuscripts on Hasidism and forty on Habad.

In the nineteenth century, Hasidism was greatly maligned. The champions of the Jüdische Wissenschaft (Science of Judaism) sided with Hasidism's bitter opponents, the *mitnagdim*, and were equally irrational in their condemnation. The historian Heinrich Graetz (1817-91) was groping in the dark when he dealt with the movement which was making such headway in his own lifetime. The Besht was merely 'a wonder-worker', and R. Dov Baer of Mezeritz was dismissed as 'a jester'. Graetz stated:

It was an accepted fact that the zaddik had to be enthusiastic in prayer, had to have ecstatic dreams and visions. How can a clever plotter appear inspired? Alcohol ... now had to take place of the inspired demon ... To predict the future was a more difficult task, yet it had to be accomplished; his reputation depended upon it ... Among his intimates were expert spies, worthy of serving the secret police.

He spoke of the zaddik as 'the papal vicar of God upon earth'.

So extreme was Graetz's contempt for Hasidism that it defeated its purpose. 'There arose in Poland, a new Essenism with forms similar to those of the ancient cult', he wrote,[4] 'with ablutions and baths, white garments, miraculous cures, and prophetic visions. Like the old movement, it originated in ultra-piety, but soon turned against its own parent and, perhaps hidden within itself, contained germs of peculiar kinds which being in course of development cannot be defined.' Similarly, Isaac Erter (1792-1851) ridiculed the strange dealings of the zaddikim and their so-called miracles. In his *Megillat Temirim (Revealer of Secrets)*, Joseph Perl (1773-1839) attacked the Hasidim for their ignorance, crudity and lack of culture. Perl puts R. Israel Baal Shem Tov on a par with Sabbatai Zevi.

Altogether, Hasidism had a bad press. As late as 1880 the London *Jewish Chronicle*[5] was writing:

All these sects, however, have one principle in common; they shun civilization as a contagious malady, disregard those who do not participate in their doctribes, prohibit the reading of any profane book or newspaper, even when written in Hebrew, and maintain themselves as well as their children, in profound ignorance and superstition. They live for the greater part in poverty, sometimes misery, but believe they are certain to be rewarded in the future life for their studies.

Not until the end of the nineteenth century did Hasidism receive a realistic evaluation. The theorist of Jewish autonomism, Simon Dubnow (1860-1941), was the first to paint a more objective factual picture. Dubnow, who was killed on 8 December 1941, wrote essays on Hasidism in the Russian Jewish periodical *Voskhod* in 1888. In his preface to the Yiddish edition[6] of his *History of Hasidism*, he wrote[7]

I had to gather the building material all by myself, dig for sand and clay and make bricks, and then erect the building according to a definite architectural plan. I used the entire Hasidic literature, both the learned works and the legendary materials, and I attempted to find some system in the name of various Hasidic currents and tried to reveal the kernel of truth present in the folk tales.

For forty years Dubnow collected material for his history of Hasidism, the only work he wrote in Hebrew. He aimed at a scientific analysis, writing with clarity and insight. He maintained that by 'an immense psychic influence, Hasidism created a type of believer for whom feeling was more important than external observance.'[8] He exhibits scepticism and occasionally fails to grasp the inner depth of the movement. He even asserted that R. Israel Baal Shem Tov in his youth went through an inner struggle as he was drawn to Sabbatianism. He even dismissed the tales of R. Nahman as uncontrolled phantasy, 'the product of a man sick in body and in mind', and stated that 'in vain have recent scholars tried to discover a scrap of an idea in this heap of nonsense.'[9]

To the Yiddish writer Isaac Leib Peretz (1852-1915), Hasidism was 'a movement which sprang apart from the heart of the people as a protest against the deadening hardness of Rabbinic Judaism, against the rigidity of living religion by the mass of dry ceremonial laws.' The essayist and philospher, Ahad Ha-Am (the pen-name of Asher Ginzberg, 1856-1927) also realised that Hasidism had been mis-represented:[10]

To our shame we must admit that if today we want to find even a shadow of our original Hebrew literature, we must return to the literature of Hasidism; there, rather than in the literature of the Haskalah, one occasionally encounters, in addition to much that is purely fanciful, true profundity of thought which bears the mark of the original Jewish genius.

Today, Israel is a thriving centre of Hasidic publishing, and many of the Hasidic classics have been reprinted; indeed, in all, more than 500 volumes have appeared in the last twenty-five years.[11] The noted writers and historians who have written about Hasidism in the last three decades include Shmuel Yosef Agnon (1888-1970), the son of a Hasid of Czortkow, and the Nobel Laureate in literature for 1964. He settled in Germany at the outbreak of World War I, returning to the Holy Land in 1924. Agnon's literary work reflects Jewish tradition and Jewish folklore. *Sippurim Shel Zaddikim* (1931) and *Days of Awe* are rooted in childhood reminiscences of his native Galicia. In his book *In the Heart of the Seas* we have a glimpse of the Hasidic way of life as the Sabbath is ushered in: 'They all put their Sabbath garments on and adorned themselves in honour of the Lord, taking great care that none of the dust of the Exile should be upon their clothing, that they might enter the land pure.' In describing a Hasidic pilgrimage to the Holy Land, he graphically sketches the mighty fury of the sea. 'Their prayers achieved one half and the ship's men achieved the other half, and the Holy One blessed be He, in His blessed mercy, achieved the whole. Within a few moments the fury of the Prince of the Sea died down, and the face of the waters changed for the better.'

Yitzhak Alfasi, born on 14 October 1929 in Tel-Aviv, studied in the yeshiva of Hebron, and now works as a secretary to the Bnai Brith. He is the author of *Rabbi Menahem Mendel of Kotzk*, *Nahman of Braclav*, *Rabbi of Ger*, *The Holy Grandfather of Shpola*, *Toledot Ha-Hasidut*, *Sepher Admorim* and *Tipheret She-Be-Malchut* (on Vizhnitz). He does not attempt new interpretations of Hasidism, but simply provides a summary of recent research. He is generally accurate, factual, clear and concise. His works are major works of reference from which those who seek to learn about Hasidism for whatever purpose will cull something of value.

Abraham Yitzhak Bromberg (1898-1975), a descendant of R. Abraham of Ciechanow, studied at the Rabbinic Seminary of Warsaw where he was ordained by R. Samuel Abraham Posnanski (1864-1921). He was a regular contributor to the Polish Jewish newspaper *Nasz Przeglad*, and later acted as chaplain to the Polish forces under General Anders, seeing action in Tobruk and accompanying the Jewish troops in Iraq and Persia. Since 1954 he has published twenty-four brief monographs on the major Hasidic rabbis of the last two centuries.[12] With expertise and experience he assembled useful information and offered his readers a penetrating insight into the lives of the Hasidic leaders. He often made good use of original sources, but his personal involvement with the subject-matter limited his detachment.

Martin Buber (1878-1965) was born in Vienna and grew up in the home of his scholarly grandfather Solomon Buber (1827-1906). He spent the summer months in the town of Sadagura and Czortkow, citadels of Hasidism, and this explains the fusion of eastern and western European influence that is so marked a feature of Buber's personality and works. When he visited the rabbi of Sadagura, he wrote:[13]

The palace of the Rebbe, in its showy splendour, repelled me. The prayer house of the Hasidim with its enraptured worshippers seemed strange to me. But when I saw the Rebbe striding through the rows of the waiting, I felt 'here is a leader', and when I saw the Hasidim dance with the Torah, I felt a sense of community. At that time there rose in me a presentiment of the fact that common reverence and common joy of soul are the foundations of a genuine human community.

At the age of twenty-six he read *The Testament of Rabbi Israel Baal Shem*, and felt an urge to proclaim it to the world.[14] His first work on Hasidism was *Die Geschichte des Rabbi Nahman (The Tales of Rabbi Nahman)*, followed by *Tales of the Hasidim*. Buber found truth and beauty in these stories, and he brought Hasidism to the attention of the world at large. It was this book that led the German-Swiss novelist and poet, Hermann Hesse, to nominate him for the Nobel Prize in literature for 'enriching world literature with a genuine treasure as has no other living author'.

But Buber was not merely a story-teller. For him religion was a dialogue between God and man. Hasidism was Cabbalah transformed into Ethos. In *The Origin and Meaning of Hasidism*, he wrote:

The Hasidic movement takes over from Cabbalah only what it needs for the theological foundations of an enthusiastic but not over-exalted life, with responsibility of a single individual for the piece of the world entrusted to him ... Hasidism itself wished to work exclusively within the boundaries of Jewish tradition. Yet something hid itself in Hasidism that should go out into the world ... I consider the truth of Hasidism vitally important at this particular hour, for now is the hour when we are in danger of forgetting for what purpose we are on earth, and I know of no other teaching that reminds us of this so forcibly.

Like Kierkegaard, Buber felt 'an unprecedented shaking of the foundations of man as man'. The Hasidic teaching was to Buber the consummation of Judaism, and it was the inspiration of his dialogic philosophy. Buber, however, believed in a religion without *mitzvot*, and was more deeply rooted in the New Testament than in the Testament of R. Israel Baal Shem Tov. He had not been an observant Jew since early boyhood, and was a Hebrew humanist whose interests became increasingly social rather than theological. Hasidism is indebted to him for making it a valued part of world literature, but denies that his formulations are true to the doctrines of its founders. He was 'a self-appointed Apostle to the Gentiles, carrying to them a metamorphosed message of Hasidism.'

Ben Zion Dinur (1884-1973) was born in Khrol in the Ukraine. He studied in the yeshivot of Belz and Slabodka and then at the universities of Bonn, Berlin and Petrograd (1911-17). He settled in the Holy Land in 1921, and became Professor at the Hebrew University in 1952. He was one of the founders of Yad Vashem, a memorial to the victims of the Holocaust, which he headed from 1956 to 1959. In his book *Be-Mifneh Ha-Dorot* (which deals with the origins of Hasidism and its social and Messianic foundations), he stressed that the Hasidic movement represented a revolt against the social oligarchical structure of the Jewish communities. His work is a genuine contribution to Jewish historiography. Known and new sources have been meticulously consulted and admirably presented.

Simon Federbush (1892-1969), a native of Narol in Galicia, studied in Vienna's Rabbinic Seminary under Samuel Krauss and Avigdor Aptowitzer. From 1923 to 1928 he was an elected deputy to the Polish Seym. In 1930 he became Chief Rabbi of Finland. He lived from 1940 in the United States, and under the auspices of Mosad Ha-Rav Kook edited *Ha-Hasidut Ve-Eretz Yisrael*, a collection of authoritative and lucid articles. His skill was in presenting information rather than in analysing it or drawing conclusions.

Israel Halpern (1910-71) studied in Warsaw's Tachkemoni and in Berlin. He settled in Israel in 1934, producing several erudite works on Hasidism, including *Aliyot Ha-Rishonim Shel Ha-Hasidim L'Eretz Yisrael (The Hasidic Immigrations to Palestine during the Eighteenth Century)* and *Bet Yisrael Be-Poilin*.

Samuel Abba Horodezky (1871-1957), a direct descendant of R. Nahman of Braclav, published his German dissertation, *Rabbi Nachman von Bratzlaw: ein Beitrag zur Geschichte der juedischen Mystik* (Berlin, 1910), and later prepared popular Hebrew anthologies of Nahman's tales and discourses. In his *Ha-Hasidut*

Ve-Ha-Hasidim, a collection of essays on Hasidic personalities, he sees Hasidism as a revolt against the legalism of the Rabbis:

Legal and practical Judaism is hemmed in within the narrow bounds of the law and within the four ells of *Halachah*. This is the God of Rabbi Akiva, who derived numerous laws from every letter and iota of the Torah. He is the God of Maimonides, of Joseph Caro, of Isserles [*Rema*] and the God of the Gaon of Vilna. It is the Cabbalah which supplied Judaism with mystery, poetic feeling and complete devotion to God.

To Horodezky, the Cabbalah supplies Judaism with its spiritual life.[15] He did not write profoundly but his works are permeated with great sensitivity. His background material is conventional, but the style is refreshingly different. His book is not a comprehensive study of Hasidism but a lively account of key periods and personalities.

Yisrael Klapholtz was born in Sanz in 1910, and studied in the yeshiva of Belz and at Baranowicze under R. Elhanan Wasserman (1875-1941). He was the personal attendant of R. Aaron of Belz in Tel-Aviv and until 1964 he headed the Belz yeshiva in Bne Brak. When Berele became the Rebbe of Belz, Klapholtz left the service of Belz and devoted himself to compiling uncritical works on R. Israel Baal Shem Tov and on Belz.

Another prolific writer is Bezalel Landau (b.1923) author of *Baal Shem Tov* (1961), *Tiferet Avot* on Biala (1962), *Elimelech of Lyshansk* and articles in various journals.[16] His ideas are interesting but the total effect is not especially illuminating. He attempts to cover too much territory without specialising in any particular field.

Raphael Mahler (b.1899), historian, lecturer in Warsaw from 1924 to 1927 and in the University of Tel-Aviv, is the author of *Der Kampf zvishn Haskalah un Hasidim in Galitzya in der ershten helft fun nayntzyn yorhundert (The Struggle between Haskalah and Hasidism in the First Half of the Nineteenth Century).*[17] He maintains that 'Hasidism was a movement of the downtrodden *petite bourgeoisie*', reflected the social deprivation and political oppression of the Jewish masses, as well as their yearnings for liberation. In 1961 he published *Ha-Hasidut Ve-Ha-Haskalah (Hasidism and Haskalah in Galicia in the Congress Kingdom of Poland)*. It is a learned and well researched book full of fascinating material, painstakingly assembled. While sympathetic to his subject, he retains an admirable impartiality.

Yitzhak Raphael (Werfel) was born in 1914 in Sassov in Eastern Galicia, and settled in the Holy Land in 1935. He became the son-in-law of R. Maimon (J.L. Fishman) (1876-1962), who wrote voluminously on religious subjects and was also the editor of *Sefer Ha-Besht* and *Mide Hodesh*, an eight-volume work which includes biographies on many Hasidic rabbis. Raphael was a member of the Vaad Leumi (National Council) and a member of the second and subsequent Knessets. From 1961 to 1964 he was Deputy Minister of Health, and since 1970 he was also a member of the Executive of the National Religious Party and of the Central Committee of the World Mizrachi, and is chairman of Mosad Ha-Rav Kook. In March 1974 he was Minister of Religious Affairs. He is an able administrator, an academic with a calm and detached approach to the hurly-burly of politics. His works *Ha-Hasidim Ve-Eretz Yisrael (Hasidim and the Land of Israel)* and *Sepher Ha-Hasidim*, with monographs of 100 Hasidic rabbis, are contributions based on original source materials.

Meir Zevi Rabinowicz (b.1908), a descendant of R. Shlomo of Radomsk, settled in the Holy Land in 1934 and studied in the Mizrachi Teachers' Seminary and at the Hebrew University. He is a professor at Bar Ilan University and the author of concise monographs on such Hasidic rabbis as the Maggid of Kozienice (1947) Jacob Isaac of Przysucha and Simhah Bunam.

Wolf Zeev Rabinowitsch was born in Pinsk in 1900. A graduate in medicine of the University of Koenigsberg in 1928, he emigrated in 1933 to Palestine, where he worked in the Hadassah Hospital, Haifa. Side by side with his medical work,

Dr Rabinowitsch has devoted himself to Hasidic studies. His book *Der Karliner Hassidismus* contains an introduction by Simon Dubnow. It is based on the large collection of documents which he found in the archives of the court of Karlin, and he succeeded in tracing Lithuanian Hasidism in all its various aspects, from its beginnings in the middle of the eighteenth century down through the Holocaust to its surviving descendants in Israel and the United States. His correspondence with Dubnow appeared in *In Memoriam: Essays and Letters of Simon Dubnow*.[18]

Gershom (Gerhard) Scholem, born on 5 December 1897 in Berlin, comes from an assimilated background. He acknowledged the influence of both Bialik and S.Y. Agnon. In 1922 he presented his doctoral dissertation, 'A Commentary and Translation of *Sepher Ha-Bahir*', and in 1925 he was appointed Professor of Jewish Mysticism at the Hebrew University. He is the author of such works as *Major Trends in Jewish Mysticism*, *Sabbatai Zevi*, and a host of learned articles. In 1928 he published a pioneering bibliography of Naham of Braclav's works, *Kuntres Ele Shemot*. He characterises R. Nahman as 'a man whose Cabbalistic terminology conceals an almost modern hypersensitivity to problems'. For nearly half a century Scholem has been one of the world's leading scholars in mysticism, and the guide for generations of students. His authority is rarely challenged.

Rivka Schatz-Uffenheimer, the successor of Gershom Scholem as Professor of Mysticism at the Hebrew University, now has the distinction of being one of the few women to make an original contribution to the study of mysticism. Her work, *The Quietistic Elements in Eighteenth-Century Hasidic Thought*, is an excellent guide to the teachings of R. Dov Baer of Mezeritz and his disciples. One may disagree with many of her conclusions, but one cannot afford simply to dismiss them.

Malka Shapira (1894-1971), daughter of R. Yerahmiel Moses of Kozienice, married Abraham Elimelech Shapira of Grodzisk. The couple settled in the Holy Land where Malka, mother of three children, attended courses at the Hebrew University under Dr Joseph Klausner. Her friend, and the founder of the Hapoel Hamizrachi, Yehoshua Radler Feldman (better known as 'Rabbi Binyamin'), without telling her, sent her first essay to the periodical *Doar Ha-Yom* (ed. Ithamar ben Zevi) and to *Davar* (ed. Berl Katznelson). She wrote a number of Hasidic stories such as *Midin Le-Rachamim*. 'Wisdom lies not in knowing what to write,' she used to say, 'but in knowing how much to leave out.'

The most prolific writer on Hasidism was Eliezer Steinmann (1892-1970). Born in Obdovka in Russia, he studied and worked in Warsaw with David Frischmann. Then he settled in the Holy Land, working as a journalist for the newspapers *Ha-Olam* and *Ha-Aretz*. He began writing on Hasidism ('Bi Yeme Ha-Besht') in the periodical *Ha-Zephirah*. His work *Beer Ha-Hasidut (Well of Hasidism)* runs to ten volumes (1958-62). There is nothing particularly novel in what he says, but he writes with flair. Although many interesting insights emerge, there is a certain poverty of ideas. He does not claim to be a historian and does not cite his sources. There is also a fair sprinkling of errors of fact, not to mention judgment, which are at odds with available evidence. He has failed to apply the standards of serious scholarship to material which both merits and needs them. But he possesses psychological insight and a philosophical bent of mind, and he succeeds in arousing the reader's interest.

Isaiah Tishby (b.1908) who was born in Hungary and settled in the Holy Land in 1933, is a scholar who treats his themes objectively and clearly. His monographs make a distinct contribution to the understanding of the movement, and his *Mishnat Ha-Zohar* (in two volumes) and other works are a notable contribution to mysticism and Hasidism.

Johanan Twersky, (1900-1967), a descendant of Rabbi Johanan Twersky was born in Spikov in Russia and studied in Odessa and in the United States. From 1948 he was one of the editors of the Dvir Publishing House in Tel-Aviv. His historical romance *Ha-Lev Ve-Ha-Herev (The Heart and the Sword)* is based on Nathan's account of Nahman's pilgrimage to the Holy Land during Napoleon's Egyptian Expedition. His other writings have centred on the Baal Shem Tov and 'the Maid of Ludomir'.

Rabbi Dr Israel Weinstock was born in Brody in 1909. During World War I he came with his parents to Vienna, where he pursued Jewish and general studies. He attended Yeshivot in Hungary and Poland and obtained *Semichah* from outstanding Rabbinic authorities. He graduated with distinction from the University of Vienna as well as from the Rabbinic Seminary there. In 1934 he began to teach Hebrew language and literature at the Chajes College in Vienna and at the Volkschoch-schule. Four years later he emigrated to England, where he served as rabbi at the Hampstead Garden Suburb Synagogue in London. In 1949 he went with his family on aliyah to Israel and taught at the Mizrachi Teachers' Seminary. He has published scholarly works in many periodicals, *Tarbiz*, *Sinai* and *Shana be-Shana*, and studies in Jewish philosophy and mysticism *(Be-Maagale Ha-Nigla Ve-Ha-Nistar)*, and is the editor of the periodical *Temirin*, texts and studies in Cabbalah and Hasidism, the first volume of which appeared in Jerusalem in 1972.

Dr Aaron Wertheim was born in Bessarabia in Romania on 18 January 1902, and settled in the United States in 1927. In his book *Halachot Ve-Halichot Ba-Hasidut*, he deals graphically with many relevant topics in a refreshing and original manner. In his accurate, immensely painstaking study, he deals with the origin of Hasidic liturgical customs. No one can effectively discuss Hasidic customs without reference to it.

Solomon Joseph Zevin (1884-1978), a native of Kazimierz, studied in the yeshiva of Mir and under R. Shemariah Noah Schneersohn of Kapust. He was ordained by R. Joseph Rosin (1858-1936) of Dwinsk in Latvia, who was known as the 'Rogatchover Gaon', one of the greatest rabbinic authorities of the twentieth century. Zevin was rabbi of several Russian communities including that of Kasimirov (where he succeeded his father). He was politically active on the eve of the Russian Revolution and in 1918 was elected to the Ukrainian Parliament as a Jewish deputy. In 1934 he emigrated to the Holy Land, became president of Yad Harav Herzog, the World Academy for Torah Research, in 1960 and in 1965 was elected as a member of the Supreme Rabbinical Council. He was the author of *Ha-Moadim Be-Halakhah* and *Sippurei Ha-Hasidim*. He edited the monumental *Talmudic Encyclopedia*. In his study in Jerusalem he had two photographs on his desk, one of R. Shneur Zalman of Lyady and one of the Gaon, Elijah of Vilna. His life was a synthesis of the scholarship of Lithuania and the fervour of Hasidism. His style makes the most complex research read as vividly as fiction, and he was awarded the Israel Prize for his contribution to Jewish scholarship.

Great interest in Israel is focused on Hasidic records and songs with Hasidic themes. The musical, *Once There Was a Hasid*, ran for 650 performances. The cast of eight young men and women, dressed in jeans and sweaters, sang Hasidic songs and related Hasidic lore to the accompaniment of a guitar. 'This musical demonstrates that in Hasidism there is no difference between the rich and the poor,' said the director. 'The Hasidim dance in a circle, because all the dancers are equal.' The steady output of long-playing albums of the Hasidic song and dance is tangible evidence of the timelessness of the Hasidic melodies which poignantly expresses the strivings of the Jewish soul.

GENEALOGICAL TABLES
OF HASIDIC DYNASTIES

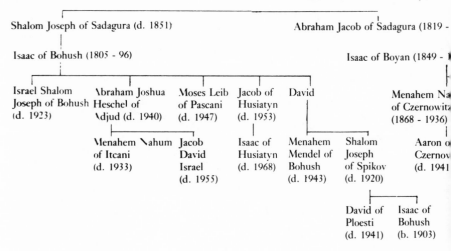

Israel Friedman of Ruzhin (d. 185

Shalom Joseph of Sadagura (d. 1851)

Abraham Jacob of Sadagura (1819 -

Isaac of Bohush (1805 - 96)

Isaac of Boyan (1849 -

Israel Shalom
Joseph of Bohush
(d. 1923)

Abraham Joshua
Heschel of
Adjud (d. 1940)

Moses Leib
of Pascani
(d. 1947)

Jacob of
Husiatyn
(d. 1953)

David

Menahem Na
of Czernowitz
(1868 - 1936)

Menahem Nahum
of Itcani
(d. 1933)

Jacob
David
Israel
(d. 1955)

Isaac of
Husiatyn
(d. 1968)

Menahem
Mendel of
Bohush
(d. 1943)

Shalom
Joseph
of Spikov
(d. 1920)

Aaron o
Czernov
(d. 1941

David of
Ploesti
(d. 1941)

Isaac of
Bohush
(b. 1903)

288

			Israel of Sadagura (d 1907)			

| el of ozig 9 - 1951) | Abraham Jacob of Lvov (1884 - 1942) | Mordecai Shlomo of Boyan (New York) (1891 - 1971) | Aaron of Sadagura (1850 - 1912) | Shalom Joseph of Czernowitz (1879 - 1936) | Abraham Jacob of Sadagura (1884 - 1960) | Isaac of Rymanow (1885 - 1924) |

Mordecai Shalom
Joseph of
Sadagura-Przemysl
(Tel-Aviv)
(1896 - 1970)

Abraham Isaac

DYNASTY OF SATMAR

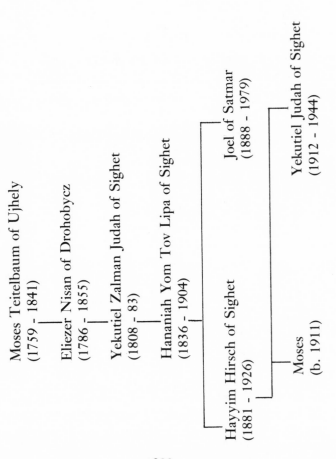

Moses Teitelbaum of Ujhely
(1759 - 1841)

Eliezer Nisan of Drohobycz
(1786 - 1855)

Yekutiel Zalman Judah of Sighet
(1808 - 83)

Hananiah Yom Tov Lipa of Sighet
(1836 - 1904)

Hayyim Hirsch of Sighet
(1881 - 1926)

Joel of Satmar
(1888 - 1979)

Moses
(b. 1911)

Yekutiel Judah of Sighet
(1912 - 1944)

DYNASTY OF LELOV

David b. Solomon Biderman
(1746 - 1813)

Moses (1776 - 1850)

Eliezer Menahem Mendel
(1827 - 1883)

David Zevi Solomon
(1844 - 1918)

Simon Nathan Nata
(1870 - 1929)

Moses Mordecai
(b.1903)

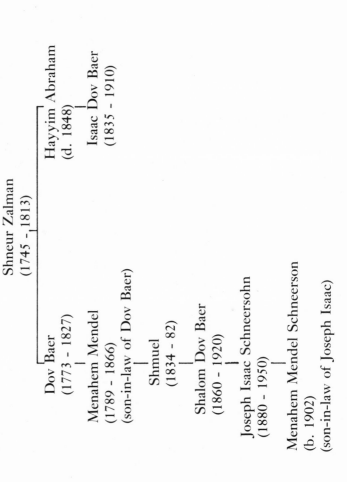

DYNASTY OF LUBAVITCH

Shneur Zalman
(1745 - 1813)

Hayyim Abraham
(d. 1848)

Isaac Dov Baer
(1835 - 1910)

Dov Baer
(1773 - 1827)

Menahem Mendel
(1789 - 1866)
(son-in-law of Dov Baer)

Shmuel
(1834 - 82)

Shalom Dov Baer
(1860 - 1920)

Joseph Isaac Schneersohn
(1880 - 1950)

Menahem Mendel Schneerson
(b. 1902)
(son-in-law of Joseph Isaac)

DYNASTY OF GER

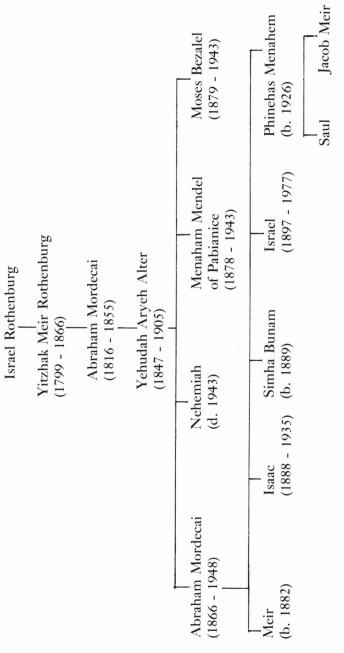

DYNASTY OF VIZHNITZ

Jacob Kopul (d. 1787)

Menahem Mendel of Kosov (1768 - 1826)

David of Zablatov (1797 - 1863)

Hayyim Hager of Kosov (1795 - 1854)

Joseph Alter (d. 1879)

Hayyim Simshon (1832 - 1900)

Jacob Simeon

Menahem Mendel of Vizhnitz (d. 1885)

Baruch of Vizhnitz (1845 - 93)

Israel of Grosswardein (1860 - 1935)

Hayyim of Itinia (1873 - 1935)

Phinehas of Borsa (d. 1941)

Hayyim Meir of Vizhnitz (1888 - 1972)

Eliezer (1891 - 1946)

Baruch (1895 - 1963)

Menahem Mendel (1885 - 1941)

Moses Yehoshua (b. 1916)

Mordecai (b. 1922)

Eliezer

Moses

Israel (b. 1948)

DYNASTY OF SANZ

Hayyim Halberstam of Sanz (1793 - 1876)

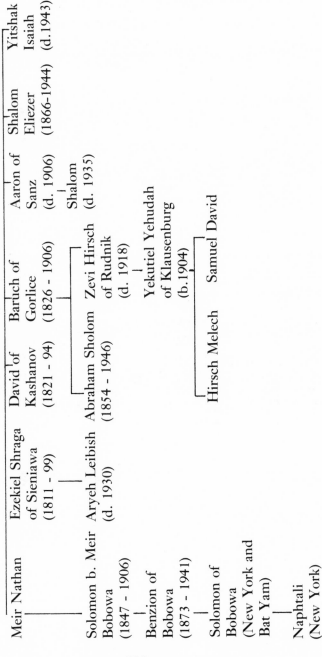

Meir Nathan

Ezekiel Shraga
of Sieniawa
(1811 - 99)

David of
Kashanov
(1821 - 94)

Baruch of
Gorlice
(1826 - 1906)

Aaron of
Sanz
(d. 1906)

Shalom
Eliezer
(1866-1944)

Yitshak
Isaiah
(d.1943)

Aryeh Leibish
(d. 1930)

Abraham Sholom
(1854 - 1946)

Zevi Hirsch
of Rudnik
(d. 1918)

Shalom
(d. 1935)

Solomon b. Meir
Bobowa
(1847 - 1906)

Yekutiel Yehudah
of Klausenburg
(b.1904)

Benzion of
Bobowa
(1873 - 1941)

Hirsch Melech   Samuel David

Solomon of
Bobowa
(New York and
Bat Yam)

Naphtali
(New York)

THE DYNASTY OF SLONIM

R. Noah of Lachowicze
(1774 - 1832)

Moses of Kobrin
(1784 - 1858)

Abraham Weinberg of Slonim
(1804 - 84)

Michael Aaron
(d. 1894)

Samuel of Slonim
(1850 - 1916)

Yissachar Aryeh of Slonim
(1873 - 1928)

Abraham the Second of Slonim
(1884 - 1933)

Shlomo David Joshua (brother of Abraham)
(1912, killed in Holocaust in 1943)

THE DYNASTY OF BELZ

Rabbi Shalom b. Eliezer Rokeah
(1779 - 1855)

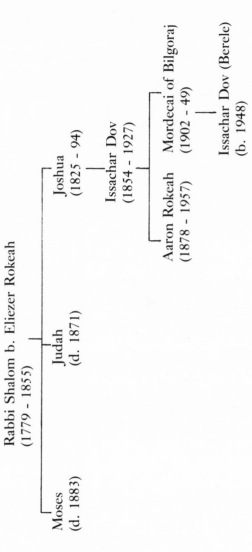

Moses
(d. 1883)

Judah
(d. 1871)

Joshua
(1825 - 94)

Issachar Dov
(1854 - 1927)

Aaron Rokeah
(1878 - 1957)

Mordecai of Bilgoraj
(1902 - 49)

Issachar Dov (Berele)
(b. 1948)

BIALA DYNASTY

Jacob Isaac (1765 - 1814)
The Holy Jew of Prezysucha

├─ Joshua Asher of Porisov (1804 - 62)
│   │
│   └─ Nehemiah Yehiel of Bohova (1808 - 60)
│
└─ Yerachmiel of Przysucha (1784 - 1834)
    │
    └─ Nathan David of Szydlowiec (1814 - 1866)
        │
        └─ Isaac Jacob of Biala (1847 - 1905)
            │
            ├─ Meir Shlomoh Yehudah of Mezeritz (1863 - 1933)
            │
            ├─ Nathan David of Parczew (1866 - 1930)
            │   │
            │   └─ Baruch Yehoshua of Munkacs (Holon)
            │
            └─ Abraham Joshua Heshel of Lublin (1875 - 1933)
                │
                ├─ Yerachmiel Zevi of Siedlice (1880 - 1906)
                │   │
                │   └─ Yehiel Joshua (Jerusalem) (b. 1900)
                │
                └─ Nathan David (London) (1899 - 1947)

298

GLOSSARY

Adar: twelfth month of the Hebrew calendar, preceding the spring month of Nisan, approximating to February-March

Adar sheni: additional month occurring in the Hebrew calendar in a leap year. There are seven leap years in every nineteen years in the Hebrew calendar

additional prayer: *see* Musaph

Admor: Hebrew acronym for 'Addonenu, Morenu Ve-Rabbenu', 'Our teacher, scholar and Rabbi'

Aggadah (pl. Aggadot): lit. 'narration' - the non-legal part of rabbinic literature; homiletic sections of rabbinic literature

aleph, bet: first two letters of the Hebrew alphabet

aliyah: lit. 'Going up' - term used in connection with being called up to the Torah in the synagogue; also used in connection with immigration to the Holy Land

Amida: lit. 'standing' - name given to the eighteen benedictions (*Shemone Esre*) which are recited in a standing position; a central element in the three daily services, Shaharit, Minhah and Maariv; it is spoken of in the Talmud as Tephillah, the prayer *par excellence*

amora (pl. amoraim): lit. 'speaker', 'interpreter' - title given to the Jewish scholars of Palestine and especially of Babylon in the third to the sixth centuries whose work and thought is recorded in the Gemara (*see also* Talmud)

apikorsus: heresy, from the Greek *'epikoureios'*

Arba Minim: lit. 'four species' - i.e. palm branch, citron, willow and myrtle, used for the Festival of Tabernacles

Ari: acronym of 'Ashkenazi Rabbi Isaac' Luria (1534-72)

Ashkenazim: term applied to the Jews of Germany, or of western, central or eastern Europe

Av: fifth month of the Hebrew calendar, corresponding to July-August

Baal Shem: lit. 'Master of the Name' - name given to a man who works miracles through piety and uses the Divine Name in accordance with the concepts of the Cabbalah

baal tephillah: lit. 'Master of Prayer' - a Reader who leads public prayer.

baale batim: house-owners, members of the community

bahur (pl. bahurim): a youth; generally applied to a youth attending a Yeshiva

bar mitzvah: lit. 'son of a Commandment' - celebration of the occasion at which at thirteen a boy becomes a member of the adult community and religiously responsible for his own conduct

ben (b.): 'son of'

ben Torah: 'son of the Torah', a young scholar

Besht: popular name by which Rabbi Israel Baal Shem Tov is known; acronym of Baal Shem Tov

Bet Din: lit. 'House of Law' - assembly of three or more learned men acting as a Jewish court of law

Bet Hamidrash: lit. 'house of study' used for study and prayer

Bilu: spearhead group of Hovevei Zion ('Lovers of Zion') among the first pioneers to settle in the Holy Land

bimah: dais or platform in the centre of the synagogue where the Torah is read

CE: Common Era; term used by Jews to describe the period of the current calendar

Codes: systematic compilation of Talmudic law and later decisions of rabbinic authorities composed at various periods

dayyan: a judge, a member of the Bet Din

devekut: 'cleaving to God', from Hebrew *davak*, to cleave, denoting meditative as well as ecstatic communion with God

Diaspora: *see* Galut

dybbuk: restless soul of a person who possesses a living man or woman; the concept was current in Judaism in the sixteenth and seventeenth centuries

Elul: sixth month of the Hebrew calendar, corresponding to September-October

En Soph: that which is Infinite ('without', 'end' or 'limit'); the hidden impersonal aspect of God

etrog: citron, 'the fruit of the goodly tree'; one of the four species used during the Festival of Tabernacles

Eretz Yisrael: the land of Israel

Eruv: general term for rabbinic enactment intended to promote the sanctity of the Sabbath

Fast of Esther: fast day instituted in memory of Queen Esther's fast before she pleaded with the king for her people

gabbai (pl. gabbaim): honorary officer of a synagogue, originally a charity collector; among the Hasidim, he also assists the Rabbi

Galut (Yiddish, Golos): Exile; dispersion of the Jewish people after the conquest of Palestine by the Romans in 70 AC, referring to the collective lands of Jewish dispersal

Gaon (pl. Geonim): title of the head of the Babylonian academies from the end of the sixth to the eleventh centuries, also given to outstanding Talmudic scholars

gartel (Yiddish word): cord worn round the waist by Orthodox Jews

Gemara: discussions and rulings of the amoraim commenting on the Mishnah and forming part of the Babylonian and Palestinian Talmuds

glat kosher: lit. 'smoothly kosher' - indicates that the meat or meat products are kosher without any shadow of doubt

groschen: small German silver coin

gulden: Austrian silver florin

Habad: acronym of the initial letters of Hebrew words *Hochmah* (wisdom), *Binah* (understanding) and *Daat* (knowledge); name of the Lubavitch Hasidic movement founded by Rabbi Shneur Zalman of Lyady

Haggadah: lit. 'telling' - the Haggadah is the book which tells the story of the Exodus from Egypt; it is read at the family table on the first two nights of Passover

hakkaphot: lit 'circuits' - processions with the Torah round the bimah on Simhat Torah

Halachah (pl. Halachot): lit. 'walking' - term used for guidance, law, traditional practice, in contradistinction to Aggadah, which includes ethical teachings and everything in rabbinic literature not of a legal nature

Halitzah: the ceremony of release from levirate marriage

Halukah: lit. 'division' - relief system for distribution of funds in the Holy Land; each of the Halukah organizations in the Holy Land was called a Kolel

halutz: lit. 'pioneer' - vanguard, specifically a pioneer in modern Israel

Hanukah: lit. 'dedication' - holiday celebrating the victory of the Maccabees in 165 BCE; celebrated for eight days beginning 25 Kislev

Hasid: (pl. Hasidim): lit. 'pious one' or 'saint' - member of the religious mystical sect founded by Rabbi Israel Baal Shem Tov; in the post-Exile period we hear of Hasidim who were followers of Judas Maccabeus; after the fall of the Temple (70 CE), the term was applied to anyone of a saintly and pious character

haskalah: lit. 'enlightenment' - movement originating in late eighteenth-century Germany to break away from the narrow limits of Jewish life and acquire the culture and customs of the outside world; an adherent was called a maskil

Havdalah: lit. 'division' - prayer recited at the conclusion of the Sabbath and festivals signifying that the Sabbath or festival is over

hazan: Reader who leads the synagogue service

heder: lit. 'a room' - private Hebrew school, usually a room in the teacher's home where the curriculum is exclusively religious; junior school preparatory to a yeshiva

herem: excommunication; Jewish authorities frequently punished certain misdeeds with excommunication and social ostracism

Heshvan: seventh month of the Hebrew calendar, corresponding to October-November

Hevrah Kadisha: lit. 'Sacred Society' - title applied to a group formed for burying the dead and supervising burial arrangements

hinuch: education

hitlahavut: fervour, esctasy

Hol Ha-Moed: the half-festive days between the first and last days of Passover and of Tabernacles on which only essential work may be performed

Hoshanah Rabba: the seventh day of Sukkot is called 'the great Hoshanah' because of the seven processions formed around the synagogue. It is a day on which according to tradition the ultimate fate of each Jew was decided in the Heavenly Court

Humash: the Pentateuch

illui: title given to an exceptionally brilliant student of the Talmud

Iyyar: second month of the Hebrew calendar, approximating to April-May

Kaddish: lit. 'sanctification' - a prayer which marks the end of a unit of the service and refers to the doxology recited in the synagogue. Also a prayer recited in memory of a dead person

kaftan: long coat

kahal: Jewish community. The ruling body hereof

kamea (pl. kameot): amulet

kapote: long black coat, formerly common among Jews of eastern Europe

kavanah (pl. kavanot): spiritual concentration, devotion in prayer

kelipot: lit. 'shells' or 'husks' - the spirit of impurity or the principles of evil

kest: old practice whereby the young bride's parents supported in their home their daughter and son-in-law for specified periods of time after their marriage

Kiddush: benediction recited to inaugurate the Sabbath and festivals usually over a cup of wine, before the meal

Kislev: eighth month of the Hebrew calendar, usually coinciding with November-December

kittle: white robe worn by officials on special occasions

klaus: prayer-room of a private congregation

Knesset: the Assembly (the Israeli Parliament)

Kol Nidre: the Evening Service of the Day of Atonement is preceded by the chanting of the Kol Nidre (lit. 'All Vows')

Kolel: each of the Halukah organisations in the Holy Land was called a Kolel or national group maintained by the communities in the countries of origin in the Diaspora. Today, it is also used to describe an institute for higher learning where students pursue rabbinic studies after their marriage

kopek: copper coin, 100 to 1 rouble

kosher (or kasher): fit to eat; term applied to food which is ritually clean and edible

kugel: noodles, or bread suet pudding frequently cooked with raisins

Lag Ba-Omer: thirty-third day of the counting of the Omer, corresponding to the eighteenth day of the month of Iyyar; observed as a minor holiday

Lubavitch: in the Mogilev region of White Russia; became the residence of the heads of the Lubavitch Habad movement in 1814 when R. Dov Baer settled there. Hence the leaders of Habad became known as 'the Lubavitcher Rebbes'

maaseh merkavah: lit. 'work of the Chariot' - speculation about the Divine Chariot

Maariv: evening prayer

maggid (pl. maggidim): popular preacher

marrano: Spanish crypto-Jew

maskil (pl. maskilim): intellectual; adherent of the Haskalah movement

matmid: very ardent student, bookworm

matzah shmurah: lit. 'guarded matzah' - matzah baked from flour that has been carefully kept from the time of the cutting of the wheat so that no moisture should touch it

Megillah: lit 'scroll' - term commonly applied to the Book of Esther

Melave Malkah: lit. 'escorting the Queen' - applied to the meal after the termination of the Sabbath; accompanied by community singing and often by a discourse from the Rabbi

Menorah: seven- or eight- branched candelabrum

meshulah: lit. 'messenger' - emissary sent to collect funds for religious or charitable institutions mezuzah: small parchment inscribed with the first two paragraphs of the shema (Deut. 6: 4-9, 11, 13-21) that is attached to the right-hand doorpost of an orthodox Jewish home

Midrash (pl. Midrashim): lit. 'expositions' - from Hebrew root meaning 'to teach', 'to enquire' - is a generic term for rabbinic expositions of the Bible; many collections are to be found, the products of different schools and periods

mikva: indoor ritual bath or pool required for Jewish ritual purification

minhag (pl. minhagim): custom, synagogue rite

minchah: the afternoon prayer

minyan (pl. minyanim): required quorum of ten Jews above the age of thirteen for communal prayer

Mishnah: lit. 'repetition' - collection of the oral law and rabbinic teachings compiled by Rabbi Judah Ha-Nasi during the early part of the third century which, with the Gemara, forms the text of the Talmud

mitnaged (pl. mitnagdim): lit. 'opponent' - i.e. opponent of Hasidism in eastern Europe

mitzvah (pl. mitzvot) - religious precept; applied also to a good and charitable deed

mohel: religious functionary who performs circumcisions

mosdot: institutions

Musaph: on the Sabbath, Rosh Hodesh and festivals, an additional service corresponding to the additional offering sacrificed in the Temple

musar: ethical literature; study of topics on admonition and repentance

Nasi: lit. 'Prince'.

Neilah: lit. 'closing' - concluding service of the Day of Atonement

nigun (pl. nigunim): lit. 'melody'

Ninth Av: anniversary of the destruction of the First and Second Temples

Nisan: first month of the Hebrew calendar, corresponding to March-April

notarikon (Greek) - shorthand-writer: used in rabbinic literature to denote a shorthand system which employs single letters to signify whole words; every letter of a word is taken as an initial or abbreviation of a word

nusah: lit. 'pattern' - term applied to distinguish different liturgical rites

olim (pl. oleh): immigrant to the Holy Land

Omer: lit. 'sheaf' - the beginning of the grain harvest in the land of Israel was celebrated on the second day of Passover, 16 Nisan, when a sheaf of new barley was reaped and offered as a meal-offering in the Temple

Pale of Settlement: twenty-five provinces of Tsarist Russia (in Poland, Lithuania, White Russia, Ukraine, Bessarabia and the Crimea) where Jews were permitted permanent residence

Pesah: Passover; the festival commemorating the liberation of the Jews from their bondage in Egypt

phylacteries: *see* tephillin

pidyon: lit. 'redemption' - money followers give to their Rebbe when visiting him

pilpul: analytical method used in Talmudic study; form of Talmudic debate consisting in a display of dialectical skill

piyyutim: liturgical poetry for the Sabbath and festivals

Poale Agudat Israel (Workers of the Union of Israel): orthodox workers' party which in 1955 and 1959 campaigned with Agudat Israel as the Torah Religious Front

pogrom: Russian 'destruction': term used to describe an organised massacre, applying particularly to attacks on the Jews in Russia

Purim: lit. 'lots' - festival celebrated on 14 Adar in commemoration of the deliverance of the Jews in Persia from the hands of Haman, as recorded in the Book of Esther

quittel: petition given to a Rebbe

Rabbi: lit. 'my teacher' - qualified rabbinic legal authority

Rav: religious leader appointed by the community; an ordained teacher of Jewish Law, a graduate from a Yeshiva or ordained by scholars

Reb: teacher, also equivalent to 'Mr'

Rebbe: religious leader of the Hasidic community, as distinct from the rabbi proper or the Rav who discharges the rabbinic functions as spiritual leader of the whole community

Rebbetzin: wife of a Rabbi

Responsa: written replies given to questions on all aspects of Jewish law by qualified rabbinic authorities

Rosh Hashanah: New Year, the first and second day of Tishri

Rosh Hodesh: new moon marking the beginning of the Hebrew month

Rosh yeshiva: head of a Talmudic college

Sabbath Bereshit: the Sabbath when the reading of the first chapters of Genesis is begun

Sabra: Hebrew term applied to a person born in Israel

Sanhedrin: assembly of ordained scholars which functioned as a supreme court before 70 CE, consisting of seventy-one members

Seder: lit. 'order' - the order of the festive meal at home on the first and second nights of the Passover

Selihot: penitential prayers recited on certain days of the Jewish calendar

Semichah: conferring of the title of 'Rabbi'

Sephardim: Jews of Spain and their descendants

Sepher Torah: Scroll of the Law

sephirot: lit. 'numbers' - from Hebrew root meaning 'to count' - technical term in the Cabbalah, employed from the twelfth century on, to denote the ten potencies or emanations through which the Divine manifests itself

seudah: lit. 'meal'

shadchan: professional marriage-broker

Shaharit: morning service

shaitl: wig worn by Orthodox Jewish women after marriage

Shalom Aleichem: well-known Hebrew greeting, 'Peace be upon you'

Shalosh Seudot: third meal, eaten after the afternoon service on the Sabbath, accompanied by community singing and discourses

shamash: minor synagogue official; a beadle

shatnez: mingling of fabrics. Garments containing mixed wool and linen are forbidden

Shavuot: Pentecost or the Feast of Weeks, celebrated on 6 and 7 Sivan, commemorating the giving of the Torah and the ingathering of the first fruits

Shechinah: Divine Presence: the manifestation of God; in the Cabbalah, the Shechinah is the tenth sephirah, representing the feminine aspect of Divinity; also used as a synonym for God

Shehitah: the Jewish method of slaughtering animals for food

Shema: 'Hear, O Israel' (Deut. 6:4) - the Jewish profession of faith, recited during morning and evening prayers

Shemini Atzeret: eighth day of Assembly, the concluding day of Sukkot, regarded as a separate festival

Shemitah: the term, used in connection with a sabbatical year, comes from a verb which means 'to detach' or 'to let drop'. Hence the year of Shemitah denotes the year of relaxation of debts, the sabbatical year during which the land was to lie fallow and be withdrawn from cultivation

Shevat: ninth month of the Hebrew calendar, corresponding to January-February

shevirat ha-kelim: lit. 'breaking of the vessels'. Evil and darkness entered the world when the impact of the Divine Light proved too strong for the sephirot (emanations), and seven out of the ten sephirot were broken, thus bringing about an endless confusion of light and darkness. Man can release the holy sparks from defilement by observance of the divine precepts, Torah study and deep meditation

shikun: colony or settlement

shirayim: remains of the Rebbe's meal shared by his followers

shohet: ritual slaughterer

shtetel: lit. 'village' - small town or village in eastern Europe

shtiebel (Yiddish, 'small room'): Hasidic term for a place of worship (also *'klaus'*)

shtreimel: fur hat with fox tails worn by Hasidim

shul: synagogue

Shulhan Aruch: lit. 'set table' - standard code of Jewish Law compiled by Joseph Caro (1488-1575), in four parts: *Orah Hayyim, Yoreh Deah, Hoshen Mishpat*

Shushan Purim: day succeeding Purim (15 Adar), regarded as a minor holiday

Simhat Torah: lit. 'rejoicing of the Law' - name given by the Diaspora to the second day of Shemini Atzeret, when the reading of the Pentateuch is completed

Sivan: third month of the Hebrew calendar, corresponding to May-June

Siyyum: lit. 'completion' - celebration marking completion of a course of a study

sukkah: festive booth for Tabernacles; wooden hut covered with branches in which all meals are taken during the festival

Sukkot: festival commemorating the wanderings of the children of Israel in the wilderness, observed from 15 to 23 Tishri

tallit: lit. 'cloak' - commonly used as designation of a prayer-shawl with fringes at four corners worn by males in synagogues at Morning Service (Num. 15:38)

talmid haham: scholar versed in the Talmud

Talmud: title applied to the two great compilations distinguished as the Babylonian Talmud (*Bavli*) and Palestinian Talmud (*Yerushalmi*), in which the records of academic discussion and of judicial administration of post-Biblical Jewish law are assembled. Both Talmuds also contain Aggadah or non-legal material. The Palestinian Talmud was edited in the fourth century CE and the Babylonian in about 500 CE

talmud torah: Hebrew school

Tammuz: fourth month of the Hebrew calendar, approximating to June-July

tanna (pl. *tannaim*): teacher mentioned in the Mishnah or in the literature contemporaneous with the Mishnah, living during the first two centuries CE

Tanya: philosophical work by Rabbi Shneur Zalman, expanding the principles of Habad; name is derived from the initial word of the work; also called *Likkute Amarim (Collected Sayings)*

tephillin: lit: 'phylacteries' - two black leather boxes fastened to leather straps worn on the arm and head by an adult male Jew during the weekday morning prayer; the boxes contain four portions of the Pentateuch (Exod. 3:1-10; 11-16; Deut. 6:4-9; 9:13-21) written on parchment

Tevet: tenth month of the Hebrew calendar, approximating to December-January

Third Meal: *see* Shalosh Seudot

Tishri: seventh month of the Hebrew calendar, approximating to September-October

Torah: word variously used for the Pentateuch, the entire Scripture or the Oral Tradition, as well as for the whole body of religious truth, study and practice

Tosaphot: lit. 'addenda', critical and explanatory notes on the Talmud by French and German scholars of the twelfth to the fourteenth centuries known as tosaphists

Turim: lit. 'rows', 'tiers' - a legal code by Rabbi Jacob ben Asher, in four sections or 'rows': *Orah Hayyim, Yoreh Deah, Even ha-Ezer* and *Hoshen Mishpat*

Vaad Leumi: national council of the organised Jewish Community in Palestine

yahrzeit: anniversary of a death

yeshiva: academy of Jewish studies

yeshiva ketana: academy for young students

Yevsektzia: the Jewish branch of the Russian Communist Party, 1918-30, which was responsible for the destruction of Jewish institutions

yishuv: Jewish community in the Holy Land

zaddik: lit. 'righteous' - a leader of a Hasidic group

zloty: large silver Polish coin

Zohar: lit. 'brightness' - chief work of the Cabbalah; commentary on sections of the Pentateuch and parts of the Hagiographa, traditionally ascribed to the tanna Simeon bar Yochai (second century CE), 'discovered' by the Spanish Cabbalist Moses de Leon at the end of the thirteenth century

NOTES

CHAPTER I THE CHOSEN LAND

1 Kilayim 1:2.

2 Lev. R. 13:21.

3 Num. R. 23:6.

4 Baba Batra 112a and Exod. R. 32:2. It is also called 'the land of the living' (Shoher Tov 56) or 'special land' (Mechilta 19:28).

5 *Kuzari*, 1:115.

6 A.H. Silver, *A History of Messianic Speculation in Israel*, p.8.

7 *Kovetz Teshuvot Ha-Rambam* (Leipzig, 1859), vol.2, p.26.

8 Abraham Berger, 'The messianic self-consciousness of Abraham Abulafia', in J.L. Blau *et al.* (eds), *Essays in Jewish Life and Thought* (New York, 1959); also Adolf Jellinek, in *Jubelschrift Dr. H. Graetz* (Breslau, 1887), Hebrew edition, pp. 56-85.

9 *Sepher Ha-Mefoar* (Amsterdam, 1709), 31, 17a-b.

10 D. Kaufmann (ed.), *Die Memoiren der Glückel von Hameln* (Frankfurt-am-Main, 1896), pp. 80-2.

11 *Sepher Ha-Geula* or *Sepher Ha-Ketz*, ed. Jacob Lipschitz (London, 1909), pp. 20-1.

12 *Sepher Paaneah Raza* (Prague, 1607).

13 Zohar, Vayyera, 116b-119b; Shemot 9b and 10a.

14   *Ateret Zekenim* (Warsaw, 1899) 88a; Simon b. Zemah Duran (1361-1444) identifies the year as 1850: *Ohev Mishpat*, commentary on the book of Job (Venice, 1589), pp. 201b-202a.

15   Treatise on Daniel (*Mashre Kitrin*, Constantinople, 1510), 18a.

16   Commentary on Daniel (Amsterdam, 1648), 7:25; 12: 11-12.

17   3:72b, 79b, 65b.

18   *Shne Luhot Ha-Berit* (Jerusalem, 1969), pp. 249-367; Eugene Newman, *The Life and Teachings of Isaiah Horowitz*, p.66.

19   Newman, op. cit., pp. 50-60.

20   Abraham Rivlin, 'Hurvah R. Judah He-Hasid Bi-Yerushalayim', *Sinai*, 38, 1968, pp. 151-66.

CHAPTER II   THE HASIDIC TRAIL-BLAZERS

1   S.M. Dubnow, *History of the Jews*, trans. M. Spiegel (New York, 1971), vol.4, p.117.

2   F.L. Nussbaum, *The Triumph of Science and Reason 1660-1685* (New York, 1953), p.144.

3   R. Mahler, *A History of Modern Jewry, 1780-1815*, p. 279.

4   Ibid., p. 301.

5   S.A. Horodetzky, 'The genealogy of Simon Dubnow' *Yivo Annual of Jewish Social Sciences* (New York), vol. 6, 1952, p.25.

6   Jacob Joseph of Polonnoye, *Toledot Yaakov Yosef*, 28a.

7   Dubnow, op. cit., p. 396.

8   Frankfurt, 1709, ch.2, p. 83b.

9   *Discorso circa il stato degli Hebrei* (Venice, 1638), pp.79-80.

10   Yaffa Eliach, 'The Russian dissenting sects and their influence on Israel Baal Shem Tov, founder of Hasidism', *Proceedings of the American Academy for Jewish Research*, 36, 1968, pp.57-82.

11   S. Dubnow, *Toledot Ha-Hasidut*, p. 68. Other historians maintain that he merely prepared the pleadings, but did not participate in the debate.

12   Commentary on Sanhedrin, ch. 10; see also Judah He-Hasid, *Sepher Hasidim*, ed. J. Wistinetzki (Berlin, 1891), 769-77, p. 212.

13   *Keter Shem Tov* (Jerusalem, 1968).

14 Eizig Judah Yehiel of Komarno, *Ozar Ha-Hayyim*, *Ki-Tetze* (Lvov, 1858).

15 *Midrash Ribash Tov*, ed. Jehudah Leib Abrahams (Kecskemet, 1927), p. 29.

16 Moses Ephraim of Sudylkow, *Degel Mahane Ephrayim* (end).

17 *In Praise of the Baal Shem Tov: Shivhei Ha-Besht*, ed. Dan Ben-Amos and J.R. Mintz, p. 23.

18 *Adat Zaddikim*, ed. Michael Levi Frumkin (Lvov, 1865), p. 5.

19 Jacob Joseph of Polonnoye, *Ben Porat Yosef* (end).

20 ibid., p. 36.

21 M.E. Gutman, *Baal Shem Tov* (Jassy, 1922), p. 44.

22 Yitzhak Raphael, *Ha-Hasidut Ve-Eretz Yisrael*, p. 13.

23 *Luhot Edut* (Altona, 1755), p. 57.

24 Responsa *Noda Bi-Yehudah*, *Even Ha-Ezer* (Prague, 1776), p. 73.

25 Nathan Michael Gelber, *The History of the Jews in Brody* (Jerusalem, 1955), pp. 51, 71, 333.

26 Abraham J. Heschel, 'R. Gerson Kitover', *Hebrew Union College Annual*, vol. 23 (2), 1950-1, p. 32; also B.D. Kahana, *Birkhat Ha-Aretz*, p. 326.

27 *In Praise of the Baal Shem Tov*, p. 19a.

28 ibid., p. 8a.

29 He had six sons and two daughters.

30 The author of *Sepher Emet Ve-Shalom* (Salonica, 1806).

31 Author of *Kedushat Yom Tov* (Jerusalem, 1843).

32 Author of *Hasdei David* (Leghorn, 1776-90), 2 vols.

33 A. Benzion, *R. Shalom Sharabi* (Jerusalem, 1930); G. Scholem, *Major Trends in Jewish Mysticism* (New York, 3rd ed., 1954), p. 328.

34 Mahler, op. cit., p. 674.

35 D. Frankel, *Mikhtavim Me-Ha-Besht Ve-Talmidav* (Lvov, 1932).

36 See Kahana, op. cit., p. 325.

37 S.M. Horodetzky, *Ha-Hasidut Ve-Ha-Hasidim*, vol. 3, p. 60.

38 JT, Sheviit 6: 136b; BT, Gittin 7b, 76b.

39 *Or Ha-Hayyim* (Vienna, 1858), Lev. 25: 25.

40 A.L. Frumkin, *Toledot Hahmei Yerushalayim*, vol. 3, p. 56.

41 Heschel, op. cit., pp. 56-62; also Gershom Scholem, 'Two letters from Palestine, 1760-61', *Tarbiz* (Jerusalem), 25, 1956, pp. 429-36. The two letters are contradictory. In one (no.8) it appears that he had been there before.

42 A.M. Luncz, *Luah Eretz Yisrael* (Jerusalem, 1885-1914), vol. 2, pp. 151-48; Abraham Ya'ari, *Sheluhe Eretz Yisrael*, p. 529.

43 According to Joel Masterbaum, *Galicia* (Warsaw, 1929), p.106, he was buried in Kitov; see Heschel op. cit., p. 56, n. 165.

44 His teachings were published in *Darkei Yesharim Ve-Ha Hanhagot Yesharot* (Zhitomir, 1805); in *Likkute Yekarim* (Lvov, 1865); and in *Yosher Divrei Emet* (Muncacz, 1905) of Rabbi Meshullam Feivush of Zbarasz.

45 Author of *Ahavat Zion* (Grodno, 1790).

46 *Seder Ha-Dorot He-Hadash* (Lvov, 1865).

47 A Ya'ari, *Iggerot*, p. 30b; Joel Diskin, *Iggerot Kodesh* (Jerusalem, 1933), pp. 15-16.

48 Printed in Amsterdam in 1740.

49 See *In Praise of the Baal Shem Tov*, p. 330. According to tale 129, this was his second trip to the Holy Land (p. 152). It is possible that R. Nahman in fact travelled to the Holy Land before 1740.

CHAPTER III   THE FIRST HASIDIC ALIYAH

1 The *Toledot Yaakov Yosef*, the first Hasidic work was not printed before 1780 (Miedzyborz and Koretz), eight years after the *herem* was promulgated.

2 *Sepher Ha-Shanah Li-Yehude Eretz Yisrael* (Tel-Aviv, 1934), p.228.

3 *Kovetz Mikhtavim Mekorayim* (Vienna, 1923), no.18.

4 B. D. Kahana, *Hibbat Ha-Aretz* (Jerusalem, 1897), p. 75a.

5 H.M. Hielmann, *Bet Rabbi*, pp. 17-18.

6 Israel Halpern, *The Hasidic Immigrations to Palestine during the Eighteenth Century*, p. 24; also I. Schipper, *Zydzi Polsko-Litewscy a Palestyna* (Vienna, 1917), pp. 18-19.

7 Yitzhak Raphael, *Ha-Hasidut Ve-Eretz Yisrael*, p.69.

8 R. Mahler, *A History of Modern Jewry, 1780-1815*, p. 658.

9   A. Ya'ari, *Sheluhe Eretz Yisrael*, p. 616.

10 Mahler, op. cit., p. 539.

11 *Pri Ha-Aretz* (Kopust, 1814), p. 10.

12 Ibid.

13 Hielmann, op. cit., pp. 17-18.

14 Halpern, op. cit., p. 33.

15 Ibid.

16 *Pri Ha-Aretz, Shelah*.

17 *Menahem Zion*, Ruth 5 (Przemysl, 1885).

18 Shabbat 104a; *Pri Ha-Aretz, Beshallah*.

19 *Edut Be-Yosef* (Frankfurt-am-Main, 1763); Mahler, op cit., p.663.

20 Mahler, op. cit., p. 653.

21 Kurt Wilhelm, *Roads to Zion* (New York, 1948), pp.14, 16.

CHAPTER IV   THE FLAME OF RABBI NAHMAN

1   *Likkute Tephillot* (Jerusalem, 1956), p. 107a.

2   *Sihot Ha-Ran* (Jerusalem, 1961), p.166.

3   *Shivhe Nahman Mi-Braclav* (Jerusalem, 1961), p.26.

4   Ibid., p. 14a.

5   *Maggid Sihot* (Warsaw, 1900), p.30.

6   *Shivhe*, p. 8b.

7   Ibid., p. 9a.

8   Ibid., p. 113a.

9   Jacob I. Dienstag, 'Maimonides' *Guide* and *Sepher Ha-Madda* in Hasidic literature', *Abraham Weiss Jubilee Volume* (New York, 1964), p. 307.

10 *Likkute Tephillot*, p. 107a.

11 *Maggid Sihot*, p. 4.

12 A. Rapoport, 'Two sources of R. Nahman's journey to the Holy Land', *Kiryat Sepher* (Jerusalem), 46 (4), 1970-1, pp. 147- 53.

13 F. Kobler, 'Napoleon and the restoration of the Jews to Palestine', *New Judea*, September 1940; Mahler, *A History of Modern Jewry, 1780-1815*, p. 687.

14 Mahler, op. cit., p. 650.

15 *Likkute Etzot* (Warsaw, 1875), p.7.

16 Khaim Liberman, 'Rabbi Nakhman Brattislaver un die Maskilim fun Uman', *Yivo Annual of Jewish Social Studies* (New York), vol. 6, 1952, pp. 287-301.

CHAPTER V   EXILE AND REDEMPTION

1 *Maggid Devarav Le-Yaakov* (Koretz, 1874); *Likkute Amarim* or *Or Torah* (Lvov, 1803).

2 *Or Ha-Meir* (Warsaw, 1910).

3 *Or Torah*, Ve-Era.

4 *Maggid* (Zolkiew, 1849), p. 4; *Or Ha-Meir*, Esther, Ki-Tetze.

5 *Or Ha-Meir*, Sephirat Ha-Omer.

6 Ibid. on Terumah, Ruth.

7 *Divrat Shlomoh* (Jerusalem, 1955), *Shelah*.

8 Berachot, 34b.

9 *Code of Maimonides*, Book XIV: *The Book of Judges*, 5, ch.XII, Yale Judaica Series (New Haven, 1948), p.240.

10 Commentary on the Song of Songs printed in Altona in 1764. Some attribute the authorship to Azriel ben Solomon (J. Zedner, *Catalogue of the Hebrew Books in the Library of the British Museum* (London, 1867), p. 140.

11 Commentary on Psalms (Naples, 1487). Also Joseph b. Abba Mari ibn Kaspi (1279-1340), *Tam Ha-Keseph* (London, 1913): 'It is possible that in the near future the Almighty will inspire the rulers of the earth to allow us to return to the land of Israel when the Jews will be gathered from four corners of the earth'.

12 Commentary to Num. 24:17.

13 *Toledot Yaakov Yosef* (Miedzyborz and Koretz, 1780; *Ben Porat Yosef* (Koretz, 1781); *Zofnat Paneah* (Lvov, 1782) *Ketonet Passim* (Lvov, 1866).

14 *Ketonet Passim*, p. 178.

15 *Keter Shem Tov* (Lvov, 1857), p.2.

16 *Toledot*, Emor.

17 *Zofnat Paneah*, p. 36.

18 *Toledot*, Va-Yetze.

19 *Ben Porat Yosef*, p. 109.

20 *Ketonet Passim*, p. 64.

21 *Midrash Phinehas* (Warsaw, 1876), p.10.

22 *Noda Bi-Yehudah*, Yoreh Deah, p. 96.

23 *Noam Elimelech* (Lvov, 1874), Mishpatim.

24 Ibid., Be-har.

25 Slavuta, 1798.

26 Va-Yehi.

27 Author of *Semikhat Hakhamim* (Frankfurt-am-Main, 1706). Issachar was the author of *Mevasser Zedek* (Lvov, 1850).

28 Ethanan 97b.

29 Author of *Yismah Lev* and *Meor Einayim* (Slavuta, 1798).

30 Ibid., Be-Shalah.

31 He was the author of *Bat Ayin* (Jerusalem, 1847).

32 *Korot Ha-Ittim*; cf. Y. Raphael, *Le-korot Ha-Kehillah Ha-Ashkenazit Be-Eretz Yisrael*, p.44.

33 A. Rivlin, *Ha-Aretz*, 8 Sivan 1938; Samuel Klein, *Toledot Ha-Yishuv Ha-Ivri Be-Eretz Yisrael* (Tel-Aviv, 1935), p. 231.

34 Albert M. Hyamson (ed.), *The British Consulate in Jerusalem in Relation to the Jewry of Palestine 1838-1914* (London, 1939-41), part 1, p. 237.

35 Ibid., part 2, p. 405

36 *Underground Jerusalem* (London, 1876), pp. 360-1, 365-6.

CHAPTER VI   CHARITY DELIVERS FROM DEATH

1 Midrash Kohelet 2; Rosh Hashanah 25a.

2 *Iggerot Ha-Kodesh*, ed. Joel Diskin (Jerusalem, 1933).

3 Baba Batra 8a.

4 *Bet Joseph* to Tur 251:8.

5 G.H. Skipwith, 'Samuel Portaleone's proposed restrictions on games of chance', *Jewish Quarterly Review* (London), 5, 1893, pp. 505-15.

6 Cecil Roth, *History of the Jews in Venice* (Philadelphia, 1930), p. 167.

7 Mahler, A., *History of Modern Jewry, 1780-1815*, p. 251.

8 Israel Halpern, 'The relation of the Jewish Councils and the communities in Poland to Palestine' (Heb.), *Zion* (Jerusalem), 1, October 1935, p. 84; see also *Acta Congressus Generalis Judaerorum Regni Poloniae 1580-1764* (Jerusalem, 1945).

9 Ibid., n. 656.

10 Albert M. Hyamson, *The Sephardim of England* (London, 1951), p. 32.

11 Cecil Roth, *History of the Great Synagogue* (London, 1950), p.9.

12 *Iggerot Ha-Kodesh*, pp.41, 44a.

13 *Pri Ha-Aretz*, p.32.

14 *Iggerot Baal Ha-Tanya*, p. 27.

15 *Iggerot Ha-Kodesh*, p. 30.

16 Ibid., ch.XIV

17 *Birkat Ha-Aretz*, p. 337.

18 Ibid.

19 *Seder Tephillot* (Warsaw, 1867), p.57

20 Ibid., 18:16; *Likkute Torah*, Re'eh.

21 *Iggerot Ha-Kodesh*, p. 37.

22 M. Teitelbaum, *Ha-Rav Mi-Ladi U-Mifleget Habad*, 1:14.

23 W.Z. Rabinowitsch, *Lithuanian Hasidism*, pp. 72-3.

24 Swet Gerson, 'Russian Jews, Zionism and the Building of Palestine', in *Russian Jewry: 1860-1917*, ed. Jacob Frumkin (New York, 1966), pp. 176-7

25 N. Sokolow, *History of Zionism* (London, 1919), vol. 2, pp. 242-3.

26 Ibid., pp. 262-3.

27 A. Ya'ari, *Masot Sheliche Safed Be-Arzot Ha-Mizrach* (Jerusalem, 1942).

28 Sokolow, op. cit., p. 254.

29 Volhynia, 770; Habad, 200; Karlin, 138; Austria, 470; Romania, 330; see A.M. Luncz, *Yerushalayim* (Vienna, 1882), p. 64.

30 'Sketches of the present condition of the Jews of Jerusalem', *Jewish Chronicle* (London), 26 March 1880, p.12, 2 April 1880, p.10.

31 120 Hasidim from Karlin; 400 from Habad; 450 from Romania, 1,000 from Volhynia. By 1906, the annual income of the Kolelim was 132,750 dollars.

CHAPTER VII   HASIDISM AND ZIONISM

1 *Ha-Maggid* (Lyck), 17 March 1874, no.12, pp. 107-8.

2 Israel Klausner, *Hibbat Zion Be-Rumania* (Jerusalem, 1958), pp. 61-2.

3 A.I. Bromberg, *R. Abraham of Sochaszew* (Jerusalem, 1955), pp. 101-5.

4 Piotrkow, 1925.

5 Willy Aron, 'Herzl and Aaron Marcus', *Herzl Year Book* (New York), vol.1, 1958, p. 184.

6 Ibid., pp. 185-6; also in Leon Kellner (ed.), *Theodor Herzls Zionistische Schriften* (Jüdischer Verlag, Berlin, 1905), part 1, p. 172.

7 Aron, op cit., pp.190-1.

8 T. Herzl, 'The Zionist Congress', *Contemporary Review* (London), October 1897, p. 595.

9 Israel Cohen, *Theodor Herzl* (New York, 1959), p. 160; Kellner, op. cit., pp. 158-9.

10 Raphael Patai (ed.), *The Complete Diaries of Theodor Herzl* (New York, 1960), vol. 1, p. 347; Marian Lowenthal (ed.), *Diaries of Theodor Herzl* (London, 1958), p. 128; Aron, op. cit., p. 185.

11 Patai, op. cit., vol. 2, p. 506.

12 J. Rappoport, 'A letter from Dr. Herzl to the Rabbi of Czortkov', *Zion* (Jerusalem), April 1939.

13 Patai, op. cit., vol. 2, p. 495. Nisan Bak (1815-89) had three sons, Samuel, Meir and Hayyim. Samuel was born in 1834.

14 Author of Responsa *Even Yekarah*, Drohobycz, 1913.

15 Hartmann's *Induktive Philosophie im Chassidismus*, vol. 1, Vienna, 1888, vol. 2, Cracow, 1890. His 387-page book *Der Chassidismus*, under the pseudonym 'Verus', was published Pleschen in 1901.

16 Willy Aron, 'The western European Jew who turned Hasid', *Yivo Bleter* (New York), 39(1), 1947, pp. 143-8; *Krakauer Jüdische Zeitung*, April 1899, pp. 8-10.

17 Y. Raphael, *Rishonim Ve-Aharonim* (Tel-Aviv, 1957), pp. 381-5.

18 Moses Hayyim Ephraim Bloch, *Dovevei Siftei Yesharim* (New York, 1959), pp. 230-1.

19 Ibid., p. 356.

20 Patai, op. cit., vol. 2, pp. 640-2.

21 Samuel Ha-Kohen Weingarten, 'Ha-Hasidut Ve-Zion', *Sinai*, 28, 1963-4, p. 342.

22 A.Y. Bromberg, *Sefat Emet* (Jerusalem, 1957), p. 108; S. Federbush, *Ha-Hasidim Ve-Zion* (Jerusalem, 1953), p. 52.

23 Patai, op cit., vol 1, p. 285; Joseph Adler, 'Religion and Herzl: fact and fable', *Herzl Year Book* (New York), vol. 4, 1962, p.278.

24 Joseph Nedava, 'Herzl and Messianism', *Herzl Year Book* (New York), vol. 7, 1971, p.9.

25 Patai, op. cit., vol. 1, p. 278.

26 Ibid., p. 283.

27 'I would have gladly driven the half hour's distance from the station to the hotel but the gentlemen made long faces so I had to resign myself to walking to the city, weak with fever though I was' (Patai, op. cit., vol. 2, p. 744; Adler, op. cit., p.301). See the letter of R. Joseph Isaac Schneersohn of Lubavitch who criticised Herzl's behaviour in the Holy Land, in I. Domb, *The Transformation*, p.223.

28 Patai, op. cit., vol. 2, p. 747; Adler, op. cit., p. 302.

29 Adler, op. cit., p. 289.

30 Ibid., p. 291; *Zionistische Schriften* (Berlin, 1924), vol. 1, p. 260

31 Bromberg, op. cit., p. 108.

CHAPTER VIII THE RETURN TO ZION

1 Bilgoraj, 1858.
2 Aaron Twersky, *Toledot Ha-Hinuch Ha-Torati* (Bne Brak, 1967), p. 250.
3 *Jewish Weekly* (London), 1 July 1949.
4 *Jewish Chronicle* (London) 31 August 1923, p.15.
5 R.H. Dratton (ed.), *Jewish Community Rule: the Laws of Palestine*, London, Government of Palestine, 1934, vol.3, pp. 2132-44.
6 Emile Marmorstein, *Heaven at Bay*, p. 87.
7 *Jewish Chronicle*, 27 September 1929, p.38.
8 Philip Henderson, *The Life of Laurence Oliphant*, p. 204.
9 Lucy S. Davidowicz, *The Golden Tradition*, pp. 197-8.
10 *Trial and Error*, p.398-9.
11 Alex Bein, *The Return to the Soil* (Jerusalem, 1953), p. 378.
12 Author of *Imrei Elimelech* (Warsaw, 1876).
13 D. Tidhar (ed.), *Encyclopaedia La-Halutzei Ha-Yishuv* (Tel-Aviv, 1958), vol.3, pp.1328-30.

CHAPTER IX THE POWER OF GER

1 Author of *Sifte Zaddik* (Piotrkow, 1924).
2 Benjamin Minz, *Ha-Rebbe Mi-Ger* (Tel-Aviv, 1950), pp. 57-60.

CHAPTER X KIRYAT VIZHNITZ

1 *Ahavat Shalom* on the Pentatauch (Lvov, 1833); *Ahavat Shalom Tinyana* on the Festivals (Lvov, 1933) and *Rezon Menahem* on the Holy Days (Sighet, 1874).
2 Author of *Torat Hayyim* (Lvov, 1855).
3 *Zemah Zaddik* (Czernowitz, 1885).
4 Kolomyja, 1912.
5 Author of *Imrei Noam* on the Pentateuch (Przemysl, 1877).
6 Grosswardein, 1943.

7   *Ahavat Yisrael, Lech Lecha,* 62

8   On the Pentateuch and Festivals (Jerusalem, 1949) and on Psalms (Jerusalem, 1958).

9   R. Meir Meiri (Fürwerger) was the author of *Humash Torah Meiri* on the Pentateuch (London, 1948) and *Ezrat Nashim* (3 vols, Basle, 1950; London, 1965).

10 Avot 3: 21.

11 Author of *Mahazeh Le-Avraham,* Responsa on *Orah Hayyim* (Brody, 1927).

12 Grosswardein, 1943.

13 *Birkhat Ha-Shabbat.*

CHAPTER XI   THE SABRA RABBI

1   Also *Kol Mahzikei Ha-Dat* (Lvov, 1879-1913).

2   *Nine Gates,* p. 18.

3   Charles Raddock, 'The Bachelor Chosid from Prague', *Jewish Life* (New York), 37, 1970, 42

4   *She'Arim* (Tel-Aviv), 23 January 1964

5   *Kol Yisrael,* Jerusalem, 1926.

6   Lam.3:56, and verses from the Psalms.

7   Responsa collection *Arugot Ha-Bosem* (Suliva, 1912), a study of the Talmudic principle *Issur Hal Al Issur* (Budapest, 1928) and a commentary on the Pentateuch (Huszt, 1913).

8   Baba Batra 75a.

9   Amsterdam, 1740.

CHAPTER XII   HE DREAMED A DREAM AND BUILT A CITY

1   On the four parts of the *Shulhan Aruch* (Lvov, 1875).

2   Author of *Divre Yehezkel* (novellae and sermons on the Pentateuch and High Holydays), printed in Sieniawa in 1906.

3   Author of *Yitev Lev* on the Pentateuch (Sighet, 1875), Festivals (Lvov, 1882) and a Responsa collection *Avne Zedek* on *Shulhan Aruch* (Lvov, 1885).

4   Author of *Atzei Hayyim* on the Torah (Sighet, 1927), Responsa
    on the *Shulhan Aruch* (Sighet, 1933) and on *Mikvaot* (Sighet,
    1939).
5   *Jewish Review* (London), 29 June 1961.
6   Gen. 12:9.
7   Avot 2:9
8   J. T. Sheviit 4.

CHAPTER XIII   THE KOTEL AND THE REBBE

1   M. Benayahu, 'The printing press of R. Israel Bak in Safed', in
    Aresheth (Jerusalem, 1966), vol.4, p. 271.
2   *Diaries of Sir Moses and Lady Montefiore* (London, 1890), vol.1,
    p. 165.
3   Abraham Ya'ari, *The Goodly Heritage* (Jerusalem, 1958),
    pp. 43-4.
4   A.R. Malachi, 'Le-Toldot Bet Ha-Arigah shel Montefiore Bi-
    Yerushelayim', in *Abraham Weiss Memorial Volume* (New York,
    1964).
5   A.G. Geshuri, *Ha-Yehudim Ve-Ha-Yahadut Bivrit Ha-Moatzot*
    (Jerusalem, 1970).

CHAPTER XV   SLONIM IN JERUSALEM

1   W.Z. Rabinowitsch, *Lithuanian Hasidism*, pp. 158-9.
2   M.H. Kleinman, *Or Yesharim* (Piotrkow, 1924), p. 142.
3   M.M. Meirson, *Ha-Shalshelet Ha-Kobrina'it (The Korbin Dynasty)*,
    Kobrin Memorial Volume, ed. B. Schwartz and Y.H. Bilecki
    (Tel-Aviv, 1951), p. 221.

CHAPTER XVI   REBBES IN THE ALL-JEWISH CITY

1   Warsaw, 1913.
2   Avot 2:11.

CHAPTER XVIII   THE TORAH CITADEL OF BNE BRAK

1   Zohar, Naso 134.

2   Avot 4: 18.

3   New York, 1952; *Ma'amar Shefune Temune Hol* (Jerusalem, 1963); also *Ma'amar Ein Techelet* (Jerusalem, 1963).

4   Menahot 44a.

CHAPTER XIX   THE LION OF THE TWENTIETH CENTURY

1   Ps. 45: 'For the Leader; upon Shoshannim'; Ps. 67: 'For the Leader; with string-music'.

2   22 Dunsmure Road, N. 16.

3   Esser Kedushot, p. 94.

4   Nasa 125a.

5   *Panim Meirot* and *Panim Masbirot* (Jerusalem, 1927, 1930); *Ha-Sullam*, 10 vols (London, 1971).

CHAPTER XX   HABAD IN ISRAEL

1   H.M. Hielman, *Bet Rabbi*, p. 189.

2   Vilna, 1860.

3   Avot 2: 12.

4   Pesahim 68b.

5   For additional information on Habad in Israel, see *Challenge: an Encounter with Lubavitch-Chabad* (London, 1970), pp. 135-51 (published by the Lubavitch Foundation).

CHAPTER XXI   A HASIDIC ISLAND IN A SECULAR SEA

1   Jerusalem, 1964.

CHAPTER XXII THE LOVE-HATE SYNDROME OF SATMAR

1 Lvov, 1848.
2 Lvov, 1898; Sighet, 1875.
3 Sighet, 1927.
4 *Va-Yoel Moshe* (New York, 1959); *Kuntres al Ha-Geulah Ve-al Ha Temurah* (New York, 1967).
5 *Va-Yoel*, p. 14
6 Ibid., p. 124.
7 Ketubot 111a.
8 *Va-Yoel*, p. 10.
9 *Al Ha-Geulah Ve-al Ha-Temurah* (New York, 1968).
10 *Va-Yoel*, p.10.
11 JT. Megillah 1:7.
12 London, 1955.
13 Aaron Cohen, *Israel and the Arab World* (London, 1970), p. 377.
14 Charles S. Liebman, 'Orthodoxy in American Jewish life', *American Jewish Year Book*, 66, 1965, pp. 83-5; also see ibid., 58, 1959, pp. 387-8 and ibid., 60, 1959, p. 62.

CHAPTER XXIII FROM DAN TO BEERSHEBA

1 Hayyim b. Jacob Palagi, *Arzot Ha-Hayyim* (Izmir, 1851), ch. 4, p. 3.
2 Rosh Hashanah 31b.
3 Avot 1: 12.
4 Sighet, 1895.
5 Munkacs, 1883.
6 Bergsasz, 1921.

CHAPTER XXIV THE REBBES OF SPINKA

1 Sighet, 1910.
2 Author of *Shulhan Aruch, Orah Hayyim* (Sighet, 1898).

CHAPTER XXV   THE HASIDIC COMMUNITY

1 *General Report, Palestine and Transjordania for 1936* (HMSO, London, 1937), p. 150.

2 State Education Act 5713-1953: Regulations Concerning Recognised Educational Institutions (Jerusalem, 1954), section 9a.

3 Mark Wischnitzer, 'Documents on the yeshivot of eastern Europe', *Talpiyot* (New York), 6, 1953, nos 1-2; Zerah Warhaftig, *The Yeshivot in Israel* (Jerusalem, Ministry of Religious Affairs, n.d.); J. Bentwich, *Education in Israel*, pp. 109-11; M.B.B. Steinberg, 'The Emergence of the Contemporary Jewish Educational System: a Comparative Study, with Special Reference to Israel and the USA', unpublished thesis, University of London, 1968.

4 S. Grueineman (ed.), *Kovetz Iggerot Hazon Ish* (Jerusalem, 1954), part 1, letter 86.

5 *Jerusalem Post*, 3 January 1973, p.2.

6 E. Marmorstein, *Heaven at Bay*, pp. 87-8.

7 *Jewish Weekly* (London), 22 August 1947.

CHAPTER XXVI   HASIDIC LITERATURE

1 There is a microfilm catalogue available in the Library of the Hebrew University, Jerusalem.

2 No. 472.

3 Nos 475 and 474.

4 *History of the Jews* (Philadephia, 1895), vol. 5, p. 374.

5 16 July, p. 12.

6 It is also the preface to the German edition, vol. 1, p. 151.

7 *Geshikhte fun Khasidism oyfn yesod*, vol. 1, Introduction, p. 2.

8 *Toledot Ha-Hasidut (History of Hasidism)* (Tel-Aviv, 1932), vol. 1, pp. 35, 36.

9 Ibid., vol. 2, p. 307.

10 *Al Parshat Ha-Derachim* (Berlin, 1913), vol. 2, p. 129.

11 Abraham Rubinstein in *Temirin*, ed. Israel Weinstock, vol. 2 (Jerusalem, 1972), pp. 327-61.

12 See the Bibliography.

13 Seymour Siegel, 'Martin Buber, an appreciation', *American Jewish Year Book*, 67, 1966, p. 40.

14 M. Buber, *The Way of Man According to the Teachings of the Hasidism*, p. 59.

15 Introduction, p. xl.

16 Tel-Aviv, 1947.

17 New York, 1942.

18 Simon Rawidowicz (ed.), London, 1954.

BIBLIOGRAPHY

HASIDIC WORKS (in alphabetical order of titles)

Avodat Yisrael, Israel of Kozienice, Lvov, 1858.

Ben Porat Yosef, Jacob Joseph of Polonnoye, Koretz, 1781.

Degel Mahane Efrayim, Moses Ephraim of Sudylkow, Jerusalem, 1963.

Divrat Shlomoh, Solomon of Lutsk, Jerusalem, 1955.

Hayye Moharan, Nathan of Nemirov, Lvov, 1872.

Iggerot Shomer Emunim, Aaron Roth, Jerusalem, 1942.

Kedushat Levi Ha-Shalom, Levi Yitzhak of Berdichev, Jerusalem, 1958.

Keter Shem Tov, Aaron of Opatow, Zolkiew, 1784.

Likkute Yekarim, Lvov, 1865.

Maggid Devarav Le-Yaakov, Solomon of Lutsk, Jerusalem, 1962.

Meor Einayim, Kalonymos Kalman Epstein of Cracow, Tel-Aviv, 1965.

Meor Einayim, Nahum of Czernobil, Jerusalem, 1960.

Noam Elimelech, Elimelech of Lyshansk, Lvov, 1874.

Nofet Tzufim, Phinehas of Koretz, Lvov, 1874.

Or Ha-Meir, Zeev Wolf of Zhitomir, New York, 1968.

Pri Ha-Aretz, Menahem Mendel of Vitebsk, Jerusalem, 1965.

Pri Kodesh Hillulim, Zeev Hirsch of Zhydachov, Tel-Aviv, 1960.

Tanya, Shneur Zalman of Lyady, Slavuta, 1797.

Toledot Yaakov Yosef, Jacob Joseph of Polonnoye, Warsaw, 1881.

Zavaat Ha-Ribash, Jerusalem, 1948.

Zimrat Ha-Aretz, Nahman of Braclav, Lvov, 1876.

Zophnat Paneah, Jacob Joseph of Polonnoye, Lvov, 1866.

WORKS ON HASIDISM

Abelson, J., *Jewish Mysticism*, London, 1913.

Agnon, S.Y., *The Bridal Canopy*, London, 1968.

——,*A Guest for the Night*, London, 1968.

——,*Twenty-One Stories*, London, 1970.

Alfasi, Yitzhak, *Rabbi Me-Kotzk*, Tel-Aviv, 1952.

——,*Rabbi Nahman Me-Braclav* Tel-Aviv, 1953.

——,*Ger*, Tel-Aviv, 1954

——,*Rishon Le-Ziyyon*, Tel-Aviv, 1956.

——,*Ha-Saba Ha-Kadosh*, Tel-Aviv, 1957.

——,*Toledot Ha-Hasidut*, Tel-Aviv, 1960.

——,*Sepher Admorim*, Tel-Aviv, 1961.

——,*Tipheret She-Be-Malchut*, Tel-Aviv, 1961.

——,*Hozeh Mi-Lublin*, Tel-Aviv, 1961.

——,*Ha-Hasidut*, Tel-Aviv, 1974

Araten, Israel, *Sepher Emet Ve-Emunah*, Jerusalem, 1940.

Badi, Joseph, *Religion in Israel Today*, New York, 1956.

Baron, Salo Wittmayer, 'Hasidism', in *A Social and Religious History of the Jews*, New York, 1937, vol. 2, pp. 153-63.

Ben-Amos, Dan and Mintz, Jeremy R. (eds), *In Praise of the Baal Shem Tov: Shivhei Ha-Besht*, Indiana University Press, 1970.

Benayahu, M., 'The printing press of R. Israel Bak in Safed', *Areshet* (Jerusalem) 4, 1966, pp.271-95 (Heb.).

Bentwich, Joseph, *Education in Israel*, Philadelphia, 1965.

Berger, Israel, *Esser Atarot*, Piotrokow, 1910.

——, *Esser Kedushot*, Warsaw, 1925.

Bihovsky, H.A., *Ginze Nistarot*, Jerusalem, 1924.

Braver, A. J. 'Al Ha-Machlokot She-bein Shneur Zalman Mi-Liadi Ve-Rabbi Avraham Mi-Kalisk', *Kiryat Sepher*, Jerusalem, 1924, vol. 1(1) pp. 142-50, and (3), pp. 226-38.

Bromberg, Abraham Yitzhak, *The Rabbi of Sanz and his Sons*, Jerusalem, 1949.

——, *Rabbi Zaddok Ha-Kohen*, Jerusalem, 1950.

——, *Rabbi Judah Leib Alter*, Tel-Aviv, 1951.

——, *Alexander*, Jerusalem, 1952.

——, *Sochaszew*, Jerusalem, 1953.

——, *Rabbi Israel of Ruzhin*, Jerusalem, 1953.

——, *Admorei Alexander*, Jerusalem, 1954.

——, *Rabbi Moses Teitelbaum*, Jerusalem, 1954.

——, *Admorim Le-Beit Belz*, Jerusalem, 1955.

——, *Amshinov*, Jerusalem, 1956.

——, *Mishpachat Eiger*, Jerusalem, 1958.

——, *Bet Kozienice*, Jerusalem, 1961.

——, *Hozeh Mi-Lublin*, Jerusalem, 1962.

——, *Rabbi Abraham Mordecai Alter*, Jerusalem, 1966.

——, *Admor Rabbi Yeshayahu Mushkat*, Jerusalem, 1968.

——, *Rabbi Elijah Guttmacher*, Jerusalem, 1969.

Buber, Martin, *Tales of the Hasidim, The Early Masters*, trans. Olga Marx, New York, 1947.

——, *Tales of the Hasidim, The Later Masters*, trans. Olga Marx, vol. 2, New York, 1948.

——, *Hasidism*, trans. Greta Hort, New York, 1948.

——, *The Way of Man According to the Teachings of the Hasidim*, London, 1950.

——, *The Eclipse of God*, New York, 1952.

——, *Israel and Palestine*, London, 1952.

——, *The Legend of the Baal Shem*, trans. Maurice Friedman, London, 1955.

——, *The Tales of Rabbi Nachman*, trans. Maurice Friedman, New York, 1956.

——, *Ha-Hasidut Ve-Zion*, Jerusalem, 1963.

Finn, James, *Stirring Times or Records from Jerusalem Consular Chronicles of 1853-1856*, Jerusalem, 1878.

Fishman, Judah Leib (ed.) *Sepher Ha-Besht*, Jerusalem, 1960.

Fleer, Gedalia, *Rabbi Nachman's Fire*, New York, 1972.

Friedman, Maurice S., *Martin Buber*, London, 1955.

Frumkin, Aryeh Leib, *Toledot Hahmei Yerushalayim* (with additions by A. Rivlin), 3 vols, Jerusalem, 1928-30.

Gersh, Harry, and Miller, Samam, 'Satmar in Brooklyn; a Zealot Community', *Commentary* (New York), November 1959, 28, pp. 389-99.

Geshuri, Meir Shimon, *Ha-Niggun Ve-Ha-Rikkud Ba-Hasidut*, 5 vols, Tel-Aviv, 1953.

Goldman, Eliezer, *Religious Issues in Israel's political life*, Zionist Organisation Youth and He-Halutz Department, Jerusalem, 1964.

Goldman, Jacob, *Yalkut Eretz Yisrael Ha-Shalem*, Warsaw, 1894.

Graetz, H., *Geschichte der Juden von den altesten Zeiten bis auf die Gegenwart*, vol. 9, Leipzig, 1970.

Halevi, Judah, *Kuzari*, Hanover, 1836.

Halpern, Israel, *The Hasidic Immigrations to Palestine during the Eighteenth Century* (Heb.) *Studies and Texts in Jewish Mysticism*, vol. 4, Jerusalem and Tel-Aviv, 1946.

——, 'Association for the study of the Torah and for Good Deeds and the spread of the Hasidic movement', *Zion* (Jerusalem), 12, 1957, pp. 195-213 (Heb.).

Hanover, Nathan Nata, *Yeven Metzula*, Lvov, 1851.

Henderson, Philip, *The Life of Laurence Oliphant*, London, 1956.

Herzl Year Book, ed. Raphael Patai, vols 1-6, Herzl Press, New York, 1958-65.

Heschel, Abraham J., 'A biographical note on Rabbi Phinehas of Koretz', *Alei Ayin; The Salman Schocken Jubilee Volume . . . Issued on the occasion of his seventieth birthday . . .* , Jerusalem, 1948, pp. 213-44.

——, 'Reb Pinkhes Koritser', *Yivo Bleter*, vol. 23, New York, 1949, pp. 9-48.

——, 'Rabbi Gershon Kitover: his life and immigration to the land of Israel', *Hebrew Union College Annual*, 23 (2), 1950-1, pp. 17-71.

——, *The Origin and Meaning of Hasidism*, trans. Maurice Friedman, New York, 1960.

Challenge: an Encounter with Lubavitch-Chabad in Israel, Lubavitch Foundation of Great Britain, London, 1974.

Cohen, Israel, *Theodor Herzl*, New York and London, 1959.

Dancyger, Yehudah Moses, *Hashurah Le-Tovah*, Piotrkow, 1933.

Davidowicz, Lucy S., *The Golden Tradition*, New York, 1967.

Dinur Ben Zion, *Israel in Dispersion*, 3 vols, Jerusalem, 1925-36.

——, 'The beginning of Hasidism and its social and messianic elements', *Zion* (Jerusalem), 8, 1934, pp, 107-15; 117-34; 179-200; 9, 1943, pp. 39-45; 9, 1945, pp. 89-108; 186-97; 10 (1944-5), pp. 67-77; 149-96 (Heb.).

——, *Be-Mifneh Ha-Dorot*, Jerusalem, 1955.

Domb, I., *The Transformation: the Case of the Neture Karta*, London, 1958.

Don Yehia, S. Daniel, *Yeshayah Shapira Ha-Admor Ha-Halutz*, Jerusalem, 1966

Dresner, S.N., *The Zaddik*, New York, 1960.

Dubnow, S.M., *History of the Jews in Russia and Poland from the Earliest Times until the Present Day*, trans. I. Friedlaender, 3 vols, Philadelphia, 1916-20.

——, *Pinkas Medinat Lita*, Berlin, 1925.

——, 'Iggerot Ha-Besht Ve-Talmidav', *Kiryat Sepher* (Jerusalem), 2, no.3, pp. 204-11.

——, *Toledot Ha-Hasidut*, Tel-Aviv, 1960.

Ele Ezkerah, Research Institute of Religious Jewry, 6 vols, New York, 1956-65.

Encyclopaedia of the Jewish Diaspora (Heb.): *Warsaw* (ed. Yitzhak Gruenbaum), Tel-Aviv, 1953-8, *Lublin* (ed. N. M. Gelber), Jerusalem and Tel-Aviv, 1956.

Eshkoli, A. Z., 'Ha-Hasidut Be-Polin', *Bet Yisrael Be-Polin*, (ed. I. Halpern), part 2, Jerusalem, 1953.

Federbush, Simon, *Hazon Torah Ve-Zion*, Jerusalem, 1960.

—, 'Unknown documents on the history of Hasidism', *Yivo Bleter*, vol. 36, New York, 1952, pp. 113-35.

—, 'Rabbi Nahman of Kosov, the Besht's Friend', *Harry Austryn Wolfson Jubilee Volume*, ed. Saul Libermann, New York and Jerusalem, 1965, pp. 113-141.

—, *The Earth is the Lord's*, New York, 1968.

—, *A Passion for Truth*, London, 1973.

Hielmann, H. M., *Bet Rabbi*, Berdichev, 1903.

Hillmann, D. Z., *Iggerot Baal Ha-Tanya*, Jerusalem, 1953.

Horodetzky, Samuel Abba, *Leaders of Hasidism*, trans. Maria Horodetzky-Magasanik, London, 1928.

—,*Ole Zion*, Jerusalem, 1947.

—, *Torat Ha-Kabbalah shel R. Moshe Cordovero*, Jerusalem, 1950.

—, *Ha-Hasidut Ve-Ha-Hasidim*, 2 vols, 3rd ed., Tel-Aviv, 1953.

—(ed.) *Shivhe Ha-Besht*, Tel-Aviv, 1947, 2nd ed., 1960.

Jacobs, Louis, 'The concept of Hasid in the Biblical and Rabbinic literature', *Journal of Jewish Studies* (London), 6, 1957, pp. 143-54.

—(trans.), *Tract of Ecstasy*, London, 1963.

—, *Seeker of Unity*, London, 1966.

—, *Hasidic Prayer*, London, 1972.

Kahana, Baruch David, *Birkhat Ha-Aretz*, Jerusalem, 1904.

Kamelhaar, Y.D., *Dor Deah*, Bilgoraj, 1933.

Klausner, Israel, *Vilna Bi-Tkufat Ha-Gaon*, Jerusalem, 1942.

—, *Hibbat Zion Be-Romania*, Jerusalem, 1958.

Klausner, Joseph, *The Messianic Idea in Israel*, London, 1948.

Lamm, Norman, 'The ideology of the Neturei Karta', *Tradition* (New York), 13, (1), Fall 1971, pp. 38-53.

Landau, Bezalel, *Rabbi Elimelech Mi-Lishansk*, Jerusalem, 1963.

Landau, Bezalel and Urenter, N., eds, *Harav Ha-Kadosh Mi-Belza*, Jerusalem, 1967.

Langer, Jiri, *Nine Gates*, London, 1961.

Lipshitz, Max A., *The Faith of a Hasid*, New York, 1967.

—, 'The Hasidic School of Gur', dissertation, University of Wisconsin, 1964.

Mahler, Raphael, *Ha-Hasidut Ve-Ha-Haskalah*, Merhavya, 1961.

——, *A History of Modern Jewry, 1780-1815*, London, 1971.

Marmorstein, Emile, *Heaven at Bay*, London, 1969.

Maybaum, Ignaz, *Trialogue between Jew, Christian and Muslim*, London, 1972.

Mindel, Nissan, *Likkutei Amarim (Tanya)*, New York, 1962.

Minkin, Jacob S., *The Romance of Hasidism*, 2nd ed., New York, 1955.

Mintz, Jerome, *The Legends of the Hasidim*, Chicago, 1968.

Montefiore, Lady Judith, *Notes from a Private Journal of a Visit to Egypt and Palestine*, London, 1844.

Montefiore, Sir Moses, *Diaries*, ed. L. Loewe, London, 1890.

Newman, Eugene, *The Life and Teachings of Isaiah Horowitz*, London, 1972.

Newman, Louis I., *The Hasidic Anthology*, New York 1934.

Orian, Meir, *Ha-Hasidim Be-Ispeklariah shel Buber*, Haifa, 1970.

Patai, Raphael (ed.), *Encyclopaedia of Zionism and Israel*, New York, 1971.

——, *Herzl Year Book*, 6 vols, New York, 1958-65.

Patterson, David, 'The portrait of Hasidism in the nineteenth-century Hebrew novel', *Journal of Semitic Studies* (London), 15, 1960, pp. 359-77.

Pinson, K. S., *Nationalism and History*, Philadelphia, 1958.

Poll, Solomon, *The Hasidic Community of Williamsburg*, New York, 1962.

Rabinowicz, H., *A Guide to Hasidism*, London, 1960.

——, *The Slave Who Saved the City*, New York, 1960.

——, *The Legacy of Polish Jewry*, New York, 1965.

——, *The World of Hasidism*, London, 1970.

Rabinowitsch, W. Z., *Der Karliner Hassidismus*, Tel-Aviv, 1935.

——, *Ha-Hasidut Ha-Litait*, Jerusalem, 1961.

——, *Lithuanian Hasidism*, London, 1971.

Rabinowitz, I. M., *Ha-Maggid Mi-Koznitz*, Tel-Aviv, 1947.

Raphael, Y., *Ha-Hasidut Ve-Eretz Yisrael*, Jerusalem, 1940.

——, *Sepher Ha-Hasidut*, 2nd ed., Tel-Aviv, 1955.

Rothschild, M. M. *Ha-Halukah*, Jerusalem, 1969.

Rubin, Israel, *Satmar, an Island in the City*, Chicago, 1972.

Schatz-Uffenheimer, Rivka, *Ha-Hasidut Ke-Mistikah* (Quietistic Elements in Eighteenth-Century Hasidic Thought), Jerusalem, 1968.

Scholem, G., *Major Trends in Jewish Mysticism*, 3rd ed., New York, 1954.

——, 'Baal Shem' (Heb.), in *Encyclopedia Hebraica*, vol. 9, pp. 263-4.

——, 'Martin Buber's Hasidism', *Commentary* (New York), 32, 1961, pp. 218-25.

——, *On the Kabbalah and its Symbolism*, London and New York, 1965.

——, *The Messianic Idea in Judaism*, New York, 1971.

——, *Sabbatai Sevi*, London and New York, 1973.

Shapira, Malka, *Shanine Be-Moginim*, Tel-Aviv, 1952.

——, *Belev Ha-Mistorim*, Tel-Aviv, 1955.

——, *Midin Le-Rachamim*, Jerusalem, 1969.

Silver, Abba Hillel, *A History of Messianic Speculation in Israel*, London, 1928.

Sokolow, Nahum, *History of Zionism*, 2 vols, London, 1919.

——, *Hibat Zion*, Jerusalem, 1941.

Steinmann, Eliezer (ed.), *Brisk De-Lita (Brest-Litovsk Memorial Volume)*, Jerusalem, 1954.

——, *Shaar Ha-Hasidut*, Tel-Aviv, 1957.

——, *Sepher Ha-Hasidut*, Tel-Aviv, 1958.

——, *Rabbi Israel Baal Shem Tov*, Jerusalem, 1960.

——, *The Garden of Hasidism*, trans. Haim Shachter, Jerusalem, 1961.

Stewart, Desmond, *Theodor Herzl*, London, 1974.

Teitelbaum, M., *Ha-Rav Mi-Ladi U-Mifleget Habad*, part I, Warsaw, 1910.

Tidhor, David, *Encyclopaedia Le-Halutzei Ha-Yishuv*, Tel-Aviv, 1947.

Tishby, I., *Mishnat Ha-Zohar*, 2 vols, 2nd ed., Jerusalem, 1957-61.

——, 'The Messianic idea and Messianic trends in the growth of Hasidism', *Zion*, 23, Jerusalem, 1967, pp. 1-45 (Heb.).

Tishby, I., and Dan, Y., 'Torat Ha-Hasidut Ve-Siftrutah', offsprint from *Hebrew Encyclopedia*, vol. 17, Jerusalem, 1966, pp. 769-822.

Twersky, Johanan, *Ha-Lev Ve-Ha-Herev*, Tel-Aviv, 1955.

Unger, Menashe, *Sepher Kedoshim*, New York, 1967.

Weiner, Herbert, *The Wild Goats of Ein Gedi*, New York, 1961.

——, *Nine and a Half Mystics*, New York, 1969.

Weinryb, B.D., *The Jews of Poland*, Philadelphia, 1973.

Weiss, Joseph G., 'The beginnings of Hasidism', *Zion*, 16, 1951, pp. 46-106 (Heb.).

——, 'The Kavvanoth of Prayer in early Hasidism', *Journal of Jewish Studies* (London), 9, 1958, pp. 163-92.

——, 'Via Passiva in early Hasidim', *Journal of Jewish Studies*, 11, 1960, pp. 137-55.

Weizmann, Chaim, *Trial and Error*, London, 1949.

Wertheim, Aron, *Halachot Ve-Halichot Ba-Hasidut*, Jerusalem, 1960.

Wilensky, Mordecai, *Hasidim U-Mitnaggedim*, Jerusalem, 1970.

Wolf, Lucien, *Sir Moses Montefiore*, London, 1884.

Ya'ari, A., *Iggerot Eretz Yisrael*, Tel-Aviv, 1943.

——, *Sheluhe Eretz Yisrael*, Jerusalem, 1951.

Yehezkeali, Moses, *Nes Ha-Hatzalah Shel Ha-Rebbe Mi-Ger*, Jerusalem, 1959.

——, *Hatzalat Ha-Rebbe Mi-Belz Mi-Gei Ha-Harigah Be-Polin*, Jerusalem, 1962.

Zeitlin, Hillel, *Be-Pardes Ha-Hasidut Ve-Ha-Kabbalah*, Tel-Aviv, 1965.

Zevin, S.J., *Ha-Moadim Be-Halakhah*, Tel-Aviv, 1955.

——, *Sippure Ha-Hasidim*, Tel-Aviv, 1957.

INDEX

Aaron of Czernobil, 75
Aaron of Karlin. *See* Karlin
Arbarbanel, Isaac, 18
Abraham Dov Baer of Ovruch, 62
Abraham "the Angel", 41
Abraham Gershon of Kutow, 29, 31-34
Abraham of Kalisk, 42, 44, 51, 68, 70, 72, 74, 58, 245
Abraham of Slonim. *See* Weinberg
Abraham of Sochaczew. *See* Bornstein
Abulafia, Abraham, 15
Abulafia, Hayyim, 35
Acre, 32, 33, 35, 39, 51, 52, 158
Adel, 30, 46
Adler, Herman, 87, 204
Adler, Nathan, 74
Agnon, Shmuel Yosef, 277, 283
Agudat, Yisrael, 90-93, 105, 109, 110, 111, 116, 117, 121, 126, 127, 133, 134, 146, 178, 184, 186, 188, 191, 200, 237, 238, 239, 246, 254, 263, 264, 267, 268, 269, 271
Ahad Ha-Am. *See* Ginsberg
Aharanowitz, Reuven, 200
Alexander. *See* Dancyger
Alexander, Michael Solomon, 63
Alexandrow. *See* Dancyger
Alfanderi, Solomon, 255
Alfasi, Isaac, 151, 277
Algazi, Yomtov, 32

Alroy, David, 15
Alshech, Moses, 61
Alter, Abraham Mordecai, 93, 108, 109-15, 116, 117, 133, 200, 211, 261, 272
Alter, Isaac Meir, 65, 73, 86, 117, 254
Alter, Israel, 105-7, 114, 115, 116, 191, 263, 269
Alter, Menahem Mendel, 113
Alter, Nehemiah, 116
Alter, Phinehas Menahem, 114, 116
Alter, Simhah Bunem, 114, 116
Alter, Yehudah Leib, 81, 108-9, 117, 151
Amdur, 54
America. *See* United States
Amshinov. *See* Karlin
Amsterdam, 16, 21, 25, 26, 68, 70, 91, 139
Annopol, 54, 58
Antwerp, 123
Aptowitzer, Avigdor, 278
Arama, Isaac, 29
Ari. *See* Luria
Arik, Meir, 127, 143
Asch, Sholem, 87, 246
Asher of Karlin, 72
Ashkenazi, Zevi Hirsch, 141
Ashlag, Baruch Shalom, 209
Ashlag, Solomon Benjamin, 209
Ashlag, Yehudah Leib Halevi, 209-11

337

Attar, Hayyim b. Moses, 33, 56, 151, 182
Auerbach, Meir, 75, 78
Auschwitz, 114, 122, 144, 167, 186, 233, 234, 248, 252, 259
Austria, 67, 94, 114, 120, 181, 186
Azulai, Abraham, 142, 151
Azulai, Hayyim Joseph David, 32, 69, 161, 243
Azulai, Yizhak Zechariah, 32

Baal Shem Tov. *See* Israel
Bak, Israel, 85, 160-61
Bak, Nisan, 95, 160, 161, 163-64
Balfour, Arthur James, 97, 160
Balfour Declaration, 92, 160
Bamberg, 167
Baranowicze, 166
Baruch of Miedzyborz, 43, 46, 70, 72, 273
Bar Ilan University, 273, 282
Bar Kochba. *See* Simon
Bash, Jacob, 257
Bat Yam, 245
Becker, Tanhum, 191
Belsen, 225
Belz. *See* Rokeah
Belzec, 91
Ben Gurion, David, 147, 211, 251, 268
Ben Yehuda, Eliezer, 55
Berab, Jacob, 243, 264
Beregszaz, 171
Bergen-Belsen, 233, 234
Berger, Getzel, 235
Bergman, Dov, 259
Berkowitz, Michael, 84
Berlin, 77, 189, 192, 205, 206, 280, 283
Berlin, Meir, 113
Bernadotte, Count Falke, 241
Bernard, Hermann Hedwig, 52
Besht. *See* Israel Baal Shem Tov
Bet Jacob, 105, 124, 138, 199, 252
Biala. *See* Rabinowicz
Bialik, Xhaim, 283
Biberfeld, Phinehas, 187
Biderman, David b. Solomon, 158, 159
Bidermen, Eliezer Menham Mendel, 159

Biderman, Jacob Meir, 113, 115
Biderman, Moses Mordecai, 155, 202-3
Biderman, Nehemiah, 158
Biderman, Simon Nathan Nata, 159-60
Binyamin. *See* Radler
Birk, Baroness, 221
Birnbaum, Nathan, 221
Blank, Joseph, 238
Blau, Amram, 174, 237, 240, 241
Balu, Moses, 91
Bloom, Sol, 114
Bne Brak, 9, 10, 53, 106, 117, 119, 122, 123, 127, 128, 137, 138, 139, 141, 147, 151, 156, 160, 167, 177, 191, 199-208, 225, 241, 242, 250, 260, 261, 266, 270, 281
Bobow. *See* Halberstam
Bochnia, 132, 248
Bornstein, Abraham, 80-81, 159, 205, 253
Bornstein, Shlomoh Menahem, 205
Boyna. *See* Friedman
Brand, Joel, 233
Brandeis, L. D., 114, 208
Brander, Shalom, 137
Brandwein, Yehudah Sevi, 193
Breuer, Isaac, 91, 109, 239
Brody, 35
Brosovsky, Abraham Yizhak, 278
Buber, Martin, 278-80
Buber, Solomon, 278
Bucharest, 252
Budapest, 123, 132, 172, 185, 233, 234, 255, 258
Bukovina, 124, 127, 196, 197

Cabbalah, 28, 37, 135, 211, 243, 262, 279, 281, 283, 285
Cahana, Joseph Elimelech, 261
Cahana, Joseph Meir, 261-62
Cahana, Moses Eliakim Briah, 261
Cahana, Nahman, 260-61
Cahana, Zevi, 261
Carlebach, Emanuel, 109
Caro, Joseph, 61, 68, 151, 243, 280

Chajes, Zevi Hirsch Perez, 96
Checiny, Hayyim Samuel, 190
Chelmno, 114
Chmielnicki, Bogdan, 24
Ciechanow. *See* Landau
Cluj. *See* Klausenberg
Cordovero, Moses, 243
Council of the Four Lands, 69
Cracow, 85, 132, 186, 206, 248, 264
Cremieux Adolphe, 78
Czechoslovakia, 120, 131, 232, 234, 248, 258
Czernobil. *See* Nahum
Czernowitz, 79, 85, 122, 196

Dachau, 189
Dancyger, Isaac Menahem Mendel, 201
Dancyger, Jerahmiel Isaac, 159, 201
Dancyger, Shraga Feivel, 200-201
Daneyger, Yehiel, 201
Dancyger, Yehudah Moses, 202-2
Dembrowski, Bishop, 50
Dher el-Amr, 39
Dinur, Ben Zion, 280
Diskin, Yizhak Yeocham, 91, 111
Dollfuss, Engelbert, 186
Domin, Nicholas, 68
Dov Baer, Maggid of Mezeritz, 37-38, 39, 54-55, 56, 61, 62, 71, 72, 130, 213, 274, 283
Drohobycz. *See* Shapira
Dubno, 25
Dubnow, Simon, 26, 28, 275-76, 283
Duwaik, Saul Ha-Kohen, 255
Dzikov. *See* Horowitz

Eda Haredit, 174, 237
Eger, Abraham, 204
Eger, Akiva b. Moses, 78, 204
Eger, Shlomoh, 204
Eibeschutz, Jonathan, 31
Eichenstein, Yizhak Eisig, 257
Eichmann, Adolf, 233
Einstein, Albert, 181
Eisenberg, Akiva, 269

Eisenhower, D. D., 145
Eliashar, Jacob Saul, 159
Elijah b. Judah of Chelm, 27
Elijah b. Solomon, Gaon of Vilna, 37-38, 148, 281, 286
Elimelech of Lyzhansk, 58, 60, 87, 120, 148, 174, 186, 223, 256, 281
England, 69, 70, 74, 164, 187, 190, 205, 234, 259, 285
Ephraim Baer of Husiatyn, 46
Ephraim of Sudylkow, 34
Epstein, Abraham Shlomoh, 190
Epstein, Aryeh Yehuda Leibish, 190
Epstein, Moses Yehiel, 190-91, 267
Epstein, Phinehas, 127
Eretz Yisroel. *See* Holy Land
Erter, Isaac, 274
Etrog, 31, 80, 108, 169
Ettlinger, Jacob, 78

Farhi, Hayyim, 39
Feder, Joshua, 137
Federbush, Simon, 280
Feinstein, Hayyim Jacob Ha-Kohen, 74
Feinstein, Moses, 204
Finn, James, 63
Fischer, Josef, 233
Frank, Jacob, 17
Frank, Zevi Pesah, 239
Frankists, 28, 37, 50
Franks, Yehudah Leib, 90
Freshwater, Osias, 249
Friedman, Aaron, 185
Friedman, Abraham Isaac, 187
Friedman, Abraham Jacob, 94, 163, 183-84, 263
Friedman, David Moses, 85
Friedman, Israel of Czortkow, 188
Friedman, Israel of Husiatyn, 182
Friedman, Israel of Ruzhin, 61, 79, 86, 120, 158, 160, 163, 164, 180
Friedman, Israel of Sadagura, 180
Friedman, Jacob of Husiatyn, 211
Friedman, Mendel of Bohush, 189
Friedman, Mordecai Shalom Joseph of Sadagura-Przemysl, 263, 267

Friedman, Mordecai Shalom of Boyan, 189
Friedman, Mordecai Shraga Feivish, 182
Friedman, Moses David of Czortkov, 84
Friedman, Nahum Mordecai, 211
Friedman, Shalom Joseph, 185-87, 189
Friedman, Shlomoh, 95
Friedman, Shlomoh (Tel Aviv), 180-81, 188
Friedman, Yisrael Aaron, 187
Friedman, Yizhak of Bohush, 79-80, 82, 83, 182, 189
Frischmann, David, 284
Frumer, Aryeh Leib, 206
Frumkin, Gad, 216
Frumkin, Israel Dov, 162
Fucks, Benjamin, 121
Furher, Samuel, 247

Galati (Galatz), 39, 52, 79
Galacia, 37, 86, 131, 140, 172, 228, 246, 265, 277, 280, 282
Gedaliah of Siemiatycze, 41
Ger. *See* Alter
Germany, 34, 40, 73, 78, 109, 113, 145, 146, 167, 184, 233, 246, 277
Gerstenkorn, Yizhak, 199
Gestapo, 181, 206, 248
Ginzberg, Asher, 188, 276
Glasner, Akiva, 144
Glasher, Moses Samuel, 143
Glick, Zevi Hayyim, 137
Gluckel of Hamelin, 16
Goldman, Mordecai, 153
Goldman, Nahum, 146
Goldman, Solomon, 153
Goodman, Harry, 93
Goren, S., 261
Gorlice. *See* Halberstam
Gottlieb, Jacob, 261
Graetz, Heinrich, 274-75
Grodzisk. *See* Shapira
Gross, Moses, 234
Gross, Samuel, 231
Grosswardein, 121, 122, 123, 126, 248

Gruenbaum, Yizhak, 268
Grunwald, Joseph Elimelech, 253
Grunwald, Judah, 230, 231
Grunwald, Moses, 137, 138, 230
Gudemann, Moritz, 87
Gutman, M. L., 274
Gutterman, Aaron Menahem, 100-101
Gutterman, Jacob Aryeh, 78-79, 167, 200, 273
Guttmacher, Elijah, 74, 78-79, 273

Habad, 38, 72, 73, 75, 86, 191, 274
Hager, Baruch, 89, 127-28, 263, 267
Hager, Baruch of Haifa, 122, 126
Hager, Baruch of Vizhnitz, 89
Hager, Eliezer, 121, 122, 123
Hager, Hayyim, 120
Hager, Hayyim Meir, 122-26, 127, 138, 263, 267
Hager, Israel, 121-22, 127
Hager, Joseph Alter, 120
Hager, Menahem Mendel, 90, 120
Hager, Mordecai, 127
Hager, Moses, 137
Hager, Moses Yehoshua, 126
Hager, Phinehas of Borsa, 123
Haidamacks, 24
Haifa, 51, 96, 99, 120, 128, 133, 139, 184, 209, 270
Halberstam, Baruch of Gorlice, 142
Halberstam, Benzion, 246, 247
Halberstam, Ezekiel Shraga, 142, 146, 168
Halberstam, Ezekiel Shraga Lipshitz, 167
Halberstam, Hayyim b. Leibish 86, 141-42, 159, 167, 223, 246
Halberstam, Hayyim Joshua 247
Halberstam, Judah Jekutoel, 138
Halberstam, Menahem Mendel, 168
Halberstam, Moses Aaron, 247
Halberstam, Naphtali, 249
Halberstam, Shalom, 168
Halberstam, Solomon, 246, 247-48
Halberstam, Zevi Hirsch, 142

Halpern, Israel, 280
Halukah, 9, 44, 70, 75, 78, 80
Hanover, Nathan Nata, 23
Haskalah, 82, 130
Hayyim Aaron (son of R. Gershon), 31, 34
Hayyim Heikel of Amdur, 54
Hayyim of Krasni, 58
Hayyim of Sanz. *See* Halberstam
Hebron, 21, 30, 31, 66, 70, 74, 203, 207, 214, 277
Heilperin, Joel, 27
Heller, Samuel, 173
Herzl, Theodor, 77, 82-87, 91, 215
Herzog, Joel Leib, 101, 115, 133, 182, 234, 286
Heschel, Abraham Jacob of Sadagura, 75
Herschel, Moses, 162
Heshel, Abraham Joshua, 73, 208, 272
Hinden, Joseph, 217
Hinuch Atzmai, 152, 186, 188, 190, 199, 263-64
Hirschensohn, Jacob Mordecai, 79
Hitler, Adolf, 33, 133
Hofstein, Israel, 94, 99, 107
Hofstein, Israel Eliezer, 98-99, 101
Holy Land, 29-36, 38-44, 47, 49-52, 56-65, 107, 110, 113, 146, 176, 205, 212, 225, 236, 239, 242, 255, 259, 261, 271, 277, 280, 282, 283, 286
Holstock, Meir Jehiel, 98, 143, 201
Hornistopol, Jacob Israel, 75
Hornstein, Samuel, 179
Horodezky, Samuel Abba, 280, 281
Horowitz, Abish, 260
Horowitz, Abraham Abish, 229
Horowitz, Abraham Hayyim, 228
Horowitz, Isaiah, 19, 20, 27, 65, 172
Horowitz, Jacob Isaac, 58, 60, 157, 190, 228, 244
Horowitz, Joshua, 121
Horowitz, Kopel, 244
Horowitz, Meir, 121, 147
Horowitz, Nephtali Hayyim, 147
Horowitz, Shmelke, 222

Horowitz, Simon Zevi, 66
Hovevei Zion, 79
Hungary, 92, 120, 131, 144, 146, 172, 223, 224, 232, 233, 234,237, 248, 261, 284, 285
Hurvah, synagogue, 121, 163
Hurwitz, Hirsch Bwe, 52

Israel b. Eliezer Baal Shem Tov, 10, 28-34, 38, 45, 46, 47, 49, 50, 54, 56, 61, 69, 70, 119, 121, 148, 173, 208, 222, 256, 273, 274, 275, 279, 281
Israel Ber of Lubavitch, 40
Issahar Dov Baer of Zloczow, 61
Istanbul, 30, 31, 35, 39, 50, 51, 52, 112, 255

Jabotinsky, Vladimir, 92-93
Jacob Joseph of Polonnoye, 45, 56
Jacob Samson of Shepetivka, 51, 57, 70
Jaffa, 35, 51, 96, 108, 110, 111
Jassy, 52, 79
Jerusalem, 9, 14, 16, 19, 30, 31, 33, 45, 52, 58, 63, 65, 66, 69, 70, 71, 73, 75, 87, 95, 97, 98, 112, 114, 115, 123, 127, 130, 133, 134, 137, 141, 147, 153, 157-70, 171, 175, 190, 200, 210, 215, 220, 237, 242, 250, 260, 263, 266, 270, 285
Jewish Agency, 292, 93, 181, 239, 244, 263, 268
Jewish Chronicle, the, 238, 275
Jewish Colonial Trust, 95
Jewish National Fund, 97, 99
Jewish National University Library, 273
Joint, 217, 233
Jordan, Samuel Zangwill, 231
Judah Halevi, 14, 45
Judah Hasid Segal, 20-21, 116
Judah Low b. Bezalel, 29
Judenrat,114
Jung, Leo, 94
Jung, Meir, 92
Jungreiss, David, 127, 239
Justman, P. M. E., 108

Kafka, Franz, 132
Kahan, Abraham Yizhak, 173-74
Kahan, Israel Meir, 93, 132
Kahaneman, Joseph, 199, 249
Kalish, Jerahmiel Yahudah Meir, 168, 170
Kalish, Joseph Zevi, 200
Kalish, Simha Bunem, 159
Kalish, Simon Shalom, 168-69, 170, 200
Kalischer, Zevi Hirsch, 74, 77, 79
Kamenets-Podolski, 28, 50
Karlin, 54, 73, 75, 159
Karlitz, Abraham Yehshyahu, 191, 266
Kasher, Menahem Mendel, 114
Katznelson, Berl, 284
Katzhelson, Isaac, 207
Kfar Ata, 100
Kfar Belz, 139
Kfar Eliyahu, 267
Kfar Habad, 212, 217-19, 226
Kfar Hasidim, 100, 207
Kfar Pekiin, 33, 42
Kfar Pines, 98
Kimhi, David, 56
Kiryat Ata, 195
Kiryat Bobow, 249
Kiryat Kalev, 148, 223-27
Kiryat Sanz, 10, 141-56, 245
Kiryat Vizhnitz, 10, 119-29, 199, 245
Kiryat Yismah Mosheh, 250-61
Klapholtz, Yisrael, 281
Klausenberg. *See* Halberstam
Klausner, Joseph, 284
Kliers, Moses, 178, 245
Kobryn, Moses of, 177
Kohn, Pinchas, 109, 239
Koidanov. *See* Perlow
Koidanover, Zevi Hirsch, 26
Kolel, 43, 73, 74, 75, 100, 116, 121, 124, 139, 150, 156, 159, 164, 171, 179, 189, 190, 205, 208, 217, 226, 235, 239, 242, 252, 255, 260, 261, 266-67
Kook, Abraham Yizhak, 94, 110, 112, 194, 201, 211, 216, 238, 242, 273, 274
Kopul, Jacob, 119

Kopycience. *See* Heschel
Kossov, 73
Kotler, Aaron, 237
Kozienice. *See* Hofstein
Krasni, Hayyim of, 196, 252
Krauss, Samuel, 280
Kretschnov. *See* Rosenbaum
Kunstlicher, Zevi Hirsch, 261

Lachowicze, Noah of, 176-77
Landau, Abraham, 78, 90
Landau, Bezalel, 281
Landau, Ezekiel b. Judah, 31, 57
Landau, Jacob, 200
Landau, Leibish Mendel Halevi, 84
Landau, Menahem Mendel Hayyim, 90
Langer, Frantisek, 132
Langer, Jiri, 131-32
Latvia, 92
Leifer, Abraham Abba, 195
Leifer, Joseph, 195
Leifer, Yehudah, 195
Leiner, Eliezer, 86
Leiner, Gershon Heinoch, 207, 211
Leiner, Mordecai Joseph, 205, 272
Leiner, Solomon, 207
Lelov. *See* Biderman
Lemberg. *See* Lvov
Levi Yizhak of Berdichev, 54, 59-60, 70, 73, 139, 227, 272
Levin, Heinoch, 111, 112
Levin, Phinehas, 112
Levin, Yizhak Meir, 114, 117-18, 133
Lippe, Karpel, 79
Lipshitz, Aryeh, 228
Lithuania, 25, 37, 54, 92, 283, 285
Loanz, Elijah ben Moses, 27
Lodz, 9, 106, 111, 116, 190, 201
Loewe, Eliezer, 62, 161
London, 21, 74, 92, 126, 165, 167, 181, 205, 210, 217, 235, 248, 249
Lubavitch, 116, 205, 210, 211, 217
Lubin, 9, 53, 58, 73, 157, 192, 204, 207, 265
Ludomir, Maid of, 64-65, 285

Luria, Yizhak, 19-20, 32, 37, 47, 153, 156, 228, 243
Luzzatto, Moses Hayyim, 36
Luzzatto, Simone b. Isaac, 27
Lvov, 25, 58, 85, 142, 247
Lyzhansk. *See* Elimelech

Mahler, Raphael, 281-82
Mahzikei Ha-Dat, 130, 134, 139, 180
Maidanek, 114
Maimon (J. L. Fishman), 85, 268, 274, 282
Maimon, Solomon, 26, 48
Maimonides, Moses, 15, 29, 56, 151, 160, 172, 280
Malbim, Meir Loeb, 18
Manasseh Ben Israel, 29
Marcus Aaron, 82-84
Margaliot, Mordecai, 273
Mayer, Solly, 233
Meir Baal Ha-Nes, 67, 68, 100, 177, 178, 230, 245, 255
Meir Yaakov, 94, 216, 238
Meiri, Meir, 124
Memorial Foundation of Jewish Culture, 274
Menahem Mendel of Kotsk, 45, 65, 66, 107, 135
Menahem Mendel of Lubavitch, 65
Menahem Mendel of Peremysslany, 34-35
Menahem Mendel of Rymanov, 60
Menahem Mendel of Vitebsk, 37, 38-49, 51, 54, 68, 159, 213, 245
Mendelsohn, Moses, 48
Meron, 162
Meshel of Bialystok, 65
Messiah, 15, 16, 29, 30, 33, 47, 53, 55, 59, 65, 71, 87, 145, 204, 229, 237, 245, 247, 259
Michelson, Ezekiel, 253
Michener, James A., 244
Miedzyborz, 30, 38, 45, 72
Minz, Benjamin, 270, 272
Mishkovsky, Joseph, 100

Mizrachi, 89, 90, 92, 98, 100, 113, 132, 133, 144, 181, 182, 200, 241, 251, 253, 256, 264, 268, 282, 285
Montefiore, Sir Moses, 60, 62, 74, 77, 78, 159, 162, 163, 214, 215, 244
Morgenstern, David, 80-81, 206
Morgenstern, Hayyim Israel, 80-82, 108, 273
Morgenstern, Isaac Zelig, 111
Morgenstern, Menahem Mendel, 80, 205
Morgenstern, Zevi Hirsch, 81
Mosad Ha-Rav Kook, 273, 280, 282
Moses ben Naman (Nsjmanides), 14, 17, 56, 148, 160
Myers, Asher, 87
Mysticism. *See* Cabbalah

Nahman of Braclav, 45-53, 60, 157, 144, 276, 277, 279, 280, 283, 285
Nahman of Horodenka, 54, 61, 208
Nathanson, Joseph Saul, 142
Nazis, 113, 114, 135, 144, 146, 181, 183, 186, 189, 192, 197, 207, 208, 211, 246, 247, 252
Nemirov, 49, 244
Netanyah, 10, 127, 141, 147-53, 186, 258
Neture Karta, 10, 174, 188, 237-38, 239, 271
New York, 94, 117, 133, 146, 167, 170, 181, 187, 189, 191, 197, 203, 225, 236, 242, 247, 248, 259, 260, 271, 274
Nissenbaum, Isaac, 98
Nordau, Maz, 85
Nurock, Mordecai, 241

Odessa, 50, 73, 76, 161, 205, 284
Oliphant, Sir Lawrence, 94-95
Ornstein, Jacob, 66
Ostropoler, Samson, 27, 57, 273

Peretz, L. L., 276
Perl, Joseph, 274
Perlow, Alter, 166
Perlow, Elimelech, 203
Perlow, Johanan, 203

Perlow, Israel, 203
Petah Tikvah, 156, 260
Petlura, Simon, 189, 195, 247
Pineles, Samuel, 79
Pinsker, Leon, 76-77
Plotzki, Meir Dan, 265
Poale Agudat Yisroel,133, 261, 267,270, 271
Podolia, 24, 26, 37, 45
Poland, 23-26, 37, 91, 92, 94, 98, 101, 105, 111, 113, 114, 116, 148, 158, 166, 169, 178, 192, 201, 206, 246, 253, 265, 269, 272, 282, 285
Ponentine Community, 69
Portaleone, Samuel, 68
Porush, Menahem, 274
Poznanski, Samuel Abraham, 278
Posner, Chaim, 233
Przesucha. *See* Rabinowicz

Rabinowicz, Baruch, 208, 253, 255
Rabinowicz, Jacob Isaac, 66, 94, 139, 164, 165, 253, 256, 282
Rabinowicz, Jerahmiel Zevi, 164-65
Rabinowicz, Joshua Asher, 209
Rabinowicz, Meir Zevi, 282
Rabinowicz, Moses Yehudah Leib, 266
Rabinowicz, Nathan David (London), 165-66
Rabinowicz, Nathan David (Parczew), 253
Rabinowicz, Shlomoh Ha-Kohen, 82, 158, 206, 265, 282
Rabinowicz, Yehiel Joshua, 164-65
Rabinowitsch, Wolf Zevi, 282-83
Rachmystrivka, Johanan, 75
Radler, Yehoshua, 284
Radzyn. *See* Leiner
Ramat Gan, 195, 250
Ramat Vishnitz, 127-29
Raphael, Abraham, 41
Raphael, Yizhak, 274, 282
Rehovot, 195, 252, 256
Reines, Jacob, 89, 199
Rokeah, Aaron, 137-39, 141, 174, 226, 252, 281
Rokeah, Berele (Issahar Dov), 127, 137-39
Rokeah, Eleazar b. Samuel, 35-36

Rokeah, Issahar Dov, 131-32, 209, 230, 254
Rokeah, Joshua, 130-33
Rokeah, Mordecai, 133, 137
Rokeah, Shalom b. Eliezer, 130, 142
Romania, 80, 86, 92, 113, 120, 131, 143, 144, 172, 182, 189, 195, 196, 197, 202, 225, 228, 232, 234, 248, 252, 260, 261, 285
Rosenbaum, David Moses, 252
Rosenbaum, Dov Baer, 202
Rosenbaum, Hayyim Mordecai, 195, 262
Rosenbaum, Israel Nisan, 253
Rosenbaum, Issachar Baer, 195
Rosenbaum, Ithamar, 195-98
Rosenbaum, Mordecai, 195, 252
Rosenbaum, Nathan Eliezer Zeev, 253
Rosenbaum, Menahem Eliezer Zeev, 253
Rosenbaum, Zevi Hirsch, 120, 195, 198
Rosenblatt, Josele, 186, 246
Rosenblatt, Levi, 186
Rosenheim, Jacob, 90, 93
Roth, Aaron, 170, 201
Roth, Abraham Hayyim, 173-74
Roth, Cecil, 273
Rothschild, Anschel, 77
Rothschild, Baron Edmund de, 99
Rubin, Aryeh Leib, 249
Rubin, Elijah, 254
Rubin, Schlomoh, 247
Rubinstein, Abraham, 273
Russia, 40, 41, 42, 61, 72, 73, 75, 76, 86, 108, 109, 162, 182, 216, 219, 247, 269, 284
Ruzhin. *See* Friedman

Sabbatai, Zevi, 6-17, 36, 37, 42, 275
Safed, 19, 20, 30, 39, 42, 51, 52, 61, 62, 69, 70, 74, 79, 83, 120, 137, 147, 156, 157, 158, 159, 161, 173, 182, 193, 214, 243-44, 255
Samuel, Sir Herbert, 111, 192
Sanz. *See* Halberstam
Sasov, Moses Leib, 120
Sassoon, Sir Albert, 215
Sassoon, Elias, 215
Sassoon, Ezekiel Reuben, 163
Sassoon, Solomon David, 209
Satmar, 112, 142, 228-42

Schatz, Rivka, 283
Schenierer, Sarah, 264
Schyneershon, Dov Baer, 214
Schneershon, Hayyim Zevi, 74
Schneershon, Joseph Isaac, 133, 200, 212, 216, 219, 265
Schneershon, Sholem Dov Baer, 215-16
Schneerson, Menahem Mendel, 214-15
Scholem, Gershom, 28, 283
Schwadron, Sholem Mordecai, 257
Sephardim, 40, 42, 43, 69, 70, 151, 189, 214
Shalom Shin, 96, 99
Shapira, Abraham Elimelech, 28
Shapira, Abraham Jacob, 96
Shapira, Aviezer Zelig, 94
Shapira, Elimelech, 97
Shapira, Hayyim Eleazar, 172, 254
Shapira, Hayyim Meir Yehiel, 94, 95, 96
Shapira, Isaiah, 97, 99, 206
Shapira, Kalonymus Kalmish, 97
Shapira, Malka, 283-84
Shapira, Meir, 53, 265
Shapira, Phinehas of Korets, 57, 272
Shapira, Shlomoh Menahem, 207
Shapira, Solomon, 253
Shapira, Zevi Elimelech, 172
Shapira Zevi Hirsch, 253-54, 255
Shapotsnik, Joseph, 211
Shazar, Zalman, 181, 219
Shneur Zalman of Lyady, 38, 39, 41, 52, 54, 71-72, 74, 212, 214, 286
Silberfarb, Heinoch Dov, 193
Silberfarb, Meshullam Zalman Joseph, 193
Simha Bunem of Przysucha, 60, 66, 107, 282
Simhah ben Joshua of Zalosce, 35, 40
Simon bar Yohai, 47, 52, 189, 211, 227
Smolenskin, Perez, 168
Sokolow, Nahum, 87
Solomon of Lutsk, 54, 55, 130
Soloveichik, Joseph Ber, 207
Sonnenfeld, Joseph Hayyim, 91, 94, 111, 170, 194, 211, 216, 238

Spinka. See Weiss, Cahane
Spira, Nathan, 69
Spiro, Nathan, Steinmann, and Eliezer, 284

Talno. See Twersky
Taub, Ezekiel, 96, 99, 112, 191
Taub, Israel, 191-92
Taub, Israel Dan, 193
Taub, Jacob, 96
Taub, Menahem Mendel, 148, 223-27
Taub, Saul Yedidiah Eleazar, 192
Taub, Samuel Elijah, 192
Taub, Shlomoh Elijah, 191
Taub, Yedhuda Yehiel, 225
Taubes, Hayyim Zevi, 181
Teitelbaum, Eleazar Nisan, 229
Teitelbaum, Hanaiah Yom Lipa, 229, 230, 232, 250-61
Teitelbaum, Hanoch Heinoch, 250
Teitelbaum, Hayyim Hirsch, 143, 230, 231
Teitelbaum, Hayyim Jacob, 247
Teitelbaum, Hayyim Zev, 121
Teiltelbaum, Joel, 10, 148, 197, 228, 250, 251, 254, 260
Teiltelbaum, Joseph David, 251
Teitelbaum, Mordecai David, 262
Teitelbaum, Moses, 228, 229, 237, 247
Teitelbaum, Yekuteil, Zalman Judah, 229
Tel Aviv, 30, 35, 42. 44, 51, 57, 62, 70, 74, 137, 156, 157, 169, 178, 182, 245-46, 263
Tishby, Isaiah, 284
Transylvania, 121, 261
Twersky, Aryeh Leib, 205
Twersky, David Mordecai, 170
Twersky, Hayyim Zizhak, 206
Twersky, Jacob Joseph, 95, 137
Twersky, Johanan, 170, 244, 284-85
Twersky, Mordecai, 61, 62
Twersky, Phinehas, 137
Twersky, Zevi Aryeh, 188
Twersky, Zusya, 127, 208

Ukraine, 24, 39, 54, 75, 188, 247, 280, 286
Ungar, Samuel David, 146, 151
United States, 74, 79, 86, 100, 108, 114, 127, 137, 138, 139, 145, 152, 164, 170, 187, 190, 191, 195, 202, 208, 218, 225, 237, 242, 250, 265, 271, 280, 283, 284
Uris, Leon, 244

Vilna, 37, 38, 72, 85, 86, 89, 166, 170
Vizhnitz, 73, 89, 116
Vital, Hayyim, 20, 142, 228, 273
Volhynia, 24, 26, 37, 39, 73, 75

Warsaw, 9, 24, 73, 98, 105, 109, 113, 114, 144, 165, 185, 192, 199, 205, 206, 209, 246, 253, 273, 278, 280, 281, 283
Washington D.C., 271
Wasserman, Elhanan, 90, 281
Weinberg, Abraham, the First, 115, 176, 177
Weinberg, Abraham, the Second, 177
Weinberg, Michael Aaron, 177
Weinberg, Samuel, 177, 245
Weinberg, Shlomo David Joshua, 177
Weinberg, Yehiel Jacob, 189

Weiss, Dov Berish, 153,
Weiss, Israel Hayyim, 259
Weiss, Jacob Joseph, 259
Weiss, Joseph Meir, 257, 260
Weiss, Yitzak Eisig, 258
Weisz, Benjamin Aryeh, 85
Weizmann, Chaim, 97
Webermacher, Hannah, 64
Williamsburg, Brooklyn, New York, 145, 234, 236
Wolffsohn, David, 77

Yabolna. *See* Taub
Yadler, Benzion, 264
Yeshiva, 26, 112, 115, 116, 124, 138, 139, 145, 150, 151, 164, 167, 170, 171, 174, 189, 193, 196, 199, 202, 216, 220, 230, 232, 235, 242, 244, 245, 246, 250, 252, 258, 260, 265-66

Zaddik, 46, 48, 49, 55, 58
Zewill. *See* Goldman
Zinz, Areyeh Leib, 107
Zionism, 82, 84, 86, 87, 90, 94, 96, 112, 132, 148, 181, 182, 183, 188, 215, 233, 234, 241, 254, 264, 268
Zohar, 33, 37, 142, 161, 172, 210, 245, 284
Zysia of Annopol, 58